The Existence of God

RICHARD SWINBURNE

CLARENDON PRESS · OXFORD

Oxford University Press, Walton Street, Oxford OX2 6DP

Oxford New York
Athens Auckland Bangkok Bombay
Calcutta Cape Town Dar es Salaam Delhi
Florence Hong Kong Istanbul Karachi
Kuala Lumpur Madras Madrid Melbourne
Mexico City Nairobi Paris Singapore
Taipei Tokyo Toronto

and associated companies in
Berlin Ibadan

Oxford is a trade mark of Oxford University Press

Published in the United States by
Oxford University Press Inc., New York

First edition published 1979
First issued in paperback 1984
Revised paperback edition published 1991
© Richard Swinburne 1979
Appendices © Richard Swinburne 1991

British Library Cataloguing in Publication Data
Swinburne, Richard.
The existence of God.   1. God—Proof.   I. Title.
211   BT102   79-40606
ISBN 0-19-823963-7

5 7 9 10 8 6

Printed in Great Britain
on acid-free paper by
J. W. Arrowsmith Ltd, Bristol

Preface to Revised Edition

The Existence of God was first published in 1979. Eleven years later, I remain convinced of the cogency of its main lines of argument. This new edition contains two additional appendices. Appendix A is a shortened version of a paper originally published in *Religious Studies* in 1983, responding to the criticisms of my arguments made in J. L. Mackie's *The Miracle of Theism*. I am grateful to all the many writers who have given critical attention to my arguments. It would not have been possible to reply to them all, but since Mackie's book has been read more widely than any other book or article which has criticized my arguments in any detail, I chose to reply to him, and hope that this reply will serve to allay some of the concerns of other critics too.

Appendix B is a shortened version of a paper first published in 1989 (in J. Leslie (ed.), *Physical Cosmology and Philosophy*), which seeks to assess the evidential force of recent scientific discoveries of the extent to which the universe is 'fine-tuned' to the production of animals and men, so that any very slight difference in the constants of its laws or its boundary conditions would have led to a universe in which there were no animals and men. These scientific discoveries had not been published or at any rate well publicized by the late seventies, and so I took no account of them when writing the book. They do, however, I claim, provide an additional argument of some strength, of the same general pattern as the other arguments which I discuss, for my conclusion that there is a God.

My thanks to the editors and publishers (Cambridge University Press and MacMillan, New York) concerned for permission to reprint this additional material.

RICHARD SWINBURNE

Oriel College, Oxford
June 1990

Preface

THIS book is based on two series of Wilde Lectures given in the University of Oxford in Hilary Term 1976 and in Hilary Term 1977. Some of the material was also used in two Forwood Lectures given in the University of Liverpool in February 1977. I am most grateful to those who elected me to these lectureships and gave me the opportunity to develop the ideas which receive here their published form. I am especially grateful to the President and Fellows of St. John's College, Oxford, who provided me with extended and very generous hospitality during the terms in which I delivered the Wilde Lectures.

Earlier versions of parts of the book have previously been published in article form, and I am grateful to the editors and publishers of the journals concerned for permission to reuse the material. The articles were: 'Whole and Part in Cosmological Arguments', *Philosophy*, 1969, **44**, 339-40; 'The Argument from Design', *Philosophy*, 1968, **43**, 199-212; 'The Argument from Design—A Defence', *Religious Studies*, 1972, **8**, 193-205; 'The Problem of Evil' in S. C. Brown (ed.), *Reason and Religion* (Ithaca, NY, 1977); 'Natural Evil', *American Philosophical Quarterly*, 1978, **15**, 295-301. I am grateful to the many philosophers who have criticized earlier ideas of mine on the topics discussed in this book, either in print or in oral discussion, and thereby forced me either to abandon them or to develop them in more adequate ways. I am also most grateful to Mrs Yvonne Quirke for her patient typing and retyping of various versions of the book; and to my wife for reading the proofs.

Contents

Introduction

The Existence of God is a sequel to *The Coherence of Theism*, published in 1977. *The Coherence of Theism* was concerned with what it means to say that there is a God and whether the claim that there is a God is internally coherent. *The Existence of God* is concerned with whether the claim is true; it is concerned to assess the weight of arguments from experience for and against this claim, and to reach a conclusion about whether on balance the arguments indicate that there is a God or that there is not. The present book assumes that the claim that there is a God is not demonstrably incoherent (i.e. self-contradictory), and hence that it is proper to look around us for evidence of its truth or falsity. For argument in justification of this assumption I must refer to the earlier work. However, it is in no way necessary for a reader to have read the earlier work in order to understand this one; nor, with the exception just described, does this work in any way presuppose the results of the earlier one. The issues discussed in *The Existence of God* are ones of more general concern than those discussed in *The Coherence of Theism*. Most men have usually supposed that they understood in some very vague way what it meant to say that there was a God; and, so long as they supposed that human words were only a rough guide to what was claimed, that the claim was not demonstrably incoherent. Intense concern about the exact meaning of the claim and whether it is coherent has been primarily the concern of professional theologians and philosophers. But what has worried ordinary men down the centuries is whether the evidence of human experience shows that the claim is true or that it is false. That issue is the topic of this book. The book aims to discuss the topic in depth and with rigour.

The book is written in deep conviction of the possibility of reaching fairly well justified conclusions by rational argument on this issue, perhaps the most important of all deep issues which stir the human mind. It is a conviction which was explicitly acknowledged by the vast majority of Christian (and non-Christian) philosophers from the thirteenth to the eighteenth centuries; and, I believe, shared, although acknowledged less explicitly, by many Christian (and non-Christian) philosophers from the first to the twelfth centuries. By the nineteenth century, however, philosophical theology began to feel the powerful sceptical influence of Hume and Kant. These philosophers produced principles designed to show that reason could never reach justified conclusions about matters much beyond the range of immediate experience, and above all that reason could never reach a justified conclusion about the existence of God. In recent years many others have argued in the same spirit, so that both among professional philosophers and outside their narrow circle, there is today deep scepticism about the power of reason to reach a justified conclusion about the existence of God.

As I construct my positive arguments, I shall briefly give my grounds for thinking that the principles of Hume and Kant are mistaken and that reason can reach justified conclusions outside the narrow boundaries drawn by those philosophers. Those who believe in the ability of modern science to reach justified (and exciting) conclusions about such things far beyond immediate experience, as subatomic particles and nuclear forces, the 'big bang' and cosmic evolution, ought to be highly sympathetic to my enterprise; Hume and Kant would not, on their own principles, have had a very sympathetic attitude to the claims of modern theoretical science.

I shall, however, argue that although reason can reach a fairly well justified conclusion about the existence of God, it can only reach a probable conclusion, not an indubitable one. For this reason, there is abundant room for faith in the practice of religion, and I hope to complete this trilogy on philosophical theology with a volume on *Faith and Reason*.

Recent developments in philosophy which I shall describe, especially developments in inductive logic, often called confirmation theory, provide tools of great value for the investigation of my topic. Confirmation theory involves some occasional use of symbols. I introduce these symbols in the text and explain their meaning with the aid of examples. There is no need for any reader unfamiliar with such symbols to take fright at them. My use of confirmation theory enables me to express my arguments with the rigour appropriate to any detailed presentation of the evidence for and against a large-scale theory of the universe; and also enables me to bring out the close similarities which exist between religious theories and large-scale scientific theories. I do, however, owe an apology, as well as an explanation, to those who find it difficult to cope with symbols. The symbols are not very frequent, and I have been careful to express the main argument of the passages in which symbols occur, in words as well.

1

Inductive Arguments

An argument starts from one or more premisses which are propositions taken for granted for the purpose of the argument, and argues to a conclusion. An argument is a valid deductive argument if it is incoherent to suppose that its premisses are true but its conclusion false. For example, the following argument is a valid deductive argument:

(Premiss 1) No material bodies travel faster than light.
(Premiss 2) My car is a material body.

(Conclusion) My car does not travel faster than light.

In a valid deductive argument the premisses make the conclusion certain. There are arguments which are not deductively valid, but in which the premisses in some sense 'support' or 'confirm' or 'give strength to' the conclusion, and some or all arguments of this general kind are often characterized as 'good' or 'correct' or 'strong' inductive arguments. However, we need here to distinguish carefully between two different kinds of argument. There are arguments in which the premisses make the conclusion probable, that is, more probable than not—e.g.

P_1: 70% inhabitants of the Bogside are Catholic.
P_2: Doherty is an inhabitant of the Bogside.

C: Doherty is Catholic.

The conjunction of the premisses makes the conclusion probable. However, many arguments which are called 'correct' inductive arguments are hardly to be regarded as of this type. Take the following argument:

P: all of 100 ravens observed in different parts of the world are black.

C: all ravens are black.

The normal way to construe this conclusion, in the context of a discussion of inductive arguments, is to suppose that it is about all ravens at all moments of time and points of space—and, even if you suppose that nothing on a distant planet would count as a raven, that means all ravens at all times in the earth's history and at all places on its surface. But, when the conclusion is interpreted this way it becomes implausible to suppose that P makes C more probable than not. For it is not improbable to suppose that the blackness of observed ravens arises from a particular feature of modern ravens, a particular feature of their make-up not present in older ravens. To suppose that all ravens are always black seems to go a long way beyond the evidence recorded in P. C may, however, be true; and, most of us suppose, P increases the probability that it is true, but P does not make C probable.

Most of the arguments of scientists from their observational evidence to conclusions about what are the true laws of nature or to predictions about the results of future experiments or observations are not deductively valid, but are, it would be generally agreed, inductive arguments of one of the above two kinds. (I do not mean that they have the simple pattern of the easy examples given above, but only that they are arguments which have the defining characteristics of one of the two kinds.) The various astronomical observations made by Tycho Brahe, Kepler, Galileo, and other men of the seventeenth century were observations which favoured Newton's theory of motion, in the sense that they made it more likely to be true, more probable, than it would have been otherwise. The various botanical, geological, and breeding data described by Charles Darwin in *The Origin of Species* added to the probability of his theory of the evolution of animal species by natural selection of variations. It is an interesting question to which I shall need to allude at a later stage, whether in a typical scientific argument from various data of observation and experiment to a conclusion about what are the laws of nature, the premisses make the conclusion probable or merely add to its probability. Laws of nature are normally supposed to be generalizations which not merely hold at all times and places, but would continue to hold under unrealized or unrealizable circumstances (e.g. however men interfere with the universe). Newton's theory of motion consists of his three laws of motion and his law of gravitational attraction. Did the various observations of the seventeenth century make it more probable than not that his theory was true? I pass no judgement on this matter at this stage. However, on our normal way of looking at these matters, clearly observational evidence often makes more probable than not a particular prediction about the future. All the observational evidence about the past behaviour of sun, moon, planets, etc. makes it more probable than not that the earth will continue to spin on its axis for the next twenty-four hours and so that the sun will rise over the earth again tomorrow.

Let us call an argument in which the premisses make the conclusion probable a correct P-inductive argument. Let us call an argument in which the premisses add to the probability of the conclusion (i.e. make the conclusion more likely or more probable than it would otherwise be) a correct C-inductive argument. In this case let us say that the premisses 'confirm' the conclusion. Among correct C-inductive arguments some will obviously be stronger than others, in the sense that in some the premisses will raise the probability of the conclusion more than the premisses do in other arguments.

The point of arguments is to get people, in so far as they are rational, to accept conclusions. For this purpose it is not sufficient that their premisses should in some sense necessitate or probabilify their conclusion. It is also necessary that the premisses should be known to be true by those who dispute about the conclusion. There are plenty of valid arguments to the existence of God which are quite useless, because although their premisses may be true, they are not known to be true by men who argue about religion—

e.g. P_1: If life is meaningful, God exists.

P_2: Life is meaningful.

C: God exists.

This argument is certainly valid. If the premisses are true, the conclusion must be true. The premisses may be true; but atheists would deny either the first premiss or the second one. Since the premisses are not common items of knowledge to those who argue about religion, they do not form a suitable jumping-off ground for such argument. What are clearly of interest to men in an age of religious scepticism are arguments to the existence (or non-existence) of God in which the premisses are known to be true by men of all theistic or atheistic persuasions. I therefore define arguments from premisses known to be true by those who dispute about the conclusion which are valid deductive, correct P-inductive, or correct C-inductive arguments, respectively good deductive, good

P-inductive, and good C-inductive arguments. In investigating arguments for or against the existence of God, we need to investigate whether any of them are good deductive, good P-inductive, or good C-inductive arguments.

I take the proposition 'God exists' (and the equivalent proposition 'There is a God') to be logically equivalent to 'there exists a person[1] without a body (i.e. a spirit) who is eternal, is perfectly free, omnipotent, omniscient, perfectly good, and the creator of all things'. I use 'God' as the name of the person picked out by this description. I understand by God's being eternal that he always has existed and always will exist. There is an alternative understanding of 'eternal' in the Christian tradition as 'timeless' or 'outside time'. This understanding did not however arrive in the Christian tradition under the fourth century AD; it is very difficult to make any sense of it, and, for reasons which I have given elsewhere,[2] it seems quite unnecessary for the theist to burden himself with this understanding of eternity. By God's being perfectly free I understand that no object or event or state (including past states of himself) in any way causally influences him to do the actions which he does—his own choice at the moment of action alone determines what he does. By God's being omnipotent I understand that he is able to do whatever it is logically possible (i.e. coherent to suppose) that he can do. By God's being omniscient I understand that he knows whatever it is logically possible that he know. By God's being perfectly good I understand that he does no morally bad action. By his being the creator of all things I understand that everything which exists at each moment of time (apart from himself) exists because, at that moment of time, he makes it exist, or permits it to exist. This will suffice for present purposes as an account of what the claim that there is a God means. The meaning of the claim will be developed in somewhat greater detail at points in later chapters, especially in Chapter 5—where we shall need to investigate the relation between the various properties ascribed to God.[3] The claim that there is a

---

[1] I am using this word in its modern sense. I do not think that many Christians wish to deny that in this sense, very loosely speaking, God is a person. Traditionally orthodox Christians do however normally also wish to claim that in a certain special sense of 'person', God is (in the traditional formula) 'three persons in one substance'. But in claiming this they are using 'person' as a translation of the Latin *persona* and the Greek ὑπόστασις, in a sense which is not, I think, intended to rule out the former claim.

[2] See *The Coherence of Theism* (Oxford, 1977), Ch. 12.

[3] For more thorough analysis I must refer the reader to *The Coherence of Theism*.

God is called theism. Theism is of course the core belief of the creeds of Christianity, Judaism, and Islam.

In the course of human history many men have taken for granted the existence of God, and many others no doubt have taken for granted his non-existence. They have not had consciously formulated reasons for their beliefs. They have just believed. However, others who have believed have had reasons for their beliefs. As with most men's reasons for most of their beliefs, these reasons have often been very vague and incohate. Sometimes, however, men have formulated some of their reasons for belief in a sharp and explicit form. Then we have something clearly recognizable as an argument for or against the existence of God. Those arguments which have been frequently discussed have been given names—and thus we have 'the cosmological argument', or 'the argument from religious experience'. Other arguments exist which have not been discussed frequently enough to gain a name. And men have had other reasons for belief or disbelief which have never been formulated explicitly enough to constitute an argument.

In the course of this book I shall discuss various of the reasons which men have had for believing in the existence of God, or in the non-existence of God, some of which have received a sufficiently precise form already to be codified in named arguments and others of which will need to be knocked into a clear shape. I shall discuss only arguments in which the premisses report what are (in some very general sense) features of human experience—e.g. evident general truths about the world or features of private human experience. Such arguments I shall term *a posteriori* arguments. They claim that something which men experience is grounds for believing that there is a God or that there is no God. I shall not discuss *a priori* arguments—these are arguments in which the premisses are conceptual truths, viz. propositions which would be true whether or not there was a universe of material or spiritual beings other than God. Among conceptual truths are the truths of mathematics or logic. Hence I shall not discuss the traditional ontological argument[1] for

[1] The traditional version of the ontological argument was put forward by Descartes and probably originally by St. Anselm. It runs roughly as follows: 'God is by definition a most perfect being. A being which exists is more perfect than one which does not. Therefore, God, being most perfect, exists.' For ancient and modern versions of the argument and criticisms of it see (e.g.) the collection edited by A. Plantinga, *The Ontological Argument* (London, 1968). For a very careful analysis leading to a rejection of the argument see J. Barnes, *The Ontological Argument* (London, 1972).

the existence of God, or any variants thereof. Nor shall I discuss arguments against the existence of God which claim that there is something incoherent or self-contradictory in the claim that there is a God. I think that ontological arguments for the existence of God are very much mere philosophers' arguments and do not codify any of the reasons which ordinary men have for believing that there is a God. The greatest theistic philosophers of religion have on the whole rejected ontological arguments and relied on *a posteriori* ones.[1] Arguments against the existence of God which claim that theism is incoherent do, however, I admit, have some basis in the thought of ordinary people. I shall not, however, of course be able to discuss all the *a posteriori* reasons which men have had for believing that there is or that there is not a God. But I shall consider those which, in my view, are the most plausible and have had the greatest appeal in human history. In reaching my final conclusion about how probable it is that there is a God, I assume that no *a priori* arguments of either species,[2] and no *a posteriori* arguments other than those which I discuss, have any significant force.

Although my theme is arguments for and against the existence of God, it will seem from the chapter headings that I concentrate on arguments for the existence of God. I do discuss in a separate chapter the main argument against the existence of God—the argument from evil, which claims that the existence of pain and suffering in the world shows that there is no perfectly good and all-powerful being. But, apart from that reason, the main reasons which atheists have for believing that there is no God have been their claims that there is insufficient evidence, that the theist's arguments do not work, do not make the existence of God probable to any significant degree. The atheist's arguments, apart from the argument from evil, have been largely in the form of criticisms of the theist's arguments. I therefore discuss such arguments in the course of discussing each of the main arguments for the existence of God. In discussing arguments for the existence of God, I shall consider forms of cosmological and teleological argument, the argument from the existence of consciousness, the moral argument, arguments from miracle and revelation, and the argument from religious experience. A cosmological argument argues that the fact that there is a universe needs explaining and that God's having made it and

---

[1] e.g. St. Thomas Aquinas. See his *Summa Theologiae*, I. 2.1.
[2] I attempt to prove this for arguments which purport to show that theism is incoherent in *The Coherence of Theism*.

kept it in being explains its existence. An argument from design argues that the fact that there is design in the world needs explaining, and that God's action provides that explanation. There are various forms of argument from design, according to the kind of design to which it draws attention. I discuss two different genera of the argument under the headings 'the teleological argument' and 'the argument from providence', and different species of each genus. The argument from the existence of consciousness argues that the fact that there are conscious beings is mysterious and inexplicable but for the action of God. Arguments from miracle and revelation cite various public phenomena in the course of human history as evidence of God's existence and activity. The argument from religious experience claims that various of men's private experiences are experiences of God and thus show his existence.

There are two evident respects in which my discussion will, for reasons of space, be incomplete. First, when I discuss the form of teleological argument which I call the argument from providence and when I discuss the problem of evil, I do assume that it is not demonstrably false that man has free will of a certain kind. The position which I take has, I believe, a certain plausibility; but to defend it adequately against some current arguments would need a discussion of freewill of book-length. The integrated nature of philosophy is such that full discussion of one issue inevitably forces a man to take a position on other issues, and for this reason one book on one philosophical topic is almost always incomplete. Secondly, when I discuss arguments from miracles, I have space only to discuss which strange public phenomena (e.g. a dead man coming to life) if they occurred would be evidence for the existence of God; but I do not have space to discuss the historical evidence for and against the occurrence of particular public phenomena. So in effect I here discuss only the form of an argument which would need filling out with detailed historical material.

Kant produced a threefold classification of arguments for the existence of God which has had a permanent and to my mind far from beneficial influence on the subsequent discussion of this topic. He wrote:

There are only three possible ways of proving the existence of God by means of speculative reason. All paths leading to this goal begin either from determinate experience and the specific constitution of the world of sense as thereby known, and ascend from it, in accordance with the laws of causality, to the supreme cause outside the world; or they start with experience which is purely indeterminate, that is from experience of existence in general; or finally they abstract from all experience, and argue completely a priori, from mere concepts, to the existence of a supreme cause. The first proof is the *physico-theological*, the second the *cosmological*, the third the *ontological*. There are, and there can be, no others.[1]

The distinction is made in terms of the nature of the premiss. Either you start from a conceptual truth—in which case you have the ontological argument; or from 'existence in general'—in which case you have the cosmological argument; or from the details of what Kant calls 'determinate experience', how things are in the world—in which case you have the 'physico-theological' argument.

My reason for claiming that this doctrine of Kant has had a far from beneficial influence on discussion of this topic is that by his use of the word 'the' Kant tends to assume that there can only be one argument of each type—whereas in fact there can quite clearly be many different arguments under each heading which are so different from each other that it would be misleading to call them forms of the same argument at all. There is for example no reason to suppose that all arguments to the existence of God in which the premisses are in some sense conceptual truths need have the form of the traditional ontological argument. Above all, there is no reason to suppose that all arguments from how things are in the world need have the form of the argument which Kant calls 'physico-theological', and has elsewhere been called the argument from design. This latter argument may itself have many forms. It may argue, for example, from the regular behaviour of objects in the world codified in laws of nature, or from the ready availability in the world of the things which men and animals need to survive. In both cases there is an argument from a very general order in nature. But there are arguments too, as we have noted, from particular miracles, from the development of human history, or from particular religious experiences. Not all of these may be particularly good arguments, but they deserve to be considered on their merits— Kant's classification obscures their existence.

So then we shall consider the worth of various *a posteriori* arguments, not merely two, as listed by Kant. When we have our arguments in clear form, we shall need to ask—are they good deductive arguments, or good P-inductive arguments, or good C-inductive arguments? Sometimes the proponents of such arguments have not been clear whether the arguments were intended to be

---

[1] I. Kant, *Critique of Pure Reason*, B 618–19.

deductive or inductive, let alone about the kind of inductive arguments which they were intended to be.

One unfortunate feature of recent philosophy of religion has been a tendency to treat arguments for the existence of God in isolation from each other. There can of course be no objection to considering each argument initially, for the sake of simplicity of exposition, in isolation from others. But clearly the arguments may back each other up or alternatively weaken each other, and we need to consider whether or not they do. Sometimes however philosophers consider the arguments for the existence of God in isolation from each other, reasoning as follows: the cosmological argument does not prove the conclusion, the telelogical argument does not prove the conclusion, etc. etc., therefore the arguments do not prove the conclusion. But this 'divide and rule' technique with the arguments is inadmissible. Even if the only kind of good argument was a valid deductive argument from premisses known to be true it would be inadmissible. An argument from *p* to *r* may be invalid; another argument from *q* to *r* may be invalid. But if you run the arguments together, you could well get a valid deductive argument; the argument from *p* and *q* to *r* may be valid. The argument from 'all students have long hair' to 'Smith has long hair' is invalid, and so is the argument from 'Smith is a student' to 'Smith has long hair'; but the argument from 'all students have long hair and Smith is a student' to 'Smith has long hair' is valid.

That arguments may support and weaken each other is even more evident, when we are dealing with inductive arguments. That Smith has blood on his hands hardly makes it probable that Smith murdered Mrs Jones, nor (by itself) does the fact that Smith stood to gain from Mrs Jones's death, nor (by itself) does the fact that Smith was near the scene of the murder at the time of its being committed, but all these phenomena together (perhaps with other phenomena as well) may indeed make the conclusion probable.[1]

---

[1] Among those who seem to have assumed that there are no good arguments other than deductive ones, and that arguments are not cumulative are both Alistair MacIntyre and Antony Flew. Thus MacIntyre: 'One occasionally hears teachers of theology aver that although the proofs do not provide conclusive grounds for belief in God, they are at least pointers, indicators. But a fallacious argument points nowhere (except to the lack of logical acumen on the part of those who accept it). And three fallacious arguments are no better than one.' A. MacIntyre, *Difficulties in Christian Belief* (London, 1959), p. 63. This passage is quoted with approval by Flew in his *God and Philosophy* (London, 1966), p. 167, who remarks himself in another very similar passage: 'It is occasionally suggested that some candidate proof, although admittedly failing as a proof, may sometimes do useful service as a

In order to consider the cumulative effect of arguments, I shall consider them one by one, starting with the cosmological argument and including the argument from evil against the existence of God, and ask how much the premisses of each argument add to or subtract from the force of the previous arguments. To give advance notice of some of my conclusions—I shall argue that (neither separately nor in conjunction) are any of the arguments which I consider for or against the existence of God good deductive arguments. There are of course, as I have pointed out, valid deductive arguments to the existence of God, but they start from premisses which are far from generally accepted. On the other hand I shall argue that most of the arguments (taken separately and together) for the existence of God are good C-inductive arguments—that is to say, their premisses make it more likely that God exists than it would otherwise be. I shall also argue that the argument from evil to the non-existence of God is not a good C-inductive argument. That is, contrary to popular belief and the beliefs of many theologians, evil of the kind which flourishes on earth does not count against the existence of God, renders it no less probable than it was that God exists. If that is right, then the net effect of taking together all the premisses of the arguments which I consider is that we will have a good C-inductive argument to the existence of God. (I shall of course argue that some of the separate arguments confirm the proposition 'God exists' much more strongly than do others.) The crucial issue however is whether all the arguments taken together make it probable that God exists, whether the balance of all the relevant evidence favours the claim of theism or not. For clearly, in so far as the probability of a hypothesis is relevant to whether or not we ought to act on it, we ought to act on a hypothesis in so far as it is

pointer. This is a false exercise of the generosity so characteristic of examiners. A failed proof cannot serve as a pointer to anything, save perhaps to the weaknesses of those who have accepted it. Nor, for the same reason can it be put to work along with other throwouts as part of an accumulation of evidences. If one leaky bucket will not hold water that is no reason to think that ten can.' (op. cit., pp. 62f.)

But of course arguments which are not deductively valid are often inductively strong; and if you put three weak arguments together you may often get a strong one, perhaps even a deductively valid one. The analogy in Flew's last sentence is a particularly unhappy one for his purpose. For clearly if you jam ten leaky buckets together in such a way that holes in the bottom of each bucket are squashed close to solid parts of the bottoms of neighbouring buckets, you will get a container that holds water. The cumulative nature of arguments for the existence of God was clearly perceived by Butler: 'The truth of our religion, like the truth of common matters, is so judged of by all the evidence taken together.' J. Butler, *The Analogy of Religion* (first published 1736, London, 1902), p. 307.

rendered probable by the total evidence available to us, all we know about the world, not just some limited piece of knowledge. The religious man claims that his religious viewpoint makes sense of the whole of his experience; and his atheistic rival is liable to make a similar claim. In the last chapter I shall reach a conclusion on whether or not the balance of all the relevant evidence favours theism. I shall be fairly brief in dismissing the suggestions that any of the arguments separately or all the arguments taken together constitute a good deductive argument. I shall be fairly brief because many other philosophers have devoted their technical skills to this task, and relatively few philosophers today would accept that there are good deductive arguments to be had here. I shall devote most of my time to assessing the inductive strength of such arguments. I shall consider of each argument whether it is a good C-inductive argument, but only when we have all the arguments shall I ask whether taken together they make a good P-inductive argument. I proceed in this way because, as will appear, it is a lot easier to see when we have a good C-inductive argument than when we have a good P-inductive argument.

It will be useful to introduce at this stage the symbols of confirmation theory,[1] which I shall use from time to time in subsequent chapters. I represent by lower-case letters such as e, h, p, and q propositions. $P(p/q)$ represents the probability of p, given q. Thus p might represent the proposition: 'The next toss of this coin will land heads', and q might represent the proposition: '505 of the last 1,000 tosses of this coin have landed heads.' Then $P(p/q)$ represents the probability that the next toss of the coin will land heads, given that 505 of the last 1,000 tosses have landed heads. (The value of $P(p/q)$ would then generally be supposed to be 0.505.) However, the relation between p and q may be of a much more complex kind; and clearly we normally assess the probability of claims on evidence other than that of relative frequencies. p may be some scientific hypothesis—say, Einstein's General Theory of Relativity—and q may be the conjunction of all the reports of the evidence of observation and experiment which scientists have collected relevant to the theory. A hypothesis up for investigation is often represented by h. Then $P(h/e \cdot k)$ represents the probability of a hypothesis h given evidence e and k.[2] It is often useful to divide the

---

[1] For a detailed study of confirmation theory see my *An Introduction to Confirmation Theory* (London, 1973).

[2] '$e \cdot k$' is the conjunction of e and k, the proposition 'both e and k'.

evidence available to an observer into two parts—new evidence and background evidence; if this is done, the former is often represented by e and the latter by k. Background evidence (or background knowledge, as it is sometimes called) is the knowledge which we take for granted before new evidence turns up. Thus suppose that detectives are investigating a murder. h could represent the hypothesis that Jones did the murder; e could represent the proposition which reports all the new evidence which detectives turn up—e.g. that Jones's fingerprints were found on the weapon, that he was near the scene of the murder at the time it was committed, etc. etc. k could represent the proposition reporting the detectives' general knowledge about how the world works—e.g. that each person has a peculiar set of fingerprints, that people who touch metal and wood with bare hands usually leave their fingerprints on them, etc. etc. Then $P(h/e.k)$ represents the probability that Jones did the murder, given the detectives' total evidence.

For all propositions p and q $P(p/q) = 1$ if (and only if) q makes p certain, e.g. if q entails p (that is, there is a deductively valid argument from q to p); and $P(p/q) = 0$ if (and only if) q makes $\sim p$ certain, e.g. if q entails $\sim p$.[1] $P(p/q) + P(\sim p/q) = 1$. So if $P(p/q) > \frac{1}{2}$, then $P(p/q) > P(\sim p/q)$ and it is on q more probable that p than that $\sim p$. So (for background knowledge k) an argument from e to h will be a correct C-inductive argument if (and only if) $P(h/e.k) > P(h/k)$, and a correct P-inductive argument (and only if) $P(h/e.k) > \frac{1}{2}$. The division between new evidence and background can be made where you like—often it is convenient to include all evidence derived from experience in e and to regard k as being what is called in confirmation theory mere 'tautological evidence', that is, in effect all our other irrelevant knowledge.

Clearly whether or not an argument is a good C-inductive argument will depend on how the evidence is divided between e and k. When I come to discuss any argument I will consider what is the most appropriate division of evidence. For the moment let k be mere tautological evidence, and all the evidence of experience be contained in e. Now let h be our hypothesis—'God exists'. Let e_1, e_2, e_3, be the various propositions which men bring forward as evidence for his existence. Thus let e_1 be 'there is a physical universe'. Then we have the argument from e_1 to h—a cosmological argument.

---

[1] '$\sim p$' is the negation of p, the proposition 'it is not the case that p'. '$>$' means 'is greater than'. '$<$' means 'is less than'. I shall also subsequently be using '$\geqslant$' to mean 'is greater than or equal to', and '$\leqslant$' to mean 'is less than or equal to'.

$P(h/e_1.k)$ represents the 'probability that God exists given that there is a physical universe—and also mere tautological evidence, which latter can be ignored. If $P(h/e_1.k) > \frac{1}{2}$, then the argument from e_1 to h is a good P-inductive argument. If $P(h/e_1.k) > P(h/k)$ then the argument is a good C-inductive argument. We shall consider some six arguments, arguments from $e_1 \ldots e_6$, to the existence of God; and one argument against, from e_7. I shall claim then that for each e_n where $n = 1 \ldots 6$, $P(h/e_n.k) > P(h/k)$, and that $P(h/e_7.k) = P(h/k)$. The crucial issue to which we will eventually come is whether $P(h/e_1 \ldots e_7.k) > \frac{1}{2}$.

In using the symbols of confirmation theory I do not assume that an expression of the form $P(p/q)$ always has an exact numerical value. It may merely have relations of greater or less to other probabilities, including ones with a numerical value, without itself having a numerical value—$P(h/e_1.k)$ for example, may be greater than $P(h/e_2.k)$ and less than $P(h/k)$ and less than $\frac{1}{2}$ without there being some number to which it is equal.[1] Clearly, for example, we may judge one scientific theory to be more probable than another on the same evidence while denying that its probability has an exact numerical value; or we may judge a prediction to be more probable than not and so to have a probability of greater than $\frac{1}{2}$, while again denying that that probability has an exact numerical value.[2]

Now it is sometimes said that the different arguments for the existence of God show different things. The cosmological argument shows at most the existence of some sort of necessary being; the argument from design shows at most some sort of arch-architect;[3] the argument from miracles shows at most some sort of poltergeist —so what have they in common? This objection gets things back to front. There is no *one* thing that premises show. In a deductive argument there are many different conclusions which can be drawn from a set of premises. And in an inductive argument the premises support different conclusions with different degrees of force.

---

[1] See my *An Introduction to Confirmation Theory*, pp. 36-9 on this point.

[2] Also, I do not assume that such expressions conform in all respects to the axioms of the mathematical calculus of probability. I shall however argue in Ch. 3 that they do conform in a crucial respect—that of obeying Bayes's Theorem. I do, however, believe that they do conform in all respects, and I have argued for this in my *Introduction*, esp. Chs. 3-6.

[3] See, for example, Kant's treatment of the argument in *The Critique of Pure Reason*, B648-58. He writes (B655): 'The utmost, therefore, that the argument can prove is an *architect* of the world who is always very much hampered by the adaptability of the material in which he works, not a *creator* of the world to whose idea everything is subject.'

What does 'there is a print in the shape of a human foot on the sand' show? It shows with different degrees of force many things—that sand is shapeable, that some creature has been on the sand, that a man has walked on the sand. The evidence makes probable the different propositions to different degrees. Our concern is with the effect of various pieces of evidence on the proposition in which we are interested—'God exists'. Does each confirm it (i.e. increase its probability)? Does it make it probable? Our concern is for various pieces of evidence e_n and for h = 'God exists' with the value of $P(h/e_n)$. This may well be for some e_n less than the value for some other interesting proposition h_1, say 'there exists an impersonal cause of the universe', of $P(h_1/e_n)$. That is, e_n may make h_1 more probable than it makes h. However, even though, say, $P(h_1/e_1) > P(h/e_1)$ it certainly does not follow that $P(h_1/e_1 \ldots e_7) > P(h/e_1 \ldots e_7)$. That is, 'God exists' may gain only a small amount of probability from e_1, a small amount from e_2, a small amount from e_3, and so on. For each of e_1, e_2, e_3, there may be some other proposition h_1, h_2, h_3, which is in some sense a rival to 'God exists' for which $P(h_n/e_n) > P(h/e_n)$; but nevertheless, on the total evidence h may be more probable than each of the rivals.

A similar situation normally arises with any far-reaching scientific or historical theory. Each separate piece of evidence does not make the theory very probable, and indeed taken on its own makes some narrower theory much more probable. But the cumulative force of the evidence taken together gives great probability to the wide theory. Thus each of the various pieces of evidence which are cited as evidence in favour of the General Theory of Relativity do not by themselves make it very probable, but together they do give it quite a degree of probability. Each by itself (given the general background knowledge available in the early twentieth century) was evidence in favour of some far less wide-ranging hypothesis than General Relativity. Thus the movement of Mercury's perihelion taken by itself would suggest only that there was a hitherto unknown planet lying between Mercury and the sun or that the sun was of an odd shape, rather than that General Relativity was true. Taken by itself it would not have given much probability to General Relativity; but taken with other pieces of evidence it did its bit in supporting the latter. It is along these lines that the theist may wish to answer the accusation that an argument such as the cosmological argument does not show the existence of the God of Abraham, Isaac, and Jacob. Not by itself, he may reply, but it does its small bit together with some very diverse arguments which do their small bit, to get to this conclusion.

Note that it is no objection to a P-inductive or C-inductive argument from e to h, that some contrary hypothesis h^* is also compatible with e, as some writers on the philosophy of religion seem to think. They seem to think that if, for example, the order in the universe is compatible with 'God does not exist', then there is no good argument from it to 'God exists'. But one has only to think about the matter to realize that this is not so. In any non-deductive argument from e to h, not-h will be compatible with e; and yet some non-deductive arguments are good arguments.

Note also a further interesting feature of good C-inductive arguments. In such an argument from e to h, $P(h/e.k) > P(h/k)$. It may be the case that also for some contrary hypothesis h^* there is a good C-inductive argument from e, i.e. also $P(h^*/e.k) > P(h/k)$. The fact that certain evidence confirms a hypothesis does not mean that it does not also confirm a rival hypothesis. Once again, this should be immediately clear if one thinks about it. Suppose that a detective has background information k, that either Smith, Brown, or Robinson did the crime, and that only one of them did. Then evidence (e) turns up that Robinson was somewhere else at the time the crime was committed. e adds to the probability that Brown did the crime, and it also adds to the probability that Smith did the crime. Despite this, one sometimes reads writers on the philosophy of religion dismissing some consideration which is adduced as evidence for the existence of God on the grounds that it supports a rival hypothesis equally well.

So then our task will be to assess the worth of different arguments to the conclusion 'God exists'. How are we to do this? In the case of deductive arguments, philosophers have a moderately clear idea of what makes a valid argument, and so are in a position to look at various arguments and see if they are valid. But our main concern will be with inductive arguments. How are we to set about assessing the probability of 'God exists' on different pieces of evidence? To do this we need to know for what fillings of p and q $P(p/q)$ becomes high or low. There is however, fortunately no need to undertake any very general examination of this question. This is because all important *a posteriori* arguments for the existence of God have a common characteristic. They all purport to be arguments to an explanation of the phenomena described in the premises in terms of the action of an agent who intentionally brought about those phenomena. A cosmological argument argues from the existence of the world to a person, God, who intentionally brought it about. An argument from design argues from the design of the world to a person, God, who intentionally made it thus. All the other arguments are arguments from particular features of the world to a God who intentionally made the world with those features.

Not all inductive arguments are arguments to an explanation. When we argue from the sun having risen at intervals of approximately twenty-four hours over the last many thousand years to the claim that it will rise tomorrow, we are not arguing to an explanation. Its rising tomorrow does not explain its previous rising. Yet when the geologist argues from various deformations to the occurrence of an earthquake millions of years ago, he is arguing to an explanation; he is arguing from phenomena to an event which brought those phenomena about. However, not all arguments to an explanation are arguments to the intentional action of an agent. An intentional action is an action which some agent does, meaning to do it. It is one therefore which the agent has some reason or purpose for doing—either the minimal purpose of doing it for its own sake or some further purpose which is forwarded by doing the action. Since he acts for reasons or purposes on which he chooses to act we may term such an agent a rational agent. Persons are rational agents;[1] but they are not the only ones—animals too often perform intentional actions. By contrast, however, inanimate objects and events do not have purposes on which they choose to act and which they seek to fulfil, but rather they bring about their effects unthinkingly. The geologist's argument from deformations to the occurrence of an earthquake is an argument to an explanation of the deformations, but not an argument to an explanation in terms of the intentional action of a rational agent. However, when a detective argues from various bloodstains on the woodwork, fingerprints on the metal, Smith's corpse on the floor, money missing from the safe, Jones's having much extra money to—Jones's having intentionally killed Smith and stolen his money, he is arguing to an explanation of the various phenomena in terms of the intentional action of a rational agent. Since persons are paradigm cases of rational agents, I will term explanation in terms of the intentional action of a rational agent *personal explanation*. In Chapter 2 I shall analyse

---

[1] I understand by a person a rational agent who has at least the complexity of intentions, purposes, beliefs, etc., typical of human beings. See *The Coherence of Theism*, p. 101.

the nature of personal explanation more fully and I shall contrast it with the other accepted pattern of explaining mundane phenomena, which I shall call scientific explanation. In Chapter 3 I shall go on to consider when it is right to invoke personal explanation and when it is right to invoke scientific explanation. A crucial issue which arises there is when is it reasonable to suppose that phenomena do have an explanation, and when, by contrast, is it reasonable to suppose that phenomena are just brute facts, things which explain other things, but do not themselves have an explanation. This issue of what is the proper terminus for explanation will be discussed in Chapter 4. It is one which is crucial for theism. For the theist claims that the various phenomena which constitute his evidence, e.g. the existence of the world and its conformity to order, need explanation; and that this is provided by the action of God, whose existence and action need no explanation. So Chapter 2 will bring out the nature of the theist's explanations, and Chapters 3 and 4 will provide essential tools for answering the question of when it is right to invoke them. With these tools we shall then be in a position to look in detail at the theist's arguments.

2

The Nature of Explanation

WHEN the theist argues from phenomena such as the existence of
the world or some feature of the world to the existence of God, he is
arguing, we have seen, to an explanation of the phenomena in terms
of the intentional action of a person. Explanation in terms of the
intentional action of a person is the normal case of what I termed
personal explanation. We give a personal explanation of my being in
London, by my having gone there in order to give a lecture; or of
the letter's being on the table by my wife's having put it there in
order to remind me to post it. However, as we have seen, not all
explanations are personal explanations. Other explanations of the
occurrence of phenomena seem to have a distinct common structure
and these I will call scientific explanations. This chapter will be
concerned with analysing the structure of explanations of the two
kinds; and the next chapter will consider when each is to be
invoked.

When a man is said to have provided an explanation of the
occurrence of some phenomenon (i.e. an event or state of affairs),
this is ambiguous. What is meant may be that he has provided a true
explanation of the phenomenon, or it may be merely that he has
suggested a possible explanation of the phenomenon. Our interest in
explanations is interest in true explanations. What is it to provide a
true explanation of the occurrence of a phenomenon E? It is to state
truly what (object or event) brought E about (or caused E), and
why that was efficacious. To explain the occurrence of the high tide
is to state what brought about the tide—the moon, water, and the
rest of the earth being in such-and-such locations at such-and-such
times—and why the moon etc. had that effect—because of the inverse square law of attraction acting between all bodies. We can thus
detect two components of an explanation of a phenomenon E—the

'what' that made E happen and the 'why' that made E happen. The 'what' will be what I may term some other independent actual factors—other events, processes, states, objects, and their properties at certain times. By these factors' being independent I mean that the 'what' is not the same event or process as E nor part of it; nor is it an object which is a participant in E at the time of E, nor is it a state or property of E or the objects which participate in E at the time of E's occurrence. Only something different from E can make E happen. By the factors' being actual I mean only that any events, processes, and states cited occurred; that any object cited existed and had the properties cited, which were occurrent as opposed to dispositional properties. I understand by a property's being dispositional that to say that an object has that property is to say that it would behave in certain ways under certain conditions—thus brittleness, irascibility, and irritability are dispositional properties. For to say that an object is brittle is to say no more than that it will break under certain circumstances. In contrast I mean by a property's being an occurrent property that to say that an object has that property is not to say that it would behave in certain ways under certain circumstances, but to say something else—the 'else' I can only describe as saying how the object is now. Thus to say that an object is square or large, or (probably) to say that it is blue or loud is to ascribe to it an occurrent property. This is an important distinction which I shall use subsequently. The point of this restriction that the factors of the 'what' cited in explanation must be actual is that only something which actually happened, only properties which actually characterized objects, can bring about effects; what merely 'would happen if' cannot bring about effects.

To say that certain factors $A \ldots D$ brought about E entails at least that each, in the conditions of its occurrence, made it more probable that E would occur; it influenced E's occurrence. Normally perhaps each of the factors are necessary, given the others and the world being in other ways the same, for the occurrence of E—i.e. without any one of them, the world otherwise remaining the same, E would not have occurred. Normally perhaps too the set of factors together are sufficient for the occurrence of E—i.e. given their occurrence E must necessarily occur. We may call all the factors together which make up the 'what', the cause of E. Alternatively, and more usually, we distinguish one as the 'cause' of E (the effect), and call the others the conditions which were necessary for the cause to have its effect (or at least made it probable that it would have the effect); which we call the cause is sometimes a somewhat arbitrary matter. Normally it will be the most unexpected member of the set of factors, or the one, the occurrence of which involves the sharpest change from the previous state of the world. Thus suppose someone lights a match close to petrol at a certain temperature and a certain pressure, and all of this produces an explosion. We may describe the ignition of the match and the petrol's being at that temperature and pressure as jointly the cause of the explosion. But it would be more natural to describe the ignition of the match as the cause of the explosion, and the petrol's being at that temperature and pressure conditions necessary for the cause to have its effect. My terminology will be as follows. I shall call a set of factors which together were sufficient for the occurrence of an event E *a full cause* of E. Any member of a set of factors which bring a phenomenon E about I shall call *a* cause of E.

To set out the 'why' of an explanation is to say why the cause, under the specified conditions, had the effect that it had. Thus it might be to cite a law of nature that all events of a certain kind exemplified by the cause bring about events of a certain other kind exemplified by the effect. To cite the 'why' is to cite what I shall call the *reason* why the cause under the conditions of its occurrence had the effect that it had. I am thus using the word 'reason' in a wide but natural sense—in a wider sense than the sense in which a reason for something is always someone's reason for bringing it about. In saying that something was *the* reason for some effect I do not necessarily imply that it was *someone's* reason for bringing about the effect.

Now if there is a full cause C of E and a reason R which guarantees C's efficacy, there will be what I shall call a *full explanation* of E. For given R and C, there will be nothing remaining unexplained about the occurrence of E. In this case the 'what' and 'why' together will deductively entail the occurrence of E. But if there is no full cause of E (e.g. there occur factors which facilitate the occurrence of E, but do not necessitate it) or no reason which ensured that the cause would have the effect which it did, there will be at most what I shall call a partial explanation of E. Any explanation involving factors or reasons which have some responsibility for the occurrence of E I will term a partial explanation. E may be given a partial explanation because there is no full explanation of E. Alternatively, it may well be the case that even if a full explanation exists, men are in no position to provide it, yet they can give some explanation—they can state some of the causes which make up the 'what' and some of the reasons for their efficacy. In that case they are providing an explanation, but only a partial one.

Also, of course, men may take for granted or not be interested in certain aspects of a full explanation and for that reason give only a partial explanation. A geologist interested in the history of geological formations may explain a present formation by telling the historical story of successive stages in its evolution. In telling this story he may not bother to cite the physico-chemical laws which are responsible for one stage succeeding another, simply because he is not interested in these. For that reason his explanation is only partial. The context often determines which answers to our questions about 'the explanation' of some phenomena will satisfy us. But while in other contexts of discussion we may not need to give full explanations even if they are available, in the contexts of scientific and metaphysical discussion, it is often of crucial importance to know whether there is a full explanation of some phenomenon and what its character is.

Scientific Explanation—Hempel's Analysis

Explanations are of different patterns according to the different kinds of cause and reason which feature in them. Explanation of the kind used in science I shall call scientific explanation. The classical account of the nature of scientific explantion, to which I suspect that the majority of philosophers still adhere, is that set out carefully by C. G. Hempel and P. Oppenheim, and subsequently championed by Hempel.[1] On the Hempelian account the causes are a group of events or states, C, known as the 'initial conditions', one of which we may arbitrarily select as 'the' cause. The 'why' is a set of natural laws L. In the normal case these will be universal generalizations, having the form 'all A's are so-and-so' or 'all A's do so-and-so'—e.g. 'all copper put in nitric acid dissolves under such-and-such conditions of temperature and pressure'. C and L then explain E if E follows deductively from them. We explain a particular explosion by the ignition of a particular volume of gunpowder in certain conditions of temperature, pressure, and humidity, and the generalization

[1] For a simple exposition see C. G. Hempel, *Philosophy of Natural Science* (Englewood Cliffs, NJ, 1966), Ch. 5. The original article dealing only with what is called deductive-nomological explanation is C. G. Hempel and P. Oppenheim, 'Studies in the Logic of Explanation', *Philosophy of Science*, 1948, 15, 135-75.

that under such circumstances ignited gunpowder explodes. We explain a particular piece of litmus paper's turning red by its having been immersed in acid and the generalization that litmus paper being immersed in acid always turns red. Sophisticated scientific explanations invoke many laws or generalizations and a complex description of previous events, of which it is a somewhat remote deductive consequence that the event or state to be explained occurs. It is a consequence of Newton's laws and arrangements of the sun and planets thousands of years ago, that they are in the positions in which they are today, and the former explain their being in those positions.

This normal pattern of scientific explanation is called by Hempel deductive-nomological explanation, or D-N explanation—'deductive' because E is deduced from L and C, and 'nomological', from the Greek '*nomos*', 'law', because laws are involved in the explanation. A D-N explanation of an event is a full explanation. However, sometimes the law involved may be a statistical generalization, i.e. claim that '$n\%$ A's are B' where n is intermediate between 100 and 0. It may be a law of genetics that '90% offspring of such-and-such a mating have blue eyes' (or 'there is an 0.9 probability of an offspring of such-and-such a mating having blue eyes'. The probability in this case is a statistical probability, which is a matter of long-run frequency; the statement states that if you take a large enough sample of such offspring, 0.9 of them will have blue eyes).

Such a law L together with initial conditions C will explain E if L and C make it highly probable that E. (The high probability is in this case an epistemic probability, a measure of how much evidence supports some hypothesis, in this case that E occurs.) Thus if an individual a is an offspring of the stated mating, this together with the cited law makes it probable that a has blue eyes, and, Hempel holds, explains this. This pattern of explanation has been called inductive-statistical or I-S explanation—'inductive' because L and C only make E probable and 'statistical' because the laws involved are statistical. Clearly explanation which involves statistical laws is only partial explanation, for you cannot deduce from the law and initial conditions the thing to be explained. There is still something unexplained in why the initial conditions were on this occasion efficacious.

Science does not explain only particular events, but it may also explain laws. If it is a consequence of L_1 that, perhaps under particular conditions C, L_2 operates, then L_1 (together with C)

explains the operation of L_2. (If the consequence is deductive , the explanation is a full one; if L_1 only makes the operation of L_2 probable, the explanation is only partial.) More fundamental laws explain the operation of less fundamental laws. Given a certain assumption about the constitution of gases, Newton's laws of motion explain the operation of the Van der Waals gas law. One set of laws is often said to explain another also when a slightly looser relation holds. L (perhaps together with some C) may entail and render it probable that phenomena will be as predicted by L_2—to a high degree of approximation. It then follows that the true laws of nature in the realm of L_2 are very slightly different from L_2, but that L_2 is a very close approximation to them. Newton's laws of motion have the consequences that, given the distribution of sun and planets through space, Kepler's laws of planetary motion will hold to a high degree of approximation. I shall follow common usage and say that in such circumstances L_2 operates to a high degree of approximation, and that L_1 explains the operation of L_2.

Hempel's account of the nature of scientific explanation has been subjected to weighty criticisms in recent years. I believe that these criticisms can be met, but only at the cost of making Hempel's account less illuminating than it might at first sight appear. First, there is the criticism that we only count a Hempelian explanation as an explanation if the 'laws' involved really are laws of nature or statements deducible therefrom, and not mere 'accidental' generalizations. A universal generalization 'all ravens are black' and 'this is a raven' would not explain 'this is black' unless the generalization were a claim that there is some sort of causal connection between being a raven and being black, viz. that ravens must be black—of physical (or natural) necessity. Hempel himself makes the point that not every true universal generalization will count as a law, though making the distinction between laws and mere 'accidentally' true generalizations in terms of the physical necessity involved in the former is not his way of making the distinction. However, he allows that laws give rise to counter-factual conditionals, i.e. tell you what would have happened under circumstances which did not in fact occur. Thus if it is a law that copper always dissolves in nitric acid, then not merely do all actual specimens put in nitric acid dissolve, but if copper had been put yesterday in nitric acid, when it was not, it would have dissolved. Such an inference is surely only justified if there is some sort of necessary connection between being copper and dissolving in nitric acid.[1] (Note that for Hempel the concept of 'law' remains wider than does the concept of 'law' for many scientists. For Hempel any true universal non-accidental generalization—in our terms any true generalization affirming a physically necessary connection—is a law, whereas for many scientists only the most wide-ranging of such generalizations are dignified with the title of 'law'.)

Similarly, we need to add that a statistical generalization '$n\%$ of A's are B' does not explain a particular A's being B unless it asserts some sort of causal connection between being A and being B. This will be if it is deducible from more basic laws of nature affirming physical necessity or physical probability, that being A is among the factors which physically necessitate or make physically probable being B. Thus John's being a juvenile delinquent would be explained by his being the child of a broken home in a rough area and a generalization that eighty per cent of children of broken homes in rough areas become juvenile delinquents—under the following conditions. There must be basic laws of human behaviour showing how behaviour is determined by genes and environment, and eighty per cent of actual children of broken homes in rough areas have such genetic and other characteristics that when coming from a broken home in a rough area are added to those characteristics, together they physically necessitate the children becoming juvenile delinquents. Alternatively, the physical connection may be a matter not of physical necessity, but of physical probability. By a physical probability I mean a certain 'would be' or tendency in nature. If nature is deterministic, the only physical probabilities in nature are probabilities of 1 (physical necessity) or 0 (physical impossibility). But if there is a certain amount of indeterminism in nature, then there are physical probabilities between 1 and 0.[2] When statistical

[1] Hempel makes the distinction in terms of laws' being those true generalizations which are grounded in accepted theory. But this is unsatisfactory since some laws may never be discovered and so never become part of accepted theory. For a general criticism of distinctions between laws of nature and other true generalizations on Hempelian lines see F. I. Dretske, 'Laws of Nature', *Philosophy of Science*, 1977, **44**, 248–68.

[2] I thus distinguish the physical probability of an event which is a matter of the extent to which the event's occurrence is causally determined, from its epistemic probability which is a matter of the extent to which evidence makes it likely that the event occurred, and from the statistical probability of an event of some kind which is a matter of the proportion of events in the long run which are events of that kind. For amplification of this distinction see my *An Introduction to Confirmation Theory*, Chs. 1 and 2. Most of what I have to say about probability in this book is concerned with epistemic probability.

generalizations are concerned with these then we may call them statistical laws—many interpreters of Quantum Theory[1] for example, claim that the basic formulae of Quantum Theory are such laws.

In the latter case '$n\%$ A's are B' together with 'this is an A' would (partially) explain this is a B if its being an A made it physically more probable that that thing would be a B. There must in one or other way be a physical connection between being an A and being a B if '$n\%$ A's are B' is to explain an A's being a B; and someone who puts the latter forward as an explanation of an A's being B must be claiming that there is such a connection.[2] By contrast John's voting conservative is not to be explained by the fact that his name appears on page 591 of the telephone directory and seventy per cent of those on that page vote conservative. For the latter generalization just states how things happen to be; it is not to be understood as stating that being on that page pushes people in the direction of voting conservative.

A second criticism of Hempel is that even if we allow that laws must be statements of physical necessity (or probability), the Hempelian model allows us to explain effect by cause, as well as cause by effect. It does not pick out the direction of causation. The law L may be such that it allows us to deduce E from L and C,

---

[1] It is a matter of philosophical and scientific dispute whether the laws of Quantum Theory are basic laws; whether perhaps there may be some more fundamental deterministic laws which explain the statistical regularities which Quantum Theory reports. There follow from the basic formulae of Quantum Theory such results as that there is a probability of $\frac{1}{2}$ of a given atom of radium disintegrating within 5,600 years, but there follows nothing more specific which will enable us to predict when the atom will disintegrate. If the laws of Quantum Theory are basic natural laws, that probability is a physical probability, and nature has a bias of $\frac{1}{2}$ in favour of any given atom of C-14 disintegrating within 5,600 years; it is biased strongly against any given atom disintegrating within the next minute. The laws of Quantum Theory are concerned with very small-scale goings-on, but they have consequences for large-scale goings-on, which are after all composed of small-scale goings-on. In general (though with exceptions), given plausible assumptions about initial conditions, they have the consequences that successions of the kind which human beings can recognize will have probabilities close to 1 or close to 0. That is to say, laws about large-scale objects such as bricks and planets and baths of water are virtually deterministic.

[2] A. W. Collins, 'The Use of Statistics in Explanation', *British Journal for the Philosophy of Science*, 1966, **17**, 127–40, makes this point that the statistical propositions which function in explanation must be 'potential statistical causal assessments'. The factors which they cite must be ones which make a difference to whether or not the effect occurs. It follows from this that they must be what Salmon has called 'statistically relevant' factors. See W. C. Salmon (ed.), *Statistical Explanation and Statistical Relevance* (Pittsburgh, 1971).

which latter consists of two states C_1 and C_2, where we can also deduce C_1 from L, E, and C_2. But causality is only one way. If C is wholly or partly causally responsible for E, E cannot be wholly or partly causally responsible for C. To take a well-discussed example,[1] we may be able to deduce from the laws of light (L) and the position (C_2) and the height of a certain flagpole (C_1), the length of a shadow (E); and also to deduce C_1 from L_1, C_2, and E. Yet, intuitively, the height of the flagpole in part explains the length of the shadow, but not vice versa. We can largely deal with this problem by stipulating, as Hempel did, that the initial conditions must be prior to or simultaneous with the effect. But this is not a complete solution, for it still does not allow us to discriminate between cause and effect where two events are simultaneous, and the occurrence of each can be deduced from a law and 'initial conditions' which include the other event. To meet this point, the obvious thing to say is that the law must not state merely that certain events are connected of physical necessity, but it must have built into it the direction of causation, i.e. it must state which events physically necessitate which other events. (Given that events cannot occur earlier than their causes, it will then be redundant to add that the initial conditions must be prior to or simultaneous with the effect.)

Modified in the light of these two criticisms, the Hempelian account of scientific explanation now runs as follows. A state of affairs or event E is explained if some state of affairs or event C together with a law of nature L entail that C physically necessitates (or makes it physically probable that) E. Laws of nature state that states or events of a certain kind physically necessitate or make probable events of a certain other kind.[2] The position of the sun, flagpole, etc. and the laws of light necessitate the occurrence of a shadow; and so they explain its occurrence. But the laws of light contain no statements about shadows necessitating anything, and so the shadow explains nothing. Similarly Laws L_1 explain the operation of L_2, under circumstances C, if L_1 and C make it physically necessary that L_2 operates (at any rate to a high degree of approximation).

However, in this modified form Hempel's account is much less exciting than it might at first sight have appeared. For explanation retains (in the precise forms of 'physically necessitates' and 'makes

---

[1] First put forward in S. Bromberger, 'Why-Questions', in R. G. Colodny (ed.), *Mind and Cosmos* (Pittsburgh, 1966).

[2] This account of laws of nature will receive a further slight modification in Ch. 12.

physically probable'), the concept of bringing about or 'causing'; it does not analyse it away in radically different terms. Many philosophers following Hume[1] have wished to analyse 'C causes E' in terms of events like C as a matter of fact being followed by events like E, without such a concept as the concept of physical necessity appearing in the analysis (and so to analyse laws of nature as simply statements about what happens, not about what must happen). We have in effect seen some of the difficulties in the way of such an analysis. These may be superable, and my modified Hempelian analysis does not preclude the possibility of analysing the concept of 'bringing about' in radically different terms. For my own part, however, I am fairly pessimistic about the ability of philosophers to produce any useful such analysis. It would not be surprising if this concept was so basic to our conceptual scheme that useful analysis of it in very different terms could not be provided.

It is Hempel's claim that explanation which does not at first sight seem to fit into this scientific pattern can really quite easily be so fitted. Thus we use this scientific pattern of explanation not only when doing science of any degree of sophistication but in much everyday explanation of happenings. We explain the cheese's being mouldy by its having been left in a warm place for two weeks and by the generalization that almost always cheese turns mouldy within two weeks if it is in a warm place. It is important in this pattern of explanation that the initial conditions C include only what I called earlier actual features of the world. If we list among C not merely that the cheese had been left in a warm place but also that it was putrescent, and mean by this 'very likely to turn mouldy within two weeks if left in a warm place' we should not need the generalization at all in order to infer the effect.

Also, we often explain some phenomenon as brought about, not by an event, but by an object. We may say that the breaking of the window was brought about by a brick, but what we are saying here, it is plausibly urged, is that the breaking was caused by some event involving the brick, e.g. its fast motion; and this reduction to the scientific pattern seems plausible enough. But although much ordinary explanation is not implausibly analysed in terms of the Hempelian schema of scientific explanation, we also use in ordinary everyday explanation of happening explanation of the pattern which I called personal explanation and which seems to be very

---

[1] D. Hume, *An Enquiry Concerning Human Understanding* (first published 1748), Sect. 7.

different in kind from scientific explanation. I will describe the structure of personal explanation at a little length and then show why it cannot be knocked into a Hempelian shape.

Personal Explanation

In personal explanation the occurrence of a phenomenon E is explained as brought about by a rational agent P doing some action intentionally. The central case of this, with which we shall be primarily concerned, is where P brings about E intentionally, i.e. brings E about, meaning so to do. The other case is where P brings about E unintentionally in consequence of doing something else intentionally—we shall come to this case briefly later. In the central case E occurred because P meant E to occur through what he was doing. What an agent meant to occur through his agency may be called the intention J in the agent's action, e.g. that E occur. E is then explained by P having intention J. E may be the motion of my hand, P be myself, and J my intention that E occur. E is then what I shall call the result of an intentional action A of bringing E about.[1] In the example cited, A is my moving my hand. However, E is only partially explained by P's having intention J. For a man may have the intention to bring about some effect and yet fail to do so. I may mean my hand to move through my agency, and yet the hand may fail to move because someone is holding it down; in consequence the only action which I perform is that of trying to move my hand. If E does result from P and J a full explanation will tell us why, how it was that P's intention was efficacious.

This leads us to the well-known distinction[2] among intentional actions between basic actions and mediated actions. Roughly speaking—a basic action is something which an agent just does, does not do by doing anything else. A mediated action is an action which is not a basic action, one which an agent does by doing something else. I signal by moving my hand. I break the door down by giving it a kick. The former are mediated actions; the latter basic actions. Now if bringing about E is a basic action, one answer to the

[1] The occurrence of the result of an action is thus entailed by the performance of the action. The result of an action is to be distinguished from a consequence of the action. A consequence of an action is something brought about but not necessarily entailed by performance of the action. This distinction is due to Von Wright. See G. H. Von Wright, *Norm and Action* (London, 1963), pp. 39 ff.

[2] First set out by A. C. Danto in his 'Basic Actions', *American Philosophical Quarterly*, 1965, **2**, 141–8.

question how it was that P's intention was efficacious, will simply be that bringing about E was among the basic powers or capacities X which P had at that time, i.e. was among the basic actions which P could do at will. Bringing about the motion of our arms or legs, lips, or eyes, or eyebrows, etc. are for most of us most of the time among our basic powers.

E is fully explained when we have cited the agent P, his intention J that E occur, and his basic powers X which include the capacity to bring about E; for given all three, E cannot but occur. Of course often in such cases it is so obvious why E occurred that we do not bother to give the explanation, but the explanation is true nevertheless. We may not bother to comment, when a man is walking along, that his legs moved because he moved them (i.e. brought about their motion, meaning so to do), but it is true nevertheless. Sometimes however, this sort of explanation is not at all obvious—it may on occasion be the explanation of a man's ears wiggling or his heart's stopping beating that the man brought about these things intentionally.

If bringing about E is a mediated action the answer to the question how it was that P's intention was efficacious will be more complicated. It will be that E was the intended consequence of some basic action of P's, A^1, i.e. a consequence which P meant to occur through his performing a certain basic action A^1 which consists in bringing about some state of affairs S. P has the intention J that E occur as a consequence of the occurrence of A^1 (and so J contained within it the intention that S occur). The explanation of how P's intention was efficacious is that bringing about S is among P's basic powers X, and that the bringing about of S had as a consequence the occurrence of E. There will often be a scientific explanation of the latter. S may cause E in accord with natural laws L, because it is a consequence of L that in circumstances D (which in fact hold) S is followed by E. So in this case, P, J, X, D, and L fully explain the occurrence of E. E is brought about by P having a certain intention J, which in consequence of his basic powers X brings about some state of affairs S in circumstances D, which laws of nature L then ensure will bring about E. Thus a full explanation of the door being flat on the ground is that I, exercising my basic powers, brought it about that my foot moved quickly into contact with the door, meaning this to occur and it to cause the door to be flat; the door hinges, the mass of the door, the mass and velocity of my foot were in fact such that it was a consequence of the laws of mechanics that the impact of my foot with the door was followed by the flattening of the door. In the above analyses I use the word 'consequence' in a wide sense. E is a consequence of A^1 if E would not have happened if A^1 had not occurred. This may be, as in the above example, because S, the result of A^1, causes E. It may also be because, given current circumstances D, the performance of A^1 constitutes bringing about E. Thus, given the current conventions in motoring and banking, my writing my name in a certain place has as a consequence that a cheque bears my signature, and my putting my arm out of the car window has as a consequence that a signal indicating a turn to the right is made.

So, to summarize, in the central case of personal explanation we explain a phenomenon E as brought about intentionally by a rational agent P. If the bringing about of E is a basic action A, we need to cite further an intention J of P that E occur and to state that bringing about E is among the things which P is able to do at will, viz. among P's basic powers X. P, J, and X provide a full explanation of E. Of course we can often go further and explain how it is that P has intention J (e.g. by stating what his intention is in doing the basic action, what he seeks to achieve by moving his hand), or how it is that P has those powers (e.g. by stating which nerves and muscles need to be operative for P to have these powers). But P, J, and X suffice to explain E—whether or not we can explain how it is that J and X hold. If the bringing about of E is a mediated action, things are more complicated. We cite P and his intention J to bring about E as a consequence of a basic action A^1; we explain that the performance of A^1 was among P's basic powers, and we explain how the performance of A^1 had E as a consequence. Again, the occurrence and operation of the factors cited here may themselves be explained further; but they do not need to be for us to have a full explanation. When there is only a basic action involved, the agent P is the cause of the effect; his intention and powers provide the reason for the efficacy of the cause. Where the action is a mediated action, further factors are added. The two figures at the top of the diagram on p. 36 summarize these results for basic actions, and for mediated actions in cases where a natural law L brings it about that S has E as a consequence. Causes and the conditions for their operation (the 'what') are shown to the left of arrows; reasons (the 'why') are shown above arrows; effects are shown to the right of the arrows.

There is, I claimed earlier, a second kind of personal explanation.

Here we explain the occurrence of E as brought about unintentionally by a rational agent P bringing about something else intentionally; E is an unintended consequence of an intentional action. There are various cases of this, to which I should briefly draw attention. The most usual one is where E is an effect caused by the result S of an intentional action, brought about in virtue of scientific laws (i.e. where a scientific explanation can be given of how S caused E). For example, in standing up I may unintentionally knock over a cup. Here the knocking-over of the cup is caused by my occupying a certain standing position, which was a state of affairs brought about intentionally by me. I did not mean the cup to be knocked over, but given the circumstances (the original position of cup, etc.), my occupying the standing position causes the knocking-over of the cup in virtue of the laws of mechanics L. There are however other cases of unintentional action. One is where the performance of the intentional action constitutes a certain action in virtue of current conventions. I may intentionally sign a form without reading the small print and thereby unintentionally sign away various rights. Another interesting case is where the effect E is not caused by the result of the action, but only by the performance of the action. By standing up intentionally I may bring it about that an electro-chemical current passes through the nerves leading to my leg, and my leg muscles contract and expand in various ways. This is not an effect of my coming to occupy a standing position, for the current passes and the muscles contract and expand before I occupy the standing position. These things, however, are consequences of my intentional action of standing up, for they happen after the beginning of my action, but not after the beginning of the occurrence of its result.[1] Having mentioned these secondary cases of an effect being brought about by an agent acting intentionally, I shall henceforward (except where I state this explicitly) confine myself to the primary case where the effect is brought about intentionally.[2]

[1] Some philosophers might say that these things are consequences of an initial action which is a component of the whole action of standing up—viz. my action of 'setting myself' or 'trying' or 'intending' to stand up—but each of these verbs may carry misleading implications, of which they must be purged before such claims are accurate. For example it may be said that if I 'try' to stand up, this carries the implication that it needed an effort to stand up, or that I failed to stand up—and neither of these things may be the case.

[2] For longer and careful analysis of the various components and kinds of intentional and unintentional action along lines somewhat similar to mine see R. M. Chisholm, 'On the Logic of Intentional Action', in R. Binkley *et al.* (eds.), *Agent, Action, and Reason* (Oxford, 1971).

Personal Explanation Unanalysable in Terms of Scientific Explanation

So a full explanation of a phenomenon as the result of an action has a complicated pattern, not all elements of which may be deployed explicitly when a man explains the occurrence of some event. But in so far as he does not deploy some element, a man's explanation is inadequate—for there is clearly some further factor at work which makes it the case that E occurs. Now, superficially, personal explanation looks very different from scientific explanation. In scientific explanation, as we have seen, we explain an event E by past (or present) events or states C and natural laws L. In personal explanation we explain E as brought about by an agent P (not by an event or state) in order to realize intentions for the future. Despite the apparent difference it has, however, been argued by some philosophers, seminally by Donald Davidson[1] and by many others at greater length, that really personal explanation conforms to the scientific pattern. In my terminology a Davidson-like suggestion amounts to the following.

Suppose first that E is the result of a basic action. Then to say that P brought E about intentionally is just to say that a state of P or an event involving P, P's intention that E occur, J, brought it about.

$$P \xrightarrow{\;J \text{ and } X\;} E$$	$$P \xrightarrow{\;J \text{ and } X\;} S \xrightarrow{\;L\;} E$$
Structure of the central case of personal explanation of E, when E is the result of a basic action.	Structure of the central case of personal explanation of E, when E is the result of a mediated action. (One scheme.)
$$\left.\begin{array}{l} J \\ Y \\ Z \end{array}\right\} \xrightarrow{\;L\;} E$$	$$\left.\begin{array}{l} J \\ Y \\ Z \end{array}\right\} \xrightarrow{\;L_1\;} S \xrightarrow{\;L_2\;} E$$
Attempted analysis of the above in the 'scientific' pattern.	Attempted analysis of the above in the 'scientific' pattern.

To say that P had the power to bring about E about is just to say that P's bodily condition Y (brain-states, muscle-states, etc.) and environmental conditions Z (no one having bound P's arm, etc.) and psycho-physiological laws L are such that an intention such as J is followed by the event intended, E. We then have a scientific explanation as set out in the diagram. Suppose next that E is the result of a mediated action. Then to say that P brought it about is

[1] D. Davidson, 'Actions, Reasons, and Causes', *Journal of Philosophy*, 1963, **60**, 685–700.

to say that a state of P or event involving P, viz. P's intention J under the current bodily and environmental conditions Y and Z bring about (in accordance with psycho-physiological laws L_1) the result of the basic action S, which has as a consequence E. We have seen that there are various ways in which S may have E as a consequence. One way is that S may bring about E in accord with the normal scientific pattern of causation—i.e. in virtue of some law of nature L_2. This is the scheme depicted in the diagram. The other ways in which S may have E as a consequence can also, it is suggested, easily be fitted into the scientific pattern of explanation. So on this reductionist view, personal explanation is in essence really scientific explanation. There are not explanations of events of two kinds—only explanations of one kind. Events brought about by actions are just those which include intentions among their causes. Proponents of this type of reductive analysis of personal explanation by scientific explanation may sometimes describe the states of P or events involving P which I have called 'intentions' in another way. Originally instead of talking of 'intentions', they talked of 'volitions', which were supposed to be something like decisions. Sometimes, now, instead, they talk of 'desires' or 'wants'.

I do not believe that in any of its forms this reduction works. The difficulty is just what are these states or events which are supposed to replace agents and what they mean to do by their actions. If these states or events are to function in scientific explanation, they must be occurrent states or events. From the seventeenth century to the twentieth century many writers supposed that they were mental acts of willing, to which they gave the name 'volitions'. On this view, actions are movements caused by volitions; my moving my hand is a volition to move my hand causing a subsequent motion of my hand. One difficulty with this view is that volitions, being themselves actions, ought to be analysable in a similar way. But if each volition involves another one, we would have an infinite series of volitions involved in every action—which is absurd.

An alternative is to suppose that the causal factors involved are conscious mental events, but happenings rather than actions. On this view an action is a movement caused by an occurrent want or desire. My moving my hand is an occurrent want to move my hand causing the movement of my hand. This view is involved in the sophisticated account of action developed by Alvin Goldman.[1] He writes of the causal factors involved in the explanation of action as

[1] A. I. Goldman, *A Theory of Human Action* (Englewood Cliffs, NJ), 1970.

occurrent 'wants'.[1] A crucial difficulty however, for both volitional theory and occurrent mental cause theory is that they vastly overpopulate our mental life. People perform vast numbers of intentional actions all the time without there being all these conscious 'findings-attractive' going on. Within a few seconds I tip my chair, I dip my pen into the ink-well, I write 'I' and 'tip' and 'my' and 'chair' meaning to do so (as well as the occasional word which I do not mean to write). There just are not all these 'findings-attractive' going on. The crucial causal factors are clearly not conscious occurrent mental events, whether actions or mere happenings.

One might suppose that the crucial causal factors are brain-states. We might find when people intentionally bring about an effect, that that effect is caused (in the way describable by normal scientific explanation) by a series of neural states beginning with a character-istic brain-state. We might then conclude that the initial brain-state was the intention to bring about the effect. Such a theory may be called an 'identity' theory of human action. It claims that human actions just are (are identical with) series of neural events terminat-ing in bodily movements and beginning with brain-states of certain kinds. Theories of this kind have recently been put forward by both A. C. Danto[2] and L. H. Davis.[3] However, the identity between actions and series of events, and between intentions and brain-events will be at most a logically contingent identity.

It will be appropriate at this stage to explain these crucial philosophical terms. An analytic or logically necessary proposi-tion is one which it would be incoherent to suppose to be false; 'all squares have four sides' and 'red is a colour' are logically necessary, because it would be incoherent, would make no sense to suppose that red could be anything else except a colour, or that a square could have only three sides. A synthetic or logically contingent proposition is one which it is coherent to suppose to be true and coherent to suppose to be false. 'The moon is more than 200,000 miles from the earth' is true, but it is not incoherent to suppose it false—we can make sense of the supposition that it is false. (It contains no contradiction.) 'The moon is less than 200,000 miles

[1] 'To have an *occurrent* want is to have an *occurrent* thought of X as attractive, nice, good, etc., a favourable, regarding, viewing, or taking of the prospect of X.' Goldman, op. cit., p. 94.

[2] A. C. Danto, *Analytical Philosophy of Action* (Cambridge, 1973).

[3] L. H. Davis, 'Actions', *Canadian Journal of Philosophy*, Suppl. Vol., No. 1, Part 2, 1974.

from the earth' is false, but it is coherent to suppose that it is true. Both propositions are logically contingent ones.[1] Logical necessity is to be distinguished from the physical necessity which we saw to be involved in causation. Laws of nature such as Newton's laws of motion, state what must happen necessarily; material bodies necessarily attract each other with certain forces; and so if I throw something out of the window, necessarily it will fall downwards rather than rise upwards. But the necessity is not logical—for it is coherent to suppose that things could be otherwise. An identity proposition is one that states that two objects are identical, e.g. 'Dr Jekyll is Mr Hyde' or 'Mr Callaghan is the Prime Minister'. An identity is logically necessary if the proposition which affirms it is logically necessary. Thus the identity of 7 and the numeral next greater than 6 is logically necessary, since '7 is the numeral next greater than 6' is logically necessary. Whereas the identity of Jimmy Carter and the present President of the USA is logically contingent. Jimmy Carter is the President, but someone else could have been President, and it is coherent to suppose that Jimmy Carter is not the President.

Now even if intentions are always brain-states, it is coherent to suppose that they are not—it is coherent to suppose that a man may have some intention without as a result his brain's being in a certain specific state. It is not a logical consequence of a man's having an intention to have a drink that his brain is in a certain specific state (although these things may always go together). Nor is it a logical consequence of some agent P bringing about an effect E, meaning so to do, that a certain specific series of neural states caused E. So the identity between intentions and brain-states, intentional actions and series of neural states is at most a logically contingent one.

However, the philosopher is looking for an analysis of what it *means* to give a personal explanation, and such an analysis will be true of logical necessity. So even if intentions were brain-states, an explanation in terms of an intention is not analysable in terms of an explanation by brain-states. A different claim is being made when we explain an effect by the action of a person bringing about the effect intentionally from that which we make when we explain an effect by a series of brain-states. It is that claim which we are seeking to elucidate; identity theory does not elucidate the philosophical

[1] For a much fuller account of logical necessity, logical contingency, and coherence see *The Coherence of Theism*, Chs. 2 and 3.

problem of what we are committed to in giving a personal explanation of events.

If the crucial causal factors are not brain-states nor mental
events of which the agent is conscious, the remaining alternative
seems to be to suppose that they are (occurrent) states of mind, or
mental events of which the agent is not necessarily conscious. This
notion needs a little clarification—what is this mind which has
occurrent states? However, it is not implausible to suppose that
desires, wants, intentions, etc. are such states. Davidson holds that
the 'attitudes' i.e. desires which bring about actions are 'states, or
dispositions, not events'. If he is to provide a scientific explanation
he must, I think, hold that they are states, not dispositions; and if
his account is to be plausible he must hold that they are mental
states. Desires may, Davidson admits, need some event such as a
perception or neural event, to trigger them off, but this does not stop
them being causes. So very roughly, actions are states which have
occurrent mental states, desires for their occurrence, among their
causes. Personal explanation is analysable in terms of the production of effects by such desires.

Despite the fact that it is the most plausible form of reductionist
theory, like all the others, Davidson's theory is open to a fatal
objection. The basic idea of all the theories is that an agent's
bringing about an effect intentionally, i.e. meaning so to do—which
is how we defined the agent's bringing about an effect having an
intention so to do—is to be analysed as the causing of that effect by
some state of the agent or some event involving him. But all such
analyses fail because an intention (or wish or desire) of P to bring
about E, if it is some occurrent state or event, could bring about E
without P's having intentionally brought about E. Causation by an
intention does not guarantee intentional action.

The classic objection to the reductionist theory was formulated
as follows by Richard Taylor. Here the causal factor is termed
a 'desire', but it could equally well be termed a 'want' or an
'intention'.

Suppose . . . that a member of an audience keenly desires to attract the
speaker's attention but, being shy, only fidgets uncomfortably in his seat
and blushes. We may suppose, further, that he does attract the speaker's
attention by his very fidgeting; but he did not fidget *in order* to catch the
speaker's attention, even though he desired that result and might well have
realized that such behaviour was going to produce it.[1]

[1] R. Taylor, *Action and Purpose* (Englewood Cliffs, NJ, 1966), pp. 248 f.

Here we have a case of desire for E causing E, and yet there being no action. The basic point is that intentions, desires, wants—as occurrent states—may occur and yet the agent for some reason may not act on his intention or seek to fulfil his desire or want. Nevertheless, in such a case, possibly unbeknown to the agent, the intention may bring about the intended effect—without the agent's bringing about the effect intentionally. An agent's bringing something about intentionally is not analysable as his intention's bringing that thing about, if an intention is supposed to be an occurrent mental event or state. The same applies if we substitute for 'intention', 'desire', 'want', or any similar term.[1] So a Davidson-type analysis seems to fail. To say that P brought something about intentionally is not to say that some state of P or event involving P, such as an intention, brought that thing about. There seems to be no other plausible way in which personal explanations can be analysed into the scientific pattern, and so it would appear that personal explanation is of a distinct type from scientific explanation.

It seems to me that the basic mistake which these reductionist analyses make is (in the terminology introduced at the beginning of the chapter) to treat intentions as belonging to the 'what' rather than to the 'why' of explanation. When one explains an occurrence as brought about by an agent's having some intention one is not by the word 'intention' describing some occurrent state or event, but one is explaining *why* the cause, the agent, brought about the effect which he did—viz. because he intended to bring about that effect or some other effect. Like laws of nature, such intentions explain why things have the effects which they do.[2]

[1] Goldman's main answer to Taylor's objection is to admit that intentional acts have to be caused by 'action plans' or desires 'in a certain characteristic way', and to claim that in Taylor's example we do not have a case of that way. And what is this characteristic way? Goldman writes: 'To this question, I confess, I do not have a fully detailed answer. But neither do I think that it is incumbent on me, *qua* philosopher, to give an answer to this question. A complete explanation of how wants and beliefs lead to intentional acts would require intensive neurophysiological information, and I do not think it fair to demand of a *philosophical* analysis, that it provide this information.' (op. cit., p. 62.) But this really will not do. For hundreds and hundreds of years men have been able to distinguish, among cases where wants cause the events wanted, those cases where an action was performed. We have distinct concepts here which we know how to apply. It is indeed incumbent upon a philosopher to analyse the difference—although it is not up to him to say which neurophysiological goings-on are physically necessary to produce a case of an action being performed. Goldman has not analysed the difference.

[2] It is important to distinguish the intention in an agent's action or the intention with which he acts from an intention to do something at some future date. The latter

An intention—to avoid a puddle, say—explains why at a certain time a man with normal capacities (and that involves, physically, a normal brain and the operation of normal psycho-physiological laws) acted as he did, made such movements as in fact led to his feet bypassing the puddle. That this account is correct is brought out by the linguistic fact that explanations in terms of intentions can easily be paraphrased in terms of explanations in which there occur no nouns which could conceivably be regarded as denoting occurrent states or events. To say that a man's intention in making certain movements was to avoid the puddle is to say that he made them in order to avoid the puddle, or so as to avoid the puddle. But no such paraphrase is possible for the initial conditions which are cited in normal scientific explanations.

Although intentions, like laws of nature, belong to the 'why', the reasons, of explanation, there are of course vast differences between laws of nature and intentions. Intentions are such that necessarily the agent whose they are 'goes along with them' (may even have deliberately chosen at some time to have them), is aware of them, and has privileged access to them in the sense that he is in a better position than outsiders to know about them. Laws of nature are not necessarily known to anyone, nor necessarily does any person 'go along with them' or have privileged access to them. But that the 'why' is here known and adopted by an agent is one of the differences between personal and scientific explanation. The other main difference is that in personal explanation talk about an object which explains, viz. a person, is not reducible to talk about occurrent states of or events involving that person.

Scientific Explanation Reanalysed

In arguing thus that personal explanation is explanation of a different kind from scientific explanation, I used an amended version of Hempel's account of scientific explanation which I developed carefully at the beginning of the chapter.

According to this the occurrence of a phenomenon E is explained in terms of initial events or states C (the 'initial conditions' including the cause) and natural laws L, when C and L conjointly physically

---

is not something manifested in action and may be a state of some sort. The former exists only in so far as an agent performs some intentional action—even if only the minimal action of trying to do something. The account in the text is meant only to apply to intentions in actions.

necessitate or make highly probable the occurrence of *E*. Although not false, in some ways this remains not a very satisfactory account of scientific explanation. For it tends to hypostatize laws of nature, to suggest that there are two sorts of thing in the world, events or states (normally consisting in states of or changes in or of material bodies) and laws of nature. But laws of nature are not things which exist independently of material bodies. Talk about laws of nature is really only talk about the powers and liabilities of bodies. Talk of laws of nature only came into science in the seventeenth century, and, although it has proved very useful to science, one must not misunderstand such talk. Earlier scientists, instead of talking of events and natural laws, talked instead of material bodies and their powers and liabilities. A power of a body is a capacity of it to bring about effects. A liability of a body is a disposition of it to suffer change under various circumstances—among the liabilities of a body are that it has (of physical necessity or probability) to exercise its powers when subjected to various stimuli. Thus instead of saying that the ignition of a certain mass of gunpowder plus a natural law of chemistry explained some explosion, earlier scientists would have said that the gunpowder caused the explosion, the power to cause an explosion being among the powers of the gunpowder, and a liability necessarily to exercise that power when ignited being among the liabilities of the gunpowder; and the explosion was to be explained by the gunpowder's exercising its powers in virtue of its liabilities. In this way of talking it is always an object, not a state or event, which causes events. In general, if on the Hempelian model a state or event *C* in circumstances *D* brings about *E* in virtue of *L*, then on the more ancient model the object of which *C* is a state or change of state brings about *E* in virtue of its powers *P* which it has a liability to exercise when it is in the state in question and under the circumstances as described by *L*.

This more ancient way of talking is in some ways more satisfactory because it brings out that the only things in the universe described in laws of physics or chemistry are material bodies; they interact and have properties, including their powers and liabilities. But that is all there is; the Hempelian way of talking suggests that laws of nature are on a parallel with material bodies, but outside them. However nothing which is not inherent in the gunpowder makes it do what it does. Each body has its own powers, and liabilities; each lump of gunpowder has its power to cause an explosion. But the world is full of bodies with similar powers and liabilities; there may be many lumps of gunpowder each with qualitatively identical powers (and liabilities). There are many lumps of iron each with qualitatively identical powers (and liabilities), and so on.[1] The objects in their states and surrounding circumstances are causes; their powers and liabilities reasons for the efficacy of those causes. Personal explanation differs from scientific explanation as thus characterized in that the cause is a rational agent (normally a person) and not any object, and instead of an object's liabilities we have an agent's intention. Since we have translated one account of scientific explanation into a more satisfactory one, and since we cannot (apparently) translate personal explanation into the first account of scientific explanation, it follows that we cannot translate personal explanation into the second account either. The basic difference is that intentions are not a species of liabilities.

Having shown reason for preferring the powers-and-liabilities account of scientific explanation to that in terms of natural laws, I shall often—where nothing turns on it—revert to the latter and easier mode of exposition.

Can there be two explanations of a phenomenon?

So far in this chapter I have been concerned to characterize the structures of the two types of explanation which we use in explaining the occurrence of phenomena, and to show that they differ greatly from each other in structure. I now turn to the question of whether there can only be one true explanation of some phenomenon. For if so, then if there is a personal explanation of some event, there cannot be a scientific one, and conversely. I suggest that there can be two true distinct explanations of some phenomenon *E*, if one or other of two conditions is satisfied, but that otherwise there cannot be.

Clearly there can be two true distinct explanations of *E*, when one or other or both are partial explanations of *E*. For the one may combine with the other to make a fuller explanation. Thus a man's death from cancer may be explained by (1) his smoking and a generalization about the proportion of smokers who die from cancer, and by (2) his parents' having died of cancer and a

---

[1] I owe many of these points to an important book which develops at length a 'non-Humean' or 'non-Hempelian' scheme of causality—R. Harré and E. H. Madden, *Causal Powers* (Oxford, 1975).

generalization about the proportion of those whose parents die of cancer who themselves die of cancer. Since (1) and (2) only make probable but do not necessitate the man's death from cancer, they are only partial explanations. Clearly they can be combined into a fuller explanation in terms of the man's smoking and his parents' having died of cancer and the proportion of those who smoke and whose parents have died of cancer who die of cancer.[1]

But can there be two different full explanations of a phenomenon? The answer is still yes—if the occurrence of the causes (the 'what') and the operation of the reasons (the 'why') cited in one explanation are to be explained at least in part by the occurrence of the causes and the operation of the reasons cited in the other explanation. For example, the present position of Mars is explained by its positions in the last six days and the laws of planetary motion, formulated more or less correctly by Kepler. Where it has been and the laws stating how planets move determine where Mars will be today. Yet the present position of Mars is also explained by its position and velocity last week and those of all other heavenly bodies, and Newton's laws of motion. Newton's laws state how material bodies change their velocities under the influence of other bodies. Both are full explanations, and yet they are clearly compatible. This is because Newton's laws and the positions and velocities of the planets explain their (approximate) conformity to Kepler's laws. Kepler's laws operate because Newton's laws operate and the sun and the planets have the initial positions and velocities which they have, and are far distant from other massive bodies. It is for this reason that the motion of a human hand is often explicable both by personal and by scientific explanations. The motion of my hand may be fully explained by goings-on in the nerves and muscles of my arm, and physiological laws. It may also be fully explained by my bringing it about, having the intention and power so to do. Yet in this case the causes and reasons cited in each explanation provide a partial explanation of the occurrence and operation of the causes and reasons cited in the other. The goings-on in my nerves and muscles are, as we saw earlier, brought about unintentionally by my bringing about the motion of my hand intentionally. Also, the operation of physiological laws provides part of the explanation of my having the power to move my hand—only because nervous

[1] It is however a difficult question how the former generalizations are to be combined to yield generalizations of the latter kind, which I discuss in my *An Introduction to Confirmation Theory*, Chs. 8 and 9.

discharges are propagated as they are, am I able to move my hand. So there is a twofold reason why two full explanations can each fully explain the motion of my hand.

But can there be two distinct full explanations of some phenomenon E, when neither in any way explains the occurrence or operation of the causes and reasons involved in the other? The answer to that question is No. For suppose that causes and reasons F_1 and also causes and reasons F_2 each fully explain E, and neither in any way explains the other. Then F_1 is necessary and sufficient for the occurrence of E. Given F_1, E cannot but occur. Now suppose F_1 not to have occurred; suppose a deity to have intervened suddenly to stop F_1 occurring. Then since F_1 in no way explains the occurrence of F_2, the non-occurrence of F_1 would in no way affect whether or not F_2 occurs. So F_2 will still occur. Since F_2 provides a full explanation of E, it is necessary and sufficient for the occurrence of E. So E will occur. E will occur, even though F_1 does not occur. So F_1 cannot be necessary and sufficient for the occurrence of E, and so the causes and reasons involved in F_1 cannot fully explain E— contrary to our original supposition. I conclude that if there are two full explanations of E, one must, at least in part, explain the occurrence and operation of the causes and reasons involved in the other. It follows that there can be a full personal explanation and a full scientific explanation of some phenomenon, only if one in part explains the occurrence and operation of the components of the other—either the scientific at least in part explains the causes and reasons in the personal, or conversely.

Explanation by the Action of God

In this chapter so far I have been concerned to analyse the structure of personal explanation, and to show its relation to scientific explanation. I have done this because when the theist claims that the action of God explains various phenomena, such as the existence and orderliness of the world, he is proposing a personal explanation of these phenomena. However, personal explanations of phenomena by the action of God differ from most mundane personal explanations in two important respects, on which I must now comment in conclusion of this chapter.

The first is that a personal explanation of the occurrence of a phenomenon E in terms of God's bringing it about, meaning so to do, cannot be even in part explicable scientifically. We have seen that a personal explanation may often, at any rate in part, be explained by a scientific explanation—and conversely. Thus a man's having the powers which he has may be explained in part by his having nerves and muscles and by the operation of various physiological laws. His having the intentions which he has may also be given a scientific explanation, and perhaps a man's existence may also be explained in this way. The fact that personal explanation cannot be analysed in terms of scientific explanation does not mean that its operation on a particular occasion cannot be given a scientific explanation.

However, it seems coherent to suppose that there should be a personal explanation of the occurrence of some event E by the agency of an agent P having the intention J to bring about E and the power so to do, without all this being in any way susceptible of a scientific explanation. To start with, an agent might have the power to perform certain basic actions without his having that power being dependent on any physical states or natural laws. His capacity to perform these actions might be an ultimate brute fact (or only explicable by another personal explanation). Likewise an agent's having the intentions in actions which he does, his choice of intentional actions, may not be susceptible of scientific explanation.

Also, there might not be a scientific explanation of the existence of the agent—this too might be an ultimate brute fact. Yet personal explanation explains, whether or not an agent's powers, intentions, or existence are dependent on physical conditions. Men have given and accepted explanations, in terms of agents' intentions, of the actions which they have performed, for many millennia without knowing anything about the physical conditions which are necessary for an agent to possess the power in question, and even without believing that there were any such conditions. You are not committed to any beliefs about bones, nerves, and muscles, if you accept that my having the intention to move my arm and my power to do so explain the motion of my arm. Because I moved it intentionally explains why it moved. Again, when presented with a purported demonstration of telekinesis, we may accept a man's having the intention to bend a fork and his power so to do as explaining why a fork at some distance from himself bent, without our having any idea of what his power depended on, and indeed even if we deny that it depends on anything. Of course we may reject this explanation, but the point is—it is a logically possible explanation and we do not need to have a belief about some physical state or law being necessary for the exercise of the power in order to accept the purported explanation. Similar points apply with respect to the other factors involved in personal explanation. Personal explanation may explain without there being a scientific explanation of the occurrence and operation of the factors involved in it.

When the theist claims that the existence of the world and its various features is to be explained by the action of God bringing these things about meaning so to do, he will claim that God's action cannot be explained scientifically, even in part. God is supposed to be perfectly free. God's existence and powers do not depend on the states of the physical world or the laws of its operation—rather, vice versa. Nor are God's intentions scientifically explicable. But all this, as we have now seen, does not in any way weaken the explanatory value of the personal explanation. God's bringing about some event may be explicable by a wider personal explanation. He may bring about *E* in order thereby to bring about *F*; *F* may be an event which takes a considerable period of time, and *E* may be the first stage of *F*. But the theist claims that this kind of explanation is the only kind of explanation of God's actions which can be provided. God's own intentions alone explain his doing what he does.

As with humans, many of the actions which God performs will be basic actions. Keeping the universe in existence and keeping the behaviour of things conforming to natural laws are presumably basic actions of God. Some of the acts attributed by the theist to God are acts of creating *e nihilo* (i.e. not out of pre-existing matter); others are acts of moving, or changing the characteristics of, existing things. Creating matter *e nihilo* is not something which men are able to do, but it is easy enough to conceive of their doing it. I could just find myself able as easily to make appear before me an ink-well or to make a sixth finger grow, as I am at present able to move my hand. Various tests (e.g. sealing off the room and keeping its contents carefully weighed) could show that the ink-well or finger were not made of existing matter. Creating *e nihilo* is a perfectly conceivable basic act.

The other important respect in which personal explanations of phenomena by the action of God differ from most mundane personal explanations is that God is supposed to be a person without a body, i.e. a spirit. It is important to make clear at this stage what it is for a person not to have a body. We can best do so by asking a different question—what is it that I am saying when I say that this body, the body behind the desk, is *my* body? First, that

I can move, as basic actions of mine, many parts of this body—whereas I can only move parts of some other body or thing by moving parts of this body. To move the arm over there I have to grasp it with this arm, but I can move this arm straight off. Secondly, that I am aware of goings-on in this body. I know the position of these limbs and feel the emptiness of this stomach. However I come to know about things outside this body, only through their effects on this body. I see the desk and so know where it is, only because light rays from the desk impinge on these eyes. I learn what you tell me only because by talking you set up air vibrations which impinge on these ears. Thirdly, and I think less fundamentally, that I look out on the world from where this body is. It is things around this body which I see well, things further away which I see less well. Fourthly, that my thoughts and feelings are affected by goings-on in this body. Disturbances in it cause me pains, aches, tingles, etc.; whereas disturbances in the table or the body over there are unfelt by me.[1]

Now clearly a person has a body if there is a material object to which he is related in all of the above four ways. And clearly a person does not have a body if there is no material object to which he is related in any of the above ways. But what are we to say if a person is related to different material objects in each of these ways, or is related to a material object in only some of these ways? Presumably, that he is embodied only to some degree.

Clearly God is not supposed to be embodied in either the third or fourth way. There is no one place from which God looks out on the world. Nor is there any material object, disturbances in which cause God pains, or whose state affects the way in which God thinks about the world (except to the extent that it makes him have knowledge of its state). As regards the first way, God is supposed to be able to move any part of the material universe as a basic action. He does not have to move anything as a mediated action. And as regards the second way, there is no part of the material universe through which God gains knowledge of other parts. His knowledge of all parts of the universe does not depend on the operation of any causal mechanism. So God is embodied in the very limited respect that he can move and has knowledge of all parts of the material universe. But the claim that God has no body is the denial of more substantial embodiment, and above all, the denial that God controls

[1] I owe these points in part to J. Harrison, 'The Embodiment of Mind, or What Use is Having a Body?', *Proceedings of the Aristotelian Society*, 1973-4, **74**, 33-55.

and knows about the material universe by controlling and getting information from one part directly and other parts indirectly. So when the theist claims that he is arguing to a non-embodied agent, we must bear in mind that it would be perhaps less misleading to say that he is arguing to the existence of a rational agent who is far less embodied (tied down to matter) than we are, but one embodied to the extent and in the ways which I have just described.

So then in the arguments to the existence of God the theist argues from the existence and order of the world and various features of it to an agent, God, who brought these things about, having some intention in so doing. The theist may or may not claim to know what that intention was. We have seen that if, in explaining the occurrence of some event *E*, we can say only who brought it about intentionally, but not why he did so, our explanation is only partial. We have given an explanation none the less. In this chapter I have been concerned to analyse what it is to explain an event as brought about by some agent meaning so to do; and in conclusion I have drawn attention to two special features of personal explanations in terms of the action of God.

Having investigated in this chapter the structure of personal explanation, my concern in the next chapter will be with the circumstances which justify us in putting it forward, with the circumstances which make it probable that an explanation of the personal type rather than one of the scientific type is the true explanation of some phenomenon. We will then be in a position to see whether the circumstances recorded in the premises of arguments to the existence of God constitute such circumstances.

3

The Justification of Explanation

WHAT are the grounds for believing that some proposed explanation of a phenomenon E is a true explanation? (I write 'a' true explanation rather than 'the' true explanation, for as we have seen there may be many true explanations of the same phenomenon.)

The Justification of Scientific Explanation

To start with, what are the grounds for supposing that a proposed scientific explanation is a true one? In answering this, I assume, to start with, the amended Hempelian account of scientific explanation (outlined on pp. 42 ff.). My answer will be very brief, since my concern is more with personal explanation, but I think that it is sufficiently general to be acceptable to most philosophers of science. On the amended Hempelian account the occurrence of a phenomenon E is explained if laws of nature L and other particular phenomena, C, called the initial conditions, physically necessitate (or make highly probable) the occurrence of E. A proposed explanation will be a true one if the purported law L which it cites is in fact a law of nature and the cited initial conditions in fact occurred (and L and C do entail that it is physically necessary or highly probable that E occur). A proposed explanation will be probably true in so far as (given the entailment, just mentioned) it is probable that L is a law of nature and probable that C occurred. Our grounds for believing a general statement such as 'all material bodies attract each other with forces proportional to the product of their masses and inversely proportional to the square of their distance apart' to be a law of nature will be that it belongs to a scientific theory which has high prior probability and great explanatory power.

The prior probability of a theory is its probability before we consider the detailed evidence of observation cited in its support. Prior probability depends on simplicity, fit with background knowledge, and scope. A theory is simple in so far as it postulates few mathematically simple laws holding between entities of an intelligible kind. By a theory postulating 'entities of an intelligible kind', I mean that it postulates entities of a kind whose nature and interactions seem natural to us.[1] Thus it may postulate that there exist very small particles, atoms, which interact by bouncing off each other in the way that billiard balls do. (I am not of course saying that if a theory postulates unobservable entities, it *has* to postulate ones of an intelligible kind. Clearly good theories often postulate entities which behave in very strange ways. I am saying merely that a theory which postulates entities of an intelligible kind, as opposed to other entities, will have greater prior probability, and so, *other things being equal*, will be more likely to be true.)

A theory fits with our general background knowledge of how the world works in so far as the kinds of entities and laws which it postulates are similar to those which we reasonably believe to hold in other fields. Thus a theory about the behaviour of potassium at low temperatures would fit well with background knowledge in so far as it postulated similar behaviour for potassium to that postulated by other accepted theories for similar substances at low temperatures. The more simple a theory, and the better it fits with background knowledge, the greater its prior probability.

Yet, a theory's prior probability is diminished in so far as its scope is great. What I mean by this is that in so far as it purports to apply to more and more objects and to tell you more and more about them, it is less probable. Clearly the more you assert, the more likely you are to make a mistake. The force of this criterion is to render theories less probable in so far as they are about all material bodies rather than (e.g.) just all bodies near the earth, or all metals. But typically if a theory loses scope it loses simplicity too, because any restriction of scope is often arbitrary and complicating. Why an arbitrary restriction to all bodies near the earth? A claim about the behaviour of all material bodies seems simpler. For this reason I do not think that the criterion of small scope is of great importance in determining prior probability; and so I shall concen-

[1] Such a theory is often said to have a comprehensible model. For discussion of the role of models in science see M. B. Hesse, *Models and Analogies in Science* (London, 1963).

trate largely on the other two criteria of prior probability, referring to this one only at crucial points. The criterion of fitting in with background knowledge is clearly of less and less importance in so far as the theory postulated is of wider and wider application (i.e. claims to tell us what there is in all fields), for then there are less and less other fields with whose theories it has to fit. For large-scale theories the crucial determinant of prior probability is simplicity.

A theory has explanatory power in so far as it entails or makes probable the occurrence of many diverse phenomena which are all observed to occur, and the occurrence of which is not otherwise to be expected.

Thus, Newton's theory of motion, as put forward in his *Principia* in 1689, consisting of his three laws of motion and his law of gravitational attraction, satisfied these criteria very well; which made it probable that each of the proposed laws was indeed a law of nature. The theory was simple because there were only four very general laws of very great mathematical simplicity stating the mechanical relationships which hold between all material bodies. Thus the law of gravitation stated that all material bodies attract each other in pairs with forces proportional to the product of the masses of each, m and m^1, and inversely proportional to the square of their distances apart $(r) - mm^1/r^2$. The relationship is simple because the distance is not raised to a complicated power (e.g. we do not have $r^{2.0003}$ or $r^{\log m}$), there is only one term (e.g. we do not have $mm^1/r^2 + mm^1/r^4 + mm^1/r^6$), and so on. Newton's law is a very natural one, for given his law and only given his law, the total force exerted by a body on a hollow sphere of given uniform thickness and density centred on the body remains the same, whatever the inner radius of the sphere. This means that the force exerted by a body can be regarded as a sort of bubble spreading out from the body, getting thinner as it grows in size. Since the theory purported to cover all the mechanical behaviour of earthly and heavenly bodies, there was not much other scientific knowledge with which it could fit. Its scope is very great in so far as it tells us about all material bodies, but it is concerned only with their mechanical interactions, not, for example, with their chemical or electrical interactions. The theory also had enormous explanatory power in that it predicted with great accuracy the behaviour of bodies of very different kinds in very different circumstances—the motions of planets, the rise and fall of tides, the interactions of colliding bodies, the movements of pendula, etc. etc.—which but for Newton's theory would not be expected to behave in the detailed way which it lays down. So except for the point about its enormous scope, it satisfied the stated criteria very well. The fact that over all it was judged enormously probable illustrates my point that the criterion of scope is of less importance than the other criteria.

Our grounds for believing that initial conditions C occurred are either that they were observed to occur; or less directly, that the supposition that C occurred has itself great prior probability and explanatory power. It is for a reason of the latter kind that we suppose unobserved entities such as distant planets to exist. We observe a distant star moving in a certain way, and we can explain this if we suppose that there is close to it a massive planet which in accordance with Newton's laws is exerting on it an attraction so as to make it move in that way. If we suppose that Newton's laws operate (for which there is the vast amount of evidence which I have just outlined), we can account simply for the behaviour of the star by postulating at least one unobserved body which is exerting a gravitational force on the star. Such behaviour would otherwise be very mysterious.[1] It is clearly simpler to suppose that there is only one such body, and so this is the supposition with maximum prior probability and explanatory power.

It is also for a reason of this kind that we suppose unobservable entities such as atoms, molecules, photons, and protons, to exist, to interact, and to have effects. We can explain the occurrence of certain clicks of Geiger counters and spots on photographic plates by the supposition that certain such particles have produced them.[2] So then, to summarize, our grounds for judging a proposed scientific explanation h of a phenomenon E to be probably true,

[1] e.g. if we were to postulate that some force of attraction other than the gravitational force were at work, we should be postulating the operation of a force determining star-motion other than the force which determined all other star-motion, and this would lead to a more complicated world-picture than the supposition in the text.

[2] These and similar examples which will be discussed in Ch. 4 point to the obvious fact that science is often able to locate the cause of phenomena in some unobservable entity or process. Both Hume and Kant wrote when science had not had the success which it has had today in discovering the unobservable causes of observable events; and their philosophy of religion is often vitiated by the implicit or explicit principle that we could only be justified in postulating a cause of some observable event if that cause was also something observable. Thus Kant: 'If the empirically valid law of causality is to lead to the original being, the latter must belong to the chain of objects of experience.' *Critique of Pure Reason* (trans. N. Kemp-Smith), A636. It is sufficient to reflect on the evident success of chemistry and physics, in providing good grounds to believe in the existence of atoms, electrons, photons, etc., to realize that that principle is quite mistaken.

where *e* is our observational knowledge which includes *E*, are the prior probability of *h* and its explanatory power with respect to *e*.

I stress the enormous importance of the criterion of simplicity, an importance which is not always appreciated. Sometimes people ignore it and say that what makes a theory probable is its explanatory power, or worse still, simply the fact that we can deduce from it our evidence, that is statements reporting the phenomena which have been observed. The trouble with this claim is that for any finite collection of phenomena there will always be an infinite number of different theories such that from each (together with statements of initial conditions) can be deduced statements reporting the phenomena observed with perfect accuracy (and it may be that but for some one of these theories these phenomena are not to be expected). The theories agree in leading us to expect what has been observed so far, but disagree in their subsequent predictions. We may wait for new observations of phenomena to enable us to choose between theories; but however many theories we eliminate by finding them incompatible with observations, we will always be left with an infinite number of theories between which to choose, on grounds other than explanatory power. If there are no theories of neighbouring fields with which some theories may fit better than others, the crucial criterion is that of simplicity. (And when our theories are very large-scale, there will be little in the way of theories of neighbouring fields.)

This point may be illustrated by what is known as the 'curve-fitting' problem. Consider Kepler studying the motion of Mars. Imagine, that he has a large finite number of past locations of Mars.[1] He wishes to know the path along which Mars is moving, knowledge which will enable him to predict its future positions. He can mark on a map of the sky the past positions; but through those positions he can draw an infinite number of different curves which diverge from each other in the future. One theory is of course that Mars moves in an ellipse. Another is that Mars moves in a spiral which diverges hardly at all from an ellipse during the period studied so far, but will diverge significantly hereafter. Another is that Mars moves along a path which describes increasingly large ellipses which eventually becomes parabolic in shape. And so on. Of

---

[1] This supposition of course gives far more knowledge than the historical Kepler had. The historical Kepler knew only the bearing of Mars from the earth at various times, not its distance from the earth as well. But I make my supposition to make exposition easier.

course very few of these theories would have been set out and seriously considered by Kepler or anyone else investigating the field. But my point is that if the sole criterion for judging between theories was their ability to predict, all of these theories would be equally likely to be true, for all of them are equally successful in predicting. The fact that many of the theories were not seriously considered is grounds for supposing that some other criterion was at work, and clearly it was the criterion of simplicity. Most of the theories which predict the data are theories which describe Mars as moving in a very contorted curve which can only be described by a very complicated equation. The theory that Mars moved in an ellipse was a very simple one.

There must be a criterion to choose between the infinite number of theories which are equally successful in predicting the observations already made, if we are ever to be able to make any justified predictions for the future. If we are to predict that the sun will rise tomorrow, we need in order to do so, a theory about how the sun moves. To obtain such a theory we need a criterion for selecting among theories of its motion which would have been equally successful in predicting past observations. The history of science reveals that, in the absence of background knowledge, that criterion is basically the criterion of simplicity. It is true that our understanding of when one theory is simpler than another is very much the product of our scientific and mathematical upbringing, but that does not mean that our understanding is in error. We must make the judgements which seem to us to be intuitively right. Without using this criterion we could make no progress at all in rational inquiry. *Simplex sigillum veri* ('The simple is the sign of the true') is a dominant theme of this book, as will become apparent in due course. All that I have been concerned to show here is the crucial influence of the criterion of simplicity within science. If we are to adopt in our investigations into religion the criteria of rational inquiry which are used in science and ordinary life, we must use this criterion there.

In my description so far of the criteria for determining the probability of a scientific explanation I have used the Hempelian account of scientific explanation, supposing that science explains in terms of laws and initial conditions. We saw in Chapter 2 that this is not a very satisfactory account of science, and that it is better to think of science explaining by objects and their states, their powers and liabilities. The results of this section may be rephrased in this terminology as follows. We explain a phenomenon E by the action of an object O in state S with powers P and liabilities K. In virtue of K and being in a state S, O had to exercise P, the exercise of which was the bringing about of E. Necessarily (or with high physical probability) an object with K in state S has to exercise P, and an object which does so brings about E. Our grounds for supposing that O existed and was in state S are either that this was observed or that this supposition has great prior probability and explanatory power. Our grounds for supposing that O has P and K are that O is an object of a certain type and the supposition that all or most objects of this type have P and K has great explanatory power and prior probability.

We shall return to these results later. I pass now to the question of the justification of personal explanation which lies closer to the centre of our interest. When does evidence make a personal explanation probable?

Justification of Personal Explanation

I distinguish between standard cases and non-standard cases of personal explanation of some phenomenon E. By a standard case I mean one where we ascribe the occurrence of E to the action of a man (or animal) P using standard capacities.

By a man's standard capacities I mean the normal powers to perform basic actions which most men have—the abilities to move arms, legs, mouth, eyes, lips, etc. in the way in which most people can. I do not have space to discuss at any length the grounds on which in such standard cases we attribute phenomena to the action of a person. Clearly we pick out certain phenomena (e.g. a man's hand moving) as normally the results of basic actions, and assume that those phenomena are the results of basic actions in the absence of counter-evidence. Such results are by definition intended. We then learn to distinguish among the consequences of a man's basic actions those which were intended and those which were unintended. We perhaps come to see the knocking-over of a cup as an unintended consequence of some basic action of a man and so not as the result of an intentional action. Or perhaps we come to see the occurrence of a war caused by a politician's speech as an intended consequence and so as the result of an intentional action. In so doing we come to acquire views about the intentions and beliefs of various men. Our grounds for characterizing some phenomena as intended results of actions and others as unintended consequences of actions are many and diverse. For example, other things being equal, we believe what a man says about what his intentions are. (If he says that he did not intend to knock the cup over, we believe him.) Of course in order to use this criterion, we need to assume that we know what the man is saying, that the sounds which he utters have the meaning which we attribute to them. We do however, also have criteria for judging what a man means by what he says, and so for judging that one translation of a hitherto unknown language is the correct one.

I suggest as plausible, although I shall not argue for this at any length, that we seek to build up a picture of other men with intentions and ways of acquiring beliefs as similar as possible to our own (principle of charity) and as simple as possible (principle of simplicity), a picture which leads us to expect the public behaviour which in fact we find. Thus we suppose, other things being equal, that others who receive the same visual sensations as ourselves will come to hold the same beliefs; e.g. that someone who has the sensations which we have when we see an aeroplane land will come to hold the belief that an aeroplane has landed (although of course it is possible that he may not, if he has never seen or heard of an aeroplane before). We suppose, other things being equal, that other people have similar intentions to ourselves—e.g. to convey true information by what they say, when it is not too inconvenient. It is by making this assumption that we learn to interpret strange languages.[1] And we suppose that people do not change their intentions and beliefs suddenly and at random—that their intentions remain constant over a period, and that their beliefs change under the reception of sensory stimuli in regular ways. This is an application of the principle of simplicity. But the picture which we build up of people must be such as to lead us to expect the behaviour which we find. If we suppose that a man has the sole intention of posting a letter and believes that the post-box is up the road to the left, our supposition must be withdrawn if he walks down the road to the right. The principle of charity is really an application of the principle of simplicity as I have defined it—for in making the assumption that the intentions of others and their ways of acquiring beliefs are similar to our own we make a simpler assumption than the assumption that they differ, as well as a more comprehensible one. So what I am suggesting, though not attempting to prove at

[1] I develop this point in more detail on pp. 271 f.

length, is that in giving explanations of phenomena brought about by men of standard capacities, we seek explanations which result from the simplest picture of the intentions and beliefs of men which we can build up which leads us to expect the public behaviour which in fact we find.

We extend this general account to include animals. We follow the principles of simplicity and charity in the powers which we attribute to animals. To animals with appendages (e.g. mouth, legs, etc.) similar to our own, in so far as we can we attribute similar powers to move those appendages. Likewise in so far as we can we attribute to animals intentions and ways of acquiring beliefs similar to our own—e.g. an intention to get food when the animal has not eaten for some time, and if visual stimuli keep landing on the animal's eye from food in a cupboard, a belief that there is food in that cupboard. However our picture must lead us to expect the behaviour which we find, and must be modified or extended in order so to do. We attribute to animals powers other than our own—e.g. the power to move a tail as a basic action—and we deny to them intentions similar to ours—e.g. the intention to utter a complicated statement—in order to have a simple picture of their powers, intentions, and beliefs which leads us to expect the animal movements which we find.

I now suggest that a similar account applies to non-standard cases of personal explanation, and for this I shall produce more in the way of arguments by example. By non-standard cases of personal explanation of some phenomenon E, I mean ones where we ascribe the occurrence of E to the action of a rational agent other than a man or animal using standard capacities. (By an animal's standard capacities I mean the powers to perform basic actions possessed by most animals of its species.) The basic idea behind such ascriptions is, I believe, that we seek to postulate agents with intentions, capacities, and ways of acquiring beliefs, as similar as can be to recognized rational agents, viz. humans (and animals)[1] and the intentions, capacities, and ways of acquiring beliefs which we believe them to have. In so far as what we observe of their movements is similar to human movements, we are justified in doing this. But in so far as there are differences, we have to postulate differences in the rational agents and their intentions, capacities, and ways of acquiring beliefs, which we suppose to exist. The

---

[1] For the sake of simplicity of exposition, I shall hereafter ignore the role of comparison with animals in the justification of personal explanations.

greater and the more complex the supposed differences, the less plausible it is to suppose their existence. Our suppositions are justified nevertheless, in so far as they lead us to expect the movements which we in fact observe.

The non-standard cases are of various kinds. First, we may claim some movement E to be the result of a basic action of a recognized rational agent, even though an agent using only standard capacities could not bring about E. E may be a movement of or in the agent's body—e.g. his ears waggling or his heartbeat changing—or outside it—e.g. a spoon bending. Our justification for making such attribution will turn on whether we can fit easily into what we know of P's intentions and beliefs, and capacities, the supposition that the movement E results from his actions. Clearly we would have to suppose that P has capacities different from those of his fellows and that is superficially to add to the complexity of our picture of the world. We would only do this if that adds to the explanatory power of that picture—viz. if it renders probable the occurrence of events such as E, when otherwise their occurrence would be very improbable. Clearly if we have no other explanation of E, the supposition that P has the capacity to produce E does this. The explanatory power of the theory would be greatly increased if not merely did it render probable the occasional occurrence of an event such as E but if it enabled us to predict more or less exactly when such events would take place. If we have reason to believe that P is like many other agents, in having the intention to do what others ask him to do, when what is asked is not immoral or too demanding, and if we suppose that (e.g.) ear-waggling is not too immoral or demanding, then we would expect P's ears to waggle when we ask P to waggle his ears. If this happens on many occasions, and if it is very improbable that P's ears would waggle otherwise at just those times, then we have good grounds for supposing the original waggling, E, to be a result of P's action.

More difficult is the case where we have some material object P which undergoes various changes of bodily state and makes movements, such as a movement of some appendage E, but it is open to question whether P is a rational agent. P may be some creature from another planet very dissimilar from the rational agents with which we are familiar and some of whose movements constitute our standard cases of the results of actions. If we are to suppose P to be a rational agent and E to be a result of an action, we are clearly making a supposition which does not fit in very well with our background knowledge of the world. We are going to suppose the existence of a rational agent very different in its history, appearance, and physiology from the ones with which we are familiar. We may need also to suppose that P has capacities, intentions, and ways of acquiring beliefs (e.g. not via stimuli impinging on sense-organs) very different from those of humans. The suppositions about P may also need to be complex ones—e.g. we may need to suppose that P has inconsistent and quickly changing intentions. Now clearly the greater the differences which we suppose between P and known rational agents, and the less simple our picture of P, the less probable it is that P is indeed as supposed. Yet however initially improbable our suggestion, its explanatory power could be so great as to render it probable nevertheless. If a certain supposition about P, how he acquires beliefs, and what are his capacities and intentions made very probable certain movements in or of his body which would otherwise be very improbable (e.g. it made certain very successful detailed predictions), then we would have good grounds for believing it true. Thus among the suppositions about P's intentions, beliefs, and capacities may be a detailed supposition about P's language, viz. that he utters certain syllables with the intention thereby of conveying certain information and that he believes that the uttering of those syllables will convey that information, and so on for various other syllables. If this supposition makes probable his utterance of various syllables rather than various other syllables under certain circumstances, and he does utter the former syllables, then that raises the probability of the supposition about P. Much evidence of this type would raise that probability greatly.

Yet more difficult (and most relevant to our concerns) is the case where we have certain otherwise inexplicable phenomena which we seek to attribute to the action of a non-embodied agent, such as a ghost or a poltergeist. The phenomena to be explained may be that books, chairs, ink-wells, etc. start flying about my room. We postulate a poltergeist P with certain intentions, beliefs, and capacities to be responsible. Clearly we have to suppose P to be very unlike other rational agents known to us both in his capacities and his ways of acquiring beliefs. (This cannot be, for example, via sense-organs.) But we can suppose P to have beliefs influenced as are ours by how things are, and to have intentions of the kind which we have, e.g. intentions of a kind typical of human beings with certain characters and histories. For example, we can suppose P to have previously been a certain embodied person who had been greatly injured by X and who had greatly loved Y, X and Y both being still alive. Then we suppose P to be like many of us if we suppose him with such a history to have the intention to harm X and to save Y from harm, and to communicate with Y. If we suppose P to be in these ways similar to us, the supposition that P exists fits in to some extent with our background knowledge, although in postulating a non-embodied person, clearly to a large extent it does not. The supposition is more probable in so far as it is simple, that is, postulates a few constant intentions, simple ways of acquiring beliefs, and unchanging capacities. Above all, the supposition will be rendered probable if it has high explanatory power. It would have this, for example, if the books, chairs, ink-wells, etc. hit X, or form themselves into words which warn Y of impending danger; and so on. We would expect this kind of thing to happen if P is as we have supposed, far more than we would ordinarily expect it to happen. It is crucial that there does not exist a plausible scientific explanation of the goings-on (apart from any which explains or is explained by the intentions of poltergeists). The phenomena of books, chairs, and ink-wells flying around must not be due to a hurricane or to my having suddenly acquired great mass and so great power of gravitational attraction, where these latter are explicable by normal scientific explanation; for they would then bring about the goings-on without doing so via intentions. It is also crucial that there should not exist a personal explanation in terms of the action of an embodied agent (other than one which is explicable by or explains the action of a poltergeist). If an embodied agent moved the chairs by telekinesis, then a poltergeist did not.

The examples which I have taken so far of cases where we may claim some phenomenon to be the result of an action of a rational agent, other than a human being using standard capacities, are cases where we claim the phenomenon to be the result of a basic action. If we are to claim a phenomenon to be the result of a mediated action, we must find a basic action of which it is an intended consequence. So if we are to discover the results of mediated actions of agents other than humans, we must first discover the results of their basic actions. Once we have found basic actions other than standard ones, we can use criteria of the kind to which I referred earlier to determine whether their consequences were intended by the agent, and so whether they are to be considered the results of mediated actions.

In all this we see the investigator using the criteria of prior probability and explanatory power to judge the worth of proposed theories of personal explanation, just as with proposed theories of scientific explanation. The prior probability of a theory is, we saw, a matter of its fit with background knowledge, its simplicity, and its lack of scope. Fit with background knowledge in the case of theories of personal explanation, is a matter of postulating persons similar to known persons in their history and physiology, their capacities, their intentions, and ways of acquiring beliefs.[1] We saw that the less similar to known persons (viz. humans) were the postulated persons, the less probable it was that they exist. Simplicity, in the case of theories of personal explanation, was a matter of postulating constant intentions, continuing capacities, and simple ways of acquiring beliefs. Clearly the less detail a theory provides about a person's intentions, capacities, etc. the more likely it is to be true; but, even if it is a detailed theory, we could have enough evidence to make it likely to be true. The explanatory power of a theory of personal explanation is, first, a matter of its ability to predict the phenomena which we in fact observe. Thus our theory that P has the power of bending spoons at a distance and the intention of doing what people ask him to do, leads us to predict that when we ask him to bend the spoons, the spoons will bend. If our predictions come off that is indeed evidence for the theory. This aspect of a theory's explanatory power, I will call in future its predictive power. However, we saw that for a theory to have great explanatory power, the phenomena which it predicts must be such that but for it they would not otherwise be expected. I shall make this point in future by saying that our evidence must have low prior probability. A theory has high explanatory power in so far as it has high predictive power and the evidence has low prior probability, that is, low probability unless we suppose our theory to be true. It was for this latter reason that it was of great importance if we were to accept theories about poltergeists or men with the ability to bend spoons at a distance, that there should be no other plausible explanation of these phenomena. That is, it should be very improbable, unless the strange theory were true, that the phenomena should occur—they must be very much not to be expected given our normal background

[1] Or rather this is so where, as in the cases discussed in the text, the background knowledge includes some knowledge of what sort of persons there are. If we take only tautological background knowledge, this consideration will not be relevant. In considering the arguments for the existence of God, we shall begin with a situation of tautological background knowledge, and so the dissimilarities between human persons and the postulated God will not as such affect the prior probability of theism.

of the world and how things work in it, including our current
scientific knowledge.

Bayes's Theorem

We can now put our points about the probability of a theory h on
evidence e depending directly on the prior probability of h and the
predictive power of h, and inversely on the prior probability of e,
into symbolic form. Where k is our general background knowledge
of what there is in the world and how it works, e is our phenomena
to be explained and other relevant observational evidence, and h is
our hypothesis, $P(h/e.k)$ is a function of the prior probability of h,
$P(h/k)$; and of its explanatory power with respect to e. This latter is
a factor which increases with the predictive power of h, $P(e/h.k)$;
and decreases with the prior probability of e, $P(e/k)$. $P(e/h.k)$ is a
measure of how likely the evidential phenomena e are to occur if the
hypothesis h is true (given our background knowledge k). So the
more h makes e probable, to be expected, the greater is $\dfrac{P(e/h.k)}{P(e/k)}$.[1]
$P(e/k)$ measures the prior probability of e, how likely e is to occur
anyway, whether or not h, given only k. Clearly the more evidence
we have, and the more diverse and otherwise inexplicable is our
evidence, the lower $P(e/k)$, and so again the greater is $\dfrac{P(e/h.k)}{P(e/k)}$.

These points are made explicit by a basic theorem of confirmation
theory, Bayes's theorem, which runs as follows:

$$P(h/e.k) = \frac{P(e/h.k)}{P(e/k)} \times P(h/k).$$

This theorem follows directly from the axioms of the mathematical
calculus of probability, for the truth of which there are good
independent grounds.[2] But in putting it forward I do not appeal
much to these latter grounds, but mainly to the ones given so far in
this chapter (although the particular way in which $P(h/e.k)$ increases with $P(h/k)$ and $P(e/h.k)$, but decreases with $P(e/k)$ does not
depend on anything which I have said so far, but must depend on
this derivation).

---

[1] '$\dfrac{P(e/h.k)}{P(e/k)}$' of course means '$P(e/h.k)$ divided by $P(e/k)$'.

[2] For the derivation of Bayes's theorem from the axioms of the calculus, and for
independent grounds for the truth of these axioms see my *An Introduction to
Confirmation Theory*, Chs. 3–6.

$P(h/k)$, the prior probability of h, depends as we have seen, in the normal case both on the internal simplicity of h (and its narrowness of scope) and also on how well h fits in with our general background knowledge of the world contained in k. However, as we saw in Chapter 1, any division of evidence between e and k will be a somewhat arbitrary one. Normally it is convenient to call the latest piece of observational evidence e and the rest k; but sometimes it is convenient to let e be all observational evidence and let k be mere 'tautological evidence'. In the latter case the prior probability $P(h/k)$ is what I shall call the intrinsic probability of h, and will depend mainly on the simplicity of h (as well as to a lesser extent on its narrowness of scope). But if k contains logically contingent evidence of what there is in the world and how it works, $P(h/k)$ will depend also on how well h fits in with that evidence. Where k is mere 'tautological evidence', $P(e/k)$ will be what I shall call the intrinsic probability of e.

I have claimed that Bayes's theorem is true, but I had better make clear what I mean by saying this. I mean that in so far as for various e, h, and k, the probabilities occurring in it can be given a numerical value, it correctly states the numerical relationships which hold between them. In so far as they cannot be given precise numerical values, my claim that Bayes's theorem is true is simply the claim that all statements of comparative probability which are entailed by the theorem are true. By statements of comparative probability I mean statements about one probability being greater than, or equal to, or less than another probability. (Such statements are sometimes all that we can justifiably assert about some probabilities—see p. 17.) Thus it follows from Bayes's theorem that if there are two hypotheses h_1 and h_2 such that $P(e/h_1 . k) = P(e/h_2 . k)$, then $P(h_1/e . k) > P(h_2/e . k)$ if and only if $P(h_1/k) > P(h_2/k)$. This says that if h_1 and h_2 both make it equally probable that we will find evidence e, given background knowledge k, then one of them h_1 will be more probable than the other on the total evidence e and k, if and only if h_1 was more probable than h_2 on the background evidence alone. Put more technically—if h_1 and h_2 have equal predictive power, h_1 will have greater posterior probability (that is, probability on the total evidence e and k) than h_2, if and only if it has greater prior probability. So if there are two scientific theories equally successful in predicting certain observations, one of them will be more probable than the other if it was more probable before the observations were made. Or again it follows from Bayes's theorem that if $P(h_1/k) = P(h_2/k)$ then $P(h_1/e.k) > P(h_2/e.k)$ if and only if $P(e/h_1.k) > P(e/h_2.k)$. This says that if two hypotheses are equally probable before certain evidence e is obtained, one of them will only be more probable than the other on the total evidence, if given that hypothesis it is more probable that e will be found than it is given the other hypothesis. (In an extreme case, h_1 may entail e—it may be a deductive consequence of h_1 that e will occur—and h_2 may entail $\sim e$, that e will not occur.)

Here is another example, slightly different from those used so far, to illustrate the working of Bayes's theorem. Let h be the hypothesis that Jones robbed Barclays Bank, e be the evidence that he was near the bank at the time of the crime, and k be the background knowledge that Jones robbed another bank, Lloyds Bank, on another occasion. Then $P(h/e.k)$ is determined by the explanatory power of h $\dfrac{P(e/h.k)}{P(e/k)}$, and the prior probability of h, $P(h/k)$. $P(e/h.k)$ is the probability that e, given both h and k. In this case this is 1, since if Jones robbed the bank, he must have been near the scene at the time. $P(e/k)$ is the probability that he would be near the scene at the time, given that he had robbed another bank. This will be greater than $P(h/k)$, the probability, given that he robbed another bank, that he did this job; since he might have had quite innocent reasons for being where he was. The probability that he robbed Barclays Bank is then the prior probability that he did multiplied by the extent to which the hypothesis that he did it makes e more to be expected than it would otherwise be.

It will be useful at this stage, before proceeding with the main argument, to make another important point about confirmation which can be illustrated by Bayes's theorem. It is sometimes said that we are only justified in accepting a hypothesis if we have tested it by finding that it predicts certain events and then waited to see whether or not those events happen; and only if they do, are we justified in accepting the hypothesis. Now it seems to me that although we often test hypotheses in this way, we do not have to do so if they are to be rendered probable by our evidence and so we are to be justified in accepting them. The suggestion that hypotheses must predict successfully (interpreted in the above way) if they are to be rendered probable by evidence is certainly not implied by Bayes's theorem. It is a matter of indifference, as regards that theorem, whether e is observed before or after the formulation of h. All that matters is the relations of probability holding between *e* and *h*. And surely the theorem is correct in that respect.

Newton's theory of motion was judged to be highly probable on the evidence available to men of the late seventeenth century, even though it made no new immediately testable predictions, other than the predictions which were already made by laws which were already known and which it explained (e.g. Kepler's laws of planetary motion and Galileo's law of fall). Its high probability arose solely from its being a very simple higher-level theory from which those diverse laws are deducible. More generally, whether *e* renders *h* probable surely cannot depend crucially on whether we had thought of *h* before we saw *e*. Probability would become a highly subjective matter instead of an objective relationship between evidence and hypothesis if that were so. Bayes's theorem is, however, able to explain why often, indeed *normally*, we are interested in predictions which we can check subsequently to the formulation of the theory. This is because only when we have the theory do we know just which evidence is such as to make $\dfrac{P(e/h.k)}{P(e/k)}$ very great; only then do we know which evidence we need to have in order that the theory be rendered highly probable. We are not very likely to have that evidence in our hands already—we normally need to look for it. Nevertheless, we *may* have it in our hands already. Hence it is in itself no objection to the hypothesis that there is a God, that it does not yield predictions such that we can only know tomorrow, and not today, whether they succeed. The theist's evidence may render his hypothesis probable without this condition being satisfied.

It follows immediately from Bayes's theorem that $P(h/e.k) > P(h/k)$ if and only if $P(e/h.k) > P(e/k)$. This important principle is one which Mackie has called the 'relevance criterion'.[1] It follows from it by a fairly short step of logic that $P(h/e.k) > P(h/k)$ if and only if $P(e/h.k) > P(e/\sim h.k)$. This says that a hypothesis *h* is confirmed by evidence *e* if and only if that evidence is more likely to occur if the hypothesis is true than if it is false. The result is surely correct. It is implicit in many judgements which we make in ordinary life. His fingerprints on the safe only confirm the supposition that Jones robbed the safe, if they are more likely to be on the safe if he did the crime than if he did not. If they are equally likely to

---

[1] See J. L. Mackie, 'The Relevance Criterion of Confirmation', *British Journal for the Philosophy of Science*, 1969, **20**, 27–40.

be on the safe whether or not he robbed the safe (e.g. because Jones is the manager of the shop in which the safe is situated and often opens it), they do not confirm the supposition that he robbed the safe. It follows that an argument from e to h is a correct C-inductive argument if (and only if) e is more likely to be found if h is true than if h is false.

The theist argues from the world, the fact of its existence, and its detailed characteristics to a God who brought it about. Since the structure of his argument is that of a man arguing from a narrower range of phenomena to a non-embodied person, such as a poltergeist, who brought them about as results of his actions, we must use the same criteria for judging the worth of his explanation—that is, the criteria embodied in Bayes's theorem—bearing in mind of course the differences between the range of the phenomena. The theist argues from all the phenomena of experience, not from a small range of them. We shall have to let e represent in turn the different facets of the world which the theist brings as evidence for the existence of God and the facets which the atheist brings as evidence against the existence of God. h will be the hypothesis that God exists, and, to start with, k will be mere tautological evidence. In order to assess $P(h/e.k)$ in each case we shall then need to assess $\frac{P(e/h.k)}{P(e/k)}$ and $P(h/k)$. The probability, on the evidence, of God's existence will depend on how well the hypothesis of God's existence is able to explain the occurrence of phenomena which would otherwise be highly unlikely; and on the prior probability, and for a hypothesis as all-embracing as this one that means merely the simplicity, of the hypothesis that God exists.

I shall assess in Chapter 5 the prior probability of theism on tautological background evidence, that is, the intrinsic probability of theism, $P(h/k)$. The explanatory power of theism will vary, as we have seen, with the difference e. But before discussing the evidential force of different e, that is, the different arguments, we shall need to consider general principles involved in determining its value. $P(e/k)$ is a matter of how likely the various phenomena are to occur anyway—i.e. whether or not God brings them about. They will be likely to occur anyway if some other cause could bring them about or if they could occur uncaused. I shall discuss in Chapter 4 the general principles involved here, and especially what are the grounds for claiming that some phenomena occur uncaused (i.e. have no explanation). In Chapter 6 I shall consider how $P(e/k)$ is to be compared with $P(e/h.k)$ in determining the explanatory power of theism for phenomena e; which will of course depend on how likely it is that God will bring about e.

Note that I take h simply as 'there is a God'. h is not supposed for any of the e to provide a full explanation of e. As I shall emphasize in Chapter 6, the existence of God does not fully explain, for example, the existence of the universe, which is the phenomenon cited by the cosmological argument as evidence of his existence. Only the existence of God (whence it follows, because of the kind of being which God is, that he has the capacity to bring into existence a universe) together with an intention of his to bring about a universe could fully explain the existence of the universe. The existence of God however, forms part of the explanation. We could of course have taken h as 'there is a God who had the intention of bringing about a universe', and then h would provide a full explanation of the existence of the universe and $P(e/h.k)$ would equal 1. But if we were to follow a similar procedure with each argument, the h would vary according to the argument, and so it would not be a common conclusion of different arguments, for which we could assess the support provided by each. It is more convenient to take h as I have done; and in that case of course $P(e/h.k)$ will not equal 1.

4

Complete Explanation

I ARGUED in the last chapter that the grounds for postulating a personal explanation of phenomena lie in the prior probability and explanatory power of that explanation. The explanatory power of an explanation depends crucially on the prior probability of the phenomena, how likely it is that phenomena would occur irrespective of whether the personal explanation of them is correct. So a crucial factor in determining the force of an argument from phenomena to God's existence is whether those phenomena would be at all likely to have occurred but for God's agency, and so (as a necessary condition of his agency) but for God's existence. They could exist apart from God's agency, if something else could have brought them into being—viz. if there is a scientific explanation (or other personal explanation) of their existence—or if they could exist uncaused, without there being any explanation of their existence. In this chapter I shall consider what kind of phenomena could not be given a scientific (or other personal) explanation; and then go on to consider what kind of phenomena could exist uncaused. This latter is the issue of what is the proper terminus of explanation; when do we have grounds for supposing that we have reached the end of the explanatory road, and when not. This chapter is concerned to develop general principles, which can subsequently be applied to the arguments for the existence of God. The theist claims that the phenomena which he cites, e.g. the existence of the universe, could not exist uncaused, but that God could exist uncaused. We shall need to investigate whether the existence of God is a more satisfactory terminus for explanation than the existence of the universe with its various characteristics. If there is a God, it follows, as I shall show briefly in Chapter 5, that explanation stops with him—a being would not be God if something other than God could explain his existence. But what needs to be shown is that the existence of God forms a more natural stopping place for explanation than, say, the existence of the universe.

The Scientifically Inexplicable

What, to start with, are the grounds for supposing that phenomena do not have a scientific explanation? Phenomena of two kinds can be shown not to be explicable scientifically. First, there are phenomena which are too *odd* to be fitted into the established pattern of scientific explanation, and secondly there are phenomena which are too *big* to be fitted into any pattern of scientific explanation.

To show phenomena too odd to be explicable scientifically the theist needs to show that there is good evidence for a scientific system h covering a certain range of phenomena, but that it is not a consequence of h that certain phenomena (within the general range of h) occur; and that any attempt to amend or expand h to allow it to predict e would make h so complex or for other reasons to have such low prior probability that it would be very improbable that it is true. Theists have claimed various particular phenomena to be too odd to be scientifically explicable. Among these, if we assume that they occur, are violations of laws of nature such as levitations, or people getting better from polio in a minute, or blood suddenly liquefying, or men walking on water, events which theists claim to be miracles. I shall discuss the issue of miracles in Chapter 12. A somewhat different example of a particular event which, if it occurred, would be scientifically inexplicable, would be the first event or initial state of the universe.

But the oddness of events need not be confined to the particular; there may be events of certain *kinds* which cannot be explained by science. There may be much evidence for a certain scientific system, and yet it be a consequence of this system that a scientific explanation of certain kinds of event is ruled out. Theists have sometimes claimed that the occurrence of living organisms or of conscious human beings are scientifically inexplicable. I do not think that much of a case can be made out for the former, but I do think that a substantial case can be made out for the latter and I shall discuss that case in Chapter 9. I shall analyse in detail and illustrate with examples in these two later Chapters, 9 and 12, the kind of argument used to show phenomena to be too odd to be scientifically explicable. Here I have only sketched it in schematic outline.

The other phenomena which cannot be explained scientifically are phenomena which are too *big* for science, and too big not merely for some particular well-established scientific system, but for any scientific system. In considering, in Chapter 2, the nature of scientific explanation, we saw that science explains why some event or state of affairs occurs. It does this, on the Hempelian model, in terms of a prior state of affairs and some natural law. It also explains why certain natural laws operate, and it does this in terms of more general laws of nature—e.g. it explains the operation of Galileo's law in terms of the operation of Newton's laws. But what, as I shall show more precisely in Chapter 7, science could not explain is why there are any states of affairs at all; it can explain only why, given that there are such states, this state is followed by that state. Nor could it explain, as I shall show more precisely in Chapter 8, why the most general natural laws of all hold. Either these are brute facts about the world, or they have an explanation of a different kind.

We shall see that the scientifically inexplicable, the odd and the big, form the normal starting-points for arguments to the existence of God. Cosmological and some teleological arguments argue from phenomena allegedly too big for science to explain; whereas most other arguments argue from phenomena allegedly too odd for science to explain. The arguments need to show also that there is no personal explanation in terms of the action of an embodied agent. This done, what has been shown is that an explanation in terms of a very powerful non-embodied agent is the only possible explanation of the phenomena. It then follows that either theism or something like it is true, or that the phenomena are just brute inexplicable facts, the stopping-point of explanation.

Full, Complete, Ultimate, and Absolute Explanation

The main issue of this chapter is then, what are proper stopping-points for explanation, when do we have grounds for supposing that certain phenomena constitute such stopping-points and when do we have grounds for supposing that they themselves have an explanation. Having established general principles, we can then ask whether it is right to suppose that the physical universe, or the regular operation of scientific laws, or such particular events as (assuming that it happened) the resurrection of Christ from the dead, are just brute facts, or whether they are phenomena which it is reasonable to suppose to have a further explanation.

Before I come to deal properly with the central issue, I need first to make certain distinctions. The question of what is a 'terminus' of explanation needs a more technical explication. I have already in Chapter 2 introduced the concepts of full explanation and partial explanation of some phenomenon. An explanation of E by F is a full one if F includes both a cause, C, and a reason, R, which together necessitated the occurrence of E. (Recall that on the Hempelian account of scientific explanation C are initial conditions and R natural laws; whereas in personal explanation C is a person, and R that person's intentions, beliefs, and capacities.) If C and R together provide a full explanation of E, nothing else logically contingent beside C and R needed to be so in order for the occurrence of E to be guaranteed, and so a proposition reporting C and R entails a proposition reporting E. Thus a scientific explanation of an eclipse of the moon E is a full one if it cites all the natural laws involved, L (laws of motion and laws of light propagation), and precedent states of the world C necessary for the occurrence of E, viz. the positions and masses of moon, sun, and earth, and the absence of other heavenly bodies in the region, and if L and C together entail E. An explanation of E is only a partial one if the explanation includes factors which brought about the occurrence of E, but these factors did not necessitate the occurrence of E.

Now a full explanation really does by itself explain why something happened. It does so quite independently of whether or not there is an explanation of how any states it cites came to be (e.g. why the sun was where it was) or why any reasons which it cites operate (e.g. why certain natural laws hold). To suppose otherwise is to commit a fallacy which we may call 'the completist fallacy'. Clearly it is a fallacy. For if it were really the case that F could not explain E, unless there is an explanation of F, nothing in the universe could be explained, unless there were explanations of such things as the origin of our galaxy—which is absurd. It is however a fallacy commonly committed both by opponents and (as we shall see later) by supporters of natural theology. Thus Hume objects in the *Dialogues* to postulating a God who planned the world as an explanation of its order, on the grounds that the postulated existence of a rational agent who produces the order of the world would itself need explaining. Picturing such an agent as a mind, and a mind as an arrangement of ideas, Hume phrases the objection as follows: 'a mental world or Universe of ideas requires a cause as much as does a material world or Universe of objects.'[1] Hume himself provides the obvious answer to this—that it is no objection to explaining E by F that we cannot explain F. But then he suggests that the F in this case, the mind, is just as mysterious as the ordered universe. Men never 'thought it satisfactory to explain a particular effect by a particular cause which was no more to be accounted for than the effect itself'.[2] But that is plainly false. We can give a perfectly good explanation of how it came about that Jones lost his fortune in terms of the way the Monte Carlo roulette wheel spun, while being entirely unable to explain why the roulette wheel spun as it did, and indeed while judging that there was no explanation of how the roulette wheel spun, this being something utterly beyond accounting for.

Nevertheless, although a full explanation of E (in the sense of 'full explanation' which I have delineated) leaves no facet of E un-explained, further explaining can often by done—there may be explanations of why the factors cited in the *explanans* are operative and how they came to exist. Let us concentrate for the moment on explanations of the operation of the factors at the time at which they bring about E. Let the factors be C, the cause which brings about E, and R, the reason for C's efficacy. Let C bring about E at the time t. The existence of C at t may depend on some other factor B which at time t makes C exist. Thus suppose my arm by moving makes to move the stick which I am holding, the motion of which moves a stone, and suppose that the transmission of motion is instan-taneous; then the motion of the stone (E) is brought about by the motion of the stick (C) which in turn is brought about by the motion of my arm (B). Then the present existence of a cause is dependent on the present operation of its own cause. Likewise the operation of the reason R may depend on some higher-level reason S which at the time of R's operation makes R to operate. Thus Galileo's law of fall operates on earth because earth has such and such a mass and Newton's laws operate.

I now define a complete explanation of the occurrence of E as follows. A complete explanation of the occurrence of E is a full explanation of its occurrence in which all the factors cited are such that there is no explanation (either full or partial) of their existence

[1] David Hume, *Dialogues Concerning Natural Religion* (first published 1779, H. D. Aitken (ed.), New York, 1948), p. 33.
[2] Ibid., p. 36.

or operation in terms of factors operative at the time of their existence or operation. Thus suppose that a high tide is brought about by sun, moon, earth, water, etc. being in certain positions and by the operation of Newton's laws. Here is, let us suppose, a full explanation. Suppose too that Newton's laws operate here because this region of the universe is relatively empty of matter and Einstein's laws of General Relativity operate. These factors act contemporaneously to make Newton's laws operate. Suppose too that nothing at this instant makes sun, moon, etc. be where they are (even though some past cause was responsible for their being where they are). Nor does anything at this instant make Einstein's laws operate or this region of the universe be relatively empty. Then there is a complete explanation of the high tide in terms of the operation of Einstein's laws, the universe in this region being relatively empty of matter, and sun, moon, earth, water, etc. being where they are.[1]

Complete explanation is a special kind of full explanation. I now delineate as a special kind of complete explanation what I shall call ultimate explanation. To speak loosely to start with, we have an ultimate explanation of some phenomenon E if we can state not merely which factors C and R operated at the time to bring E about, and which contemporaneous factors made C and R exist and operate at that time, and so on until we reach factors for the contemporaneous existence and operation of which there is no explanation; but also state the factors which originally brought C and R about, and which factors originally brought those factors about, and so on until we reach factors for the existence and operation of which there is no explanation. Less loosely, I define an ultimate explanation of E as a complete explanation of E, in which the factors C and R cited are such that their existence and operation have no explanation either full or partial in terms of any other factors. Those factors are ultimate brute facts. Suppose that there is no God, that the universe began with a bang in a state X at a time t, that it is governed by deterministic laws L (whose operation is not

---

[1] It may be that while C and R provide a full explanation of E, either C or R or both have no full explanation in terms of factors operative at the time of their operation, but only a partial explanation of this kind. So long as there is an end to any regress of partial explanation, there will, nevertheless, on my definition be a complete explanation of E. For suppose that event B (in virtue of a law S) partially explains the simultaneous occurrence of C, but that neither B nor S have an explanation (either full or partial) in terms of factors operative at the time of their occurrence, then a complete explanation of the occurrence of E is provided conjointly by B, C, R, and S.

further explicable); and that in accord with L, X brought about a state Y, and Y brought about a state Z, and Z brought about E. Then (X and L); and (Y and L), and (Z and L) are each complete explanations of E; but only (X and L) is an ultimate explanation of E.

Finally let us delineate as a special kind of ultimate explanation, what I shall call absolute explanation. An absolute explanation of E is an ultimate explanation of E in which the existence and operation of each of the factors cited is either self-explanatory or logically necessary. Other explanations cite brute facts which form the starting-points of explanations; there are no brute facts in absolute explanations—here everything really is explained.

I do not believe that there can be any absolute explanations of logically contingent phenomena. For surely never does anything explain itself. P's existence at t_2 may be explained in part by P's existence at t_1. But P's existence at t_1 could not explain P's existence at t_1. P's existence at t_1 might be the ultimate brute fact about the universe, but it would not explain itself. Nor can anything logically necessary provide any explanation of anything logically contingent. For a full explanation is, we have seen, such that the *explanandum* (i.e. the phenomenon requiring explanation) is deducible from it. But you cannot deduce anything logically contingent from anything logically necessary. And a partial explanation is in terms of something which in the context made the occurrence of the *explanandum* probable, without which things would probably have gone some other (logically possible) way. Yet a world in which some logically necessary truth did not hold is an incoherent supposition, not one in which things would probably have gone some other way. These are among many reasons why it must be held that God is a logically contingent being, although maybe one necessary in other ways.

So for these reasons let us leave aside consideration of absolute explanation, and return to explanations of other types. I suggest that the arguments to the existence of God with which we are concerned are arguments to a complete explanation of phenomena, but not necessarily arguments to an ultimate explanation. They all claim that God's present action (which has no explanation in terms of any other present factor) brings about certain present phenomena, while not necessarily denying that there may be partial past causes of that action—viz. God's own action in the past in keeping himself in existence may have helped to make possible his present action. The issue turns on just how temporal a being the theist claims his God to be. He may regard him as a being who keeps himself in existence the following moment by his own choice at each moment of time. Or, more traditionally he may regard him as a being who is in some sense necessarily eternal.[1] In the latter case if he exists at any time, then necessarily he exists at all times. In that case any complete explanation of any phenomena in terms of God's action at a certain time would also be an ultimate explanation. For the explanation is in terms of God's existence and his intention. His intention has no explanation; he freely chose to act on that intention at that time; and his existence at the time would not be explicable in terms of anything earlier or contemporaneous, and so not explicable at all. Whereas if God is the cause of his own subsequent existence, his existence at a certain time, which forms part of a complete explanation of some phenomena, would be explicable further. At this stage I allow the possibility that arguments to God's creative action provide only complete, but not ultimate explanations of phenomena. However, in the next chapter I shall be producing arguments in favour of God's being a necessarily eternal being.

For this reason I shall confine myself to examining our grounds for supposing that we have reached a complete explanation of phenomena. However, if God is a necessarily eternal being any complete explanation in terms of his action will also be an ultimate explanation.

Justifying a Claim to Complete Explanation

The basic considerations in judging a proposed explanation probable are, as we have seen, the prior probability and the explanatory power of the proposed *explanans*. In so far as the proposed *explanans* renders probable, or better necessitates, the *explanandum*, and the occurrence of other phenomena too, which are observed to occur, and in so far as the occurrence of the phenomena is otherwise very improbable, then it has great explanatory power. It has prior probability, basically, in so far as it is simple and fits in with our general knowledge of the world. It is simple in so far as it postulates few entities and reasons (i.e. laws or intentions) of a simple kind. It fits in with our general background knowledge

---

[1] A third possibility is to regard God as a being outside time. But in that case it is hard to see how he can be regarded as acting. I give reasons for finding this third view an incoherent view, and I develop the other two views in a full way in the last four chapters of *The Coherence of Theism*.

of the world in so far as the entities and reasons which it postulates are of a kind with entities and reasons which we have reason to believe to exist and to operate in other spheres. I would suggest that our grounds for believing that objects (events, states, etc.) or reasons do not have a further explanation in terms of factors acting at the time, and so that any explanation provided by those objects or reasons is a complete explanation, are any grounds for believing that the latter could only be explained themselves by postulating causes and reasons (acting at the time) having no more explanatory power or prior probability than the *explananda*, i.e. the things to be explained, or having more of one only if they have much less of the other.

I will now illustrate this claim with one or two examples of cases where we believe with reason that we have reached a complete explanation. For my first examples I confine myself to explanation within science. On the Hempelian model we explain a phenomenon E by initial conditions C and scientific laws L. The explanation is full if C and L together necessitate E. A complete explanation of E will cite the most fundamental laws of nature, and initial conditions which have no explanation in terms of contemporaneous states or events. I illustrate my thesis about our grounds for believing that we have reached a terminus of explanation by considering our grounds for believing that we have reached the most basic laws of nature.

We often explain the operation of one law by the operation of another—for example Galileo's law of fall is explained by the operation of Newton's laws. Our grounds for accepting such an explanation will be that there is a gain of either explanatory power or prior probability without a great loss of the other. In my example there is a gain of explanatory power in that Newton's laws successfully predict both the operation of Galileo's law (to a high degree of accuracy) and the occurrence of further phenomena. It is a deductive consequence of Newton's laws and certain true statements of initial conditions (e.g. that the earth has such and such a mass and radius) that Galileo's law operates to a high degree of approximation. Newton's laws also successfully predict the motions of the planets, the behaviour of the tides, the interactions of colliding bodies, etc. etc. Further, Newton's laws have high prior probability. As we also saw earlier, they are extremely simple. The question of fitting in with background knowledge hardly arises because Newton's theory purports to cover such a large field that there is not a great deal outside it with which to compare the entities and laws which it postulates. However the later discovery of inverse square laws of electrostatic and magnetostatic attraction (viz. laws of the same mathematical type as Newton's law of gravitational attraction) gave Newton's theory some prior probability for this reason too. So the attempt to explain Galileo's law by Newton's laws was a move which resulted in a gain of explanatory power in no way cancelled out by any loss of prior probability. Hence Galileo's law of fall is indeed explained by the operation of Newton's laws. Newton's laws in their turn are (probably) explained by Einstein's field equations of General Relativity. In passing from Newton's laws to Einstein's there is I believe a considerable loss of simplicity (though Einstein himself considered that his laws had a simple form). But there is some considerable gain in explanatory power. We can derive from Einstein's laws not merely Newton's laws of mechanics, but Maxwell's laws of electro-magnetism which enable us to predict accurately the behaviour of light and other electro-magnetic radiation; and also some moderately successful predictions about the mechanical behaviour of bodies which are different from those made by Newton's laws.

Now my thesis is that we would be justified in believing that some law or laws were the terminus of explanation, were not to be further explained, if we had grounds for believing that any gain of explanatory power would be outweighed by considerable loss of prior probability and that any gain in prior probability would be outweighed by considerable loss of explanatory power. We would have these grounds if we already had simple laws which fitted in well with our background knowledge, and if we had grounds for believing that any attempt to amend our laws or to derive them from more fundamental laws, in order to increase the explanatory power of science, would make them or other scientific laws very complicated, or not to fit in with our background knowledge, at the expense of little gain of explanatory power. I suggest that the men of the later eighteenth century who held that Newton's laws were the most basic laws of nature had just such grounds. For the phenomena, which Newton's laws did not explain were light, chemical and biological phenomena, and a few odd phenomena, such as electric and magnetic attraction. Newton had outlined a plausible account of how his laws could explain light. In chemical and biological phenomena and also in the phenomena of electric and magnetic attraction there was obviously some force or forces at work which had significant effects only over very short distances. It looked as if one could cope with these phenomena by adding a fifth law concerned with such forces to the other four, without amending the latter.[1] The fifth law would lay down the equation governing the production of such forces, which would be subject to the general propositions about forces contained in the first three laws. Because these forces were operative only over very short distances, while the gravitational force showed its strength over longer distances, and were in consequence different from the gravitational force, there was no reason to suppose that the law of gravity would require any amendment. So it looked as if there could be no gain in explanatory power by amending Newton's laws or deriving them from more fundamental laws. Nor, in view of their incredible simplicity (and, in so far as it arose, good fit with background knowledge) did it look as if they could possibly be improved on that score. For these reasons, the men of the eighteenth century were, I suggest, justified in believing that science had reached a terminus in Newton's laws.[2] However, many new phenomena first discovered by science in the twentieth century proved not at all amenable to the kind of account which would fit in with Newton's theory. A whole range of phenomena concerned with the behaviour of light and other electro-magnetic radiation, as well as sub-atomic phenomena, proved to be not at all as Newton's theory led men to expect. In consequence, a theory such as Einstein's General Theory of Relativity which led us to expect many of these phenomena, as well as the gravitational phenomena, would be a theory of much greater explanatory power than Newton's, and so some considerable loss of simplicity would be tolerable in order to obtain an over-all theory. Yet my point remains that the men of the eighteenth century had a reasonable belief when they believed that Newton's laws were not susceptible of further explanation.

So then we have seen at work the criteria of prior probability and explanatory power in giving us grounds, within scientific explanation, for believing that we have reached a terminus in regress of explanation by laws. The same considerations are, I suggest, at work in giving us grounds for believing that, within scientific

---

[1] For Newton's speculations on these matters see I. Newton, *Optics*, Queries, 29, 30, and 31.

[2] And of course many of them believed just this. Recall Halley's Ode prefixed to the *Principia*; and Pope's famous couplet:

> Nature and Nature's laws lay hid in night
> God said, Let Newton be, and all was light.

explanation, we have located initial conditions *C* which are not dependent for their present existence on some further state of affairs *B*. Thus to use again the example used at the end of Chapter 3, we may explain some phenomenon by the motion of some star *S*. Yet *S* is moving in a way which is to be expected if Newton's laws (or laws similar thereto) are the true laws of motion only if there is an unobserved planet *P* which is exerting an attractive force on *S*. It would complicate science vastly if we supposed that the laws of motion were somewhat different from Newton's, simply in order to account for the motion of *S*. It is far simpler to postulate *P*. We suppose that we have reached initial conditions which are not dependent on further states of affairs if, as far as we can see, there would be no over-all gain in explanatory power or prior probability in postulating further states. To postulate *P* increases the explanatory power of science (in enabling it to explain the motion of *S*) while keeping its laws simple, and although it adds to the entities which it postulates, the new entity is of a type (planet) well known in science—the supposition of its existence fits well with our background knowledge. However, contemporary science never postulates entities whose action is responsible for the current existence (as opposed to, e.g. the motion) of distinct material bodies. Nothing distinct from *S* keeps *S* in being by its current action. But contemporary science claims this only because there would be no gain in prior probability or explanatory power if it were to claim otherwise. (Of course, as this book suggests, there may be reasons from outside science for making such a claim.)

Similar considerations arise with the problem of determining the constituents of material objects. Science postulates that observable material objects are made of unobservable constituents, e.g. of molecules of various kinds linked in various ways. It postulates entities which make up material objects, and whose interaction constitutes the behaviour of observable material objects.

Observing thousands of macroscopic substances combining in different ratios to make other substances, chemists postulated that these substances were made of atoms of only a hundred different kinds and they postulated certain laws of their interaction sufficient to account for the behaviour of the macroscopic substances. The atomic theory was such that it led us to expect a whole host of chemical phenomena, some of which were already known and some of which were subsequently discovered, phenomena which there was no other reason for expecting. Also in postulating that macroscopic substances were made only of atoms of a hundred different kinds, it explained the phenomena in terms of a simpler picture. Seeking for greater simplicity, scientists naturally sought to give an account of how the atoms of different kinds differed from each other in terms of their being made of different numbers of yet more elementary building-blocks of, say, two or three distinct kinds. They hoped that such an account would explain the valency of the different atoms, why they entered into just the chemical combinations that they did. Much of the subsequent history of fundamental physics is the history of the failure of such attempts, the failure to find one or two distinct elementary building-blocks, such that the observable world could plausibly be regarded as composed of these and its behaviour as constituted by their interaction. At first in the early twentieth century a nice, simple picture seemed to be emerging—atoms seemed to be made of electrons and protons alone. But, alas, new phenomena turned up such that science had to postulate photons and positrons, neutrinos, π-mesons, K-mesons, muons, and so on, in order to explain the phenomena. The variety of fundamental particles became almost as great as the variety of atoms. Of course there was a gain in explanatory power involved in postulating the various fundamental particles—various physical as well as chemical phenomena were now predictable. But there was no gain in simplicity, or fit with background knowledge—though, as we have seen, this latter is hardly a consideration which arises with very fundamental theories which purport to explain everything. Physics is still devoting its attention to finding an underlying pattern in the variety of fundamental particles.

Although physics has not yet reached a situation where it can rest content, I suggest that physicists would be able to recognize grounds for believing that there were no further entities responsible for some observed or postulated behaviour. Suppose that physics had had the success that physicists of the early twentieth century hoped for. Suppose that all known chemical and physical behaviour were predictable by postulating one positive and one negative kind of particle, of equal mass but opposite charge, out of different numbers and arrangements of which all bodies were made and whose interactions constituted their behaviour. Postulating further entities could then result in no gain of explanatory power. Nor to all appearances could it result in any gain of simplicity, the crucial element determining prior probability. For I defy anyone to imagine a simpler kind of scientific explanation of the data. This is not to say that there could not be one; only that it is not very likely, and that it would not be profitable to try to find one. Here we would have a reasonable stopping-point for explanation (within science). We know with entities, as with laws, what a reasonable stopping-point would be like. In the example which I have just been discussing we have been concerned with postulating unobservables to 'account for' what we observe; but these unobservables are ones which constitute what we observe, rather than ones distinct from what we observe. But I hope that the latest example by illustrating the criteria of explanatory power and prior probability once again at work shows how one would expect them to apply to closely analogous cases.

One facet of phenomena which suggests to scientists that there is a deeper explanation is similar patterns of regularity in distinct groups of phenomena. Thus Mendeleev discovered in 1869 that if you arrange the chemical elements in order of their atomic weight, you find groups of elements which exhibit similar chemical and physical properties to those of earlier and later groups—for example, you get one or two elements of high atomic volume (volume of a gram of the element multiplied by its atomic weight) followed by groups of elements of low atomic volume, followed in turn by one or two elements of high atomic volume. This 'periodic law' was one piece of evidence in favour of subsequent theories of how atoms were made up, which sought to explain this periodicity. Regularity in the midst of complexity needs explaining.

So far I have phrased my points in terms of the Hempelian account of scientific explanation. Let me now put it in terms of the powers-and-liabilities account. To account for the existence and behaviour of observable objects science postulates that objects of observable kinds have certain powers and liabilities and often also postulates the existence of unobservable objects of various kinds with various powers and liabilities. It postulates that objects have various powers (e.g.) of attracting and repelling other objects, and various liabilities to be acted on by yet other objects so as to be made to exert their powers. It postulates that there are objects additional to ones which can be seen—e.g. distant planets known only by their effects on observable stars—and that observable objects are composed of various unobservable objects. It does all this only in order to explain what is observed. What is postulated must have considerable power to explain what is observed, and there must be greater prior probability in supposing that the postulated objects, powers, and liabilities exist than in supposing that the things to be explained exist unexplained. The basic consideration here is simplicity. The explanation is to be accepted in so far as it postulates *few* entities (as few unobserved planets as possible), entities of few *kinds* (few kinds of fundamental particles), few and simple kinds of powers and liabilities (e.g. all material bodies, not just nitrogen atoms on earth, having certain powers; and having powers describable by simple formulae, e.g. the power of attracting in accordance with Newton's mm^1/r^2 formula). We accept an explanation with postulated entities and properties in so far as it leads us to expect the phenomena to be explained and other phenomena, which latter would not be otherwise expected, and in so far as it provides or belongs to a simpler world-picture than the one in terms of the phenomena alone. We only move beyond an explanation to a new one if we can get greater explanatory power (new things are explained) or the total world-picture becomes simpler. If there are no further phenomena to be explained, and the entities and properties postulated have a simplicity which would be hard to better in the ways shown by our examples—we have good grounds for believing that we have reached a complete explanation.

Similar considerations apply to personal explanation. Here, it will be recalled, we explain an event E as brought about by a person P with certain capacities, beliefs, and intentions. The capacities, beliefs, and intentions belong to the 'why' of explanation. As with scientific laws, we seek to explain each of these factors in terms of simpler factors fitting in with background knowledge with greater explanatory power. Thus in explaining a man's behaviour, although we may begin by postulating a separate intention for each action, we seek to postulate a number of wider-ranging intentions of the kind which other men have such that, given them, it would be predictable that the man—given his beliefs—would have the lower-level intention that he has at some time. Thus we may explain a man's intention to open the door in terms of his belief that the door's being open is a necessary condition of his going out of it, and his belief that his going out of it a necessary condition of his posting a letter, and his intention to post a letter. The latter intention will (together with certain beliefs) explain not merely the former intention, but many other intentions which the man has on the way to his posting the letter (e.g. an intention to go down the stairs, an intention to cross the road, etc.). Similarly we explain beliefs by wider and simpler beliefs—a belief that this body which feels heavy will fall rapidly if I let go of it, in terms of a belief that all bodies which feel heavy will fall rapidly if I let go of them, and the latter belief in terms of a belief that all bodies which feel heavy will fall rapidly if people let go of them. The same kind of point can be made about capacities. Further, in explaining unusual phenomena (e.g. books flying about the room, as in the example discussed at the end of Chapter 3) we seek to attribute them, in so far as we can, to the agency of one person (one poltergeist) rather than many. We seek, so far as we can, to postulate intentions, beliefs, and capacities which are similar, or at any rate similarly formed, to those of other people, and which thus fit with our background knowledge. Within the limits of personal explanation, we then seek as a complete explanation of phenomena an explanation in terms of the agency of as few persons with the most general intentions, beliefs, and capacities which fit with other postulated intentions, beliefs, and capacities into as simple a picture of the agents as we can get which leads us to expect the phenomena which we find, and which we would have no other grounds for expecting. Clearly for human agents we often reach a situation where we have every reason to suppose that we have reached the end of the explanatory road: intentions than which the agent has no wider or simpler intentions, beliefs and capacities not derivable from wider or simpler ones.

Since, within scientific and personal explanation, explanations explain other explanations and are rightly judged so to do in so far as they satisfy the criteria of prior probability (determined by simplicity and fit with background knowledge), and of explanatory power, and since, as we saw in Chapter 2, scientific and personal explanations are on a level, i.e. are rivals for the explanation of phenomena, it would seem to follow that a scientific explanation could explain a personal one, and conversely; and that the criteria that it does so are any gain of prior probability and explanatory power which would result from supposing that it does. By a scientific explanation explaining a personal explanation, I do not mean the one being analysed in terms of the other—we saw in Chapter 2 that a personal explanation cannot be analysed in terms of a scientific explanation, and it is surely equally plausible to suppose that scientific explanation cannot be analysed in terms of personal explanation. What, rather, I do mean by a scientific explanation explaining a personal explanation is the existence and operation of the factors involved in a personal explanation being explained by the existence and operation of factors involved in a scientific explanation. A scientific explanation might be given of how people come to exist, and to have the intentions, beliefs, and capacities which they have. It is the programme of materialism to effect a reduction of just this kind. The theist who tries to explain why the world is and works as it does is attempting the reverse programme—to give a personal explanation in terms of the action of God, of the existence and operation of the factors involved in scientific explanation.

From our detailed consideration of the criteria operative within scientific or personal explanation for supposing that objects (events, states, etc.) or reasons do not have a further explanation in terms of factors acting at the time, and so that any explanation in terms of the former is a complete one, we may reasonably conclude that the criteria for supposing that factors have no further explanation (scientific or personal) in terms of factors acting at the time and so that any explanation is a complete explanation over all (not just a complete explanation within scientific or within personal explanation) are that any attempt to go beyond the factors which we have would result in no gain of explanatory power or prior probability. You reach a theory such that if you attempt to explain the existence and operation of the factors involved in it, you always reach a theory which explains nothing further and has no greater prior probability (in particular, is no simpler) than the theory which you already have; or if it does have more of one of these factors, it has significantly less of the other.

Let us now bring out the significance of these points by expressing them in our symbolic notation. We have as our evidence phenomena e. e will include some things e_1 which, it is probable, explain other things e_2, and perhaps also some things e_3 which have not been explained. We postulate explanations in terms of new causes and reasons only for things which probably do not have them already in terms of the phenomena which form our evidence. Hence we do not postulate new things to account for e_2, only to account for e_1 (and e_3). We may postulate h as an explanation of e_1. h must be such as to lead us to expect e_1 and so e_2)—$P(e_1/h.k)$ must be fairly high (k being tautological background knowledge). There will be a gain of explanatory power in so far as h leads us to expect e_3 as well, and so $P(e/h.k)$ is fairly high. There will be a gain of prior probability in so far as $P(h/k)$ is greater than $P(e_1/k)$.

Our grounds on evidence e for supposing that there is an h which satisfies the above demands will clearly be that our explanatory phenomena e_1 are complex and diverse (containing perhaps many low-level regularities) ($P(e_1/k)$ is low) and there are alongside e_1 distinct unconnected phenomena e_3 which have no explanation. For only if $P(e_1/k)$ is low are we likely to find an h which results in a gain of prior probability, and only if there are additional phenomena e_3 can we find an h which results in a gain of explanatory power. So, given that as we have seen for tautological background knowledge k, $P(e/k)$ is largely determined by the simplicity of e, the lower the prior probability of e, $P(e/k)$, (due either to the complexity of e_1 or its lack of fit with e_3) the more grounds there are for supposing that e is further explicable. What this chapter has done in effect is to draw attention to the kind of lack of simplicity which leads to low $P(e/k)$.

The higher the predictive power of h with respect to e, and the prior probability of h, the more grounds there are for postulating h to explain e. All of this is exactly what Bayes's theorem says:

$$P(h/e.k) = \frac{P(e/h.k)}{P(e/k)} \times P(h/k)$$

The results of this chapter are further evidence for the truth of Bayes's theorem.

APPENDIX

Aquinas and Scotus on Regress of Explanation

It may be helpful at this stage to contrast the terminology which I have introduced and the results which I have reached with those of Aquinas and Duns Scotus, who are among the few philosophers of the past who devoted much thought to this matter of explaining one explanation by another, and the latter in turn by another one. To start with, Aquinas and Scotus are concerned only with the 'what', causes; and not with the 'why', reasons; and by causes they mean not events, but objects, the states of which are the events. They then consider cases where we can order causes in series, A being caused by B, B by C, C by D, and so on. They distinguish series of two kinds—essentially ordered causes, and accidentally ordered causes. Scotus explains that 'in essentially ordered causes the second depends on the first precisely in its act of causation. In accidentally ordered causes this is not the case, although the second may depend upon the first for its existence, or in some other way.'[1] Aquinas and Scotus give as an example of a series of

---

[1] See Duns Scotus, *Opus Oxoniense*, I, Dist. II, Q1, trans. in A. Wolter (ed.), *Duns Scotus: Philosophical Writings* (Edinburgh, 1962), pp. 40f. I am indebted for this quotation and for a careful analysis of the scholastic terms which I discuss in this paragraph to P. Brown, 'Infinite Causal Regression', *Philosophical Review*, 1966, 75, 510–25.

essentially ordered causes—stone, stick, hand, when (the motion of) the hand makes the stick move the stone. The stick depends on the hand not for its existence, but for its operation in making the stone move. They give as an example of accidentally ordered causes the series of ancestors—son, father, grandfather, great-grandfather, etc. Here each member depends on the last for his coming into existence, but not for his operation in generating—the grandfather does not make the father generate the son. Then the causes which occur in any series of full explanations will be a series of essentially ordered causes, and conversely. A series of accidentally ordered causes in explaining beginnings of existence does not fully explain present existence or operation. Scotus claimed that any series of essentially ordered causes must be a series of simultaneous causes. But, this is not at all intuitively obvious. Why cannot there be causes which act at a temporal distance? Why cannot *A* make *B* do something two seconds later? Aquinas claimed that natural reason could not show that there cannot be an infinite regress of accidentally ordered causes, and so could not show that the universe had a beginning at a time. I agree with him that there can be no good deductive argument to this effect, but there might nevertheless be a good inductive one.[1] However, our concern, as was Aquinas's, in arguments to the existence of God, is with series of essentially ordered causes.

Aquinas claimed that there cannot be an infinite regress of essentially ordered causes. The present operation of *C* may be due to the operation of *B*, which may in turn be due to the operation of *A*; but this series cannot go on, he held, *ad infinitum*. Presumably Aquinas held, like Scotus, that any causes fully responsible for *E* are contemporaneous with *E*. He did not, as I have said, much consider series of reasons, but we could hold a similar thesis with respect to them. In that case we can put all this in a neat form in the form of a thesis to which, I believe, he would have assented, as the thesis that every phenomenon which has a full explanation has a complete explanation. The thesis is that if there is a full explanation of *E* by *C* and *R*, then, if there are any factors responsible for the current operation of *C* and *R*, you can find a set of such factors such that they themselves have no explanation in terms of contemporaneous factors, and no full explanation in terms of past factors (e.g. past factors could explain the beginning of existence of some factor *D*, but that could at most be part of the explanation of the present existence of *D*).

Aquinas claimed to be able to prove his thesis that there cannot be an infinite regress of essentially ordered causes on *a priori* grounds, but it is not altogether clear just what his argument is. Patterson Brown[2] claims that it is as follows: Essentially ordered causation[3] is transitive. If *W* causes *X*, and *X* causes *Y*, then *W* causes *Y*. If *V* in turn causes *W*, then *V* causes *Y*, and so on. Brown suggests that the argument is that as long as this series *V*, *W*, *X*,

---

[1] For discussion of this issue see my *Space and Time* (London, 1968), Ch. 15.

[2] Loc. cit., p. 522.

[3] Brown only considers in detail the case of 'moving', i.e. 'causing to move', but claims that his account applies to other kinds of causation. Hence I phrase my account of Brown in terms of 'causes' rather than 'moves'.

Y, continues backwards we have not found the real cause of *E*. Unless we reach a first cause we have not found the 'Aristotelian explanation' of *E*. If this is Aquinas's argument, it seems to suffer from the completist fallacy to which I alluded earlier. Surely if *C* causes *E*, *C* really does explain the occurrence of *E*, even if *C* itself needs explanation. Consider a long railway train in which each truck makes the next truck move. The motion of the last truck is certainly fully explained by the motion of the last truck but one, even if there are other things to be explained. If Aristotle thought otherwise, so much the worse for Aristotle. A fallacy committed by both Hume and Aquinas and possibly Aristotle deserves our respect, but a fallacy is a fallacy none the less.

I know of no good *a priori* argument for Aquinas's thesis that there cannot be an infinite regress of essentially ordered causes, and so for the thesis that any phenomenon which has a full explanation has a complete explanation. The thesis may nevertheless be true, but until it is shown to be true we should not assume that it is. The infinitely long railway train, in which each truck by its own motion simultaneously makes the next truck move, *seems* a coherent supposition. Yet although there may be no good *a priori* argument to show that phenomena which have full explanations always have complete explanations, it may be possible to show in particular cases that it is probable that they do. This chapter has been devoted to arguing this latter thesis and to setting out the grounds for judging in a particular case that some explanation is a complete explanation.

5

The Intrinsic Probability
of Theism

WE have seen that the theist claims that the various phenomena
which he cites in evidence of theism require explanation, and
he claims that theism allows us to understand why these occur,
and is itself a much more natural stopping-point for explanation than are the original phenomena. The argument of the
last chapter has shown that the correctness of this claim depends
on how great are the prior probability of theism and its explanatory power with respect to the phenomena. In this chapter I
shall consider the prior probability of theism. If we assume that
all our empirical data are among the things to be explained,
then our background knowledge will be mere tautological evidence; and so our concern will be with the intrinsic probability
of theism, and that, we have seen, is basically a matter of how
simple a hypothesis it is.

I shall now set out the hypothesis of theism in much greater detail
than I did in Chapter 1, and shall examine just how simple a
hypothesis it is.[1]

The Nature of God

Theism states the following. There exists now, and always has
existed and will exist, God, a spirit, that is, a non-embodied person
who is omnipresent. I considered at the end of Chapter 2 what is
meant by saying of God that he is non-embodied. To say that God
is not embodied is to deny that there is any limited volume of matter

---

[1] This chapter largely summarizes points made more fully and with greater rigour
in *The Coherence of Theism.*

such that by his basic actions he can control only it and such that he knows of goings-on elsewhere in the universe only by their effects on it. By contrast, to say that God is an omnipresent spirit is to say that he knows about goings-on everywhere without being dependent for that knowledge on anything, and can control by basic actions all states of affairs everywhere, that is, anywhere in this or any other universe. God is creator of all things in that for all logically contingent things which exist he himself brings about, or makes or permits other beings to bring about, their existence. He is, that is, the source of the being and power of all other things. He is, for example, responsible for the past, present, and future existence of material objects and of the natural laws which they follow, of persons and their powers. And whatever else logically contingent there may be—devils and angels, and other universes—he makes them exist and behave as they do, or gives to other beings the power so to do. Some theists have held that God created the world at a first moment of its history and imposed upon it then the laws of its future operation and thereafter left it to itself. This is the view of the deist. By contrast, in developing the theist's position, I shall assume the more orthodox view that God is at each moment of the world's history responsible for its operation at that moment of its history. Of course the more orthodox theist does hold that, if the universe or anything else had a beginning of existence, God it was who brought that beginning about or permitted some other being so to do. The majority of Christian theists have held that God does not make other persons do what they do; to a considerable extent he gives them freedom of choice, freedom to choose their intentions for action. However, which choices men make is obviously influenced— though, according to the majority of theists, not determined—by environment and heredity. God by contrast, according to all theists, is perfectly free in the sense (which I introduce by definition) that nothing apart from God in any way causally influences his choices. Which choices he makes, that is, which intentions he adopts, depends on himself alone.

God is omnipotent in the sense (roughly) that he can do whatever it is logically possible that he do.[1] He is omniscient, at any rate in the sense that he knows at any time whatever it is logically possible that he know at that time. (It *may* be that there are true propositions which it is not logically possible that a person P know at some time

[1] This is of course a very inadequate account of a difficult concept. For a more adequate account see *The Coherence of Theism*, Ch. 9.

t, e.g. propositions about some person's future free actions. Then to claim that God is omniscient is not to claim that at *t* he knows these propositions.) He is perfectly good. I understand by this that he is a being who does no morally bad actions, and does any morally obligatory action.

The theist holds that God possesses these properties described in some sense necessarily, and he is in some sense a necessary being. That is to say, God could not suddenly cease to be (e.g.) omnipotent. While God is God, he is omnipotent; nor could he cease to be God while remaining the same individual (as, for example, the Prime Minister can cease to be Prime Minister while remaining the same person). Further, while other things exist by chance or because of the action of yet other beings, God could not not exist. His existence is not dependent on any other being, nor is it a matter of chance. But what sort of 'could not' is this; what sort of 'necessity' is involved? It seems to me that a theist, if he is to worship a God worthy of worship, must hold that God's necessity amounts to at least what I am about to set out. He may wish to claim a deeper necessity for God, but the attribution to God of the deeper necessity is something which he will have difficulty in showing to be coherent.

My account is as follows. To say that God has necessarily the properties which I have just described, is to say that having those properties is essential to being the kind of being which God is. Let us say that *φ* is an essential kind if an individual which is *φ* cannot cease to be *φ* while continuing to be. To use Kripke's well-discussed example,[1] a person is an essential kind. If John is a person, he could not be anything else; because if John ceases to be a person, he ceases to be. Let us call a person who is omnipotent, omniscient, perfectly free, perfectly good, and creator of all things a personal ground of being. The theist must claim that God is a being who belongs to the essential kind of personal ground of being. He could not lose any of the properties analysed without ceasing to be God. There is no obvious incoherence in supposing that a kind within the kind of person is also an essential kind in the sense in which person is. So much for the necessity of the divine properties belonging to God. A somewhat different account has to be given of the necessity of God's existence. To say that 'God exists' is necessary is, I believe, to say that the existence of God is a brute fact which is inexplicable—not

---

[1] See (e.g.) his 'Naming and Necessity' in D. Davidson and G. Harman (eds.), *Semantics of Natural Language* (Dordrecht, 1972).

in the sense that we do not know its explanation, but in the sense that it does not have one—it is a terminus of complete explanation. As we saw in Chapter 4, any terminus to explanation of things logically contingent must be itself something logically contingent. However, as we also saw there, there are two ways in which God's existence being an inexplicable brute fact can be spelt out, although, as I shall argue shortly, one of them seems to me a more satisfactory one than the other. The first position is to say that God's essence is an eternal essence. Being eternal is to be added to the defining properties of a personal ground of being. Then God is a being of a kind such that if he exists at any time he exists at all times. His existence at all however, remains a logically contingent fact. The alternative position is to say that the divine essence is a temporal essence; being eternal is not to be added to the defining properties of a personal ground of being. Although God has always existed, nevertheless, God's existence at one time in no way implies his existence at a subsequent time. The inexplicable brute fact is then that there was no time before which God was not, that he existed at a time earlier than any time you like to name. His subsequent existence on this view is brought about by his continual choice. At every moment he chooses to exist at the subsequent moment. He chooses this freely, and he could if he so wished choose to commit suicide instead. This second position is much less consonant with the tradition of Christian theological thought than is the first. For this reason and for reasons which I will give shortly for believing the first view to be more likely to be true (while not ruling out the second view) we will work with the view that God's essence is an eternal essence; that there is a being who is essentially a personal ground of being (which includes being eternal) is the inexplicable brute fact, a terminus of explanation, how things are. Such necessary existence we may term factually necessary existence (in contrast to logically necessary existence).

Such is the hypothesis of theism, as I understand it. How simple a hypothesis is it? I propose to argue that it is a very simple hypothesis indeed, and I shall do this by showing how the divine properties which I have outlined fit together. A theistic explanation is a personal explanation. It explains phenomena in terms of the action of a person. Personal explanation explains phenomena as the results of the action of a person brought about in virtue of his capacities, beliefs, and intentions. Theism postulates God as a being with intentions, beliefs, and capacities, but ones of a very simple kind, so simple that it postulates the simplest kind of person that there could be.

To start with, theism postulates a God with capacities which are as great as they logically can be. He is infinitely powerful, omnipotent. That there is an omnipotent God is a simpler hypothesis than the hypothesis that there is a God who has such-and-such limited power (e.g. the power to rearrange matter, but not the power to create it). It is simpler in just the same way that the hypothesis that some particle has zero mass, or infinite velocity is simpler than the hypothesis that it has a mass of 0.34127 of some unit, or a velocity of 301,000 km/sec. A finite limitation cries out for an explanation of why there is just that particular limit, in a way that limitlessness does not. It is simpler in the way that Newton's hypothesis that all material bodies attract each other with forces proportional to mm^1/r^2 is simpler than the hypothesis that they attract each other with forces proportional to $mm^1/r^{2.000142}$. The former has about it a naturalness, as we saw in Chapter 3. For, given that law and only given that law, the total force exerted by a body on a hollow sphere of given uniform thickness and density centred on the body remains the same, whatever the inner radius of the sphere. Force can thus be regarded as a sort of bubble spreading out from the body and getting thinner as it grows in size. There is likewise a neatness about zero and infinity which particular finite numbers lack. Yet a person with zero capacities would not be a person at all. So in postulating a person with infinite capacity the theist is postulating a person with the simplest kind of capacity possible.

God's beliefs have a similar infinite quality. Human persons have some few finite beliefs, some true, some false, some justified, some not. In so far as they are true and justified (and perhaps—to allow for Gettier-type[1] counter-examples—justified in a particular way), beliefs amount to knowledge. It would seem most consonant with his omnipotence that an omnipotent being have beliefs which amount to knowledge (for without knowledge of what you are doing you can hardly have the power to do any action). The simplest such supposition is to postulate that the omnipotent being is limited in his knowledge, as in his power, only by logic. In that

---

[1] In 'Is Justified True Belief Knowledge?' (*Analysis*, 1963, **23**, 121–3), E. L. Gettier raised difficulties for the definition of knowledge as justified true belief, which have been much discussed by philosophers. They suggest that a true belief has to be not merely justified, but justified in a particular kind of way, in order to acquire the status of knowledge.

case he would have all the knowledge that it is logically possible that a person have, i.e. he would be omniscient.

For a person to act, he has to have intentions. His intentions might be determined by factors outside his control, or at any rate, as are those of humans, greatly influenced by them. It would, however, seem more consonant with his omnipotence for an omnipotent being to be entirely uninfluenced in his choice of intentions on which to act by factors outside his control, i.e. to be perfectly free. (For an omnipotence which you cannot but use in predetermined ways would hardly be worth having.) The theist postulates that God is perfectly free. Theism thus postulates a person of an incredibly simple kind—one with such capacities, beliefs, and intentions, that there are no limits (apart from those of logic) to his capacities, to the extent of his justified true belief, and to his choice of intention.

One could suppose that these three properties did not belong essentially together. But that would be to postulate a more mysterious world than one in which they do belong essentially together—for it would make it a cosmic accident that the being who had all power also had all knowledge. To avoid that, it is simpler to suppose that the properties belong necessarily together in a divine essence; as we have seen, they do have a natural affinity. A being who is essentially of this kind is necessarily a terminus of complete explanation. For if some state of affairs E is explained as brought about by God in virtue of his powers and beliefs and intentions to bring about E, how can this action be further explained? God's powers derive from his omnipotence, his beliefs from his omniscience, and his intention, if it derives from anything, can only derive from some wider intention of his. God's widest intention has no explanation except that he chose this intention—it follows from his perfect freedom that nothing in any way influences him to make that choice. God's being omnipotent, omniscient, and perfectly free is involved in his existing, given that, as we have supposed, these qualities belong to the divine essence. But his existing cannot be due to any contemporaneous factor which makes him exist or allows him to exist. For if his existence depended on some factor apart from himself, that factor could not depend for its existence on himself (for one cannot have causation in a circle). But if it did not so depend, then God would not have been able to make it exist or not exist, and so would not be omnipotent. In consequence God must be a necessary being in our sense that how things are depends on him, but he depends on nothing. He is necessarily a terminus of complete explanation. It is clearly simpler to suppose that the ultimate principle of explanation, the final source of things, has always been the same—rather than to suppose that only e.g. in 4004 BC did God come to be and reign—and so to suppose that God has existed eternally. We may suppose, as we mentioned earlier, that God's continuing in existence is due either to his choice, or to his nature.

I suggest however that the supposition that God's eternity is his by nature is to be preferred to the alternative supposition that it is his by choice, for three reasons of internal simplicity. If God's eternity belongs to his essence, we need no further explanation of why he is eternal. Otherwise his eternity is to be explained in terms of his continual choice. But why should he choose to go on existing; why should he not commit suicide? If there is some overriding reason for his not committing suicide, which he cannot in virtue of his nature go against, then eternity belongs to him by nature. Otherwise his continued existence would be a puzzle, a coincidence. The second reason is that if God is essentially eternal, then there are ultimate explanations of phenomena. For in this case God's action at a time *t* provides an ultimate explanation of that which it brings about. On the alternative supposition when you explain something by God's action at *t*, there is always something further to be explained—why God was in existence to make choices; and that has to be explained in terms of his existence and choice at a prior moment. But the latter fact also needs explaining in terms of God's existence and choice at a yet earlier moment, and so *ad infinitum*. If God is essentially eternal, our explanations of phenomena have a simplicity which otherwise they lack.

The third reason for preferring the hypothesis that God is essentially eternal is this. If God was not essentially eternal, he could, we have seen, if he so chose, at any time commit suicide. If he did, there could then come into existence, either uncaused or because God in his last moment had brought it about, another individual whom we will call Zeus, like God in being essentially omnipotent, omniscient, and perfectly free, and thus like God in all respects except in not being backwardly eternal (i.e. not having existed for ever). Zeus could move the stars as well as God could. Although Zeus could not have come into existence without God's consent, God would not be all that special, if all this is a possibility. The lordship over all things would not be tied to God so closely as to be inalienable. By contrast if God is essentially eternal, no other being could exercise complete control of the universe. God would have a logical uniqueness; the nature of things would be that how things are can be determined ultimately by God and by no one else. If God, in being essentially omnipotent, omniscient, and perfectly free, is the source of all things, he is obviously very different from things mundane. If he is essentially eternal, this seems to fit better with his other essential properties and to make sense of the difference between God and things mundane better than the alternative supposition.

Hence for three reasons, I argue that the supposition that God is essentially eternal is to be preferred to its rival.

I argue next that God's possession of the other properties ascribed to him—being an omnipresent spirit, being creator of all things, and (given a certain not implausible assumption) being perfectly good follow from his being omnipotent, omniscient, and perfectly free. His possession of the first two properties is easy enough to show. If God is omnipotent, then he must be able to control by basic actions all states of affairs everywhere. If God is omniscient, he must know what is going on everywhere. If he depended for this knowledge on the operation of nerves or eyes, then if they were to behave in unusual ways, he would lack knowledge. But since, *ex hypothesi*, God's omniscience belongs to his essence, this could not happen. Hence God is an omnipresent spirit. Since God is omnipotent, then he could prevent anything from happening if he so chose. So whatever happens, happens because he makes it or permits it to happen. Hence he is the creator of all things in the sense which I delineated.

Further, if one takes a certain view about the status of moral judgements, God's perfect goodness follows deductively from his omniscience and his perfect freedom. The view in question is the view that moral judgements to the effect that this action is morally good and that morally bad are propositions which are true or false. The truth of this view is of course a highly contentious philosophical issue,[1] but it has a certain plausibility. One is inclined to say that the man who says that there was nothing morally wrong in Hitler's exterminating the Jews is saying something false. There is no space here to argue for the view that moral judgements have truth-values, but I should comment that if they do not, it would be misleading to call perfect goodness a *property* of God, for it would be neither true

---

[1] I argue for it in *The Coherence of Theism*, Ch. 11 and in the article from which that Chapter is derived, 'The Objectivity of Morality', *Philosophy*, 1976, **51**, 5-20.

nor false to say of him that he does no morally bad acts. If my view is coi rect, it follows that an omniscient being will know the truth-value of all moral judgements, that is, will know of all moral judgements whether or not they are true or false. I now proceed to argue further that necessarily an agent who is perfectly free (that is, free in the sense that nothing in any way causally influences which choices he makes) will not do acts which he believes to be morally wrong. Thence it will follow that if this agent is also omniscient, he will not do acts which are morally wrong (for necessarily his beliefs about their status will be true ones).

To do an action an agent has to have a reason for acting. A movement brought about by an agent would not be an action unless the agent had some reason for bringing it about. The reason may be simply just to do that action, but normally an agent will have some further purpose in doing an action. Having a reason for an action consists in regarding some state of affairs as a good thing, and the doing of the action as a means to forwarding that state, and hence itself a good thing. If my reason for going to Oxford was to give a lecture, I must regard it as in some way a good thing that I give the lecture, and so a good thing that I go to Oxford. If I regarded it as in no way a good thing that I give the lecture, if I thought that giving the lecture was an event which would serve no useful function at all, giving the lecture could not have been my reason for going to Oxford. The point that to do an action I must (of logical necessity) see my performance of it as in some way a good thing is a very old one due to Aristotle, emphasized by Aquinas, and re-emphasized in our day by, among others, Stuart Hampshire.[1] God, like man, cannot just act. He must act for a purpose and see his action as in some way a good thing. Hence he cannot do what he does not regard as in some way a good thing. This is not a physical constraint, but a logical limit. Nothing would count as an action of God unless God in some way saw the doing of it as a good thing.

Now for many actions there are reasons for doing them and reasons for not doing them; in some ways it is good that the agent should do them, and in some ways it is good that he should refrain from doing them. It is good that I should watch the television, because I would enjoy doing so; yet bad because it will stop me reading a book. It is good for governments to lower taxes, because

---

[1] 'A man cannot be sincere in accepting the conclusion that some course of action is entirely mistaken, if he at the same time deliberately commits himself to this course of action.' S. Hampshire, *Freedom of the Individual* (London, 1965), p. 7.

that will give people more money to spend; and yet bad because lowering taxes will promote inflation and social inequality. Frequently, perhaps normally, there is no objective scale in which competing reasons can be weighed; one cannot say that doing A is on balance better than refraining from doing A, or conversely; or that the reasons for doing A override the reasons for refraining from doing A. In such a case a man who does A need be no less sensitive to objective values than one who refrains from doing A. But sometimes competing reasons can be compared objectively; clearly sometimes doing A is over all better than refraining from doing A, or conversely. One may think that there are some such cases where, although doing A may be better than refraining from doing A, it is unimportant, no harm is done, if the less good action is done. For example, it might be on balance better that I should read a work of literature than an aesthetically worthless book, but it might not matter if I read the latter. But often, maybe always, in these cases it is all-important that an agent should do the action which is on balance better. It matters. Such are the actions which we call morally obligatory. (If a reader does not understand these closely connected notions of actions 'mattering', being 'all-important', and being 'morally obligatory', all that can be done is to spell out the notions in similar terms and give many examples.) A morally obligatory action is certainly one which is over all better than any alternative, but it may be, as we have seen, that some actions which are over all better than alternatives are not morally obligatory.[1] Conversely, a morally bad action is one which is over all worse than any alternative, but it may be that some actions which are over all worse than any alternative are not morally bad. Although it is in some way a good thing that a sadist should torture children (because of the pleasure which it gives to him), clearly it is over all a bad thing, and indeed a morally bad thing; there are overriding reasons why he should not torture children.

We have seen that an agent has to have some reason if he is to do an action A, to see doing A as in some way a good thing. Can an agent still do action A even if he judges that on balance it would be better to refrain from doing A? What are we to make of the suggestion that a man might see doing A as a good thing in one way (e.g. by its giving sensual pleasure to himself), refraining from doing

---

[1] In *The Coherence of Theism*, Ch. 11, I wrongly ignored this possibility and, without argument, equated the action which was over all better, with the morally obligatory action.

A as a good thing in another way (e.g. by its contributing to the lifelong peace of mind of someone else), see refraining from doing *A* as over all a better thing than doing *A*, but nevertheless do *A*. When it is suggested that a case is of this sort, we may well suspect that it is not, that the agent did not really see refraining from doing *A* as over all a better thing than doing *A*. Yet we are sometimes prepared to allow that a situation is of this kind. We do seem to allow the possibility that a man might do an action which he regarded as a good thing only in some respect, but on balance a bad thing. But although we allow this possibility, we do feel that some further explanation is called for. If a man really does accept that to refrain from doing *A* would be on balance better than to do *A*, and so accepts that he has overriding reason for refraining from doing *A*, he recognizes that he has adequate reason for refraining from doing *A*, but inadequate reason for doing *A*. Rational considerations point clearly in one direction, and yet the agent goes in the other direction. Yet to say that someone recognizes that he has a reason for doing something is to say that if there are no equally good reasons for not doing that thing and if no factors other than reasons influence him, he will do that thing. We would not understand an agent who claimed to recognize 'overriding reason' for refraining from doing *A* rather than doing *A* and also claimed to be uninfluenced by anything other than the reasons which he acknowledged, and yet did *A*. For if the latter claim is taken at its face value, what on earth can the agent have meant when he said that he recognized 'overriding reasons' for refraining from doing *A*? Not what we normally mean, for normally to recognize a reason for doing something involves acknowledging an inclination, *ceteris paribus*, to do that thing. So to say of someone that he recognizes that he has overriding reasons for refraining from doing (or for doing) action *A* is to say that in so far as no factors other than reasons influence him, he will refrain from *A* (or do *A*, as the case may be). If you said that you recognized that over all it would be better for you to go home rather than to go to the cinema, and then you went to the cinema, we should have to suppose either that you were lying or had changed your mind, or that factors other than reasons influenced what you did. An explanation of your behaviour is needed, not only in terms of what you believed about the relative merits of the actions, in terms that is of reasons; but also in terms of other factors such as sensual desires and neurological impulses which led you to do what you did not recognize adequate reason for doing. If a man has strong sensual desires, it makes sense to suppose that he recognizes refraining from A as over all better than doing A, but nevertheless intentionally does A. Such non-rational factors over which the agent does not have control explain 'weakness of will', a man acting 'against his better judgement'. But the suggestion that a man might see refraining from A as over all better than doing A, be subject to no non-rational influences inclining him in the direction of doing A, and nevertheless do A is incoherent.

It follows from all this that an agent subject to no non-rational influences, that is, a perfectly free agent, can never do an action if he judges that over all it would be worse to do the action than to refrain from doing it. Hence he can never do an action which he judges to be over all a bad action, one for refraining from doing which he recognizes overriding reasons, and especially one which he judges to be a morally bad action. By a similar argument a perfectly free agent will always do any action which he recognizes to be over all better to do than not to do, and so one which he judges to be morally obligatory. These are logical limits on which actions a perfectly free agent (in the sense in which I have defined this term) can do.

Now if moral judgements have truth-values, an omniscient person will know them. His judgements about which actions are morally bad and which actions are morally obligatory, will be true judgements. Hence a perfectly free and omniscient being can never do actions which are morally bad, and will always do actions which are morally obligatory, and so he will be perfectly good. Moral judgements involve judgements about actions being such that over all it is better that an agent should do them than that he should refrain from doing them. If these have truth-values, then judgements about actions being good at all will have truth-values. It can only be true that some action is over all better than some other action if it is true that actions are in some way good. Put in the other way in which I have expressed these points, moral judgements involve judgements about there being overriding reasons for doing actions. If these have truth-values, so will judgements about there being reasons for doing things. Hence God will always do any action for doing which there is overriding reason, never do any action for refraining from doing which there is overriding reason; and only do an action if there is a reason for doing it. We may call this aspect of God's nature his complete rationality. It includes his perfect goodness, and gives us some expectations about the sort of world he will be expected to create, and so, as we shall see in the next chapter, allows us to some extent to infer from the character of the world to whether or not it is made by God.

The constraints imposed by logic upon God's choice of actions are of course quite compatible with God having a very considerable choice among actions. That there are some constraints upon God's action's resulting from his nature, but that otherwise God has very considerable choice of action, has been the view of many, but by no means all Christian theists. It was certainly the view of Aquinas[1] who held that God can do no evil (what is evil being determined in part by criteria other than what God chooses to do) but that it was entirely up to him whether or not to create a universe. However God's goodness only follows from his perfect freedom and omniscience, given that moral judgements have a truth-value.

The Simplicity of Theism

I conclude that theism postulates a person of a very simple kind—a person who is essentially omnipotent, omniscient, and perfectly free and who is eternal, perhaps essentially so. Such a being will be a necessary being and will necessarily be an omnipresent spirit, creator of all things, and (given that moral judgements have truth-values) perfectly good. Theism is also intrinsically very simple in a further respect. According to the theist, all explanation is reducible to personal explanation, in the sense that the operation and causal efficacy of the factors cited in scientific explanation is always explicable by the action of a person. A personal explanation of a scientific explanation states which persons with which intentions, beliefs, and capacities bring about the existence of the initial conditions C and the operation of laws of nature L. In the theist's view all phenomena which have a full scientific explanation have a complete explanation which is a personal explanation. Theists differ among themselves as to whether an event E which has a full personal explanation in terms of the action of a human agent P has a complete explanation solely in terms of the action of God. If one does hold this, one holds that a human agent's intention is his through God's making it the case that he had that intention. This seems to me to involve the view that man has no free will. It is, I believe, the view of a significant minority among Christian theists. The majority position however, seems to be that man has some

---

[1] See e.g. *Summa Contra Gentiles*, 2.25.

control of his own destiny, a control given to him by God, but which he exercises independently of God; that, whatever may be the case with his beliefs or capacities, at any rate a man's intentions are not all given to him by God. In that case not all personal explanations have complete explanations solely in terms of the agency of God. Nevertheless, the theist does hold that all phenomena which have full explanations have complete explanations which are personal explanations, although not all of them are explanations solely in terms of God's action.

Further, for the theist, explanation stops at what, intuitively, is the most natural kind of stopping-place for explanation—the choice of an agent. If regress of explanation ever stops, where it stops is the ultimate source of the diversity of things. We ourselves make choices, and we understand that in making a choice we ourselves are the source of one state of affairs coming about rather than another. Of course there *may* be some explanation of why we make the choices which we do. But we can understand what is happening without having to make that supposition—something which is apparent from the fact that many people do not make that supposition, and yet use the concept of choice. In our experience we are aware of ourselves as sources of things being this way rather than that. Hence we have an intelligible concept of an agent's bringing about through choice the diversity of things, which it is natural to use in this context. As we saw in Chapter 3, the intelligibility of postulated operations is a facet of simplicity.

In these respects the theist proposes a significant simplification of our world view. There are three tenable views as to the relation between scientific explanation and personal explanation. One untenable view is the occasionalist view that scientific causes never produce effects, but that all effects are brought about by rational agents, normally God. The occasionalist claims that the ignition of gunpowder does not really cause explosions; it is just that when men ignite gunpowder, God reliably produces explosions. This view is manifestly false, and the theist as such is not committed to it. Another untenable view is that persons never bring about effects in virtue of their intentions and beliefs. This view too is manifestly false. Two other untenable views are the view that scientific explanation is analysable in terms of personal explanation and the opposite view that personal explanation is analysable in terms of scientific explanation. I mentioned the former view above, only to dismiss it, since it is not a view which anyone is tempted to hold. The latter view is of course a seriously held philosophical thesis, and in Chapter 2 I produced what I regard as a compelling argument against it. Given that all these views are false, there really operate both scientific causality and personal causality and neither is analysable in terms of the other. There remain three tenable views of their relation to each other. One is the theist's view described above that the operation and causal efficacy of the factors cited in scientific explanation have a full personal explanation; a second is the materialist's view that the operation and causal efficacy of the factors cited in personal explanation have a full scientific explanation; the third is that the operation and causal efficacy of neither can be given full explanation in terms of the other. On the third view, which we may call explanatory dualism, there are just two kinds of explanation of goings-on in the world and neither can in any way be reduced to the other.

Now clearly both the theist's view and the materialist's view result in a significantly simpler world-view than the dualist world-view. At the end of the last chapter I pointed out that the rational man is ever seeking explanations of greater simplicity and explanatory power. It would be surprising and irrational if the search for simpler and more comprehensive explanations, which we have seen to be so characteristic of the advance of explanation, were to resist the natural impulse to cross the border between types of explanation. If scientific explanations can themselves be explained by wider scientific explanations, and personal explanations by wider personal explanations, surely the seeker after truth should consider whether perhaps all personal explanations are in the end themselves susceptible of a complete scientific explanation, or whether perhaps all scientific explanations are in the end susceptible of a complete personal explanation. A world-view in which all personal explanations have a complete explanation in scientific terms, or all scientific explanations have a complete explanation in personal terms would be a simpler world-view than others, and as such more likely to be true.

There are many philosophers attempting to carry through the materialist's programme, to fill out the details of his world-picture in the way in which I have filled out the details of theism. The materialist claims that a scientific explanation of personal explanation can always be given, stating which initial conditions C and laws L bring about the existence of persons P and intentions I, beliefs B, and capacities X, and thereby make it the case that persons bring about certain effects. The materialist programme has a certain initial plausibility, for clearly a man's capacities and beliefs are in part dependent on the operation of various laws of neural interaction and on the existence of nerves, brain, muscles, etc. There are, however, I believe, very considerable scientific and philosophical difficulties in effecting this reduction, and I shall discuss these difficulties in Chapter 9. My main purpose here has been to catalogue—to point out that dualism gives a very messy, unsimple, picture of the world; and that both theism and materialism are to all appearances simple world-views and as such more likely to be true. Those who have studied the voluminous literature on mind–brain identity will have seen philosophers urging rightly that dualism is a messy world-view and going on to urge that the rational inquirer ought to postulate that in some way mental events and causation can be reduced to entities and causation of the kinds with which physical science deals. I have pointed out here that equal simplicity may be gained in a different way by supposing that in the stated respect scientific explanation is reducible to personal explanation.

Note the nature of the connection which the theist postulates between personal and scientific causation. God is omnipotent. His power is not dependent on brain or nerves. His intentions are immediately operative—because that is how things ultimately are. Hence the existence of matter and the operation of natural laws. There is a natural connection between the factors cited in this personal explanation and what they effect—God's intention to bring about φ is followed by φ. (We shall see later that the materialist is going to be hard put to it to produce any similar natural connection.) Among the things which God brings about are the existence of human persons with brains, nerves, muscles, etc. and the natural laws which determine when, by what route, and within what range their intentions are efficacious. There is a similar natural connection between God's knowledge and the world. If p is a true proposition which it is logically possible that a person know, then God knows p.

One final feature of great importance about the hypothesis of theism is this. What is at stake in the various arguments which we shall be considering is whether we ought to go beyond various phenomena to postulate a God who brings them about. This is a matter of whether the hypothesis of theism has sufficient prior probability and explanatory power. But if it has, there is no similar issue of whether we ought to go beyond theism in order to provide a complete explanation. For if theism is true, then of logical necessity, God's action provides a complete explanation of what it explains (and if God is essentially eternal, an ultimate explanation as well). For as we saw earlier, it follows from God's omnipotence and perfect freedom that all things depend on him whereas he depends on nothing. If God features at all in explanation of the world, then explanation clearly ends with God.

So then theism has very considerable simplicity. Simplicity is the major determinant of intrinsic probability. We saw that another determinant is narrowness of scope. It is not quite clear how we are to assess theism on this criterion. Since it only postulates one entity, in a way its scope is very narrow; but in that it postulates that that entity has control over and knowledge of all other things, its scope is wide. However, it is clear from earlier examples that the great simplicity of a wide hypothesis outweighs by far its wideness of scope in determining intrinsic probability. Perhaps it seems *a priori* vastly improbable, if one thinks about it, that there should exist anything at all logically contingent. But, given that there does exist something, the simple is more likely to exist than the complex. Hence with k as mere tautological evidence and h as the hypothesis of theism, even if $P(h/k)$, the intrinsic probability of theism, is low, it will not be nearly as low of $P(j/k)$ for many other hypotheses j about what there is. The intrinsic probability of theism is, relative to other hypotheses about what there is, very high, because of the great simplicity of the hypothesis of theism.

6

The Explanatory Power of Theism: General Considerations

Summary of the Argument so far

I argued in Chapter 3 that the probability of a hypothesis h on evidence e and background knowledge k is a function of its prior probability ($P(h/k)$) and its explanatory power ($P(e/h.k))/P(e/k)$. By Bayes's Theorem:

$$P(h/e.k) = P(h/k) \times \frac{P(e/h.k)}{P(e/k)}$$

We saw in Chapter 3 that, with tautological background knowledge k, the major determinant of $P(h/k)$ is the simplicity of h. We saw in Chapter 4 that, with tautological background knowledge, the major determinant of $P(e/k)$ is the simplicity of e. Chapter 4 showed in some detail the kind of lack of simplicity which needed explanation and so suggested that e had some explanation in terms of some h. Now let h be the hypothesis of theism, that there is a God; let k be mere tautological evidence (and so $P(h/k)$ is the intrinsic probability of theism), and e the evidence cited in arguments for and against theism. We saw in the last chapter that although $P(h/k)$ may be low, it is significantly greater than that of alternative fillings for h. Theism postulates a God of infinite power, knowledge, and freedom, and that all complete explanation is personal explanation. Hence theism forms a natural stopping-point for explanation, a natural candidate that is for a brute fact which explains other things, but itself has no explanation. A stopping-point for explanation is of course a highly mysterious thing. That there should be anything (logically contingent) at all is overwhelmingly strange, when we think about it. But there is something logically contingent.

The issue is whether the world and its operations are the stopping-point, or whether we must go beyond the world to find the stopping-point of explanation; or whether, although we go beyond the world to find an explanation of the world, there is no stopping-point for explanation to be found. By the argument of the last two chapters the God of theism is a good candidate for a stopping-point, if the world and its operations have sufficiently low intrinsic probability ($P(e/k)$) to need explaining, and if the hypothesis of theism makes it quite likely that e will occur (if $P(e/h.k)$ is quite high).

We saw in Chapter 3 that by the 'relevance' criterion an argument from e to h is a good C-inductive argument if (and only if) $P(e/h.k) > P(e/k)$ and that this will be the case if (and only if) $P(e/h.k) > P(e/\sim h.k)$. Hence the occurrence of certain phenomena will confirm, i.e. raise the probability of, the existence of God, if and only if it is more probable that those phenomena will occur if there is a God than if there is not. How probable the phenomena will make the existence of God will depend on just how high or low are the various factors which we have been discussing. The force of the arguments from e to h will depend, as well as on the constant factor ($P(h/k)$), on the explanatory power of theism with regard to those phenomena; how much more likely does the existence of God make the occurrence of those phenomena than it would be if we do not assume the existence of God.

Principles for Assessing the Explanatory Power of Theism

With this background I come to consider the arguments to the existence of God (h) from various phenomena (e).

To show that it is unlikely that the phenomena would occur unless there was a God (that $P(e/\sim h.k)$ is low) one has to show that it is unlikely that there is any complete explanation of the phenomena—e.g. a scientific explanation or an explanation in terms of the operation of some ordinary person—other than one which involves God's agency. I have referred briefly once or twice to the importance of this consideration. One also has to show that it is unlikely that the phenomena would occur without there being an explanation of their occurrence, that it is unlikely that those phenomena would be ultimate brute facts. I considered in general terms in Chapter 4 the kind of grounds which are relevant to showing that we have reached a terminus of explanation.

To show that it is likely that the phenomena would occur if there

were a God (that $P(e/h.k)$ is high) we have to show that God with
his known character is likely to bring about or allow others to bring
about e. For clearly whatever e is, God, being omnipotent, has the
power to bring about e. He will do so, if he chooses to do so. Now it
follows from the definition of God, as I showed in the last chapter,
that he will do every action which is over all a good action (and so
every morally obligatory action), no action which is over all a bad
action (and so no morally bad action), and that whatever he does
must be in some way a good thing to do. Put another way—he will
do whatever he has overriding reason to do, he will not do whatever
he has overriding reason not to do, and whatever he does he will
have reason to do.

What follows from all this about the states of affairs which we can
expect to find in the world, if there is a God? With regard to any
state of affairs e, there seem to be seven possibilities. First, God may
have overriding reason for not allowing e to occur. (Allowing e to
occur may be morally bad.) In that case God, being omnipotent,
will not allow e to occur. In such a case $P(e/h.k) = 0$. Secondly, God
might have reason to bring about $\sim e$; and also reason to allow
either e or $\sim e$ to occur, dependent on processes which he puts
outside his control (neither of these reasons overriding the other);
yet God has overriding reason for not himself bringing about e. The
most plausible case when there is reason for God to put the
occurrence of e or $\sim e$ in the hands of processes outside his control is
where there is reason for him to allow free agents to determine what
happens by their choice. It might be good that such agents should
have the choice of which of two states to bring about, while it might
be good that God himself should bring about one of these states and
morally bad for God to bring about the other; just as, by analogy, it
is often good that parents give to children, or the law of the land
give to subjects, the opportunity of bringing about one or other of
two states of affairs, the bringing about of one of which is good and
the bringing about of the other morally bad. I shall argue positively
for the value of such freedom in Chapters 9 and 10—all that I am
doing here is to use the analogy of this kind of example in which a
man might claim that such freedom is good, to illustrate what is
being got at in the similar claim about God. In this case $P(e/h.k)$
will be intermediate between 1 and 0, but clearly closer to 0 than in
some other cases which we shall consider.

Our third, fourth, and fifth possibilities are rather similar to each
other, and give rise to rather similar values for $P(e/h.k)$. The third

one is where God has overriding reason for not bringing about e, overriding reason for not bringing about $\sim e$, but reason to allow the occurrence of e or $\sim e$ to depend on processes outside his control. The fourth possibility arises where God has reason for bringing about e, reason for bringing about $\sim e$ (neither of these reasons overriding the other), but overriding reason for not allowing the occurrence of e or $\sim e$ to depend on processes outside his control. The fifth possibility arises when God has reason to bring about e, reason to bring about $\sim e$, and reason to allow the occurrence of e or $\sim e$ to depend on processes outside his control (none of these reasons overriding any other). In all of these cases $P(e/h.k)$ will be intermediate between 1 and 0, but intuitively rather higher than under the second possibility, since there is, as it were, less bias against e.

The sixth possibility is that God might have reason to bring about e, and reason to allow the occurrence of e or $\sim e$ to depend on processes outside his control, but overriding reason not to bring about $\sim e$. In this case again $P(e/h.k)$ will be intermediate between 1 and 0, but, intuitively, closer to 1 than under the third, fourth, and fifth possibilities—since there is, as it were, more bias in favour of e. Finally, God may have overriding reason for not allowing $\sim e$ to occur. In that case he will himself bring about the occurrence of e; $P(e/h.k) = 1$.

The value of $P(e/h.k)$ in the intermediate cases will depend, more precisely, on exactly what e is, and in cases where God allows other processes the opportunity to bring about e, how many such other processes have this opportunity, and whether, although their actions are not fully dependent on God's will, they are in any way biased in favour of e or $\sim e$. For example, the less specific is e (i.e. the more distinct states of affairs involve e), the more probable it is *a priori* that e occur—whether as a result of the action of God or of some creature given by God the opportunity to determine whether or not it occurs.[1] Thus clearly *a priori* it is more probable that God bring about a universe with regular laws, than that he bring about a universe with the particular laws which our universe has. Or, if e is a state of affairs which any free agent can bring about, and God allows to each free agent the opportunity to bring e about, $P(e/h.k)$ will be greater, the more free agents there are.

It is the fact that a God will be a completely rational being, and so

---

[1]   Indeed it follows from the axioms of the calculus that for any p, where e_1 entails e_2, $P(e_2/p) \geqslant P(e_1/p)$.

a perfectly good being, which gives us some ability to predict what he will do. Only *some* ability of course, for clearly all too often there are reasons for bringing about states of affairs and reasons for not bringing them about, where neither override the other. But sometimes there are overriding reasons for doing things, and we with our limited understanding can recognize these. Of course, as ignorant and morally corrupt human beings, we may have very inadequate ideas of which actions God has reason to do and which actions he has overriding reason to do (which actions are good, and which actions are good over all). Yet clearly most of us have some understanding of this matter, for we have some understanding of what is morally good and what is morally bad (e.g. when we judge that torturing children just for fun is morally bad, we make a true moral judgement)[1] and the capacity to grow in such understanding. And clearly too our understanding of most other things discussed in this book, and in most books about most things, is very limited and prone to error, but is such that we can grow in it. We have to make tentative judgements in the light of our understanding at the time of our investigation—in this matter as in all matters—bearing in mind the possibility of future revision. With this caveat, we will move on.

With respect to different arguments for the existence of God, different factors will turn out to be of prime importance in determining the explanatory power of the hypothesis of theism. $P(e/h.k)$ may exceed $P(e/k)$ because $P(e/\sim h.k)$ is very low. This will be if e is totally inexplicable except through God's action in bringing it about (or allowing it to occur)—e.g. there is no scientific explanation of e (or personal explanation in terms of the action of an embodied agent), and if it has the kind of complexity which makes it a very unlikely stopping-point for explanation (at any rate in comparison with the simplicity of God). All this would make $P(e/k)$ low. Alternatively, although there might well be other rival candidates for explaining e, or e is a state of affairs which might well occur by chance, $P(e/h.k)$ may exceed $P(e/k)$ because $P(e/h.k)$ is large. This would be if e is the kind of state which God could be expected to bring about or to allow others to bring about, more than other states. e may be no less to be expected than many other states if natural processes above are at work, but more to be expected than other states if a God is at work. This may be because

---

[1] For further argument on the objectivity of morality see *The Coherence of Theism*, Ch. 11.

he has overriding reason not to bring about some of those other states. I shall wish to stress the first factor as of great importance for the cosmological argument, the teleological argument, the argument from consciousness, and the argument from miracles; whereas I shall wish to stress the second factor in connection with the teleological argument and the argument from providence—although I shall need to mention it in connection with other arguments.

The considerations of the last two pages enable me to meet an important objection to probabilistic arguments which is put in a fairly precise form in an article by D. H. Mellor,[1] which is one of the very few places where the application of confirmation theory to the philosophy of religion is seriously discussed. Mellor's argument is directed against the argument from design, but it could equally well be directed against almost any argument for the existence of God. I will give Mellor's argument, which is only one of a number of inter-connected arguments in his paper, a somewhat more precise form than it has there. I hope that I shall not represent him unfairly.

Mellor imagines that we find the cards in a bridge hand which has been just dealt in a certain kind of order (e), and he considers the worth of the argument from this order to a cheat's having put them in order (h) (i.e. to the shuffling having been rigged, not being a chance matter). He rightly says that we can only assess the probability of this hypothesis if we could have written down in advance of looking at the pack in what order (or orders) a cheat would be likely to have arranged the cards. In our terminology, in order to assess $P(h/e.k)$ and to see whether it exceeds $P(h/k)$ we need to know in advance of observing e, $P(e_i/h.k)$ and $P(e_i/k)$ for different e_i. This part of the argument seems to me indubitably correct. He then implies that we cannot do this where h is the hypothesis of theism, and e_i are different possible worlds since we have no idea what kinds of world God is likely to create. We cannot tell whether for some e_i $P(e_i/h.k)$ is greater or less than $P(e_i/k)$, for we have no idea what are the intentions of God, if he exists. The answers to Mellor's objection should now be clear from what has been said earlier in this chapter. First, contrary to Mellor, we do have some idea of what kinds of world God is likely to create and hence an idea of how $P(e_i/h.k)$ will differ for different e_i; and secondly, unlike in the bridge analogy, not all e_i are equally likely *a priori*. Some e_i, some worlds, have such complexity that *a priori* they

[1] 'God and Probability', *Religious Studies*, 1969, **5**, 223-34.

are not to be expected—probably only the power of God can bring them about. So $P(e_i/h.k)$ may be known to exceed $P(e_i/k)$ not only because of the known character of God (because he is known to be more likely to bring about some e_i than others) but also because of the known *a priori* improbability of certain world-states occurring uncaused.

The Best of all Possible Worlds

The answer given on pp. 109 ff. as to the kinds of states of affairs which might be expected to exist if there is a God is a somewhat complicated one, and on one well-known view, a far too complicated one. On that view God has an obligation, or at any rate an overriding reason, to create the best of all possible worlds. This answer, espoused classically by Leibniz[1] but by many others as well, has the consequence that the only states of affairs which we can expect to exist, if there is a God, will be ones belonging to the best of all possible worlds. The probability, if there is a God, that they will exist is 1; the probability that any other state will exist is 0.

This answer seems to me mistaken. A God will not necessarily bring about the best of all possible worlds.[2] For there is every reason to suppose that there is no unique best of all possible worlds. For suppose that there is such a world, *W*. Is it really plausible to suppose that every world which contained one or two more individuals than *W* would be a less good world? Again, *W* will presumably contain a finite or infinite number of conscious beings. Would a world be a worse world if instead of one of these conscious beings it contained another with the same properties—if instead of Swinburne it contained a counterpart of Swinburne who wrote an exactly similar book and in other ways had exactly similar properties and did exactly similar actions? Surely not. But then there will be no unique best of all possible worlds. It seems almost equally implausible to suppose that there is *a* best of all possible worlds, that

---

[1] 'Now this supreme wisdom, united to a goodness that is no less infinite, cannot but have chosen the best . . . If there were not the best among all possible worlds, God would not have produced any. I call "world" the whole succession and the whole agglomeration of all existing things . . . There is an infinitude of possible worlds among which God must needs have chosen the best', G. W. Leibniz, *Theodicy*, trans. E. M. Huggard (London, 1952), p. 128.

[2] This is the view of Aquinas. See *Summa Theologiae*, Ia. 25.6 ad 3. 'God could make other things, or add other things to those he has made, and there would be another and better universe.'

is, a world such that no world is better than it (although other worlds may be equally good). For again take any world *W*. Presumably the goodness of such a world, as I shall argue in more detail later, will consist in part in it containing a finite or infinite number of conscious beings who will enjoy it. But if the enjoyment of the world by each is a valuable thing, surely a world with a few more conscious beings in it would be a yet more valuable world— for there would be no reason why the existence of the latter should detract from the enjoyment of the world by others—they could always be put some considerable distance away from others, so that there was no mutual interference. I conclude that it is not, for conceptual reasons, plausible to suppose that there could be a best of all possible worlds,[1] and in consequence God could not have overriding reason to create one.

Anyway, even if there could be a best of all possible worlds, it seems highly dubious to suppose that God is under any moral obligation to create such a world. This has been well argued in an important article by Robert Merrihew Adams[2] who claims that God would not necessarily do any wrong to any one by creating a world which was not a best of all possible worlds. There might be certain beings in a best of all possible worlds, which do not exist in the world which God actually makes. Yet, Adams points out, God would not do wrong to those beings in not creating them—for you cannot do any wrong to a being which never has existed and never will exist. There might be other beings in the world which God actually makes who would not exist in a best of all possible worlds— God would hardly do them any wrong by creating them, so long as he created them so as to live a life which was better to live than to live no life at all. Finally there might be some beings who are less perfect in the world which God actually makes than they would be in a best of all possible worlds. Would God wrong them by creating them thus? So long as God has created them now in such a

---

[1] There is a good discussion of Leibniz's arguments for supposing that there is a best of all possible worlds by D. Blumenfeld, 'Is the Best Possible World Possible?', *Philosophical Review*, 1975, **84**, 163–77.

[2] 'Must God Create the Best?', *Philosophical Review*, 1972, **81**, 317–32. In discussing in a very different context the moral consequences of utilitarianism, Jan Narveson argues that there are no duties to non-existing persons, and hence no duty to increase the total happiness of the human race, and hence no duty to ensure that there is a human race at all. There is no duty to increase the number of happy persons, only a duty to increase the happiness of existing persons. See his 'Utilitarianism and New Generations', *Mind*, 1967, **76**, 62–72.

condition that it is better for them to exist than not to exist, in what way does he wrong them if he makes them less perfect than he could have made them? For he still gives them a reasonable existence which they would not otherwise have. Even if we suppose that a given embryo, if interfered with sufficiently early, could grow into a rabbit rather than a goldfish, and that this technique is available to a breeder, there is surely nothing wrong in breeding goldfish. Although, *ex hypothesi*, the breeder could have made those goldfish into rabbits, the breeder does the goldfish no wrong in not having made rabbits out of them.

However, if there *were* a best of all possible worlds, although God would be under no moral obligation to make such a world, it seems plausible to suppose that he would have overriding reason for doing so. It seems over all better to make such a world than to make any other world. Nevertheless—the previous arguments suggest that there is no best of all possible worlds, and so God cannot have any overriding reason to make one. Given that for every possible world, there is a better one, there is no world such that it is over all better that God should make that world than that he should make any other world.

However, one must be careful not to draw either of two false conclusions from this result. First, there is the conclusion that therefore God would not create any world. Leibniz argued that if there were no best of all possible worlds, God would not create any world. (See the quotation on p. 113 n. 1.) But that does not follow. He has reason to create a world, and reason to create any of many different worlds, but no overriding reason to create one of them rather than all others. In that case he surely has reason to use some process of random selection or some arbitrary feature of a world to determine which to create. A man who has reason to buy a house but no reason to buy this house rather than that house will not necessarily fail to buy a house—unlike Buridan's ass, he may make an arbitrary selection, and that will have been the rational thing to do. Secondly, it is important to avoid the alternative false conclusion that *any* possible world is such that God might make that world. Even if there is no best of all possible worlds, there may still be worlds which are such that God has overriding reason not to make them (e.g. worlds which contain unnecessary suffering)—we shall consider this issue in Chapter 10. God's choice can only be exercised between worlds which he does not have overriding reason not to make.

7

The Cosmological Argument

THE previous chapters have been concerned with elucidating the principles for assessing the worth of arguments from experienced phenomena, to the existence of God. With this chapter I begin to apply them to the consideration of particular arguments, starting with that argument which has the most general premiss of all—the cosmological argument.

Two Forms of Cosmological Argument

Kant defined a cosmological argument as one which starts from 'experience which is purely indeterminate' or 'experience of existence in general'. Let us say, more precisely, that it is one which starts from the existence of a finite object, i.e. any object other than God. However, other arguments called cosmological have in effect started from something rather more specific, the existence of a complex physical universe; and I shall concentrate mainly on these. I understand by a physical universe a physical object consisting of physical objects spatially related to each other and to no other physical object. (By 'spatially related to each other' I understand 'at some distance in some direction from each other'.) Our physical universe, *the* universe, is the physical object which consists of all physical objects including the earth, spatially related to each other and to no other physical object. It consists of the galaxies, stars, and planets, including the earth, things on them, and gases between them. The universe is the only physical universe of which we have knowledge, but I define it in such a way as not to rule out the logical possibility of other physical universes,[1] or of objects which are not

---

[1] Another physical universe would be a physical object consisting of physical objects, spatially related to each other, but not to the objects of our universe such as

part of any physical universe (e.g. God or some finite spirit, neither of which are physical objects). By a complex physical universe I understand one consisting of many physical objects of diverse and of not very natural volume, shape, mass, etc.; mostly inert objects without powers of choice. Our universe of material objects of galaxies, stars, planets, and pebbles on the sea-shore is thus a complex physical universe.

From time to time various writers[1] have told us that we cannot reach any conclusions about the origin or development of the universe, since it is (whether by logic or just in fact) a unique object, the only one of its kind, and rational inquiry can only reach conclusions about objects which belong to kinds, e.g. it can reach a conclusion about what will happen to this bit of iron, because there are other bits of iron, the behaviour of which can be studied. This objection of course has the surprising, and to most of these writers unwelcome, consequence, that physical cosmology cannot reach justified conclusions about such matters as the size, age, rate of expansion, and density of the universe as a whole (because it is a unique object); and also that physical anthropology cannot reach conclusions about the origin and development of the human race (because, as far as our knowledge goes, it is the only one of its kind). The implausibility of these consequences leads us to doubt the original objection, which is indeed totally misguided. One could perhaps circumvent it by regarding the universe as consisting of two parts, divided by an infinite plane, then reach conclusions about each of these parts, and then conjoin them. But there is no need for such subterfuge since the objection is totally misguided in ignoring the point that uniqueness is relative to description. Every object is unique under some description, if you allow descriptions which locate an object by its spatial position, i.e. by its distance and direction from other objects. Thus my desk is the one and only desk in Room 91 in Keele Hall of Keele University; and my house is the last house on the left along such-and-such a road. And even if you

the earth. For the logical possibility of other universes see A. Quinton, 'Spaces and Times', *Philosophy*, 1962, **37**, 130–47, and the more extended discussion in my *Space and Time* (London, 1968), esp. Ch. 2.

[1] Including, for example, Hume. In Hume's *Dialogues Concerning Natural Religion* (first published 1779, H. D. Aiken (ed.), New York, 1948), p. 23, Philo objects to arguments to the cause of the universe as an object which is 'single, individual, without parallel or specific resemblance'. See also Hume's *Enquiry Concerning Human Understanding* (first published 1748, L. A. Selby-Bigge (ed.), Oxford, 1902), pp. 147 f.

allow only descriptions in qualitative terms—e.g. the one and only desk of such-and-such a shape, such-and-such a weight, with such-and-such carvings on its legs, and scratches on its top—it is still plausible to suppose that most objects have a unique description.[1] In the first respect the universe is, like all physical objects, pickable out by a unique description—viz. the one which I gave above—'The physical object consisting of all physical objects including the earth spatially related to each other and to no other physical object'. In the second respect too the universe is, very probably, describable by a unique description—e.g. 'physical object consisting of physical objects, which are all spatially related to each other and to no other physical object'. In all of this the universe is no more 'unique' than the objects which it contains. Yet all objects within the universe are characterized by certain properties, which are common to more than one object. My desk has in common with various other objects that it is a desk, and with various different objects, that it weighs less than a ton, and so on. The same applies to the universe. It is, for example, like objects within it such as the solar system, a system of material bodies distributed in empty space. It is a physical object, and like other physical objects, has density and mass. The objection fails totally to make any crucial distinction between the universe and other objects; and so it fails in its attempt to prevent at the outset a rational inquiry into the issue of whether the universe has some origin outside itself.

So then, to return to the main thread, a cosmological argument is an argument to the existence of God from the existence of some finite object or, more specifically a complex physical universe. There have been many versions of the cosmological argument given over the past two-and-a-half millennia; the most quoted are the second and third of Aquinas's five ways to show the existence of God.[2]

[1] The claim that this is necessarily so for all objects is one version of the principle of the identity of indiscernibles. I do not rely on this principle, but only on the plausible empirical claim made in the text. For an introduction to the issues involved in discussion of the identity of indiscernibles see A. J. Ayer, 'The identity of indiscernibles' in his *Philosophical Essays* (London, 1954).

[2] See St. Thomas Aquinas's *Summa Theologiae*, 1a.2.2. Aquinas's first way is sometimes said to be a version of the cosmological argument, but it does not count as one on my definition of a cosmological argument, since it argues not from the existence of physical objects, but from change in them. It claims in effect that, given that there are physical objects, change in them is so surprising that we need to invoke God as its source. I cannot see that change as such is surprising at all. Given the existence of physical objects, it seems to me no more surprising that they should change than that they should remain changeless. Aquinas's supposition to the

However, Aquinas's 'five ways', or rather the first four of his five ways, seem to me to be one of his least successful pieces of philosophy.[1] In my view the two most persuasive and interesting versions of the cosmological argument are that given by Leibniz in his paper, 'On the Ultimate Origination of Things', and that given by his contemporary, Samuel Clarke, in his Boyle Lectures for 1704 and published under the title *A Demonstration of The Being and Attributes to God*.[2] The former seems to be the argument criticized by Kant in the *Critique of Pure Reason* and the latter the argument criticized by Hume in the *Dialogues*. In so far as I consider one detailed example of a cosmological argument, I shall consider Leibniz's version, but most of my remarks will apply to most versions of the argument.

The starting-points of cosmological arguments are evident facets of experience. There is no doubt about the truth of statements which report that they hold. It seems to me equally evident that no argument from any of such starting-points to the existence of God is deductively valid. For if an argument from, for example, the existence of a complex physical universe to the existence of God were deductively valid, then it would be incoherent to assert that a complex physical universe exists and that God does not. There would be a hidden contradiction buried in such co-assertions. Now, I believe,[3] the only way to prove a proposition to be incoherent is to deduce from it an *obviously* incoherent proposition (e.g. a self-contradictory proposition); and the only way to prove a proposition coherent is to show that it is deducible from an *obviously* coherent proposition, that is to spell out one obviously coherent way in which it could be true. Now notoriously, attempts to derive obviously incoherent propositions from such co-assertions have failed through the commission of some elementary logical error. Furthermore it seems easy enough to spell out in an obviously coherent way what it

contrary arises from the Aristotelian physics which is so closely meshed with his philosophy. It is more plausible to suppose that the existence of *orderly* change is surprising, but the argument from orderly change is Aquinas's fifth way and is a teleological argument which I shall discuss in the next chapter.

[1] For detailed criticism of Aquinas's five ways see the full and careful discussion in A. Kenny, *The Five Ways* (London, 1969).

[2] Clarke's argument, treated as a deductive argument, has received very full and interesting treatment in W. L. Rowe, *The Cosmological Argument* (Princeton and London, 1975). This is one reason why I concentrate on Leibniz's version.

[3] I argue for this claim about how coherence and incoherence are to be proved in *The Coherence of Theism*, Ch. 3.

would be like for such co-assertions to be true. There would be a complex physical universe and no God, if there had always been matter rearranging itself in various combinations, and the only persons had been embodied persons; if there never was a person who knew everything, or could do everything, etc. Atheism does seem to be a supposition consistent with the existence of a complex physical universe, such as our universe. Of course things may not be as they seem, but in the absence of any worthwhile argument to the contrary known to me, I shall assume that the non-existence of God is logically compatible with the existence of the universe, and so that the cosmological argument is not a valid, and so not a good, deductive argument. Our primary concern is however to investigate whether it is a good C-inductive or P-inductive argument, and just how much force it has.

An argument from the universe to God may start from the existence of the universe today, or from its existence for as long as it has existed—whether a finite or an infinite time. Leibniz considers the argument in the latter form, and I shall follow him. So let us consider the series of states of the universe starting from the present and going backwards in time, S_1, S_2, S_3, and so on. (We can suppose each to last a small finite time.) Now clearly there are laws of nature L which bring about the evolution of S_3 from S_4, S_2 from S_3, and so on. (I shall assume for the purpose of simplicity of exposition that this process is a deterministic progress, viz. that L and S_5 together provide a full explanation of S_4, L and S_4 a full explanation of S_3, and so on; we can ignore any minor element of indeterminism—nothing will turn on it.) So we get the following picture:

$$\cdot > \cdots S_5 \xrightarrow{L} S_4 \xrightarrow{L} S_3 \xrightarrow{L} S_2 \xrightarrow{L} S_1$$

The series of states may be finite or infinite—which, we do not know. Now God might come into the picture in one of two ways, as responsible for L, and so as providing a complete explanation of the occurrence of each state S; or at the beginning of the series (if it has one) as starting the process off.

Before an argument of the second type can get off the ground, we would need to give reason to suppose that the universe had a beginning. I have argued elsewhere[1] that, although there is not much hope for any *a priori* arguments to show that the universe had a beginning, there is some possible future in *a posteriori* arguments to

[1] See my *Space and Time*, Ch. 15.

show it. These would be arguments of a scientific character, showing that the universe was now in a state S_1 and that the laws of nature were L, and that extrapolation backwards from S_1 via L eventually leads to a physically impossible state or a state with no matter, at a time t; whence we could conclude that the universe must have come into existence at a time after t, and not as a result of the operation of scientific laws. Thus science might discover that among the laws of nature was a law that conglomerations of matter (including the galaxies) necessarily over time recede linearly from each other. Then we might be able to retrodict from the present state of the universe that, if the universe existed say 14,000 million years ago, its matter must have been packed together with infinite density. But this, we may suppose, is a physically impossible state. So there cannot have been conglomerations of matter subject to the law of expansion for as long as 14,000 million years. So the universe must have come into existence more recently. I do not think that a very strong inductive argument of this character could be constructed—because of the difficulty of getting any very strong confirmation for claims about what are the laws of nature in distant regions of space and time. Just how sure can we be, for example, that the laws of nature include laws of a continuous expansion of the universe, rather than laws of oscillation? Nevertheless, it is possible that the science of the future might provide us with such an argument of moderate strength for the conclusion that the universe had a beginning in time. (The science of the present, incidentally, in my view, is nowhere near providing us with a worthwhile argument either for the temporality or for the eternity of the universe.) In showing that the universe had a beginning in time, we would have shown that its first stage S_f had no scientific explanation in terms of a cause which was a prior state of the universe. There are then two alternatives—either S_f just happened (it had no cause) or S_f has a personal explanation. I shall not take this argument further here, because we are not likely to be able to show with very much force that the universe did have a first state; and because the other type of cosmological argument has much more force.

The Force of the First Form of the Argument

So let us revert to our series of states of the universe allowing for the possibility of an infinite regression. If the universe is infinitely old, then each state of the universe S_n will have a full explanation in terms of a prior state S_{n+1} and natural laws L. Clearly, since S_{n+1} consists of the state of the universe at the time in question, there can be no explanation of its occurrence in terms of any contemporaneous state. So if we take the most basic laws of nature L,[1] then, keeping ourselves within the scientific scheme, L and S_{n+1} will provide a complete explanation of S_n—in the sense in which I defined complete explanation in Chapter 4. Now L, being scientifically inexplicable, is either inexplicable totally, or it has an explanation of a non-scientific, viz. personal, kind. In the former case each state of the universe has a complete explanation, which is a scientific explanation, as the atheist believes. In the latter case there is a person, e.g. God, who brings about the operation of L at each moment of time, and a complete explanation of each state of the universe will involve reference to God who brings it about that L operates, viz. that S_{n+2} brings about S_{n+1}, S_{n+1} brings about S_n, and so on, and so keeps the universe in existence throughout infinite time.

It would be an error to suppose that if the universe is infinitely old, and each state of the universe at each instant of time has a complete explanation which is a scientific explanation in terms of a previous state of the universe and natural laws (and so God is not invoked), that the existence of the universe throughout infinite time has a complete explanation, or even a full explanation. It has not. It has neither. It is totally inexplicable. It has often been assumed and sometimes argued by philosophers, including Hume, that if we have a scientific explanation of each of a collection of states, then we have an explanation of the whole collection. Thus, Hume:

In . . . a chain . . . or succession of objects, each part is caused by that part which preceded it, and causes that which succeeded it. Where then is the difficulty? But the *whole*, you say, wants a cause. I answer that the uniting of several parts into a whole, like the uniting of several distinct countries into a kingdom, or several distinct members into one body, is performed merely by an arbitrary act of the mind, and has no influence on the nature of things. Did I show you the particular causes of each individual in a collection of twenty particles of matter, I should think it very unreasonable,

---

[1] See p. 139, n. 1 for the difficulty that there may be no most basic laws of nature, that every law may be explicable by the operation of a yet wider law (Galileo's law by Newton's laws, Newton's laws by Einstein's laws, and there be no end to this process). I shall argue there that if this were so, the situation will be equivalent to one in which there is an infinite series of most basic laws, each applicable to regions of the universe in different physical conditions. In that case L in the text of this chapter should be taken as such an infinite series.

should you afterwards ask me what was the cause of the whole twenty. This is sufficiently explained in explaining the cause of the parts.[1]

To assess the worth of Hume's claim we need to develop general principles concerning the relation of causes of parts to causes of wholes.

One principle which might be proposed in this connection is that a cause of the occurrence of a collection of states is any collection of the causes of each. More particularly, a full cause of the occurrence of a collection of states is any collection of full causes of each. This principle clearly holds for any finite set of effects, where none of the causes of any member of the collection of effects is itself a member of the collection of effects. If a full cause of a is a', of b is b', of c is c', and of d is d', a, b, c, d, a', b', c', and d' being distinct states, then a full cause of $a+b+c+d$ is $a'+b'+c'+d'$. If a full cause of one lamp's lighting up is its being connected to a battery, and a full cause of a second lamp's lighting up is its being connected to a different battery, then a full cause of the two lamps' lighting up is the connection of the two to batteries. This principle seems also to hold where the collection of effects is infinite, and none of the causes of any member of the collection of effects is itself a member of the collection of effects. If a full cause of the existence of every double-star system in the universe is the breaking-up of a single star, then a full cause of the existence of the double-star systems is still the breaking-up of single stars, even if the number of double-star systems is infinite.

However, the principle must be modified if it is to take account of cases where the cause of some member of a collection of effects is itself a member of that collection. For when b is the cause of a, and c is the cause of b, we say that the cause of $a+b$ is c, not $b+c$. If c is the lighting of a fuse, b is an explosion caused by c, and a an explosion caused by b, then the cause of $a+b$ is just c. To take account of this point, the previous principle must be expressed more generally as follows: a full cause of the occurrence of a collection of states is any collection of (full) causes of each, which are not members of the former collection. Hence if a full cause of a is b, of b is b', of c is d, and of d is d', then a full cause of $a+b+c+d$ is

[1] David Hume, *Dialogues Concerning Natural Religion* (first published 1779, H. D. Aiken (ed.), New York, 1948), pp. 59 f. The same argument is put forward, among modern writers, by Paul Edwards. He writes that 'if we have explained the individual members' of a series 'there is nothing additional left to be explained'. ('The Cosmological Argument' in *The Rationalist Annual*, 1959, pp. 63–77. See p. 71.)

$b' + d'$. If a full cause of a is b, of b is c, of c is d, and of d is e, then a full cause of $a+b+c+d$ is e. In so far as some member of the collection does not have a cause, to that extent the collection of states does not have a cause. If a has no cause, but c is a full cause of b, then there is no full cause of $a+b$, but c is a partial cause. Hence in so far as a finite collection of states has a cause, it has its cause outside the set. Hence if the universe is of finite age, and the only causes of its past states are prior past states (i.e. scientific causality alone operates), the set of past states as a whole will have no cause and so no explanation.

The principle: 'a (full) cause of the occurrence of a collection of states, is any collection of (full) causes of each, which are not members of the former collection' assumes, with the Hempelian account of scientific explanation, that causes are states, rather than objects, and it must be rephrased to allow object-causation (as in personal explanation, and in the powers-and-liabilities account of scientific explanation). The necessary rephrasing is as follows: 'a (full) cause of the occurrence of a collection of states, is any collection of (full) causes of each, whose states as they cause are not members of the former collection.' I shall in general use the original form, but shall also need to use the rephrased form shortly.

Now if the universe is of infinite age, a similar conclusion to that of the last paragraph but one applies. If the only causes of its past states are prior past states, the set of past states as a whole will have no cause and so no explanation. This will hold if each state has a complete scientific explanation in terms of a prior state, and so God is not involved. For although each state of the universe will have a complete explanation (unlike in the case where the universe is finite, where its first state will not have any explanation), the whole infinite series will have no explanation, for there will be no causes of members of the series, lying outside the series. In that case the existence of the universe over infinite time will be an inexplicable brute fact. There will be an explanation (in terms of L) of why, once existent, it continues to exist. But what will be inexplicable is the non-existence of a time before which there was no universe.

Further, the universe will have during its infinite history, certain constant features, F_1 which are such that given that the universe has these features at a certain time and given L, the universe will always have them. But they are such that the universe could have had a different set of features F_2 equally compatible with L. What kind of features these are will depend on the character of L. But suppose for example that L includes a law of the conservation of matter, then given that there is a quantity M_1 of matter at some time, there will be M_1 at all times—and not merely that quantity of matter, but those particular bits of matter. Yet compatible with L will be the supposition that there was a different quantity M_2 made up of different bits. Then it will be totally inexplicable why the quantity of matter was M_1 rather than M_2. If L does not include laws of the conservation of matter, it is hard to see[1] how it could fail to include laws formulable as conservation laws of some kind (e.g. of energy, or momentum, or spin, or even the density of matter). And so a similar point would arise. Why does the world contain just that amount of energy, no more, no less? L would explain why whatever energy there is remains the same; but what L does not explain is why there is just this amount of energy.

I conclude that if each state of the universe at each instant of time has a complete explanation which is a scientific explanation, then the existence of the universe at each instant of time and its having certain permanent features have no explanation at all. This is the point which Leibniz makes in his exposition of the argument:

Neither in any one single thing, nor in the whole aggregate and series of things, can there be found the sufficient reason of existence. Let us suppose the book of the elements of geometry to have been eternal, one copy always having been written down from an earlier one; it is evident that, even though a reason can be given for the present book out of a past one, nevertheless out of any number of books taken in order going backwards we shall never come upon a full reason; though we might well always wonder why there should have been such books from all time—why there were books at all, and why they were written in this manner. What is true of the books is true also of the different states of the world; for what follows is in some way copied from what precedes (even though there are certain laws of change). And so, however far you go back to earlier states, you will never find in those states a full reason why there should be any world rather than none, and why it should be such as it is. Indeed, even if you suppose the world eternal, as you will be supposing nothing but a succession of states and will not in any of them find a sufficient reason, nor however many states you assume will you advance one step forward giving a reason . . .[2]

---

[1] I write that this is 'hard to see', for the reason that laws of nature tell us that a value of some quantity at some time is a function of some other value at an earlier time, e.g. $x = f(y)$. They can then be written as saying that something is conserved between the two times, e.g. that $x/f(y)$ or $x - f(y)$ remains constant.

[2] G. W. Leibniz, *On the Ultimate Origination of Things*, trans. M. Morris, in *The Philosophical Writings of Leibniz*, Everyman Edn. (London, 1934), pp. 31 f.

Like Leibniz, I conclude that the existence of the universe over infinite time would be, if only scientific explanation is allowed, a brute inexplicable fact. Just the same would apply if the universe does have a first state. That state S_f would be a brute, inexplicable fact. The existence of the universe over time comes into my category of things too big for science to explain. If the existence of the universe is to be explained, personal explanation must be brought in, and an explanation given in terms of a person who is not part of the universe acting from without. This can be done if we suppose that such a person G brings it about at each instant of time, that L operates, and so brings it about for each S_{n+1} that S_{n+1} brings about S_n. We thus get this picture:

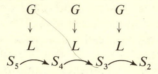

It will clarify what is at stake here to rephrase our supposition, using the powers-and-liabilities account of scientific explanation. Our supposition that there is a full scientific explanation of the existence of each state of the universe in terms of the action of an immediately prior state then amounts to the following. The universe at any given time t_n is in a state S_n. At each such time it has power P to bring about its continued existence with whatever constant characteristics it has (e.g. same matter, or same quantity of energy), and a liability K necessarily to exercise P. Our supposition that a person G acts from without to conserve it in being is the supposition that G brings it about that it has the power P and the liability K. G makes it bring about its subsequent existence, and its subsequent possession of its permanent characteristics. At any time he could make the universe bring about different subsequent permanent characteristics or not give it the power to bring about its subsequent existence.

Now my earlier principle, in its rephrased form, runs as follows: 'a (full) cause of the occurrence of a collection of states, is any collection of (full) causes of each whose states as they cause, are not members of the former collection'. It follows under the conditions described in the last paragraph, whether the universe is of finite or infinite age, that G is a full cause of the existence of the universe throughout its history (with its permanent characteristics). For he is a full cause of each state of the universe, by his making it the case (through some intention of his) that the prior state brought it about, and yet his states are not states of the universe. *G* would be the cause of the existence of the universe (with its permanent characteristics) over all the time that it exists, by a series of intentions, or rather a continuing intention to keep it in being. If we are to postulate *G* we should postulate the simplest kind of *G* for the purpose, and that means a *G* of infinite power, knowledge, and freedom, i.e. God. A *G* of very great but finite power, much, but not all knowledge, etc. would raise the inevitable questions of why he has just that amount of power and knowledge, and what stops him having more, questions which do not arise with the postulation of God. The choice is between the universe as stopping-point and God as stopping-point.

Can we rest with the universe as a brute, inexplicable fact? Leibniz cannot, because the Principle of Sufficient Reason pushes him further. He writes:

The reasons of the world then lie in something extra-mundane, different from the chain of states, or series of things, whose aggregate constitutes the world. And so we must pass from physical or hypothetical necessity, which determines the subsequent things of the world by the earlier, to something which is of absolute or metaphysical necessity, for which itself no reason can be given. For the present world is necessary physically or hypothetically, but not absolutely or metaphysically. In other words, when once it is determined that it shall be such and such, it follows that such and such things will come into being. Since then the ultimate root must be in something which is of metaphysical necessity, and since there is no reason of any existent thing except in an existent thing, it follows that there must exist some one Being of metaphysical necessity, that is, from whose essence existence springs; and so there must exist something different from the plurality of beings, that is the world, which, as we have allowed and have shown, is not of metaphysical necessity.[1]

Leibniz has here deployed the principle of sufficient reason as a metaphysically necessary truth. The principle boils down to the claim that everything not metaphysically necessary has an explanation in something metaphysically necessary. A being has metaphysical necessity according to Leibniz, if from its 'essence existence springs'; i.e. if it could not but exist. Whether this 'could not' is a logical 'could not' is, however, unclear. If the 'could not' is a logical 'could not', then the metaphysically necessary being with whom explanation is supposed to end is a logically necessary being. But against this claim that explanation ends with a logically necessary

[1] Ibid., p. 33.

being I urge the point which I made in Chapter 4—the logically necessary cannot explain the logically contingent. Further, as I argued at the beginning of this chapter, it seems coherent to suppose that there exist a complex physical universe but no God, from which it follows that it is coherent to suppose that there exist no God, from which in turn it follows that God is not a logically necessary being. If there is a logically necessary being, it is not God.[1]

If, however, Leibniz's metaphysically necessary being is not a logically necessary being, but (speaking metaphorically) the supreme brute fact, then his principle boils down to the simple claim that there is a terminus to explanation, that everything which has a full explanation has an ultimate, or at least a complete explanation. In an earlier chapter we saw no general reason for accepting this claim. Whether it is rational to suppose that phenomena have complete explanations is a matter of whether we have potential explanations for them of great simplicity and explanatory power. Leibniz claims that the universe is not metaphysically necessary, and so that its existence needs explanation. He may be right, but I cannot see how you can argue for this claim except in terms of the relatively greater simplicity and explanatory power of a potential *explanans*. Leibniz does not provide such an argument. It is up to us to see the force of an argument along these lines for the existence of God.

Peter Geach has suggested[2] that four of Aquinas's five ways really have a somewhat similar form to the form which I have represented

---

[1] If this is correct, then of course the traditional ontological argument (see p. 9 n. 1) which attempts to prove that God exists of logical necessity, fails utterly. Kant accused the cosmological argument of being the ontological argument in disguise. His criticisms only have force if we suppose that the necessary being to which the cosmological argument purports to argue is a logically necessary being. See I. Kant, *Critique of Pure Reason*, Sect. 5: The Ideal of Pure Reason. For detailed discussion of Kant's treatment of the cosmological argument, see J. Bennett, *Kant's Dialectic*, Ch. 11, and references contained there.

Kant holds that all necessity is either logical necessity or, more widely, necessity for human thought. Either way, for Kant, there is no necessity in things, only in our thought about them. ('The concept of necessity is only to be found in our reason, as a formal condition of thought; it does not allow of being hypostatised as a material condition of existence'. *Critique of Pure Reason*, trans. N. Kemp-Smith, A620.) This is another of the general principles of Kant's philosophy which he brings to the philosophy of religion, and which spoils his treatment of it. Kant's principle is quite mistaken. Clearly there is a necessity in the conformity of material bodies to laws of nature which exists in things and not in our thought. See Ch. 2; and for more extended discussion of kinds of necessity see *The Coherence of Theism*, Ch. 13.

[2] G. E. M. Anscombe and P. T. Geach, *Three Philosophers* (Oxford, 1963), pp. 109–17.

Leibniz's argument as having. He suggests, for example, that the first two ways should be understood as follows. The chain of objects *A*, *B*, *C*, etc. such that *A* brings about *B*, and *B* brings about *C* should be regarded as one big object, that is the universe which may have existed for infinite time. We look for the cause of this which is to be found outside the universe, in God. But if Aquinas's argument is to be represented in this form, the question arises as to why we should suppose that the universe has a cause. Aquinas might answer that we should suppose this because the universe is a complex whole of parts and is in the process of change.[1] But it is surely not a logically necessary truth that there is an explanation of the existence of any complex whole which is in the process of change. The argument can, surely, be only an *a posteriori* one from the simplicity and explanatory power of a postulated *explanans* in comparison with the complexity of the *explanandum*.

I commented in the last chapter on the great simplicity of theism. What now of its explanatory power with respect to the universe? Let *h* be the hypothesis of theism, and *k* be mere tautological evidence. It is important at this stage to be clear about exactly what *e* is meant to be. We have seen that different versions of the cosmological argument interpret it somewhat differently. It can be taken, most generally, as the existence of a finite object. At the other extreme, it can be taken as the existence over time of a complex physical universe. I shall take it in the latter more specific form, and then comment on the effects of taking the premiss more generally. With this understanding of *e*, how does $P(e/h.k)$ compare with $P(e/k)$? *e* could not, as we have seen, have a scientific explanation. Either *e* occurs unexplained, or it is due to the action of a person, the most likely person being, as we have seen, God. For the sake of simplicity of exposition we may, I suggest, ignore the alternative which we have shown to be *a priori* much less probable, that *e* was brought about by a person of very large but finite power, very considerable but limited knowledge, etc. Hence we may regard $P(e/ \sim h.k)$ as the probability that there be a physical universe without anything else having brought it about.

We saw in Chapter 6 that (for *h* as the hypothesis of theism) $P(e/h.k)$ may exceed $P(e/k)$ for one of two reasons. One is that $P(e/ \sim h.k)$ is very low, because *e* cannot be explained in any other way and has the kind of complexity which makes it a very unlikely

[1] Op. cit., p. 113.

stopping-point for explanation (at any rate in comparison with the simplicity of God). The other is that *e* is the kind of state which God can be expected to bring about (or allow others to bring about) more than other states. My appeal in connection with the cosmological argument is to the first reason only.

A complex physical universe (existing over endless time or beginning to exist at some finite time) is indeed a rather complex thing. We need to look at our universe and meditate about it, and the complexity should be apparent. There are lots and lots of separate chunks of it. The chunks each have a different finite and not very natural volume, shape, mass[1] etc.—consider the vast diversity of the galaxies, stars, and planets, and pebbles on the sea-shore. Matter is inert and has no powers which it can choose to exert; it does what it *has* to do. There is just a certain finite amount, or at any rate finite density of it, manifested in the particular bits; and a certain finite amount, or at any rate finite density of energy, momentum, spin, etc. There is a complexity, particularity, and finitude about the universe which cries out for explanation, which God does not have. *A priori* the existence of anything at all logically contingent, even God, may seem vastly improbable, or at least not very probable. (Hence 'the mystery of existence'.) Yet whether this is so or not, the existence of the universe has a vast complexity, compared with the existence of God. As we saw at some length in Chapter 5, the supposition that there is a God is an extremely simple supposition; the postulation of a God of infinite power, knowledge, and freedom is the postulation of the simplest kind of person which there could be. For this reason of the complexity of *e* $P(e/\sim h.k)$ is low. If something has to occur unexplained, a complex physical universe is less to be expected than other things (e.g. God).

However I do not claim that $P(e/h.k)$ is especially high. $P(e/h.k)$ measures how likely it is if there is a God that there will be a physical universe. The choice before God among worlds to create includes a world where there is just God; a world where there are one or more finite non-physical objects (e.g. non-embodied spirits); a world consisting of a simple physical universe (e.g. just one round steel ball); and a world which is a complex physical universe. There are good reasons why God should make a complex physical universe. For such a physical universe can be beautiful, and that is

[1] I shall come in Ch. 8 to the point that the building-blocks of which the chunks are made, i.e. the fundamental particles, are of only a few distinct kinds.

good; and also it can be a theatre for finite agents to develop and make of it what they will (and I shall argue in Chapter 10 that that is a good thing). But I cannot see that God has overriding reason to make such a universe. (It is not obviously superior to any other sort of world; and he certainly has no moral obligation to make such a universe, for before he creates any rational agents, there are no rational agents to wrong.) Nor can I see that he has overriding reason to make or not to make any alternative world. Maybe God will leave things with God alone modifying his own states (and the succession of his own states would be a beautiful and so a good thing), and exercising his power in that way; or maybe he will create one or more finite beings, or just one physical object. That God is under no necessity to create a physical universe, or anything at all, is of course the traditional view of theism. So I conclude that $P(e/h.k)$ does not exceed $P(e/\sim h.k)$ (and so $P(e/k)$) because God is especially likely to bring e about, although it does exceed it because e is very unlikely to come about but for God's agency. In view of the enormous number of different complex physical universes which there might be, neither $P(e/h.k)$ nor $P(e/k)$ will be very low. Since $P(e/h.k) > P(e/k)$, by the relevance criterion $P(h/e.k) > P(h/k)$, and so the argument from the existence of a complex physical universe to God is a good C-inductive argument.

The same conclusion follows, I believe, if we take e, most generally, as the existence of a finite object. In that case both $P(e/\sim h.k)$ and $P(e/h.k)$ are going to be greater, but I suggest that as before, $P(e/h.k)$ will exceed $P(e/\sim h.k)$. $P(e/\sim h.k)$ will be higher since it is more likely *a priori* that there should exist a finite object, than that there should exist a complex physical universe (a somewhat more specific hypothesis). Yet intuitively, any finite object would lack the simplicity of the God of Chapter 5. So, I suggest that $P(h/k)$ remains greater than $P(e/\sim h.k)$ and both remain low. $P(e/h.k)$ however, will also be higher in virtue of the general principle mentioned in Chapter 6 that the less specific is e, the higher is $P(e/h.k)$. For only if God refused throughout endless time to create any object other than himself could there fail, if there is a God, to be a finite object.

The argument of the last few pages can now be put in simple words as follows. There is quite a chance that if there is a God he will make something of the finitude and complexity of a universe. It is very unlikely that a universe would exist uncaused, but rather more likely that God would exist uncaused. The existence of the universe is strange and puzzling. It can be made comprehensible if we suppose that it is brought about by God. This supposition postulates a simpler beginning of explanation than does the supposition of the existence of an uncaused universe, and that is grounds for believing the former supposition to be true.

8

Teleological Arguments

I UNDERSTAND by an argument from design one which argues from some general pattern of order in the universe or provision for the needs of conscious beings to a God responsible for these phenomena. An argument from a general pattern of order I shall call a teleological argument. (The name 'teleological argument' has usually been used to characterize much the same arguments as 'the argument from design'. I am giving 'teleological argument' a narrower use.) I shall deal with teleological arguments in this chapter. I shall deal in Chapter 10 with the argument from the occurrence of provision for the needs of conscious beings, and I shall call such an argument an argument from providence. In the definition of 'teleological argument' I emphasize the words 'general pattern'; I shall not count an argument to the existence of God from some particular pattern of order manifested on a unique occasion as a teleological argument.

Two Forms of Teleological Argument

I begin with the distinction between spatial order and temporal order, between what I shall call regularities of co-presence and regularities of succession. An example of a regularity of co-presence would be a town with all its roads at right angles to each other, or a section of books in a library arranged in alphabetical order of authors. Regularities of succession are simple patterns of behaviour of objects, such as their behaviour in accordance with the laws of nature—for example, Newton's laws.

Many of the striking examples of order in the universe evince an order which is due both to a regularity of co-presence and to a regularity of succession. A working car consists of many parts so adjusted to each other that it follows the instructions of the driver delivered by his pulling and pushing a few levers and buttons and turning a wheel, to take passengers whither he wishes. Its order arises because its parts are so arranged at some instant (regularity of co-presence) that, the laws of nature being as they are (regularity of succession) it brings about the result neatly and efficiently. The order of living animals and plants likewise results from regularities of both types.

Men who marvel at the order of the universe may marvel at either or both of the regularities of co-presence and of succession. The thinkers of the eighteenth century to whom the argument from design appealed so strongly were struck almost exclusively by the regularities of co-presence. They marvelled at the order in animals and plants; but since they largely took for granted the regularities of succession, what struck them about the animals and plants, as to a lesser extent about machines made by men, was the subtle and coherent arrangement of their millions of parts. Paley's *Natural Theology* dwells mainly on details of comparative anatomy, on eyes and ears and muscles and bones arranged with minute precision so as to operate with high efficiency, and in the *Dialogues* Hume's Cleanthes produces the same kind of examples: 'Consider, anatomize the eye, survey its structure and contrivance, and tell me from your own feeling, if the idea of a contriver does not immediately flow in upon you with a force like that of sensation.'[1]

The eighteenth-century argument from spatial order seems to go as follows. Animals and plants have the power to reproduce their kind, and so, given the past existence of animals and plants, their present existence is to be expected. But what is vastly surprising is the existence of animals and plants at all. By natural processes they can only come into being through generation. But we know that the world has not been going on for ever, and so the great puzzle is the existence of the first animals and plants in 4004 BC or whenever exactly it was that animals and plants began to exist.[2] Since they could not have come about by natural scientific processes, and since they are very similar to the machines, which certain rational agents,

[1] Op. cit., p. 28.

[2] Even if they had supposed that the world had been going on for ever and had contained animals and plants for ever, the men of the eighteenth century could still have constructed an argument from the eternal existence of a universe containing animals and plants rather than a universe not containing animals and plants; but the argument would have to have been a more subtle one than the one which we are considering.

viz. men, make, it is very probable that they were made by a rational agent—only clearly one much more powerful and knowledgeable than men.

In the *Dialogues*, through the mouth of Philo, Hume made some classical objections to the argument in this form, some of which have some force against all forms of the argument; I shall deal with most of these as we come to appropriate places in this chapter. Despite Hume's objections, the argument is, I think, a very plausible one—given its premises. But one of its premises was shown by Darwin and his successors to be clearly false. Complex animals and plants can be produced through generation by less complex animals and plants—species are not eternally distinct; and simple animals and plants can be produced by natural processes from inorganic matter. This discovery led to the virtual disappearance of the argument from design from popular apologetic—mistakenly, I think, since it can easily be reconstructed in a form which does not rely on the premises shown to be false by Darwin. This can be done even for the argument from spatial order.

We can reconstruct the argument from spatial order as follows. We see around us animals and plants, intricate examples of spatial order in the ways which Paley set out, similar to machines of the kind which men make. We know that these animals and plants have evolved by natural processes from inorganic matter. But clearly this evolution can only have taken place, given certain special natural laws. These are first, the chemical laws stating how under certain circumstances inorganic molecules combine to make organic ones, and organic ones combine to make organisms. And secondly, there are the biological laws of evolution stating how organisms have very many offspring, some of which vary in one or more characteristics from their parents, and how some of these characteristics are passed on to most offspring, from which it follows that, given shortage of food and other environmental needs, there will be competition for survival, in which the fittest will survive. Among organisms very well fitted for survival will be organisms of such complex and subtle construction as to allow easy adaptation to a changing environment. These organisms will evince great spatial order. So the laws of nature are such as, under certain circumstances, to give rise to striking examples of spatial order similar to the machines which men make. Nature, that is, is a machine-making machine. In the twentieth century men make not only machines, but machine-making machines. They may therefore naturally infer from nature which produces animals and plants, to a creator of nature similar to men who make machine-making machines.

This reconstructed argument is now immune to having some crucial premiss shown false by some biologist of the 1980s. The facts to which its premisses appeal are too evident for that—whatever the details, natural laws are clearly such as to produce complex organisms from inorganic matter under certain circumstances. But although this is so, I do not find the argument a very strong one, and this is because of the evident paucity of organisms throughout the universe. The circumstances under which nature behaves as a machine-making machine are rare. For that reason nature does not evince very strongly the character of a machine-making machine and hence the analogies between the products of natural processes on the one hand and machines on the other are not too strong. Perhaps they give a small degree of probability to the hypothesis that a rational agent was responsible for the laws of evolution in some ways similar to the rational agents who make machines, but the probability is no more than that.

I pass on to consider a form of teleological argument which seems to me a much stronger one—the teleological argument from the temporal order of the world. The temporal order of the universe is, to the man who bothers to give it a moment's thought, an overwhelmingly striking fact about it. Regularities of succession are all-pervasive. For simple laws govern almost all successions of events. In books of physics, chemistry, and biology we can learn how almost everything in the world behaves. The laws of their behaviour can be set out by relatively simple formulae which men can understand and by means of which they can successfully predict the future. The orderliness of the universe to which I draw attention here is its conformity to formula, to simple, formulable, scientific laws. The orderliness of the universe in this respect is a very striking fact about it. The universe might so naturally have been chaotic, but it is not—it is very orderly.

That the world has this very peculiar characteristic may be challenged in various ways. It may be said of the order which we seem to see in the universe that we impose the order on the world, that it is not there independently of our imposition. Put another way, all that this temporal order amounts to, it might be said, is a coincidence between how things have been so far in the world and the patterns which men can recognize and describe, a coincidence which is itself susceptible of an explanation in terms of natural selection. In fact, however, the temporal order of the world is something deeper than that. The premiss of a good teleological argument is not that so far (within his life or within human history) things have conformed to a pattern which man can recognize and describe. The premiss is rather that things have and will continue to conform to such a pattern however initial conditions vary, however men interfere in the world. If induction is justified, we are justified in supposing that things will continue to behave as they have behaved in the kinds of respect which scientists and ordinary people recognize and describe. I assume that we are justified in believing that the laws of gravity and chemical cohesion will continue to hold tomorrow—that stones will fall, and desks hold together tomorrow as well as today—however initial conditions vary, however men interfere in the world. It may of course be doubted whether philosophers have given a very satisfactory account of what makes such beliefs justified (hence 'the problem of induction'); but I assume the common-sense view that they are justified. So the teleologist's premiss is not just that there has been in nature so far an order which men can recognize and describe; but there has been and will continue to be in nature an order, recognizable and describable by men certainly, but one which exists independently of men. If men are correct in their belief that the order which they see in the world is an order which will hold in the future as in the past, it is clearly not an imposed or invented order. It is there in nature. For man cannot make nature conform subsequently to an order which he has invented. Only if the order is there in nature is nature's future conformity to be expected.

An objector may now urge that although the order of the universe is an objective matter, nevertheless, unless the universe were an orderly place, men would not be around to comment on the fact. (If there were no natural laws, there would be no regularly functioning organisms, and so no men.) Hence there is nothing surprising in the fact that men find order—they could not possibly find anything else. This conclusion is clearly a little too strong. There would need to be quite a bit of order in and around our bodies if men are to exist and think, but there could be chaos outside the earth, so long as the earth was largely unaffected by that chaos. There is a great deal more order in the world than is necessary for the existence of humans. So men could still be around to comment on the fact even if the world were a much less orderly place than it is. But quite apart from this minor consideration, the argument still fails totally for a reason which can best be brought out by an analogy. Suppose that a madman kidnaps a victim and shuts him in a room with a card-shuffling machine. The machine shuffles ten packs of cards simultaneously and then draws a card from each pack and exhibits simultaneously the ten cards. The kidnapper tells the victim that he will shortly set the machine to work and it will exhibit its first draw, but that unless the draw consists of an ace of hearts from each pack, the machine will simultaneously set off an explosion which will kill the victim, in consequence of which he will not see which cards the machine drew. The machine is then set to work, and to the amazement and relief of the victim the machine exhibits an ace of hearts drawn from each pack. The victim thinks that this extraordinary fact needs an explanation in terms of the machine having been rigged in some way. But the kidnapper, who now reappears, casts doubt on this suggestion. 'It is hardly surprising', he says, 'that the machine draws only aces of hearts. You could not possibly see anything else. For you would not be here to see anything at all, if any other cards had been drawn.' But of course the victim is right and the kidnapper is wrong. There is indeed something extraordinary in need of explanation in ten aces of hearts being drawn. The fact that this peculiar order is a necessary condition of the draw being perceived at all makes what is perceived no less extraordinary and in need of explanation. The teleologist's starting-point is not that we perceive order rather than disorder, but that order rather than disorder is there. Maybe only if order is there can we know what is there, but that makes what is there no less extraordinary and in need of explanation.

So the universe is characterized by vast, all-pervasive temporal order, the conformity of nature to formula, recorded in the scientific laws formulated by men. Now this phenomenon, like the very existence of the world, is clearly something 'too big' to be explained by science. If there is an explanation of the world's order it cannot be a scientific one, and this follows from the nature of scientific explanation. For, as we saw in Chapter 2, in scientific explanation we explain particular phenomena as brought about by prior phenomena in accord with scientific laws; or we explain the operation of scientific laws in terms of more general scientific laws (and perhaps also particular phenomena). Thus we explain the operation of Kepler's laws in terms of the operation of Newton's laws (given the masses, initial velocities, and distances apart of the sun and planets); and we explain the operation of Newton's laws in terms of the operation of Einstein's field equations for space relatively empty of matter. Science thus explains particular phenomena and low-level laws in terms partly of high-level laws. But from the very nature of science it cannot explain the highest-level laws of all; for they are that by which it explains all other phenomena.[1]

At this point we need to rephrase our premisses in terms of the powers-and-liabilities account of science, which we have seen reason for preferring to the Hempelian account. On this account what the all-pervasive temporal order amounts to is the fact that throughout space and time there are physical objects of various kinds, every such object having the powers and liabilities which are described in laws of nature—e.g. the power of attracting each other physical object in the universe with a force of $\gamma mm^1/r^2$ dynes (where γ is the gravitational constant) the liability always to exercise this power, and the liability to be attracted by each other body in the universe with a force of $\gamma mm^1/r^2$ dynes and so on. From the fact that it has such general powers it follows that an object will have certain more specific powers, given the kind of object that it is. For example, given that it has a mass of 1 gram, it will follow that it has the power of attracting each other body in the universe with a force of $\gamma m^1/r^2$ dynes. This picture allows us to draw attention to one feature of the orderliness of the universe which the other picture makes it easy to ignore. Unlike the feature to which I have drawn attention so far, it is not one of which men have always known; it is one which the atomic theory of chemistry strongly suggested, and the discovery of

[1] It may be urged that we have no reason to suppose that there is a highest-level law of nature. Maybe law L operates in circumstances C because it follows from L' that it does; and L' operates in circumstances C' (which include C) because it follows from L'' that it does; L'' operates in circumstances C'' (which include C') because it follows from L''' that it does, and so on *ad infinitum*. This difficulty can, however, be avoided as follows. Either such a series ends with a highest-level law L which holds in all circumstances, or it does not. In the latter case let us represent the higher-level laws as conjunctions of laws which hold without exception under specifiable circumstances such as C. Thus to say that L', holds in C' will be to say that L holds in C and L_1 in C_1; to say that L'' holds in C'' will be to say as well as this that L_2 holds in C_2. Then the claim that there is an infinite series L, L'_1, L'', etc. is the claim that there exists an infinite series of lower-level laws L, L_1, L_2 which hold without exception in circumstances C, C_1, C_2, etc.; and that although there is an explanation of the operation of any finite sub-series, there is no explanation of the operation of the whole series. That the whole series operates will then be the starting-point for an argument from design; that it operates shows a conformity of the world to order similar to that shown by the conformity of the world to statable highest-level laws of nature which form the starting-point for the simpler argument, with which I shall henceforward deal on the not implausible assumption that there are highest-level laws of nature.

fundamental particles confirmed. It is this. The physical objects scattered throughout space and time are, or are composed of, particles of a few limited kinds, which we call fundamental particles. Whether the protons and electrons which we suppose to be the fundamental particles are in fact fundamental, or whether they are composed of yet more fundamental particles (e.g. quarks) which are capable of independent existence is not altogether clear—but what does seem clear is that if there are yet more fundamental particles, they too come in a few specific kinds. Nature only has building-blocks of a few kinds. Each particle of a given kind has a few defining properties which determine its behaviour and which are specific to that kind. Thus all electrons have a mass of $\frac{1}{2}MeV/c^2$, a charge of -1, a spin of $\frac{1}{2}$, etc. All positrons have other properties the same as electrons, but a charge of $+1$. All protons have a mass of 938 MeV/c^2, a charge of $+1$, and a spin of $\frac{1}{2}$. And so on. There are innumerably many particles which belong to each of a few kinds, and no particles with characteristics intermediate between those of two kinds. The properties of fundamental kinds, that is, which give specific form to the general powers which all objects have, belong to a small class; and the powers and liabilities of large-scale objects are determined by those of their fundamental components. Particles have constant characteristics over time; they only change their characteristics, or are destroyed or converted into other particles by reason of their own liabilities (e.g. to decay) or the action of other particles acting in virtue of their powers.

Put in these terms then, the orderliness of nature is a matter of the vast uniformity in the powers and liabilities of bodies throughout endless time and space, and also in the paucity of kinds of components of bodies. Over centuries long, long ago and over distances distant in millions of light years from ourselves the same universal orderliness reigns. There are, as we have seen, explanations of only two kinds for phenomena—scientific explanation and personal explanation. Yet, although a scientific explanation can be provided of why the more specific powers and liabilities of bodies hold (e.g. why an electron exerts just the attractive force which it does) in terms of more general powers and liabilities possessed by all bodies (put in Hempelian terms—why a particular natural law holds in terms of more general natural laws), science cannot explain why all bodies do possess the same very general powers and liabilities. It is with this fact that scientific explanation stops. So either the orderliness of nature is where all explanation stops, or we must

postulate an agent of great power and knowledge who brings about
through his continuous action that bodies have the same very general
powers and liabilities (that the most general natural laws operate);
and, once again, the simplest such agent to postulate is one of infinite power, knowledge, and freedom, i.e. God. An additional consideration here is that it is clearly vastly simpler to suppose that the
existence and the order of the world have the same cause, and the
considerations which lead us to postulate a being of infinite power,
knowledge, and freedom as the cause of the former reinforce the
considerations which lead us to postulate such a cause for the latter.

In the *Dialogues* Hume made the objection—why should we not
postulate many gods to give order to the universe, not merely one?
'A great number of men join in building a house or a ship, in rearing
a city, in framing a commonwealth, why may not several deities
combine in framing a world?'[1] Hume again is aware of the obvious
counter-objection to his suggestion. 'To multiply causes without
necessity is . . . contrary to true philosophy.'[2] He claims, however,
that the counter-objection does not apply here, because (in my
terminology) although the supposition that there is one god is a
simpler supposition than the supposition that there are many, in
postulating many persons to be responsible for the order of the
universe we are postulating persons more like to men in power and
knowledge—that is we are putting forward a hypothesis which fits
in better with our background knowledge of what there is in the
world. That may be. But Hume's hypothesis is very complicated—
we want to ask about it such questions as why are there just 333
deities (or whatever the number is), why do they have powers of just
the strength which they do have, and what moves them to co-
operate as closely as obviously they do; questions of a kind which
obtrude far less with the far simpler and so less arbitrary theistic
hypothesis. Even if Hume were right in supposing that the prior
probability of his hypothesis were as great as that of theism (because
the fit with background knowledge of the former cancels out the
simplicity of the latter)[3] (and I do not myself think that he is right),
the hypothesis of theism nevertheless has greater explanatory power
than the Humean hypothesis and is for that reason more probable.

[1] Ibid., p. 39.
[2] Ibid., p. 40.
[3] This would in fact only be so if the knowledge of the existence of men was
background knowledge. But since the existence of men is one facet of the world's
orderliness, it is surely part of the phenomena *e* which our hypothesis has to explain,
not part of background knowledge *k*. See p. 63 n. 1.

For theism leads us to expect that we will find throughout nature one pattern of order. But if there were more than one deity responsible for the order of the universe, we would expect to see characteristic marks of the handiwork of different deities in different parts of the universe, just as we see different kinds of workmanship in the different houses of a city. We would expect to find an inverse square of law of gravitation obeyed in one part of the universe, and in another part a law which was just short of being an inverse square law—without the difference being explicable in terms of a more general law. It is enough to draw this absurd conclusion to see how wrong the Humean objection is.[1]

So I shall take as the alternatives—the first, that the temporal order of the world is where explanation stops, and the second, that the temporal order of the world is due to the agency of God; and I shall ignore the less probable possibilities that the order is to be explained as due to the agency of an agent or agents of finite power. The proponent of the teleological argument claims that the order of nature shows an orderer—God.

The Force of the Second Form of Teleological Argument

The teleological argument, whether from temporal or spatial order, is, I believe, a codification by philosophers of a reaction to the world deeply embedded in the human consciousness. Men see the comprehensibility of the world as evidence of a comprehending creator. The prophet Jeremiah lived in an age in which the existence of a creator-god of some sort was taken for granted. What was at stake was the extent of his goodness, knowledge, and power. Jeremiah argued from the order of the world that he was a powerful and reliable god, that god was God. He argued to the power of the creator from the extent of the creation—'The host of heaven cannot be numbered, neither the sand of the sea measured';[2] and he argued that its regular behaviour showed the reliability of the creator, and he spoke of the

---

[1] Kant saw that in so far as the 'physico-theological' argument, as he called our argument, worked, it pointed to one deity and not many. He had no criticism of this part of the argument. 'The unity of this cause may be inferred from the unity of the reciprocal relations existing between the parts of the world, as members of an artificially arranged structure—inferred with certainty in so far as our observation suffices for its verification, and beyond these limits with probability, in accordance with the principles of analogy.' *Critique of Pure Reason* (trans. N. Kemp-Smith), A625-6.

[2] Jer. 33: 22.

'covenant of the day and night' whereby they follow each other regularly, and 'the ordinances of heaven and earth',[1] and he used their existence as an argument for the trustworthiness of the God of Jacob. The argument from temporal order has been with us ever since.

You get the argument from temporal order also in Aquinas's fifth way, which runs as follows:

The fifth way is based on the guidedness of nature. An orderedness of actions to an end is observed in all bodies obeying natural laws, even when they lack awareness. For their behaviour hardly ever varies, and will practically always turn out well; which shows that they truly tend to a goal, and do not merely hit it by accident. Nothing however that lacks awareness tends to a goal, except under the direction of someone with awareness and with understanding; the arrow, for example requires an archer. Everything in nature, therefore is directed to its goal by someone with understanding and this we call 'God'.[2]

Aquinas argues that the regular behaviour of each inanimate thing shows that some animate being is directing it (making it move to achieve some purpose, attain some goal); and from that he comes— rather quickly—to the conclusion that one 'being with understanding' is responsible for the behaviour of all inanimate things.

It seems to me fairly clear that no argument from temporal order—whether Aquinas's fifth way or any other argument can be a good deductive argument. For although the premiss is undoubtedly correct—a vast pervasive order characterizes the world—the step from premiss to conclusion is not a valid deductive one. Although the existence of order may be good evidence of a designer, it is surely compatible with the non-existence of one—it is hardly a logically necessary truth that all order is brought about by a person.[3] And

[1] Jer. 33: 20f. and 25f.

[2] St. Thomas Aquinas, *Summa Theologiae*, Ia, 2.3, trans. T. McDermott, OP (London, 1964).

[3] Hume suggested (op. cit., pp. 53ff.) that perhaps this ordered universe is a mere accident among the chance arrangements of eternal matter. In the course of eternity matter arranges itself in all kinds of ways. We just happen to live in a period when it is characterized by order, and mistakenly conclude that matter is always ordered. Hume is certainly right in claiming that this is a logical possibility, but the issue is whether it is very likely; and, as I shall urge shortly, an appeal to chance to explain order becomes less and less plausible, the more and more order there is. It is compatible with the existence of the works commonly attributed to Shakespeare to suppose that they came into being as a result of random typing by monkeys, but it is not a very probable supposition, to say the least. (As Hume phrases his objection it is directed against an argument from spatial order, but it could easily be rephrased as an argument against an argument from temporal order.)

although, as I have urged, the supposition that one person is responsible for the orderliness of the world is much simpler and so more probable than the supposition that many persons are, nevertheless, the latter supposition seems logically compatible with the data—so we must turn to the more substantial issue of whether the argument from the temporal order of the world to God is a good inductive argument. We had reached on pp. 140f. the conclusion that either the vast uniformity in the powers and liabilities of bodies was where explanation stopped, or that God brings this about by his continuous action, through an intention constant over time.

Let us represent by e this conformity of the world to order, and let h be the hypothesis of theism. It is not possible to treat a teleological argument in complete isolation from the cosmological argument. We cannot ask how probable the premiss of the teleological argument makes theism, independently of the premiss of the cosmological argument, for the premiss of the teleological argument entails in part the premiss of the cosmological argument. That there is order of the kind described entails at least that there is a physical universe. So let k be now, not mere tautological evidence, but the existence of a complex physical universe (the premiss of the version of the cosmological argument to which I devoted most attention). Let us ask how much more probable does the orderliness of such a universe make the existence of God than does the mere existence of the universe.

With these fillings, we ask whether $P(h/e.k) > P(h/k)$ and by how much. As we have seen $P(h/e.k)$ will exceed $P(h/k)$ if and only if $P(e/h.k) > P(e/\sim h.k)$. Put in words with our current fillings for h, e, and k, the existence of order in the world confirms the existence of God if and only if the existence of this order in the world is more probable if there is a God than if there is not. We saw in Chapter 6 that where h is the hypothesis that there is a God $P(e/h.k)$ may exceed $P(e/\sim h.k)$, either because e cannot be explained in any other way and is very unlikely to occur uncaused or because God has a character such that he is more likely to bring about e than alternative states. With respect to the cosmological argument, I suggested that its case rested solely on the first consideration. Here I shall suggest that again the first consideration is dominant, but that the second has considerable significance also.

Let us start with the first consideration. e is the vast uniformity in the powers and liabilities possessed by material objects— $P(e/\sim h.k)$ is the probability that there should be that amount of uniformity in a God-less world, that this uniform distribution of the powers of things should be where explanation terminates, that they be further inexplicable. That there should be material bodies is strange enough; but that they should all have such similar powers which they inevitably exercise, seems passing strange. It is strange enough that physical objects should have powers at all—why should they not just be, without being able to make a difference to the world? But that they should all, throughout infinite time and space, have some general powers identical to those of all other objects (and they all be made of components of very few fundamental kinds, each component of a given kind being identical in all characteristics with each other such component) and yet there be no cause of this at all seems incredible. The universe is complex as we urged, in the last chapter, in that there are so many bodies of different shapes, etc., and now we find an underlying orderliness in the identity of powers and paucity of kinds of components of bodies. Yet this orderliness, if there is no explanation of it in terms of the action of God, is the orderliness of a coincidence—the fact that one body has certain powers does not explain the fact that a second body has—not the simplicity of a common underlying explanation. The basic complexity remains in the vast number of different bodies in which the orderliness of identical powers and components is embodied. It is a complexity too striking to occur unexplained. It cries out for explanation in terms of some single common source with the power to produce it. Just as we would seek to explain all the coins' of the realm having an identical pattern in terms of their origin from a common mould, or all of many pictures' having a common style in terms of their being painted by the same painter, so too should we seek to explain all physical objects' having the same powers in terms of their deriving them from a common source. On these grounds alone $P(e/h.k) \gg P(e/k)$, and so $P(h/e.k) \gg P(h/k)$.[1]

I think, however, that we can go further by bringing in considerations from God's character—we saw in Chapter 6 that God will bring about a state of affairs if it is over all a good thing that he should, he will not bring about a state of affairs if it is over all a bad thing that he should, and that he will only bring about a state of affairs if it is in some way a good thing that he should. Put in terms of reasons—he will always act on overriding reasons and cannot act except for a reason. Now there are two reasons why human beings produce order. One is aesthetic—beauty comes in the patterns of

---

[1] '$\gg$' means 'is much greater than'. '$\ll$' means 'is much less than'.

things, such as dances and songs. Some sort of order is a necessary condition of phenomena having beauty; complete chaos is just ugly—although of course not any order is beautiful. The second reason why a human being produces order is that when there is order he or other rational agents can perceive that order and utilize it to achieve ends. If we see that there is a certain pattern of order in phenomena we can then justifiably predict that that order will continue, and that enables us to make predictions about the future on which we can rely. A librarian puts books in an alphabetical order of authors in order that he and users of the library who come to know that the order is there may subsequently be able to find any book in the library very quickly (because, given knowledge of the order, we can predict whereabouts in the library any given book will be).

God has similar reasons for producing an orderly, as opposed to a chaotic universe. In so far as some sort of order is a necessary condition of beauty, and it is a good thing—as it surely is—that the world be beautiful rather than ugly, God has reason for creating an orderly universe. Secondly, I shall argue in Chapter 10 that it is good that God should make finite creatures with the opportunity to grow in knowledge and power. Now if creatures are going consciously to extend their control of the world, they will need to know how to do so. There will need to be some procedures which they can find out, such that if they follow those procedures, certain events will occur. This entails the existence of temporal order. There can only be such procedures if the world is orderly, and, I should add, there can only be such procedures ascertainable by men if the order of the world is such as to be discernible by men. To take a simple example, if hitting things leads to them breaking or penetrating other things, and heating things leads to them melting, men can discover these regularities and utilize them to make artefacts such as houses, tables, and chairs. They can heat iron ore to melt it to make nails, hammers, and axes, and use the latter to break wood into the right shapes to hammer together with nails to make the artefacts. Or, if light and other electro-magnetic radiation behave in predictable ways comprehensible by men, men can discover those ways and build telescopes and radio and television receivers and transmitters. A world must evince the temporal order exhibited by laws of nature if men are to be able to extrapolate from how things have behaved in the past, to how they will behave in the future, which extrapolation is necessary if men are to have the knowledge of how things will behave in the future, which they must have in order to be able to extend their control over the world. (There would not need to be complete determinism—agents themselves could be exempt from the full rigours of determinism, and there might be violations of natural laws from time to time. But basically the world has to be governed by laws of nature if agents are consciously to extend their control of the world.) If I am right in supposing that God has reason to create finite creatures with the opportunity to grow in knowledge and power, then he has reason to create temporal order. So I suggest that God has at least these two reasons for producing an orderly world. Maybe God has reasons for not making creatures with the opportunity to grow in knowledge and power, and so the second reason for his creating an orderly universe does not apply. But with one possible, and, I shall show, irrelevant qualification, the first surely does. God may choose whether or not to make a physical universe, but if he does, he has reason for making a beautiful and so an orderly one. God has reason, if he does make a physical universe, not to make a chaotic or botched-up one. The only reason of which I can think why God should make the universe in some respects ugly would be to give to creatures the opportunity to discover the aesthetic merits of different states of affairs and through co-operative effort to make the world beautiful for themselves. But then the other argument shows that if they are to be able to exercise such an opportunity the world will need to be orderly in some respects. (There will have to be predictable regularities which creatures may utilize in order to produce beautiful states of affairs.) So, either way, the world will need to be orderly. It rather looks as if God has overriding reason to make an orderly universe if he makes a universe at all. However, as I emphasized, human inquiry into divine reasons is a highly speculative matter. But it is nevertheless one in which men are justified in reaching tentative conclusions. For God is postulated to be an agent like ourselves in having knowledge, power, and freedom, although to an infinitely greater degree than we have. The existence of the analogy legitimizes us in reaching conclusions about his purposes, conclusions which must allow for the quantitative difference, as I have tried to do.

So I suggest that the order of the world is evidence of the existence of God both because its occurrence would be very improbable *a priori* and also because, in virtue of his postulated character, he has very good, apparently overriding, reason for making an orderly universe, if he makes a universe at all. It looks as if $P(e/h.k)$

equals 1. For both reasons $P(e/h.k) \gg P(e/ \sim h.k)$ and so $P(h/e.k) \gg P(h/k)$. I conclude that the teleological argument from temporal order is a good C-inductive argument to the existence of God.

Let us look at the argument from a slightly different angle. It is basically an argument by analogy, an analogy between the order in the natural world (the temporal order codified in laws of nature) and the patterns of order which men often produce (the ordered books on library shelves, or the temporal order in the movements of a dancer or the notes of a song). It argues from similarity between phenomena of two kinds B and B^* to similarity between their causes A and A^*. In view of the similarities between the two kinds of order B and B^*, the theist postulates a cause (A^*) in some respects similar to A (men); yet in view of the dissimilarities the theist must postulate a cause in other respects different. All arguments by analogy do and must proceed in this way. They cannot postulate a cause in all respects similar. They postulate a cause who is such that one would expect him to produce phenomena similar to B in the respects in which B^* are similar to B and different from B in the respects in which B^* are different from B.

All argument from analogy works like this. Thus various properties of light and sound were known in the nineteenth century, among them that both light and sound are reflected, refracted, diffracted, and show interference phenomena. In the case of sound these were known to be due to disturbance of the medium, air, in which it is transmitted. What could one conclude by analogy about the cause of the reflection, etc., of light? One could conclude that the propagation of light was, like the propagation of sound, the propagation of a wave-like disturbance in a medium. But one could not conclude that it was the propagation of a disturbance in the same medium—air, since light pased through space empty of air. Scientists had to postulate a separate medium—aether, the disturbance of which was responsible for the reflection, etc., of light. And not merely does all argument by analogy proceed like this, but all inductive inference can be represented as argument by analogy. For all inductive inference depends on the assumption that in certain respects things continue the same and in other respects they differ. Thus that crude inference from a number of observed swans all having been white to the next swan's being white is an argument by analogy. For it claims that the next swan will be like the observed swans in one respect—colour, while being unlike them in other respects.

In our case the similarities between the temporal order which men produce and the temporal order in nature codified in scientific laws mean postulating as cause of the latter a person who acts intentionally. The dissimilarities between the kinds of order include the world-wide extent of the order in nature in comparison with the very narrow range of order which men produce. This means postulating as cause of the former a person of enormous power and knowledge. Now, as we saw in Chapter 2, a person has a body if there is a region of the world under his direct control and if he controls other regions of the world only by controlling the former and by its movements having predictable effects on the outside world. Likewise he learns about the world only by the world having effects on this region. If these conditions are satisfied, the person has a body, and the stated region is that body. But if a person brings about directly the connections between things, including the predictable connections between the bodies of other persons and the world, there is no region of the world, goings-on in which bring about those connections. The person must bring about those connections as a basic action. His control of the world must be immediate, not mediated by a body. So the dissimilarities between the two kinds of order necessarily lead to the postulation of a non-embodied person (rather than an embodied person) as cause of the temporal order in nature.

These considerations should suffice to rebut that persistent criticism of the argument from design which we have heard ever since Hume that, taken seriously, the argument ought to be postulating an embodied god, a giant of a man. 'Why not', wrote Hume, 'become a perfect anthropomorphite? Why not assert the deity or deities to be corporeal, and, to have eyes, a nose, mouth, ears, etc.?'[1] The answer is the simple one that dissimilarities between effects lead the rational man to postulate dissimilarities between causes, and that this procedure is basic to inductive inference.

[1] Ibid., p. 40. There is a similar counter-move to Hume's similar objection that there are in the universe other things than persons which bestow order. 'A tree bestows order and organisation on that tree which springs from it, without knowing the order; an animal in the same manner on its offspring' (op. cit., p. 50). It would therefore, Hume argues, be equally reasonable if we are arguing from analogy, to suppose the cause of the regularities in the world 'to be something similar or analogous to generation or vegetation' (op. cit., p. 47). This suggestion makes perfectly good sense if it is spatial order which we are attempting to explain. But as analogous processes to explain the patterns of temporal order codified in natural laws, generation, or vegetation will not do, because they only produce spatial order—and those through the operation of natural laws outside their control. The seed only produces the plant because of the continued operation of the laws of biochemistry.

It is true that the greater the dissimilarities between effects, the weaker is the argument to the existence of a similar cause; and it has been a traditional criticism of the argument from design represented as an argument by analogy that the analogy is weak.[1] The dissimilarities between the natural world and the effects which men produce are indeed striking; but the similarities between these are also, I have been suggesting, striking—in both there is the conformity of phenomena to a simple pattern of order detectable by men. But although the dissimilarities are perhaps sufficiently great to make the argument not a good P-inductive argument, this chapter suggests that it remains a good C-inductive argument. The existence of order in the universe increases significantly the probability that there is a God, even if it does not by itself render it probable.

The Argument from Beauty

We saw that God has reason, apparently overriding reason, for making, not merely any orderly world (which we have been considering so far) but a beautiful world—at any rate to the extent to which it lies outside the control of creatures. (And he has reason too, I would suggest, even in whatever respects the world does lie within the control of creatures, to give them experience of beauty to develop, and perhaps also some ugliness to annihilate.) So God has reason to make a basically beautiful world, although also reason to leave some of the beauty or ugliness of the world within the power of creatures to determine; but he would seem to have overriding reason not to make a basically ugly world beyond the powers of creatures to improve. Hence, if there is a God there is more reason to expect a basically beautiful world than a basically ugly one—by the principles of Chapter 6 (see the sixth possibility, p. 110). *A priori*, however, there is no particular reason for expecting a basically beautiful rather than a basically ugly world. In consequence, if the world is beautiful, that fact would be evidence for God's existence. For, in this case, if we let k be 'there is an orderly physical universe', e be 'there is a beautiful universe', and h be 'there is a God', $P(e/h.k)$ will be greater than $P(e/k)$; and so by our previous principles the argument from e to h will be another good C-inductive argument.

Few, however, would deny that our universe (apart from its

---

[1] See D. Hume, *Dialogues, passim*; and for a recent development of Hume's criticism, J. C. A. Gaskin, *Hume's Philosophy of Religion* (London, 1978), Ch. 2.

animal and human inhabitants, and aspects subject to their immediate control) has that beauty. Poets and painters and ordinary
men down the centuries have long admired the beauty of the orderly
procession of the heavenly bodies, the scattering of the galaxies
through the heavens (in some ways random, in some ways orderly),
and the rocks, sea, and wind interacting on earth, 'The spacious
firmament on high, and all the blue aethereal sky', the water lapping
against 'the old eternal rocks', and the plants of the jungle and of
temperate climates, contrasting with the desert and the Arctic
wastes. Who in his senses would deny that here is beauty in
abundance?[1] If we confine ourselves to the argument from the
beauty of the inanimate and plant worlds, the argument surely
works.

[1] For the argument from beauty see F. R. Tennant, *Philosophical Theology*, vol. II
(Cambridge, 1930), pp. 89–93.

9

Arguments from Consciousness and Morality

IN considering the arguments to the existence of God I am passing from those with more general premises to those with less. The cosmological argument appeals to the existence of the universe as its starting-point. Teleological arguments and the argument from beauty appeal to the universe's having some very general over-all characteristic. The subsequent arguments which I shall consider, appeal to more specific features of the universe. In fact they almost all start from the nature, experiences, and history of the conscious beings which inhabit the universe. The main argument which I shall consider in this chapter is an argument from the nature of the conscious beings of which we have knowledge. I then proceed in the next chapter to consider arguments for the existence of God from the circumstances of their existence; and I then come in Chapter 11 to consider an argument against the existence of God from their nature and circumstances. These three chapters are closely inter-dependent.

Terminology and Assumptions

I begin my discussion of the next three chapters with some points of terminology and some assumptions. I distinguish between animals and men. I assume that plants are not conscious, and so that the class of conscious beings about which we have immediate know-ledge consists of animals and men. All the conscious beings of which we have such knowledge are therefore rational agents who bring about effects in the way described in Chapter 2. (That is, all the beings of which we know who have feelings are also beings who can do something in response to their feelings.) To do this they need capacity or power to make differences to the world; and beliefs as to how these differences are to be made, beliefs which if the agent's action is to be rational and surely efficacious should amount to knowledge. Animals as well as men have limited power and knowledge; although the knowledge which animals have is obviously so much smaller than that of men, notably because men have language. However, men, and to a lesser degree some of the higher animals have the power to act so as to increase their power and knowledge. Man finds himself in his early years with limited power over his body, but in time he can, if he chooses, learn to run fast, read, write, and build television sets. In his early years too, he finds himself with very limited knowledge of the world around him, but if he chooses, he can acquire knowledge of the laws of nature, or the laws of football, or the history of ancient civilizations. Men and animals both enjoy things and dislike things, and have pleasurable and painful sensations, although in both intensity and sophistication of pleasure and pain there is presumably a steady increase as we move from the lowest animals up to man. Men are capable of kinds of enjoyment (e.g. reading good literature) and dislike (e.g. reading bad literature) of which the highest animals are not. And presumably the degree of suffering (and pleasure) increases with mental and nervous complexity—since man suffers and inanimate matter does not, one would expect increase of suffering with degree of organization.

Further, men evidently have two properties which at any rate lower animals evidently do not, and possibly a third property which animals do not possess. First, men are capable of marvelling at the natural world and worshipping God, consciously rejoicing in the beauty of the natural world and the uncreated being who, if he exists, is its source. Secondly, men have moral knowledge, knowledge of which actions are morally good and bad, and so which actions there are overriding reasons to do and which there are overriding reasons not to do.

Thirdly, it may be that men have free will. I understand by a being's having free will that he acts intentionally and that how he acts is not fully determined by prior states of the world; his choices are to some extent up to him. God is supposed to have perfect free will in that prior states of the world do not in any way causally influence how he acts, but on the definition which I have given a being has some free will if his intentional actions are not *fully* determined. (Of course 'free will' is a philosopher's technical term and philosophers can use it and have used it with definitions other than the one which I am giving it because it is useful for my purposes.)[1] If beings have free will, what they do will be in part at least up to them. Explanation of their actions terminates in part with themselves who have chosen so to act; their choice is not fully explicable in terms of factors operative long before they were born. They are therefore at least in part responsible for their actions.

Whether man has free will in our sense is disputed, but if he has, evidently it is limited free will. Man has to struggle to act rationally in a situation of temptation; and for all or at any rate most of us the range of psychological possibility is limited. Various heroic moral acts are just not live options for most of us—not because we lack the physical power to execute a choice, nor because we lack the knowledge that we do have some physical power, but because we just cannot face the prospect; we are not free enough psychologically to choose to perform them. Yet if man does have very limited free will, he seems also to have the power to grow in the extent of his freedom, to decrease the influence over himself of natural inclinations. Like St. Paul, a man can bring his 'body into subjection', or like yogis and athletes, learn to ignore much pain.

Conscious beings of limited power, knowledge, and freedom; yet with the capacity to grow in these respects, to marvel at nature, and to worship God, and who have moral knowledge, who enjoy and dislike things, I will call humanly free agents. In all respects which we can readily determine (viz. in all respects except that of possessing free will) men are evidently humanly free agents. If God has reason to create humanly free agents, he has reason to create men. I assume that animals do not have free will, but nothing in the argument turns on this—if any animals do have free will, they are to all intents and purposes to be classed as men, and the same reasons for creating or not creating them arise as for men.

Reasons for God to Create Animals

A creator of an orderly universe has good reason for not stopping with the creation of inanimate order. It is a good thing that there

[1] Many philosophers have claimed that in the ordinary sense of the words, to say that a man is 'free' to do something or has 'free will' does not entail that his actions and choices do not have causes. See, for example, most famously, David Hume, *An Enquiry Concerning Human Understanding* (first published 1748, L. A. Selby-Bigge (ed.), 2nd edn., Oxford, 1902), p. 95. But whether or not this is the ordinary use of the words, it is clearly open to a philosopher to define another sense, and, as I do, to urge that there is reason for God to create agents with 'free will' in his sense rather than the 'ordinary' sense. See A. Plantinga, *God and Other Minds* (Ithaca, NY, 1967), Ch. 6.

should exist conscious beings who have pleasurable sensations and enjoy doing things, and have wants which they are able to satisfy. And it is good that they should learn what is to their benefit or harm, and use their knowledge and capacities to care for themselves and to prolong their life. Animals are such beings. No doubt worms and fishes get pleasurable sensations from food and sex. And birds and rabbits rejoice in controlling their bodies to run and fly. They learn where food is to be had, and danger avoided, and through effort often get the food and avoid the danger. As we move up the evolutionary scale, we find animals whose actions are less a matter of instinct, and more a matter of learning and so of knowledge. It is good that there should be beings who make a difference to the world through their knowledge of how it is and their power over it, and that they should seek knowledge (e.g. of where food is to be had) in order to know how to make a difference. Animals enjoy, and control the natural world, and the fact that we find such beings is in itself evidence of a benevolent creator. Of course there is the enormous problem of animal pain and suffering, and I shall come to that in due course. But it is important to get our perspective right at the start. Nature may be 'red in tooth and claw', but most animals give every impression of enjoying themselves a great deal of the time.

Reasons for God to Create Men

It is good that there should be beings who are able to worship God and to marvel at the natural world, and who also have moral knowledge. It is good too that there should be beings who do not merely make a difference to the world, but who are not predetermined to make this or that difference, but who through their free choice are an independent source of the character and development of the world. For this a being needs three things—power, knowledge, and free will. He needs free will in the sense which I have delineated if he is to be an independent source of how things are, but he needs also power and knowledge. Freedom, as I have understood it, is freedom to choose; power is power by your choice to make another difference—e.g. to bring about the motion of your body, or the pattern of your subsequent thoughts. Freedom to make choices which were never or hardly ever efficacious—hardly ever made a difference to anything else—would hardly be worth having.

But an agent cannot choose how things are to be unless he has some knowledge—knowledge of what he does, knowledge of what are some of the alternatives between which he may choose. So, if God is to make beings who are independent sources of the character of the universe, he must make beings of at any rate limited freedom, power, and knowledge. God has reason to make such creatures who have power over things apart from themselves, over the inanimate world. They would determine the destiny of things. That there should be beings with such control of things is good. They would be higher beings than mere robots, modelled, as it were, on the divine model—little creators.

I have said that God has reason to create beings of at any rate limited freedom, power, and knowledge. He could only create a being of unlimited freedom, power, and knowledge if he could curtail his own power or commit suicide. For another being of unlimited power beside himself would be able to stop God doing things, and God's power would not then be unlimited. It is doubtful if it is logically possible for God to commit suicide or limit his power—it would not be logically possible if God's nature is eternal, as I suggested in Chapter 5. Even if it were logically possible, God could not create *beings* of unlimited freedom, power, and knowledge—he could only create one. (There can be at most one omnipotent being. For if there were two, one would have the power to curtail the power of the other, and the other would have the power to stop the curtailment—which involves a contradiction.) It is a good thing that more than one being exist with freedom, power, and knowledge—and that means that at any rate the power of such beings must be limited. Does God have reason to create beings whose knowledge and freedom are also limited? I think very much so, for the following reason.

I argued in Chapter 5 that a being of perfect knowledge and freedom would necessarily be perfectly good. Because of his perfect knowledge such a being would know which actions are right and wrong. Because of his perfect freedom nothing would inhibit him from avoiding what is wrong and doing what is right. He would not have chosen righteousness, but rather had it foisted upon him. In his discussion of the angels St. Thomas Aquinas describes beings who are *very nearly* in this situation.[1] On Thomas's doctrine, the angels were created virtually perfect. They had the opportunity, aided by grace, of making a single turn towards God. If they made that turn, they received the beatific vision of God (including, that is, sufficient knowledge and freedom) which made it impossible for them sub-

[1] See St. Thomas Aquinas, *Summa Theologiae*, Ia. 62.

sequently to sin. (The Devil of course, made the wrong turn, for he aspired to be as God.) Maybe there is a point in making creatures who are morally good from the start—for moral goodness is a good thing. And maybe there is a point in making creatures who are almost morally good from the start. But there is also surely a point in making creatures who have a considerable choice over a period of time, of whether to do what is morally right.

The reader may feel that a perfectly free and omniscient agent could choose whether or not to be morally good. But if the arguments given in Chapter 5 are correct, he could not. An agent who saw with crystal clarity what there was overriding reason to do and what there was not, and so what was right and what was wrong, and who was in no way diverted from doing the right by sensual desire or brain construction, would do what is right—inevitably and gladly; for he would have no wish to do anything else. For an agent to have a choice as to whether to be a morally good agent, that agent must be of limited freedom or knowledge. If his knowledge was limited and his freedom limitless, his failure to behave perfectly would be simply a consequence of ignorance—of not knowing which actions were right and which wrong. In so far as he grew in knowledge he would inevitably grow in moral goodness. If the choice of whether to be morally good is to be really up to him, it is his freedom which must be limited. The agent must be put in a situation where, although at any rate in part he sees what is morally right, and so what there is overriding reason to do, he is nevertheless 'pulled strongly' to do what there is much less reason to do. He must be put in what I shall term a situation of temptation. Paradoxically, *limited* freedom on my definition is a necessary condition of a creature's having a certain sort of choice.

The idea of an agent being 'pulled strongly' to do something is of course a metaphor which needs to be spelt out. In acting after mature consideration of reasons for and against doing an action, and doing what one honestly believes on balance that there is not overriding reason for not doing, one is acting on reason—to use Aristotelian terminology, one is acting on *boulesis*. But a reason which one rationally judges to be overridden by some other reason may in fact be the reason on which one acts because one has a felt desire or natural inclination to act on it. There are more and less obvious cases of felt desire. One has a felt desire if it needs an effort of will to stop one acting on that desire when one has an overriding reason for doing something else—desires for food or drink, sex or sleep are often obvious cases of felt desire. Less obvious cases of felt desire are desires for company or fame. The most obvious cases of felt desire are, in Aristotelian terminology, sense-desires; but the less obvious ones are not sense-desires. In virtue of the existence of felt desires, an agent has of course a reason for satisfying them. But there may be overriding reason for not satisfying them. Yet because the desires are felt desires, the agent who sees the overriding reason for not satisfying them, does not automatically fail to satisfy them. An agent with a felt desire for some lesser good, the satisfaction of which at the expense of some greater good would be immoral, is in what I shall call a situation of temptation. It requires an effort of will on his part to choose the greater good; whether he makes this effort is up to him.

It is perhaps a *sad* truth of logic that to have genuine choice of one's own destiny one must be in a situation of temptation. But some truths of logic are sad. There is the example, of the impossibility of being married monogamously to all of many beautiful women at once, and the example of the impossibility of time-travel. That he cannot give to agents the radical choice of destiny which I have described without subjecting them to temptation is only one of a number of logical constraints on the sort of universe which God can create, which we shall come across in this and the next two chapters. God cannot do the logically impossible, and that has not usually been supposed to be a limit on his omnipotence. (The logically impossible is something the description of which is ultimately incoherent. A logically impossible proposition is the negation of a logically necessary proposition.) I should add that although temptation allows the possibility of over-indulging felt desires, felt desires are in themselves evidently good things—for the satisfaction of felt desires is one of the main ways in which pleasure is to be had; and that is reason for giving them to animals as well as to men.

It is a good thing that an agent should have this power over the universe, the power to determine whether the morally good will prevail. Yet of course in other respects—just because of the possibility of the morally good not prevailing and the effort needed to ensure that it does prevail—the situation of temptation is an undesirable one. A morally good agent will seek to ensure not merely that his present choice is right, but also that his future choices are right ones. To do this, he must seek to make himself a morally good being. A creator has reason to allow him the opportunity to do so, to allow him through right choices to grow in freedom and morally relevant knowledge until he becomes as the angels. A creator has reason to allow him the opportunity to rescue himself from subjection to felt desires—gradually, so that the end is achieved by a process of serious commitment over time. The reason is that it allows the agent to ensure that he behaves morally in future, as, in so far as he pursues the good, he inevitably wishes to do.

Likewise in so far as both power and other knowledge are good things, there is reason for a creator to create agents with the choice of whether or not to acquire great power and knowledge. He can make them with limited power and knowledge and leave it up to them whether they grow in these. In all of these respects the creator would be giving to the agent the choice of what sort of being he is to be. He will be initially a being of very limited freedom, power, and knowledge, yet with the power through right choices to grow in these, or to abandon them. He can choose whether to return to the level of the beasts or to move in the direction of divinity. Bad choices will make good choices harder next time, and conversely. Bad choices persisted in may remove the possibility of choice at all. Good choices persisted in will enable a creature so to grow in knowledge, power, and freedom, until (although bad choices are no longer open to him) his range of choice is enormous. Such a limited being will have what I may call a genuine choice of destiny. This, as we have seen, is not to be equated with free will as such; but is a matter of the range of options which is open to an agent with free will. As we have seen, man is (if he has free will) a being of such limited freedom, power, and knowledge, including moral knowledge, and power to worship and marvel. I have not yet discussed one crucial feature of man's nature, his capacity for pain and suffering, and I shall come to that in the next two chapters. But, with that exception, man is a being such as God has good reason to make.

There are however, as we have seen, certain bad aspects of the existence of humanly free agents. Just because they are free, they may choose evil rather than good. That would seem to be some reason for God not to make them, but hardly an overriding reason; and also reason for God to make simpler beings, capable of enjoyment, who have some power and knowledge so as to perform actions, but without knowledge of moral good and evil or freedom to choose between them. Such beings too, as I have already noted, we find around us—the animals. And perhaps too God has reason for making beings of much greater power, knowledge, and freedom than men (and of course according to the majority Christian tradition down the centuries, he has done so—for he made angels).

To create embodied beings is an evident way of creating agents of limited power and knowledge with the power to increase their power and knowledge. For if an agent has a body, there is a part of the world through which his intentions are executed and through which he acquires knowledge. If the world is temporally ordered, the agent can then, as we saw in the last chapter, acquire knowledge of the regularities which govern the world, and thereby acquire knowledge of states of the world at distant places and times and learn which basic actions of his will produce which effects at distant places and times. A body is an instrument through which an agent can extend his power and knowledge.

An embodied agent, person or animal, is one whose conscious processes interact with his bodily processes, for example by his intentions causing limb-movements, and stimuli impinging on his eyes and ears giving him knowledge of the world. We have seen that God has reason for creating embodied agents. But the different ways in which the agent's intentions could be executed through a body and the ways in which his knowledge of the world could be derived are many and various. Why the particular mind-body connections which there are? What reason could God have for connecting sucrose with a brain-state giving rise to a sweet taste, and sodium chloride with a brain-state giving rise to a salty taste? I do not know. But it is not implausible to suppose that he may have some reason of which we know not. There may for example, be a beauty about the one connection which is lacking in the other. Or if he has no reason for bringing about one connection rather than the other, and yet reason for bringing about one or the other, then he would have reason for choosing one connection by some kind of mental toss-up, and so we can understand how one connection came to be.

The Scientific Inexplicability of Consciousness

So far, I have been arguing that the existence of embodied agents and especially men, is something which God has reason to bring about, although he also has reason not to bring about such agents. I now wish to argue that embodied agents of the kind which we find on earth, would be unlikely to come into existence in the normal course of things, that is, but for the action of a God. I argue that, even given the existence of an orderly inanimate universe, the prior probability of the existence of embodied agents, conscious beings who bring about effects through intentions (in the way analysed in Chapter 2) is very low, unless a God intervenes in the natural order to bring about their existence. I shall take it as an argument about men, but of course it applies also to animals. I do not know of any classical philosopher who has developed the argument from consciousness with any rigour. But one sometimes hears theologians and ordinary men saying that conscious men could not have evolved from unconscious matter by natural processes. I believe that those who have said this have been hinting at a powerful argument to which philosophers have not given nearly enough attention. In this chapter, I propose to set out and defend such an argument.

Superficially, man differs from inorganic things in at least two crucial respects. Men perform actions, which, as we have seen earlier, are explicable in a very different kind of way from the way of scientific explanation; and, secondly, there are in causal interaction with the physical events in men's bodies mental events. I understand by a mental event one which it is not logically possible should occur unexperienced; and by a physical event one which it is logically possible should occur unexperienced. Mental events are such things as thoughts, feelings, sensations, imaginings, conscious decisions, etc. Brain-events are physical events. Clearly often brain-events cause mental events (neural disturbances cause pains) and often mental events cause brain-events (decisions cause bodily movements).

The programme of materialism is to provide a scientific explanation of the occurrence of mental events, and of the occurrence and operation of the other factors involved in personal explanation (persons having the intentions and capacities which they have). I believe that there are substantial difficulties in the way of the success of this programme, and that the existence and operation of man is not ultimately scientifically explicable. If that is so, it is proper to look for another kind of explanation of the existence and operation of man. The prospects for a theistic explanation of the existence of men are, I believe, much better than the prospects for a scientific explanation.

Before coming to grips with this issue, I need first to discuss a strong thesis which has become fashionable in recent years; that there are no distinct mental events—mental events just are brain-events. There are two forms of the doctrine of reducibility of mental events to physical events. One is behaviourism—the view that all talk about a person's thoughts, feelings, etc. is analysable in terms of talk about his actual or possible behaviour. It is, I believe, fair to say that the vast majority of contemporary philosophers do not see much hope any more in the behaviourist programme. Although all the public evidence for another man's thoughts, feelings, etc. must indeed come from his public behaviour, talk about the former is not always fully analysable in terms of talk about the latter. Talk about a man's pains is not just talk about his screams; nor is talk about his thoughts merely talk about what he says aloud. The alternative form of the doctrine of reducibility is central state-materialism, alias the mind–brain identity theory.[1] On this view talk about thoughts, feelings, etc. is really talk about brain-states. It is not of course very plausible to suppose that there is identity of meaning here. One does not mean by an imaging of St. Paul's Cathedral such-and-such a brain-event. But the claim of identity theorists is that there is here a logically contingent identity (see pp. 38 ff.). Such-and-such a brain-event is in fact contingently identical with (is the same event as) an imaging of St. Paul's Cathedral—just as one does not mean by 'lightning' an electrical discharge of such-and-such a type, but there is nevertheless a contingent identity between the two. All mental events are in fact just brain-events, according to identity theory; although of course not all brain-events are mental events—there are disturbances in the brain which have nothing directly to do with consciousness.

The identity theorist claims that science often shows that an event described in one way E_1 is just the same event as an event described in another way E_2, and that our grounds for saying this are (1) E_1 and E_2 occur in the same place, (2) E_1 and E_2 occur at the same time, and (3) the supposition that E_1 is the same event as E_2 is a consequence of a scientific theory which gains in simplicity or

[1] Mind-brain identity theory was advocated in U. T. Place, 'Is Consciousness a Brain Process?', *British Journal of Psychology*, 1956, **47**, 44-50, and in J. J. C. Smart, 'Sensations and Brain Processes', *Philosophical Review*, 1959, **68**, 141-56. Since the publication of these articles there has developed a very considerable literature on the theory. The most useful articles (including the two just cited) from the early stage of the debate are collected in C. V. Borst (ed.), *The Mind/Brain Identity Theory* (London, 1970). The best full-length defence of the theory is J. W. Cornman, *Materialism and Sensations* (New Haven and London, 1971). Cornman defends a sophisticated version of the theory known as 'adverbial materialism'.

explanatory power through making this and similar suppositions. Thus our grounds for saying that a certain flash of lightning is an electrical discharge are that (1) the lightning occurs at the same place as an electrical discharge, (2) the lightning occurs at the same time as the electrical discharge, and (3) the occurrence of electrical discharges can be explained without reference to lightning, and yet lightning always occurs at the same place and time as electrical discharges of a certain kind. Physics deals in such things as electrical discharges, and if we assume that lightning is nothing but an electrical discharge we add to the simplicity of our world-view. Just as science can show events to be identical, so on similar grounds it can show objects to be identical. It can show that a certain volume of water is really a certain collection of H_2O molecules by showing (1) that wherever that water is, there are those H_2O molecules, (2) whenever that water exists, there are those H_2O molecules, and (3) whenever you have water at all, you have H_2O molecules. Physics and chemistry deal in interactions of molecules and atoms. They can explain why water behaves as it does—why it flows downhill, quenches thirst, is transparent, etc.—if we assume that the water just is the H_2O molecules. In such cases, the identity theorist claims, science affirms that there is only one event or one object because there is no need to claim that there is more than one event or object. Science follows Ockham's Razor, 'entities are not to be postulated, except when necessary', which is an aspect of the principle of simplicity, which I discussed in Chapter 3.

Are these three conditions satisfied in the case of the suggested identity of mental events with brain-events? Brain-events occur in the brain, but we do not normally think of mental events as having any very exact location. It would be odd to say that my thought that today is Wednesday occurred just two millimetres below such-and-such a spot on the cerebral cortex. Yet, the identity theorist claims[1] that our thinking of mental events as things without very precise location is purely arbitrary, and that it would involve no real change in our concept of a mental event if we adopted a convention to think of it as located at that place (if any) in the brain where that event correlated with it takes place. It is not as though we had previously thought of mental events as located anywhere else or that non-localizability was somehow of their essence. Suppose that we adopt the stated convention; in that case the first condition will be satisfied

---

[1] See J. Shaffer, 'Could Mental Events be Brain Processes?', *Journal of Philosophy*, 1961, **58**, 813–22, in Borst (ed.), op. cit.

by definition if the second and third conditions are satisfied. Would the supposition that mental events were identical with specified brain-events, occurring simultaneously, add to the simplicity or explanatory power of science? The identity theorist suggests that it would. He makes a scientific assumption, that there is a one-one or many-one correlation between kinds of brain-event and kinds of mental event. That is, for each brain-event of a given kind there is correlated a mental event of a given kind. A certain pattern of c-fibre firing is correlated with pain; a different pattern of firing is correlated with an itch; one pattern is correlated with a thought that $2 + 2 = 4$; another pattern is correlated with a thought that $3 + 3 = 6$, and so on. It may be that a mental event of some kind is correlated sometimes with a brain-event of one kind, sometimes with a brain-event of another kind; but, the assumption is, it is never the other way round. In that case it will be possible, after science has discovered these correlations, for a scientist to infer with complete accuracy from his study of a person's brain the mental life of that person. Yet brain-events are part of the network of physical events in the world, and are to be explained by and explain other physical events. The supposition that there are mental events additional to physical events would seem to add vastly to the complexity of science without allowing it to explain anything new. Given the crucial scientific assumption, the identity theorist suggests that there is as much reason here to postulate contingent identity as in normal scientific cases.

I have very considerable doubt about the cogency of some of the steps in the argument outlined above, but let us suppose for the moment that identity theory is correct. Nevertheless, a major difficulty remains that mental events are events of which the agent whose they are has privileged knowledge and which have such phenomenal properties as blueness, painfulness, and hardness. If mental events are identical with brain-events, then we have the following picture of the world. Almost all events in the world including many brain-events are physical events (i.e. events which are not experiences of an agent) which consist of interactions between objects distinguished only by their primary qualities (mass, shape, velocity, etc.); yet certain brain-events are conscious events (i.e. events which are experiences of an agent) with phenomenal properties such as blueness and painfulness. Identity theory still seems to leave us with a dualism, no longer a dualism of events, but now a dualism of properties. Identity theory now tries *either* to analyse talk about phenomenal properties into talk about physical properties *or* to claim that talk about phenomenal properties is dispensable in the new scientific world-view. The former move is made by J. J. C. Smart. He claims that such a sentence as 'I have a yellowish-orange after-image' means something like 'there is something going on which is like what is going on when I have my eyes open, am awake, and there is an orange illuminated in good light in front of me, that is, when I really see an orange'.[1] The statement does not say what is going on, but science may discover what is going on—a similar brain-process. The suggested translation seems to me implausible. The original claim was not merely that something similar was going on similar to what goes on when the agent has his eyes open, etc., but that there was something going on similar in a crucial respect—there was a particular phenomenal colour which the subject experienced—however dissimilar in other ways what is going on might be to the normal case. The latter move, espoused by R. Rorty,[2] suggests that the new over-all scientific world-view would lead us to deny—what at first sight might appear to be the case—that there are phenomenal properties to which agents have privileged access; just as the progress of science leads us to deny will-o'-the-wisps, fairies, ghosts, and witches, although there might seem to observers to be such. In the past we may have used such a term as 'witch' to refer to particular people (old women of certain appearance and habits) but what science has revealed is that the implications carried by that description do not apply to anyone (no one has the power to put successful spells on people). Similarly, Rorty suggests, we may have used the word 'after-image' or 'pain' to refer to events which certainly occur (viz. brain-events), but the implications carried by that description—that they are events with phenomenal properties distinct from physical events, known best by the agent who experiences them, etc.—may be false. However, it seems to me, as to many other writers, that the cases of witches and of mental events are very far from parallel. For at any rate some of the implications carried by 'after-image', 'pain', etc. are correct. There are phenomenal properties, blueness, painfulness, smelling of roses, which are not the same as physical properties. We cannot describe the world fully if we use only terms denoting physical

[1] Smart, op. cit., p. 148. For more thorough criticism than I give see Cornman, op. cit., p. 43.

[2] R. Rorty, 'Mind-Body Identity, Privacy, and Categories', *Review of Metaphysics*, 1965-6, **19**, 24-54; republ. in Borst.

properties. Any world-view which denies the existence of experienced sensations of blueness or loudness or pain, does not describe how things are—that this is so stares us in the face.

For these reasons, which I have of necessity had to state very tersely, it seems to me that the materialist programme of reducing talk of mental events and properties to talk about physical events and properties is doomed to failure. Some kind of dualism of entities or properties or states is inevitable. If you deny that there are mental events which interact with brain-events, you still have to say that some brain-events are very different from other bodily events in having mental properties, which cause and are caused by other brain-events. However, the main argument for identity theory was the alleged simplification of the world-view which resulted from its adoption, and yet the simplification seems to be lost if we are forced to adopt a property dualism. For this reason I revert to the more natural account of the matter: that mental events are distinct events from brain-events, but that mental events cause brain-events and brain-events cause mental events. However, if any reader prefers to think in terms of a dualism of properties, my points can easily be put in these terms.

My conclusion that there are mental events and that they are not analysable exclusively in non-mental terms parallels the conclusion which I reached in Chapter 2, that personal explanation cannot be analysed in terms of scientific explanation. Unable to get rid of mental events, the best that the materialist can do is to tame the mental events, by establishing a scientific theory showing how physical events give rise to mental events and the mental events have physical effects. That is, the materialist will try to bring mental events within the network of scientific laws, as entities governed by these. He will try to do the same, as we saw in Chapter 2, for personal explanation. Unable to analyse personal explanation in terms of scientific explanation, he tries to produce a scientific explanation of how there come to exist persons, and how they come to have and exercise the intentions, beliefs, and capacities which they do. What prospect is there for these programmes? I shall consider the programme of constructing a theory to explain the occurrence, and causal powers of mental events. It will be seen that just the same considerations apply to the programme of giving a scientific explanation of the existence and operation of the factors involved in personal explanation and I shall comment on this from time to time.

To establish a complete scientific explanation of the occurrence of mental events, the materialist needs to take three separate steps. The first is to establish (in the way which I described earlier) for all mental events and states a one–one or perhaps one–many correlation between the occurrence of mental events of specifiable kinds, and the simultaneous occurrence of brain-events of specifiable kinds—e.g. a correlation between a man's thinking about stroking a cat (whenever any man has such a thought) and a brain-event or brain-events of specifiable kinds. The establishment of such correlations is going to be a very dubious business. The suggestion that such correlations have been established is always going to be open to question for the reason that some of the data in which they are based are going to be (of logical necessity) better known to one person than to all others. A man knows about his own mental events, better than do outsiders. In general we have to take an agent's word about what his thoughts and feelings are if ever we are to correlate thoughts and feelings with brain-events. The lack of public observability of one half of the correlations means that there is a certain doubt about the data. And not merely will the data on which the theory of correlation is originally based be somewhat dubious, but it is a further consequence of the privileged access to which I have drawn attention that any predictions derived from the theory of correlations are very largely not publicly testable. For while the theory claims to predict a man's mental events, all that can be tested publicly is which mental events a man will publicly confess to having.

Suppose however, that despite these difficulties, a scientist has established as well as he can a theory of correlation between physical and mental states. I know of no adequate reason to suppose that such a theory can be established even within the logical limitations to which I have called attention. Certainly there are general correlations between certain patterns of brain-states and certain kinds of mental activity, e.g. the occurrence of dreams; but the occurrence of one brain-state for my dream that I am Napoleon the First, and a different brain-state for my dream that I am Napoleon the Third seems a bit speculative. Imagine nevertheless the task accomplished. The mere existence of a correlation between two variables shows nothing about what causes what. To show that the brain-events are the ultimate determinant of what goes on, the materialist will need to show that the occurrence of all mental events is predictable from knowledge of brain-events alone, and that the occurrence of brain-events is explicable in physiological terms (e.g.

by the occurrence of other bodily events) whereas the occurrence of all brain-events is not predictable from knowledge of mental events alone.

In the way of this second task there stand two difficulties—neither insuperable, but difficulties nevertheless. The first is that of man's experience of choice. Man often chooses his intentions, that is the intentions on which he will act. It often seems to him that he is selecting on rational grounds between alternative courses of action, choosing the intentions which he will have. It seems to him that the choice is up to him whether to be influenced by rational considerations or not, his choice not being predetermined for him by his brain, character, or environment; and that it is rational considerations, not brain-states which influence him (though not conclusively). Now if man (at any rate sometimes) chooses his intentions and this choice is not predetermined, his choices cannot be invariably predictable from prior brain-states, nor can any effects in the brain which they may have. Now certainly what seems to be so may not be so—freedom of choice may be an illusion. But it is a sound principle of reasoning[1] to suppose that things are as they seem to be, unless and until proved otherwise. If we did not suppose that, we could know nothing of the universe. The second difficulty is that Quantum Theory, at any rate on one standard interpretation, assures us that the basic physical laws are statistical or probabilistic. They only allow us to infer from one brain-event B_1 that it was (physically) very probable that a subsequent brain-event B_2 would occur, not that it was physically necessary. But this would leave open the possibility that the explanation of the occurrence of brain-event B_2 correlated with intention I_2 was to be explained fully by the joint action of brain-event B_1 and intention I_2. Further, whatever reasons we may have from the success of science in other fields to believe that universal physical determinism reigns, it seems to me hazardous to extrapolate from other fields to the brain. For the brain is clearly very different from anything else studied by science in having correlated with events in it, mental events. It would be surprising if this meant no difference to the way in which inter-actions take place in the brain.

Despite these difficulties, let us suppose the second task accomplished. We would then have one–one (or one–many) correlation between mental events and brain-events, mental events being fully

---

[1] I defend this principle, which I call there the Principle of Credulity, at greater length in Ch. 13.

predictable from brain-events, but not vice versa. We could then have a dictionary in which, observing a man's brain-events, we could look up and see which mental events he now had. Would all this mean that we had got a scientific explanation of the existence of mental events, intentions, beliefs, and indeed persons (these being beings which have mental events, intentions, and beliefs)? I think not. For to explain the existence of mental events we need to cite not merely the cause, the brain-event, which apparently brings about the mental event, but also the scientific law in virtue of which the brain-event brings about the mental event. It is at this point, I believe, that the materialist programme reaches its stiffest obstacle.

The materialist needs laws, not merely a collection of generalizations, correlating brain-events and mental events. As we saw in Chapter 2, a law is a generalization which holds of physical necessity, and so holds without exception under circumstances other than those examined, and under hypothetical circumstances as well as actual circumstances. We saw in Chapter 3, that our grounds for believing a generalization to be a law are that it belongs to a scientific theory which has high prior probability and great explanatory power. For a theory concerned with a vast area and one very different from those covered by other scientific theories, prior probability is almost entirely a function of simplicity. A theory's explanatory power is a matter of its leading us to find what we would not otherwise expect to find. I have already referred to the difficulty of testing any suggested generalization about how mental events are correlated with brain-events, arising from the fact that the only public evidence about mental events which we have is indirect evidence. This difficulty would arise in an acute form if some scientist suggested a law about the conditions under which physical states give rise to the existence of embodied persons. The law claims, say, that when you have a being with such-and-such reactions with an internal controlling centre of such-and-such electrical complexity, you have a person (i.e. a rational agent with intentions, purposes, beliefs, etc. of a certain complexity—see p. 20 n. 1).

It follows from the law, say, that some being made from wire in a laboratory or some being from a distant planet with a different physiology from ours is a person. How can we test this claim? The claim is true if the being has thoughts, has feelings, etc. But how do we know that he has? All that we can observe is his public behaviour which simulates our own, but that does not necessarily mean that behind the public behaviour are thoughts and feelings similar to our own—maybe the creature screams when you stick pins into it without its having any feeling of pain lying in the causal chain between the sticking of the pins and the emitting of the scream.

Now it may reasonably be urged that we are often in a similar position in physical science. A theory concerned with the behaviour of electrons or neutrinos can hardly be tested by observing the electrons or neutrinos in any direct way. What we can test is the laws about the interactions of electrons and neutrinos together with laws about their interactions with larger objects. The whole is testable and must give satisfactory predictions about large-scale publicly observable phenomena such as the patterns which you will find on photographic plates, if we are to have reason for believing it. Likewise certainly we can test the conjunction of a theory telling us how brain-events are correlated with mental events with a theory telling us how the mental events will be manifested (e.g. which of his intentions a man will acknowledge, which of his sensations he can and will describe, which of his beliefs will be manifested in action). However, our ground for believing the conjunction does not lie solely in its explanatory power. As we have seen before, infinitely many totally different theories about unobservables can be constructed which predict the same events as each other, events which we would not ordinarily expect to occur. The evidence that one of them is the true theory lies in simplicity, the naturalness of the connections in the laws which it postulates. The suggested laws of fundamental particles are going to be relatively simple laws which describe how the interactions of particles depend on their mass, volume, charge, spin (and perhaps charm), and give an account of why there are just the fundamental particles which there are, why their masses, volumes, and lifetimes are as they are; as well as give an account of how they interact with larger objects. Fundamental physics has not yet reached a finished theory of this kind, but it is some way towards it. My point here is that materialism is never likely to move very far at all towards such a simple theory.

For suppose that the materialist's programme of establishing correlations so far has been moderately successful. What will he have? Lots and lots of correlations of the following kind: brain-event B_1 correlated with a red after-image, B_2 with a blue one, B_3 with a green one, B_4 with an intention to move an arm, B_5 with an intention to sign a cheque, B_6 with a belief that time is going backwards, and so on. What he needs is a neat set of laws showing a natural connection between redness and this kind of brain-event, blueness and that kind, an intention to move an arm with this kind of brain-event, to sign a cheque with that kind; laws which fit together with each other in a theory from which one can deduce new correlations hitherto unobserved. If there were a theory whose generalizations postulated natural and simple connections of this kind, we would have grounds for believing those generalizations to state laws which would hold under varied conditions; and so we would have an *explanation* of why (e.g.) persons have the intentions or beliefs or after-images which they have, not merely a (slightly questionable) ability to predict them. We would be able to say *why* sodium chloride tastes salty rather than sweet in terms of the brain-event which tasting sodium chloride normally produces having a natural connection with saltiness; why grass and trees look green and sky and sea look blue as opposed to the other way round.

Mere correlation does not explain and because it does not, we never know when our predictions will go wrong. If you have found that all swans observed so far are white, but this generalization does not in any way fit into an over-all theory of animal colour (e.g. a genetic theory of which it is a consequence that swan genes always carry and must carry the gene for white colour), then there is always a considerable possibility that a black swan may turn up. In a scientific theory we demand simple connections between entities of few kinds in terms of which we can explain diverse phenomena. For example, the atomic theory of chemistry was able to give a very good explanation in terms of its basic elements of why carbon and oxygen combined in the ratio of $3:8$ by weight to make carbon dioxide. This is that a molecule of carbon dioxide consists of one atom of carbon and two of oxygen, carbon has an atomic weight of 12, and oxygen of 16. These latter postulates were used in the explanation of other combinations also. From such factors it follows that it is no *ad hoc* separate element in the theory, that the ratio of combination of carbon and oxygen to make carbon dioxide is $3:8$.

But why should not the materialist devise a theory showing the kinds of correlation discussed to be natural ones? Why should he not postulate entities and properties from whose interactions (the laws of which are simple) it would follow that you get the correlations which you do between brain-events and mental events? Although it is theoretically possible that a scientific theory of this kind should be created, still the creation of such a theory does not look a very likely prospect. Brain-states are such different things qualitatively from experiences, intentions, beliefs, etc. that a *natural* connection between them seems almost impossible. For how could brain-states vary except in their chemical composition and the speed and direction of their electro-chemical interactions, and how could there be a natural connection between variations in these respects and variations in the kind of respects in which intentions differ—say the difference between intending to sign a cheque, intending to square the circle, and intending to lecture for another half an hour? There does not seem the beginning of a prospect of a simple scientific theory of this kind and so of having established laws of mind–body interaction as opposed to lots of diverse correlations; which, just because they are unconnected in an over-all theory, are for that reason not necessarily of universal application. If we cannot have scientific laws we cannot have scientific explanation. The materialist's task of giving a full explanation of the occurrence of a man's mental events, and of his intentions, beliefs, and capacities *seems* doomed to failure. For a detailed materialist theory could not be a simple enough theory for us to have reasonable confidence in its truth.

The correlations of mental events and intentions with brain-events are too 'odd' for science to explain (in contrast to the existence and orderliness of the world which are too 'big' for science to explain). As I argued in an earlier chapter, there are two alternatives to materialism. One is to suppose that the occurrence of mental events is not fully explicable scientifically, nor is the applicability of personal explanation to some phenomena, in a world in which events are mainly explicable in the scientific pattern above. This is dualism—to suppose an essential and inexplicable plurality of entities and kinds of explanation. Dualism, is, as we have seen, a very messy world-picture; and it was the messiness of that picture which rightly drove men to attempting to construct a satisfactory materialist world-picture. Dualism is not a satisfactory stopping-point for explanation.

The other alternative is to seek a personal explanation of mind–body correlations and a personal explanation of the operation of the factors cited in scientific explanation. That there are such explanations is a central thesis of theism. The theist claims that an explanation of why brain-event of kind B_1 is correlated with mental event of kind M_1, brain-event of kind B_2 with mental event of kind M_2, and so on is that God has chosen that these kinds of events be so correlated; an explanation in so far as there is one of why I have the thoughts, feelings, etc. that I have is that my having thoughts, feelings, etc. of those kinds is correlated with certain kinds of brain-states and that God has chosen that these kinds of thoughts, feelings, etc. be so correlated; it follows from God's omnipotence that his choice will be executed. The trouble with the materialist's programme was that there was no natural connection between brain-events and correlated mental events. But the intention of an agent to join them binds them together. There is a very natural connection indeed between an agent's intention to bring about X, and the occurrence of X; for the intention has written into it one thing with which it is naturally correlated: its fulfilment—whereas a brain-event does not have written into it a mental event with which it is naturally correlated (a natural correlation with redness as opposed to greenness is not written into brain-events correlated with after-images). That is why the prospects are so much better for a reduction of all explanation to personal explanation. It can give a natural explanation of all connections in the world in terms of an agent's intention to bring about those connections.

In suggesting that the evolution of conscious beings is not explicable by normal scientific processes, I do not wish to deny that there is a story of the gradual evolution of conscious beings out of inorganic matter. My only claim is that this evolutionary story is not to be explained in scientific terms, for there are no scientific *laws* correlating the bodily and the mental, only correlations of too limited a scope to constitute laws. I do not wish to deny that there is a satisfactory scientific explanation given by the biological theory of evolution of the evolution of more and more complex beings which interact in increasingly complex ways. But there is not, I have argued, a scientific explanation of their increasing complexity of physiological organization and behavioural response giving rise to the particular conscious life to which it does give rise and which subsequently in part determines what happens in and through the body.

So then the argument of this section has been designed to show that the existence of conscious beings would not have come about by normal physical processes. The argument of the previous section was designed to show that God had reason for bringing about the existence of such beings, and so that there is some probability that he would do so. Put together, the two sections form a good C-inductive argument for the existence of God. Let k be the premisses of the arguments which we have discussed so far, viz., that there is an orderly (and beautiful) world. Let e be the existence of conscious men with brains of the kind which they have. Let h be, as before, the hypothesis of theism—that there is a God. $P(e/\sim h.k)$ is low—it is improbable that the world should just have the kind of complexity with which a dictionary of mind–body connections would set out, without some explanation. As we saw in Chapter 4 (p. 83), regularity in the midst of complexity cries out for explanation. For the reasons which I have given it does not look at all plausible to suppose that there is a scientific explanation of these phenomena. Once again, for reasons of simplicity, the most probable personal explanation is one in terms of the agency of God—both because such an explanation is in itself the simplest kind of personal explanation, and also because it is simpler to suppose one person to be responsible for the existence and order of the world as well as for the existence of conscious men than to suppose two or many separate creator persons at work, and we have seen some reason for supposing a person to be responsible for the former. A personal explanation in terms of the action of God would provide a good explanation of the phenomena, both because God has the power to create what is otherwise strange (God's intention makes a natural bridge between brain and consciousness in the way described) and because he has some reason to make conscious men. However, I am not claiming that God has more reason for bringing about e than for bringing about alternative states. We saw earlier (p. 159) that there are reasons why God might not wish to bring about conscious men. I am claiming simply that he has reason for bringing about e as well as for bringing about alternative states, but that $P(e/h.k) >$ $P(e/\sim h.k)$, because e has the sort of complexity which makes it unlikely to occur without God's action. For that reason the argument from consciousness is a good C-inductive argument for the existence of God.

The argument from consciousness which I have now set out with, I hope, some rigour, captures in a precise form the feeling of amazement which many people have when, aware of the web of physical laws governing such inanimate physical objects as electrons, protons, and photons operating through boundless space and endless time, they are also aware of something quite different, interacting with the physical objects in very limited regions of space (such as human bodies on earth) over a very limited region of time. Here, they have felt, is something outside that web of physical laws—which needs explanation of a different kind—explanation in terms of the action of an agent in certain respects similar to the human agents, whose existence needs explanation. Here, they have felt, are particular footprints of the divine. I have been arguing that this feeling is a justified one.

The Argument from Morality

Moral awareness is confined to certain conscious beings, men. Many theists have held that through morality God makes himself known intimately to men, for the voice of conscience is the voice of God. We find an argument from morality to God classically in Kant—although he would vigorously deny that he is putting forward anything which can properly be called an argument;[1] and also in writers of the late nineteenth and early twentieth centuries, who, when the argument from design was driven out of fashion, cherished this as their favourite argument. For my part, as will appear, I find 'the moral law within' considerably less good testimony to God than 'the starry heavens above'.

It is crucial to distinguish two different arguments from morality. First there is the argument from man's moral consciousness, his making moral judgements. Given the objectivist account of morality which I am taking for granted, this is an argument from man's awareness of moral truths. During the long process of human evolution man gradually came to acquire the concepts of right and wrong, good and evil, and to make judgements about which actions and states of affairs were right and wrong, good and evil. Some of these judgements were ones which we would recognize as true—e.g. the wrongness of taking from a man his handiwork, and the obligation to defend one's children's lives. Other judgements are ones which we would recognize as false. I argued earlier that clearly

[1] See I. Kant, *Critique of Practical Reason*, Bk. 2, esp. Ch. 2, Sect. 5. Kant claims that the existence of God is a 'postulate of pure practical reason', that is that the existence of God entails that the *summum bonum*, the perfection of the universe which the moral law commands us to seek, is attainable; and hence that the binding obligation upon us to keep the moral law is something that makes sense. He would, however, vigorously deny that this constitutes an argument for the existence of God since he would deny that the binding obligation to keep the moral law can in any way be formulated as a theoretical truth. We simply find ourselves feeling the force of the moral law, and try to make sense of how it can be that we are under the moral law. But I cannot see how it can be rational for us to conform to the moral law (as Kant believes that it is), unless we believe that what the moral law states is true—e.g. that murder is wrong, and promise-keeping obligatory. Hence in effect Kant seems to be putting forward an argument from the fact that there are binding moral truths.

God has reason to give to man awareness of moral truth; and I shall argue in the next chapter that he has reason to give it to men not all at once but to allow them to acquire it gradually through co-operation and experience. For this reason man's awareness of moral truth forms part of the evidence in the general argument from the existence of men and animals to the existence of God, begun above. I cannot however see that, given that there are conscious men acquiring knowledge of the world, that man's awareness of moral truth is something especially difficult to explain by normal scientific processes. Men living in close proximity and needing fellowship might well be expected to grasp concepts of fairness and justice, especially when it would be of advantage to one group to bring home to other groups their moral obligations. A long tradition of writing on human evolution beginning with Darwin's *The Descent of Man* showed how man's moral awareness might be expected to develop by evolutionary processes, as man evolved from lower animals.

Secondly, very different from the arguments which I have been considering so far in this chapter, there is an argument from the fact of morality itself, from the fact that there are binding moral truths (quite apart from whether men are or are not aware of them). An argument of this kind takes for granted moral objectivism—that moral judgements have truth-values. If there are no moral truths, then there is no fact about the world for this argument to take off from. The issue then arises, given that moral judgements are propositions with truth-values, whether true moral propositions are analytic or synthetic. An argument which claims that the best explanation of the existence of morality is the action of God who created it, must claim that many moral truths are synthetic. For the existence of the phenomena described by analytic truths needs no explanation. It does not need explaining that all bachelors are unmarried, or that if you add two to two you get four. These things hold inevitably and necessarily, whether or not there is a God. Now clearly if there are moral truths, quite a lot of moral truths are synthetic. That whatever action was done by Hitler at 10.00 a.m. on 3 December 1940 was morally wicked is, if true, clearly synthetically so; for it is coherent to suppose that Hitler might have done a good action at that time. And generally we may say, true statements of the form '*a* is wrong', and '*a* is right' and '*a* is obligatory', where '*a*' is the name of an action or a description which picks it out by its spatio-temporal co-ordinates are, given moral objectivism, synthetic truths. Yet actions cannot be just obligatory or right or wrong. They must be obligatory or right or wrong in virtue of their possessing certain natural (i.e. non-moral) properties, e.g. what made a certain action wrong may have been that it was an act of torturing children. Once one has specified fully what it is that makes the action wrong, then it will be (given that it is a truth) an *analytic* truth that an action of that kind is wrong. For if it were not it would be coherent to suppose that another action could be just like the first one in all other qualitative respects and the second be right and the first wrong—yet this is not a coherent supposition. If one action is right, and another imagined one is wrong, there must be some natural feature which the second action has and the first lacks which makes the second wrong. It is not coherent to claim that *a* is wrong, and that *b* differs from *a* in no natural property but that, unlike *a*, *b* is right. There could not be a world which was different from our world solely in the respect that murder was wrong here, but right there. There would have to be some natural features of the other world which made murder right there, e.g. that there murdered people quickly come to life again. It follows, given moral objectivism, that synthetic claims that some actions are right (or wrong) hold in virtue of synthetic truths that the action has certain natural properties and analytic truths that actions with those properties are right (or wrong, as the case may be). Fundamental moral principles must be analytic.[1] The mistake of intuitionism, as I understand it, was to suppose that the basic moral principles could be synthetic. But then a world would be coherently conceivable in which (despite the fact that they hold in our world) the basic moral principles did not hold, and such a world is not coherently conceivable.

Now if the basic moral principles are analytic, the existence of what they describe cannot provide an argument for the existence of God. An argument could only take off from the truth of some or all synthetic moral truths (e.g. from the fact that it is wrong to drop atom bombs on Japan rather than from the fact that it is wrong to kill people who will not certainly come to life again). Now the fact that certain moral truths hold can only confirm, add to the probability of, the existence of God if it is more likely that those moral truths hold if there is a God than if there is not. Now the synthetic truths that actions, *a*, *b*, *c*, *d*, are obligatory (or right or

---

[1] For further argument on these points see *The Coherence of Theism*, Ch. 11, or the article on which that chapter is based, 'The Objectivity of Morality', *Philosophy*, 1976, **51**, 5-20.

wrong as the case may be) depend on *a*, *b*, *c*, *d*, possessing certain natural properties *Q*, *R*, *S*, *T*, which analytically make them obligatory (or whatever). So if there is to be an argument to the existence of God from certain actions being obligatory it will have a structure somewhat[1] as follows: actions *a*, *b*, *c*, *d*, are obligatory; they would not be obligatory unless they were *Q*, *R*, *S*, *T*. It is more probable that there are actions which are *Q*, *R*, *S*, *T*, if there is a God than if there is not; therefore the obligatoriness of *a*, *b*, *c*, *d*, confirms the existence of God.

Now the most plausible candidates for actions which would not be obligatory unless there were a God are actions like promise-keeping and truth-telling, for the obligatoriness of which there is no easy utilitarian justification. Starting from the obligatoriness of such actions we could construct a Kantian argument along the following lines. (Although this argument is very much in the spirit of Kant's *Critique of Practical Reason*, Kant himself denies that he is putting forward *an argument* to the existence of God—see my p. 175 n. 1.) 'Promise-keeping is always obligatory. But an action is obligatory if and only if it conduces to the perfection of the universe—what Kant calls the *summum bonum*. It is more probable that promise-keeping will conduce to the *summum bonum* if there is a God than if there is not. (This, it may be urged, is because keeping secret promises to dying men would be pointless if there is no life after death, in which the promises can have the benefits of the promise being kept; and it is more probable that there is life after death if there is a God than if there is not.) Therefore the obligatoriness of promise-keeping confirms the existence of God.' This argument is valid, but its first and third premisses are highly questionable. Some will deny the first premiss—that promise-keeping is always obligatory. Others will deny the third premiss—that it is more probable that promise-keeping will conduce to the *summum bonum*, if there is a God than if there is not. For they would say that the very act of promise-keeping as such contributes to the *summum bonum*, and any consequences are irrelevant. A moralist of a teleological viewpoint will tend to deny the first premiss, and ones similar to it; and a moralist of a deontological viewpoint will tend to deny the third premiss and ones similar to it. What goes for the particular argument which I stated is liable to go for similar arguments (e.g. ones which appeal in their

---

[1] The argument could be varied in various ways such as making the step from *a*, *b*, *c*, *d*, being obligatory to their being *Q*, *R*, *S*, *T*, a mere probabilistic one, and making the next step a deductive one.

first premiss to the invariable wrongness of lying). Now of course both the first and third premisses could be true even though most people have an initial inclination to deny one or the other. But to get the moral argument off the ground you would need arguments to show the first and third premisses to be true. As it stands, the argument is not a good argument (for the reason that the premisses are not accepted by disputing parties). I am too pessimistic about the prospects to devote more time to attempting to supplement the argument by producing good arguments to support its premisses. One reason for this is that I cannot see how anyone who holds one of the first and third premisses but not the other is going to be persuaded by a process of rational argument to hold the other, unless he is *first* persuaded by some other argument that there is a God. For this reason I cannot see any force in an argument to the existence of God from the existence of morality.

The religious believer of course considers the voice of conscience to be the voice of God. In running down the argument from the fact of morality, and not being very enthusiastic about the argument from man's moral consciousness, I am not arguing that this conviction is unjustified. The religious belief that the voice of conscience is the voice of God is true if it is true that God has brought about man's moral consciousness. The latter will be true either if God does this on each occasion on which a man becomes conscious of moral truths, or if God makes to operate the natural laws by which man comes to know moral truths. My only point here is that man's moral knowledge does not wear its source on its face. We need other grounds for supposing that there is a God who brings about most things in the world in order to infer that he is the source of our moral knowledge, and so to conclude that the voice of conscience is the voice of God.

10

The Argument from Providence

I ARGUED in the last chapter that God has reason for creating animals and men, especially if the latter have free will. The nature of animals and men in their enjoying the world, having knowledge of it and power over it, power by which, if men have free will, they can begin to mould it themselves, etc., is such as a God has reason to make. If his free will is limited, then man has the possibility of moral choice, of choosing to do good or evil, and to grow into a good or evil person. A being with such a nature God has reason to make. I did not however, argue there that he has more reason for bringing about a world containing men and animals than a world without them, and that for that reason their existence was evidence of his. I argued only that the existence of men and animals was very unlikely to have come about by natural processes, and that for that reason their existence was evidence of his. In this chapter I turn to further general features of the nature and the circumstances of conscious beings, and to investigate which ones God has reason to make. In particular we shall need to inquire whether the general circumstances of the world are such as to show that a good God is providing for the basic needs of men and animals, i.e. whether the world is a providential place. I emphasize that in this chapter I shall continue to be concerned with *general* features of the world; they are pervasive features, but ones not always present on all occasions for all agents.

I shall not wish to deny that, given an orderly universe and the existence of conscious beings, the further features which I shall be discussing originate from the operation of scientific laws on pre-existing states. However, what cannot be given scientific explanation is why there are those particular laws, why the laws of nature are such as to produce these features of the universe. If there are to be laws of nature, the ones in question are no less likely to operate than any others, unless God is responsible for their operation. My argument here, however, will be (in contrast to the argument of the last chapter) that the sort of world to which they give rise is the sort of world he has more reason to make than other worlds, and so that there are grounds for supposing that he is responsible for their operation, and so that he has made this world. With k as the existence of an orderly universe (i.e. the existence of some laws of nature) and of conscious beings, h as 'there is a God' and e as the particular laws of nature which give rise to the features of the world to which I shall draw attention in this chapter, I shall claim that $P(e/h.k) > P(e/k)$ because of the character of God, but not because e are especially unlikely to be among the laws of nature, if there are laws of nature and conscious beings. However, many of the features of the natures and circumstances of conscious beings which I shall claim to be good ones do have their disadvantages, and I do not wish to claim that a God has overriding reason for giving these features to conscious beings. Nevertheless, I argue that a God has overriding reason not to bring about various alternative worlds (in which conscious beings had different natures and circumstances) which, if there were no God, would be no less likely to occur than our world, and so the existence of our world is evidence of his existence. I shall confine my argument during the chapter to the case of men, but point out at the end of the chapter that it applies to a lesser extent to animals, i.e. that a God has reason to give to animals some of the features of the nature and circumstances of conscious beings, which I discuss.

I argued in the last chapter that God has reason for making agents with the possibility of non-predetermined choice between good and evil, a choice between actions which they see to be morally good and so over all better than alternative actions, to do which they have felt desire. God could have made the world so that such choices were not of great moment, or so that they were of great moment. Clearly if it is good that agents should have a choice, it is good that they should have a significant choice, an opportunity to choose between important goods and evils and so significantly to influence the way things happen in the world.

Man's Opportunity to Provide for Himself

The first kind of influence which an agent can have is on his own future, on whether he continues to exist, and whether his future life is one of worthwhile pleasure, or lower pleasure, or even pain. Hence beings need opportunities to continue their own existence (e.g. by escaping from prey, walking in safe places, eating, drinking, caring for health), or to curtail that existence (e.g. by neglecting sustenance and health, courting danger, or even committing suicide). By and large the world is in this way an abundantly providential place, for it is full of such opportunities—even if sometimes the only opportunity before a man is the opportunity of continuing to work at a hard task or lying down to die. As we saw in the last chapter, it is good that agents should have felt desires for some of these things which are lesser goods—e.g. immediate pleasurable sensations as opposed to long-term safety. Further, it is good that agents should have the opportunity to choose whether to grow in knowledge of the world, and in knowledge of which things in it are for their benefit or harm, or whether to neglect such opportunity. But if they are to have that opportunity, they must start by being in ignorance about the consequences for themselves for good or ill of many of their actions.

In so far as the knowledge of agents is limited in this respect, they will inevitably often do actions which if continued or repeated will have disastrous long-term consequences—and they will do these actions simply because they are unaware of these consequences. In so far as these consequences would be disastrous for themselves or others, it is good that they should be deterred from doing the actions—to some extent and until they have time to discover the consequences. Further, in so far as the freedom of agents is limited, they will sometimes give in to felt desires when they know that they ought not to. They will do actions which if continued or repeated, will have known disastrous consequences. What will a God do when he sees his creatures giving in to felt desire when they ought not to, taking the wrong path?

In considering what a God will do when he sees creatures knowingly or unknowingly taking steps which lead to disaster, we have an obvious analogy in the case of the human parent in relation to his children. In the case of some of their actions children, especially very young children, are often quite unable to understand the consequences, even if the parent tells them—the consequences, for example, of swallowing Mother's pills or running into the road after a ball. And in the case of other actions although a child may understand the consequences, his will may be weak—he may give in to felt desire, not take his medicine or clean his teeth, through sloth.

What does the good parent do in these situations? With regard to the first, the parent ties a child's action to less disastrous consequences which he can understand—by giving or threatening a punishment of a comprehensible kind. ('If you run into the road, I will beat you.') With regard to the second, the parent is inevitably torn. He is anxious for his children to grow up to have increasing freedom to choose their own lives and work out what is best for themselves. Too much interference, especially as a child grows older, would be bad. Yet the parent is aware that the child's will is weak, especially when the child is young. He wishes to encourage him to do what is right, but not to force him. Hence he will to a limited extent reinforce the child's will with rewards and punishments. A good parent steers the middle course between leaving everything to the child on the one hand and on the other hand dictating what the child is to do. Analogy suggests that a good God will behave like a good parent. He will provide easily comprehensible deterrents of a less disastrous kind. If an action persisted in has bad consequences of which an agent is ignorant, God will give him more immediate reason for desisting from the action. Likewise if an action has put an agent in a state where it is bad that he should remain, God will give him immediate reason for getting out. Or if the repetition of the action is what will cause harm it is to that that God will provide a deterrent. And in so far as the agent's will is weak and reason does not immediately influence him, he will make it to some extent 'natural' for the agent to do what is right. All this will involve giving to the agent a felt desire to stop doing the action, or get out of the situation, or not to repeat the action. (Recall that by a felt desire I understand one which it needs an act of will to resist.)

A felt desire not to do an action or be in a situation I shall call an aversion. Aversions inevitably bring with them suffering. This is most apparent where the aversion is to continuing to do an action which a man is currently doing or to continuing to be in a situation. For you would not have a felt desire to stop doing an action or get out of a situation unless you found doing that action or being in that situation unpleasant. A man may find his action or situation unpleasant for various reasons. One may be that it gives rise to painful sensations. Pains are sensations of a certain kind which when we experience them in an acute form are unpleasant.[1] There

---

[1] I owe this account of the nature of pain to R. M. Hare, 'Pain and Evil', *Proceedings of the Aristotelian Society, Suppl. Vol.*, 1964, **38**, 91–106. Reprinted in J. Feinberg (ed.), *Moral Concepts* (London, 1969).

are, however, unpleasant sensations other than pains, for example the sensation of sweltering heat. And although all pains are unpleasant sensations, they are sensations of a kind which when experienced to a lesser intensity are not necessarily unpleasant—an acute ache may be unpleasant and thus painful, but a mild ache may not necessarily be unpleasant. So pains are simply sensations of a certain kind felt acutely enough to be found unpleasant. And situations may be unpleasant for reasons quite other than that they give rise to unpleasant sensations, e.g. they may be embarrassing; and the unpleasantness may be much greater in these cases. There is no special problem of pain for the theist. The problem is the problem of agents having experiences which they find acutely unpleasant—pain is only a special case of this.

An aversion to repeating an action or being again in a situation will, however, if it is to be strong and justified, also involve the occurrence of past suffering. For a felt desire not to repeat an action involves believing that the repetition of the action will be unpleasant. One could acquire that belief, and so the desire by ways other than finding the first performance of the action unpleasant. However, finding the first performance unpleasant is clearly one way of acquiring the belief that repetition will be unpleasant. I shall argue in the next chapter that past experience gives the most sure knowledge of future experience, and hence will provide the strongest and best justified felt desire. Clearly it is good that men should act on justified beliefs, not merely react instinctively. In that case it will follow that in so far as strong felt desires not to repeat actions are necessary, unpleasant sensations need to accompany the first performance.

Our world is of course full of such felt deterrents to action. Most actions, persistence in which would cause physiological damage, are painful. It is painful to push your hand against a needle. Most situations, to remain in which would be physiologically damaging for an agent, give him a felt desire to go. An agent who finds himself in a burning room finds it very painful to stay there, and an agent who finds himself in a room full of poisonous gas often finds the experience very unpleasant. There are plenty of deterrents too to repeating actions which would be damaging if repeated often—e.g. the pain which you get by swallowing boiling tea is a powerful deterrent to doing it again. Such felt desires are in the main deterrents to actions which would be physiologically damaging or lead to premature death; such desires and the pains which go with them I will term biologically useful desires and pains.

In their task of keeping men (and animals) from what is harmful, pains and other unpleasant sensations are backed up by emotions such as fear and dread. There is a natural fear of the unknown, of heights and depths, which preserves men from death and hurt; as well as acquired fear which attaches to situations of known danger.

In a world without such deterrent sensations and emotions, either people would harm themselves without warning very easily, or the world would be so cushioned that they could not harm themselves or they would be so made that they had no possibility of harming themselves inadvertently and no temptation to allow themselves to be harmed. A world of the first kind would in this respect be a bad one. A world of the second kind would be one in which man had little power over his future; and a world of the third kind would be a world in which man was born with perfect knowledge of the consequences for himself of his actions and no temptations to pursue lesser goods. Hence it would be a world in which perfect knowledge of a kind and good character were foisted upon men and men did not choose whether or not to have them. A world with deterrent sensations and emotions has a lot to be said for it.

In that the freedom and knowledge of agents is limited, not merely will they often do actions which if continued or repeated will have disastrous consequences, but they will fail to do actions necessary for their well-being. Here too there is need of felt desire to do actions whose consequences are unappreciated, and to do actions where there are competing desires to do other actions. These too I shall term biologically useful desires—desires for food, drink, and sleep are obviously biologically useful desires. But felt desires of any strength to perform actions and be in situations are also going to involve suffering. For a desire to do something involves thinking of your state of not doing it as unpleasant. The man with a strong desire to drink suffers from his present thirst; and the heroin addict suffers until he takes his heroin. (If his desire is not a strong one, the agent may still find his present situation pleasant for other reasons.)

So, I have been arguing, strong felt desires are needed to get men out of trouble when through ignorance or abuse of their freedom, they fall into trouble or are in danger of doing so. Yet it is a good thing for men to have a temporary ignorance, so that acquisition of knowledge is through their own choice; and a good thing for men to have imperfect freedom, since this puts a choice of destiny, good or bad, within their hands. True, I am suggesting both that it is a good thing that they should have a felt desire to do what is sometimes not for their good (e.g. drink a lot of alcohol) and that it is a good thing that they should have a felt desire when the former is indugled not to do it again (e.g. a desire produced by a desire to avoid a repetition of the hangover). The first is necessary in order to have a situation of temptation at all. The second is necessary to prevent things getting out of hand too quickly, to give men a second chance. The argument is that a situation of temptation with second chances is better than a situation of temptation without second chances, and there is reason for having situations of temptation. In our world temptation normally arises through a felt desire for a good which under different circumstances it would be right to pursue, but which under the particular circumstances of its occurrence there is overriding reason not to pursue. For example, the desire for alcohol is normally a good one, but there is overriding reason not to give in to it if you have already drunk too much.

I am not arguing that a God ought *always* to provide felt desires to avoid all known disasters. For if he did and was known to do so, then a human agent would know that any action would not have disastrous consequences until after he had persisted in it contrary to a strong felt desire not to do so. In that case he would have far less reason to seek knowledge of the consequences of his actions; and no opportunity to choose between desire and reason, to choose to do something contrary to a felt desire merely because there was overriding reason for doing so. For there would not be overriding reason for not doing an action which was not backed up by desire. And it is good that men should have opportunity to choose whether to act on reason or not, and not always be over-influenced in their choices by desire. Similarily, when arguing that a God might well provide second chances, I am certainly not arguing that he might well provide endless chances. One might say: if a situation of temptation with second chances is better than one with no second chances, would not situations of temptation with third, fourth, and fifth chances be even better? Sometimes, perhaps. So why not a situation of temptation with infinite chances? No. A situation of temptation with infinite chances is no situation of temptation at all. If there is *always* another chance, there is no risk. There would not be overriding reason not to do the bad act, if you are always preserved from its consequences. You do not have a choice of destiny here. If you cannot damn yourself however hard you go on trying, your salvation is inevitable—and it is not you who have chosen it. A God who wishes that all men shall be saved is a good God. But a God who makes all men to be saved is a being of more dubious moral status.

As we have seen, a strong felt desire to stop doing an action or to be out of a situation involves finding the action or situation highly unpleasant, e.g. painful. Since there is reason for a God to make a world with such felt desires, there is in this respect reason of biological or psychological utility for him to create a world containing suffering. (We shall consider other reasons why he might create a world containing suffering of this and other kinds in due course.)

Man's Opportunity to Provide for Others

So far, I have been talking about individual agents, and the desirability of their having control of their own destiny. I have been considering them as though each lived like Robinson Crusoe on his own island. But in our world of course things are not like that. Men are interdependent to an enormous degree.

The very birth of a man is due to a combined act of a man and a woman. In his infancy and childhood man depends very largely for his existence and health, for his knowledge of the world, and for encouragement to develop his character, on parents and others, including doctors and teachers. We have not only (in so far as we can see) choice of our own destiny, but also evidently responsibility for others. Does a God have reason for making a world in which men have responsibility for the well-being of each other?

Fairly evidently, to some extent yes. A world in which good things can only be attained by co-operation is one which a God has reason to make—for benefiting each other is a good thing. We are in a position to benefit each other if something which is for our well-being is attained more easily or only at all if we co-operate in a common task. Our world is clearly arranged so that men working together can bring about goals which working separately they cannot. Conception is impossible, giving birth difficult, and rearing children none too easy without co-operation between parents. If society is organized so that there is specialization of labour (one man is carpenter, one is mason, one is potter, one is farmer, and so on), a decent standard of living is reached for all which would be difficult if not impossible to attain if each man did all the jobs for himself. And of course building aeroplanes, cyclotrons, and radio-telescopes, and sending men to the moon are quite impossible without co-operation. Of course co-operation can be abused in the assembly line which gives to no man a demanding task, but that does not alter the fact that in general co-operation gets better results, and it is a good thing that the world should be constructed so that it should. If it is so constructed, then it will be so made that felt desires for food, drink, etc. can often not be immediately satisfied, but can only be satisfied in the long term as a result of co-operation; and that means some suffering until they can be satisfied. Our world of course is like this.

All that I have suggested so far is that it is good that the world should be one in which A can benefit B, and B can also benefit A if they agree to work together. In such a world, however, working for others will always have its reward for the agent. Dependence can go a lot further than that. We can for example have a situation where A can benefit B but B can confer no benefit on A, although he can benefit C. Is a world with the opportunity for unrequited benefit a good thing? Surely yes, for in such a world an agent has the opportunity to share in the work of a creator himself in benefiting others without reward. Our world has plenty of opportunity for such benefit. One obvious case is provided by the parent/child relationship. We can give material goods to our children. They can give very little such to us. Yet they in their turn can give good things to their own children.

It is a good thing too not merely that agents should need to co-operate with each other, but that they should enjoy doing so, and more generally that they should get pleasure both from companion-ship and from collaboration in work with others. Once again, our world is one in which there is plenty of such pleasure. Indeed it is one in which creatures have a variety of needs for collaboration and company, and a variety of kinds of pleasure from the satisfaction of these needs. There is the need for a parent, for a child, for a permanent mate, for a friend, for a casual acquaintance, for a colleague with whom to collaborate in working hours on a common project. The world is such that collaboration and companionship of such varied kinds is useful, gives pleasure, and is wanted for its own sake. It is good too that the world should be such that there is the opportunity for a kind of co-operation between many men over many generations to build up human knowledge and extend human power. This co-operation in the acquisition of knowledge has some-times been going on for many generations—sometimes generations of investigators (especially scientists) have helped each other forward, and worked consciously in order to add their bit to the corpus of knowledge. Yet men seem only to be beginning to take the opportunities which exist for co-operation for long-term practical ends. Planning of towns and schools and populations so as to provide for the welfare of generations long distant is not something to which politicians have so far given very much attention. But as knowledge and power increase, so the opportunity for such planning increases radically.

But, as well as being good that men should have the opportunity to benefit each other, is it good that they should have the opportunity to harm each other? I believe that it is. A God has the power to benefit or to harm. If other agents are to be given a share in his creative work, they must have that power too (although perhaps to a lesser degree). A world in which agents can benefit each other but not do each other harm is one where they have only very limited responsibility for each other. If my responsibility for you is limited to whether or not to give you a television set, but I cannot make you unhappy, stunt your growth, or limit your education, then I do not have a great deal of responsibility for you. Of course the distinction between harming and failing to benefit is by no means a very clear one. It seems to presuppose some natural standard of well-being; if I add to this, I confer benefit, and if I subtract from it, I confer harm. But in that case if I cannot harm you, you will be moderately all right whatever I do. Your well-being will not then depend greatly on me. God has reason for going beyond that. A God who gave agents only such limited responsibility for their fellows would not have given much. He would be like a father asking his elder son to look after the younger son, and adding that he would be watching the elder son's every move and would intervene the moment the elder son did a thing wrong. The elder son might justly retort that while he would be happy to share in his father's work, he could only really do so if he was left to make his own judgements as to what to do within a significant range of the options available to the father. A good God, like a good father, will delegate responsibility. In order to allow creatures a share in creation, he will allow them the choice of hurting and maiming, of frustrating the divine plan. Our world is of course one where creatures have just such deep responsibility for each other. I can not only benefit, but harm my children. One way in which I can harm them is that I can inflict physical pain on them. But there are much more damaging things which I can do to them.

I can deprive them of adequate food, of play, and, above all, of affection. They are made so as to need certain things for their well-being. If God has made me, he has given me the opportunity to deprive them of what they badly need.

One crucial way in which one agent B may depend on another A is that whether and how B grows in freedom, power, and knowledge, depends on A; and if A is to have a very deep responsibility for B, he will have that sort of responsibility. That allows A to stunt B's growth in freedom and power, give him false belief instead of knowledge, and generally make him retarded or lead him to wickedness. One may of course feel that it is a very good thing that I should have such responsibility for my children, but a very bad thing that they should have their well-being entrusted to me. Yet although the latter may be bad, it can be compensated by giving my children in their turn the responsibility for bringing up their own children.

An obvious way in which a God can give to agents the opportunity to harm or benefit each other in the long run is to produce a world which is such that agents know that if they do nothing about it, it will be in future in some ways a bad world (e.g. containing disease and inadequate food), and allowing agents the choice of co-operating to bring about a better world or of leaving it as it is. Giving to agents a felt desire to do nothing (i.e. laziness) and yet overriding reason for co-operating for mutual benefit, God would put them in a situation of temptation such as we saw necessary to give them moral choice. As I shall argue in the next chapter, the most sure knowledge that the world will be in a bad state can be provided by giving agents experience of similar bad states emerging from states like the present states if agents do nothing about it—e.g. by making the world in a bad state and by giving agents experience that such states continue unless they do something about them. Our world is one which, but for man's co-operative effort, has been in some ways a bad world, and but for man's continuing co-operative effort will remain thus. Yet it is a world in which A's pain gives reason for B's research which in co-operation with C, using money provided by D, leads to discovery of the cause of the pain which E then produces a drug to relieve, with money provided by F.

So then a God has reason for creating a world in which humanly free agents have deep responsibility for each other—provided by the opportunity to harm each other in various ways, e.g. by curtailing each other's knowledge, freedom, and power, and the opportunity to benefit each other in converse ways. In so far as he has knowledge, an agent will know that he has reason to benefit his fellows; and in so far as he has freedom (in so far as felt desires do not make him do what is wrong), he will seek to benefit those fellows. But his knowledge and freedom may be small. We saw earlier that it is no bad thing that agents should have felt desires to do what is right to counteract desires to do what is wrong with respect to themselves (e.g. the desire not to have the hangover which alcohol produces to counter the desire to drink the alcohol). This is useful in a situation where creatures do not know what is right or are of feeble will-power (and there is reason why a God should put them in that position). The same considerations apply with regard to a man's actions which concern others. It is good that men should have felt desires for the well-being of others; that there should be a natural love of parent for child, man for woman, fellow for fellow. Such a concern for well-being is of course not merely useful, but good in itself. Felt desires for the well-being of others will include felt desires to remove suffering, i.e. sympathetic concern. This concern may lead to long-term co-operation to remove the suffering. In the example given in the previous paragraph, *B*, *C*, *D*, *E*, and *F* may all have sympathetic concern for *A*.

However, there is point in such desires not occurring inevitably in certain circumstances, beyond the ability of man to control. As before, agents should have the opportunity to do what is right, without the help of desire. Further of course (and a similar point applies to self-interested desires), if desires are not automatic, they can be cultivated or repressed; and that gives agents one more kind of control over their own destiny and that of their fellows. Our world is of course one in which such control is possible. Love which comes naturally in some circumstances can be encouraged or inhibited. We can cultivate love for a child by doing things with it, or inhibit affection for a woman by avoiding her and consorting with other women instead. (Such methods are not of course infallible, but they often work. We do have limited control over such desires.)

Desires for specific ends are helped by more general emotions of affection and sympathy. And as we can cultivate good emotions, so we can cultivate bad ones, such as envy and jealousy—one more aspect of our control of our destiny. Yet some bad emotions come to us passively without our having much to do with them. They are just another aspect of our situation of temptation, having felt desires for lesser goods, necessary if we are to choose whether we are to be moral beings. Many emotions which have a natural expression in action may be good or bad according to circumstance—anger and resentment may facilitate justice or promote self-interest. Once again they provide us with a situation of temptation and an opportunity to direct the emotions for good or ill.

Because of the opportunities which others have for harming us (as well as for other reasons to which I will come in the next chapter), inevitably things may go badly wrong with us. Our plans may fail, our beloved may be taken from us by circumstances or by some other agent. How will a God arrange for us to react to such misfortune? He could of course make us turn our minds straight away to other things, make us have no feeling about things going wrong. But surely the world is better if agents pay proper tribute to losses and failures, if they are sad at the failure of their endeavours, mourn for the death of a child, are angry at the seduction of a wife, and so on. Such emotions involve suffering and anguish, but in having such proper feelings a man shows his respect for himself and others. A man who feels no grief at the death of his child or the seduction of his wife is rightly branded by us as insensitive, for he has failed to pay the proper tribute of feeling to others, to show in his feeling how much he values them, and thereby failed to value them properly—for valuing them properly involves having proper reactions of feeling to their loss. Also, only a world in which men feel sympathy for losses experienced by their friends, is a world in which love has full meaning. Once again a God would not necessarily make the expression of such emotions inevitable. It would be good if we have the opportunity to cultivate or repress them. Other emotions which are in place are emotions of regret and penitence at our wrong actions; emotions also which it would be good if agents have the opportunity to cultivate or repress.

I have been arguing for the last few pages that a God would have reason to make a world in which agents have the opportunity to benefit or harm each other and other creatures, and also to mould the inanimate world. There are a variety of different possible worlds, according to the time-scale and nature of the mutual dependence involved. First you could have what I shall call a world—I. Here there would be an unchanging set of immortal humanly free agents. The world and its inhabitants would have their evils and imperfections, but the world would be perfectible by the co-operation of agents within a finite time. By the world being perfectible I mean that all evils would be removable and the world and society could be brought to a very happy and beautiful state such that no effort of agents could make it more beautiful. For the rest of eternity all they would need to do would be to keep it ticking over. There would be reason for God to make such a world—the happiness of agents is a good thing and each agent (after enduring a little) would be able to attain it in such a world. But the trouble with such a world is that after a finite time agents would have nothing demanding to do. Although they could always tinker with the world, it would (once their initial labours were completed) as a result of the tinkering be no better a world than it was before; and having attained much knowledge, agents would realize this. For this reason God seems to me to have more reason to make what I shall call a world—II. Here once again there is an unchanging set of immortal humanly free agents, but in this case there is an infinite number of such agents, and there would be no limit to the extent to which they could go on improving each other and their world. There would be an infinite amount of world and of agents to improve, infinite knowledge and freedom to acquire; and all this in World—II would need an infinite time. However by the very description of World—II, one good thing would be barred to agents—giving birth to new agents and forming them from scratch. Clearly it is good that agents should have such power. In what I call a World—III the number of immortal agents can be increased through the activity of existing agents. If a God has reason to make a World—II, he has, *a fortiori*, reason to make a World—III.

Birth is fine, but what about death? Does a God have reason to make a world in which either by natural causes or by the action of agents, there is death? I believe that he does have a number of reasons to make mortal agents. The first is that if all agents are immortal, there is a certain harm (of a qualitatively different kind to other harms) which agents cannot do either to themselves or to others—they cannot deprive of existence. However much I may hate you or myself, I am stuck with you and me. And in this vital respect humanly free agents would not share the creative power of God. In refusing them this power, a God would refuse to trust his creatures in a crucial respect. To let a man have a gun is always a mark of profound trust. Secondly, a world without death is a world without the possibility of supreme self-sacrifice and courage in the face of absolute disaster. The ultimate sacrifice is the sacrifice of oneself, and that would not be possible in a world without death. ('Greater love hath no man than this, that a man lay down his life for his friends.') Supreme generosity would be impossible. So too would cheerfulness and patience in the face of absolute disaster. For in a world without death the alternatives would always involve continuance of life and presumably too the possibility that others would rescue one from one's misfortunes. There would be no absolute disaster to be faced with cheerfulness and patience.

Thirdly, a world with natural death would be a world in which an agent's own contribution would have a seriousness about it because it would be irreversible by the agent. If I spent all my seventy years doing harm, there is no time left for me to undo it. But if I live for ever, then whatever harm I do, I can always undo it. It is good that what people do should matter, and their actions matter more if they have only a limited time in which to reverse them. Fourthly, a world with birth but without natural death would be a world in which the young would never have a free hand. They would always be inhibited by the experience and influence of the aged.

The greatest value of death however seems to me to lie in a fifth consideration which is in a way opposite to my second one. I wrote earlier of the great value which lies in agents having the power to harm each other. Only agents who can do this have real power. Yet it may seem, despite the arguments which I gave earlier, unfair that creatures should be too much subject to other agents. Clearly for the sake of the potential sufferer, there must be *a* limit to the suffering which an agent can inflict on another. It would, I believe that we would all judge, be morally wrong for a very powerful being to give *limitless* power to one agent to hurt another. Giving to agents the power to kill is giving vast power of a qualitatively different kind from other power; but it involves the end of experience. It is very different from a power to produce endless suffering. Clearly the parent analogy suggests that it would be morally wrong to give limitless power to cause suffering. A parent, believing that an elder son ought to have responsibility, may give him power for good or ill over the younger son. But a good parent will intervene eventually if the younger son suffers too much—for the sake of the younger son. A God who did not put a limit to the amount of suffering which a creature can suffer (for any good cause, including that of the responsibility of agents) would not be a good God. There need to be limits to the intensity of suffering and to the period of suffering. A natural death after a certain small finite number of years provides the limit to the period of suffering. It is a boundary to the power of an agent over another agent. For death removes agents from that society of interdependent agents in which it is good that they should play their part. True, a God could make a temporal limit to the harm which agents could do to each other without removing them from each other's society. But that would involve agents being in mutual relation with each other while being immunized from each other's power for good or ill—and that arrangement has its own disadvantages in that the deep mutual interdependence of creatures would not hold there.

I conclude that God would have reason to make what I shall call a World—IV. In a World—IV agents are born and die and during their life give birth, partly through their own choice, to other agents. They can make a difference to the world; but there is endless scope for improvement to it, and each generation can only forward or retard its well-being a little. Agents can make each other happy or unhappy, and can increase or decrease each other's power, knowledge, and freedom. Thereby they can affect the happiness and morality of generations distant in time. Our world is clearly a World—IV. A God has reason for making such a world.

In it there is the possibility of agents damaging each other over a number of generations until they fall badly down the ladder of ascent to divinity. Such a fall is described in a pictorial form in Genesis 3. Many modern commentators seem to me to have missed the point of this story. The point is not just that we are in a mess (of course we are), but that many of us are in a mess which is not largely of our making but which is due to others, our ancestors (and that is of course also fairly evidently so). Many, perhaps all, of the tragic situations—the hatreds and the violence—in the world today result largely from the choices of generations long past—Ireland, South Africa, the Iron Curtain, and so on. And those bad choices of centuries ago themselves were partly facilitated by bad choices of centuries before that, and so on until we reach back close to the early morally conscious choices of man.

But also in a World—IV there is the possibility of man's gradual ascent up the evolutionary scale, of man gradually developing his moral and religious awareness, and of each generation handing on to the next some new facet of that awareness. Man may grow in understanding moral truths and in applying them to the care of the less fortunate; he may grow in sensitivity to aesthetic beauty and in the creation and appreciation of works of art; in the acquisition of scientific knowledge and in its application to the betterment of the human condition and to the exploration and comprehension of the universe.

Although a God would have reason to make a World—IV, such a world is obviously a very unsatisfactory one in the crucial respect that lives capable of flourishing happily for years to come, if not for ever, are cut short, deprived of future experiences and choices. God would have reason to intervene in the process to preserve in existence in some other part of this world agents who cease to exist in our part (and of course Christian theism claims that he has so intervened). But if the advantages of a world with death are to remain, the mutual interdependence in this world must cease after a finite period (to give a limit to the suffering allowed herein) and the future existence must in no way be foreknown for certain by agents (else there would be no opportunity in our part of the world for choices of great seriousness). If God did intervene in this way, our part of the world would still be, as far as appears to its inhabitants, much like a World—IV.

The Place of Animals

So far, this chapter has been concerned with the nature and circumstances which a God would have reason to give to humanly free agents. However, I suggested in the last chapter that God would have reason also to create conscious beings unburdened with the mixed blessing of free will, i.e. animals. I suggested that it was good that there should be beings who learn what is to their good and harm and seek the good and avoid the harm, and through doing so enjoy the world and have pleasurable sensations. The results of this chapter about the natures which God would have reason to give to men and the circumstances in which he would have reason to place them have limited application to animals. As they lack free will, God would have reason to give to them less responsibility, and hence less power and knowledge than he would given to men. For a substantial reason for giving great responsibility, and with it the power and knowledge of how to produce great evil, to men, was that they were not predetermined in their choices but were independent sources of how the world was to be. Since animals lack free will, they must not be given such power for evil; and in our world we find that they do not have such power. Animals can hurt and kill other animals, but they cannot indulge in genocide or atomic warfare, in giving perjured evidence in court or breaking solemn undertakings, in unjust imprisonment of their fellows for long periods, or in the subtler forms of torturing or humiliating their fellows. There are however, reasons which I shall discuss in the next chapter for giving animals limited power to hurt. One is the higher-order virtues which it allows them to exercise. Another is in terms of the knowledge which it gives to other animals and to men of how to avoid hurt. I shall argue in the next chapter that sure knowledge of how hurt is to be avoided can only be obtained by experience of the circumstances in which it occurs. With that knowledge, and with that alone, animals can do many of the things which we saw in this chapter it is good that they should be able to do—preserve themselves and their offspring, and perhaps others of their species also, from harm. The tiger, like the drought, provides the gazelle with one of its many opportunities to use its power for good ends—for its own benefit and that of its offspring—by escaping from it and helping its offspring to escape from it.

In general, God has reason for giving to animals some power and knowledge, with opportunity to use it for good ends—for their own benefit and for that of others, and knowledge of how to do this. Clearly animals are in this position. Like humans, they have the opportunity to continue their existence by escaping from prey, walking in safe places, eating, drinking, and caring for health. Lacking free will, they cannot choose whether to pursue these ends. Hence if they are to do so they must be given the desires to do so, including the desires to get out of circumstances fatal to their well-being—and that means, as we saw earlier, biologically useful pain. Animals, like humans, also have the opportunity to care for others, notably their offspring, spouses, and to a lesser extent members of their own species. The care of offspring is a very central activity in the lives of animals. Again, since they lack free will, they cannot choose whether to pursue these ends, but they must be given the desire to do so. And of course, they are in general abundantly blessed with the parental instinct.

God could have put animals in a separate world from ourselves, or he could have put them in our world and given them as an additional responsibility to men. For hundreds of millions of years there were on earth animals and no men. But latterly there have been both. There is a clear risk in having both belong to the same world—that man will abuse animals, causing them much suffering or sorrow. But there are advantages. For both men and animals there is opportunity for responsibility and a new kind of co-operation and friendship. The horse, for example, has the opportunity to do interesting work together with man that he could not do apart from him, and friendship with a different kind of being. In return man has a helper and a friend. In seeing how much the welfare of animals now depends on him, man has come to realize that animals are his responsibility. (The doctrine of Genesis 1: 28 is that God gave to man this responsibility.)

Conclusion

So then I have argued in this chapter that a God has reason to make (and so there is some probability that he will make) a world containing animals, and also humanly free agents, subject to temptation, and yet also to biologically useful felt desires—desires to avoid actions and situations which are damaging to oneself and to others. The world would be one in which agents were greatly interdependent, one in which they were born and died, were able to increase each other's power, knowledge, and freedom, to make each other happy or unhappy, and to influence in this way distant generations; a world too in which there are natural emotions, which agents can cultivate or repress. Our world is like this. It is providential in giving normally to man (and animals) the opportunity to satisfy their own biological needs for food, drink, safety, etc.; and providential in giving to man (and animals) the opportunity to satisfy the biological and psychological needs of other men and of animals, and so to satisfy their own psychological needs for co-operation, friendship, etc. The very general features of men's nature and circumstances described in this chapter are such as a God has reason for making, and so there is some reason for supposing that he made them.

There are however many other worlds, which if there were no God, would be as likely to come into existence as this one, characterized by very different general features. To take crucial examples, the world might have been one in which the laws of nature were such that there evolved rational agents like men or animals lacking perfect freedom and knowledge, but with the power to hurt each other for endless time or to an infinite intensity. Surely a good God who created men and animals would not allow others to do such hurt to them for whatever good purpose; he would have overriding reason not to allow this. (Of course our judgements on what God would or would not have reason to do are highly fallible, but as I argued on p. 111, we do have some right to pronounce on these matters and we must make our judgements on what seems to be the case.) It follows that the existence of our world rather than of these other worlds, the existence of which is incompatible with the existence of God, which would be equally likely with ours to occur if there is no God, is evidence that God made our world.

The argument of this chapter has however in three places (pp. 184, 190, and 197) depended on a claim about sure knowledge of how evils are to be avoided coming only from experience of those evils. That claim must be justified. Also of course there is pain and suffering in the world other than that which can be explained in the way outlined in this chapter. Although much of the evil in the world is either man-made or of obvious biological utility, not all of it is. There is pain which is not man-made and has no evident useful deterrent effect—such as much of the pain of incurable disease. Also there are plenty of cases of pain which under normal circumstances could be justified along the lines of this chapter, but which still occur when those circumstances do not hold—e.g. the deterrent pain caused by fire which would normally lead a man to escape from the fire but which still occurs when a man is too weak or paralysed to do so. Would a God have reason for making a world which contains such pain, or does its existence count against his? I come to these issues in the next chapter. I shall argue there that the evils which we find in this world have a certain character, such that God has reason for bringing them about or allowing them to occur, and that others which we do not find do not have this character. This will allow me to take further the argument of the last paragraph in claiming that there are many other possible worlds than the ones which I mentioned there which to all appearances God has overriding reason not to make; and hence that the existence of our world is in its general pattern of good and evil stronger confirmatory evidence for the existence of God than the argument of this chapter alone shows.

11

The Problem of Evil

I HAVE been considering the question of the kinds of world which a God would have reason to make. I have urged that a God has reason to make worlds of many different kinds, but among them a world providential in the ways described in the last two chapters. In such a world, there will inevitably be evil. For there will inevitably be biologically useful unpleasant sensations, such as the pain which a man suffers until he escapes from a fire or the feeling of suffocation which he gets in a room full of poisonous gas, and unpleasant emotions such as fear and grief. Also, since men have the power to do each other significant hurt and they are not causally determined to do what they do, it is vastly probable that in such a world there will be a lot of further suffering, inflicted by men on each other. And there will also be the moral evil of men choosing to do what they believe to be wrong, in inflicting such suffering. In these ways evil comes with the good—it would be logically impossible for God to give certain benefits (e.g. of choice of destiny and responsibility) without the inevitability or at any rate enormous probability of various accompanying evils. I suggested in the last chapter that they were worth it. A good God would have reason to create a world in which there were men with a choice of destiny and responsibility for each other, despite the evils which would inevitably or almost inevitably be presented in it, for the sake of the good which it contained.

In so far as I was explaining the existence of evil in the world by God's gift to man of free will (which was my main explanation in the last chapter for the existence of evil) I was deploying what is known as 'the free will defence' to the problem of evil. The problem of evil is of course the problem of how if God, by definition omniscient, omnipotent, and perfectly good, made the world, there is evil in it.

It has often been claimed that the existence of evil provides a conclusive disproof of the existence of God. For, the atheist argues, if God exists, then being omniscient, he knows under what circumstances evil will occur, if he does not act; and being omnipotent, he is able to prevent its occurrence. Hence, being perfectly good, he will prevent its occurrence and so evil will not exist. Hence the existence of God entails the non-existence of evil; and so the existence of evil entails the non-existence of God. The theist normally attempts to rebut this argument by denying that necessarily a perfectly good being will prevent the occurrence of evil. The free will defence claims that a perfectly good God might well create free agents and allow them to harm each other. The other main defence which I deployed in the last chapter was the defence that a perfectly good God might well allow the occurrence of biologically useful pain—to encourage free agents to make right choices, without forcing them to do so.

There are however in our world other evils which do not seem to be accountable for so easily by the devices used in the last chapter. These are many of the natural evils (i.e. evils not brought about deliberately or knowingly allowed to occur by men; they may be either evils produced by natural processes which men do not know how to prevent, or evils produced accidentally by men). There is the pain of incurable disease, and the lengthy pain of much curable disease and injury, and some natural pain such as the pain of childbirth; and also much animal pain. It is the existence of natural evils of this kind which seem to me to constitute the most awkward part of 'the problem of evil'. Would a God have reason for making a world which contains such evils, or does their existence count against his?

Three Traditional Defences

As well as the free will defence, theism has had a number of traditional defences to the problem of evil.[1] I must comment briefly on three well-known but rather unsatisfactory ones. First there is the claim that much of the evil suffered by a man is God's punishment for his sins. Although this might account for some natural evil, it is clearly quite unable to account for the suffering of babies or animals. Secondly, there is the claim that God ties to the choices of men the well-being of other men, including later generations, and

[1] For the history of Christian theological reaction to the problem of evil see J. Hick, *Evil and the God of Love* (London, 1966).

also animals. In so far as men make immoral choices, God lets others suffer for it. This seems to be the view of Genesis 3: 16-20. One major difficulty is that if man does not believe that his actions have these effects (as perhaps normally he does not), there is no gain in this tie (viz. in the responsibility gained by free agents), to outweigh the resulting evil. In any case this defence cannot explain the suffering of animals long before men arrived on earth.

More substantial is the third defence, used by many theistic writers down the centuries,[1] that natural evils have been brought about by free agents other than men, viz. fallen angels. If there is reason, as I argued in the last chapter that there is, for allowing humanly free agents to hurt other agents, then there is reason for allowing free agents other than men to inflict such hurt. This move is an old one and it certainly saves the theist from a conclusive disproof of the existence of God. However, it still leaves an argument which counts against the existence of God—at any rate so long as there is no independent evidence of the existence of such fallen angels. For if the hypothesis that these angels exist and have power over nature is added to the hypothesis of theism to save it from falsification, then it has the status of an *ad hoc* hypothesis. An *ad hoc* hypothesis added to a theory complicates the theory and for that reason decreases its prior probability and so its posterior probability. So natural evil would decrease the probability that there is a God, disconfirm the theist's claim, if the fallen angel hypothesis were the only way of saving theism from falsification. (That is not to say that despite such disconfirmation, it may not on balance remain more probable than not.)

I conclude that use of the third defence would disconfirm theism, that there is a major difficulty in the second defence, and that the first defence is not adequate to deal with many natural evils. Theism must look elsewhere for a more adequate defence.

The Argument from the Need for Knowledge

I turn now to an argument that the existence of many natural evils of the kind described is logically necessary for the existence of a world of the type which I have already described. For they are necessary if agents are to have the *knowledge* of how to bring about evil or prevent its occurrence, knowledge which they must have if

---

[1] This defence has been used recently by, among others, Alvin Plantinga. See his *The Nature of Necessity* (Oxford, 1974), pp. 191 ff.

they are to have a genuine choice between bringing about evil and bringing about good.

How are agents to acquire knowledge—in particular the knowledge of which of their actions will have pleasant consequences and which will have unpleasant consequences for themselves or others, knowledge which they must have if there is to be a world of the kind which I have described? An agent's present evidence will allow him to infer to what will probably happen in future; his knowledge of what will happen in future will come from induction, but his evidence may be of one of two kinds. The normal evidence will be of patterns of similar events in the past allowing an inductive inference to how events will probably succeed each other in future. I shall call such inference normal inductive inference. The simplest case of normal inductive inference is where I infer that a present state of affairs C will be followed by a future state E, from the fact that in the past, states of affairs like C on all occasions of which I have knowledge have been followed by states like E. Because on the many occasions of which I have knowledge a piece of chalk being liberated from the hand has fallen to the floor, I can infer that the next time chalk is liberated it will fall. However normal induction may take a more complicated form. From a vast collection of data about the positions of planets a scientist may infer a consequence of a different kind, e.g. that there will be a very high tide on earth when the planets are in such-and-such positions. Here the data provide evidence for a complicated scientific theory of which the prediction about the high tide is a somewhat remote consequence; the similarities between the data and the prediction are more remote. (But the similarities exist and are the basis of the prediction. In the data and the prediction there are material bodies attracting each other.)

Whether the normal inductive inference is simple or complicated, certain general points can be made about the claim to knowledge of the future which results from it. The first is that the more past data there are, the better established is a claim to such knowledge. This is because the data confirm a claim about the future by confirming a theory or a simple universal (or statistical) generalization (e.g. 'states like C are always followed by states like E') which in turn licenses the claim about the future. The more data there are, the more they show that the theory or generalization holds in many different circumstances and so is more likely to hold in the future instance in question. (However similar the circumstances under which the past data are observed are in many respects, they are almost bound to differ from each other in some observable or unobservable respects; if the generalization holds despite many differences, that gives it greater reliability.) Secondly, the surer my knowledge that the past data occurred as stated, the better grounded is my claim to knowledge of the future. If the data are mental experiences of mine or events which I myself have seen, then my knowledge of their occurrence is sure. If they are experiences of others or events which others have seen, then I have some doubt whether they occurred. I have more doubt still if I need to make a complicated inference from other data to prove their occurrence. Clearly in so far as an inference is licensed by certain data, then to the extent to which it is doubtful whether the data are correct, it is doubtful whether the inference is justifiable. Thirdly, in so far as the data are qualitatively rather dissimilar from what is predicted, and a complicated scientific theory is needed to generate the prediction, the claim to knowledge will be less surely based. Thus suppose that by a process of complex extrapolation from a number n of astronomical data I reach a very complex theory of mechanics, from which I conclude that in a very unusual set of circumstances (when the planets are in just such and such configurations) if I let go of a bit of chalk it will rise into the air. And suppose that these circumstances are to be manifested on earth uniquely in my study during this hour. Do I *know* that when shortly I let go of the chalk it will rise? Doubtfully so. Clearly I do know it and know it a lot better if I have already actually let go of the chalk n times during the hour, and it has risen. Fourthly, if a complex inference is needed in order to reach a prediction, then in so far as the inference is of a type which has proved successful in the past or the inference is done by persons with known predictive success from this kind of work in the past, that is grounds for believing the prediction. These four points about the strength of knowledge obtained by normal induction may be summarized by saying that our claims to knowledge are better justified, the closer they are to our experience.

Now if agents are knowingly to bring about states of affairs, or to allow states of affairs to come about through neglecting to prevent them, they must know what consequences will follow from their actions. Normal inductive knowledge of consequences, it follows from what has just been said, is to be obtained as follows. Consider an action A which I am contemplating doing in circumstances X. Suppose that A consists in bringing about a state of affairs C, the result of *A* (see p. 32 for a definition of 'result'). How am I to know what its effects will be, what will follow from it? Most certainly, by having done such an action myself many times before in similar circumstances, and having observed the effects of its result. I come to know most surely what will result from my drinking eight double whiskies—that I shall be unable to drive my car safely, by having done such an action often before. I know the effect less surely by having seen the effects of others doing the action, or by having seen the effects of the result of the action when this was brought about unintentionally, all in similar circumstances to those in which I am considering doing the action; or by others telling me what happened on different occasions when they drank eight double whiskies. I know that this will lead to inability to drive less surely, because I suspect that I am different from the others (have more will-power, am more conscious of the dangers, am a better driver than the others anyway).

Less sure knowledge still is obtained by observing the result occur in somewhat different circumstances (e.g. when drinkers drink the whiskies much more quickly, or when tired). Still less sure knowledge is obtained by having observed goings-on only somewhat similar, and having to make allowance for the difference—e.g. I may only have seen the effects of men drinking different quantities of beer or gin. Or my knowledge may depend on reports given by others; then it will be still less certain. The witnesses may have exaggerated, not noticed differences in circumstances, etc.

The least certain knowledge of all is that which is reached by a process of more complicated inference from goings-on only remotely similar to *A*. However it is difficult to see how a theory which predicted the occurrence of such evils as pain or death could have any justification unless the data on which the theory was built were cases of pain and death. If you had no knowledge of anything causing pain, how could other kinds of data substantiate predictions about pain? For pain is so different from other kinds of goings-on and has no natural connection with particular brain or nerve conditions rather than with others. (There is no reason for supposing that stimulation of this nerve will cause pain and of that one will cause pleasure, other than knowledge that that is what has happened in the past.)

So proximity to experience gives more certain knowledge. It is notorious that people are much more inclined to take precautions against disaster if they have suffered before themselves or if a similar disaster has happened to those close to them than if they are warned of the need for precaution by some impersonal distant authority. A man is far more inclined to take precautions against fire or burglary if he or his neighbours have suffered than if the police warn him that these things have happened in the next village. My point is that this is not just irrational perversity. It is the height of rationality to be influenced more by what is known better. People know better that it can happen to them if they know that it has happened to them or to others like them. With a mere police warning, they always have some reason for suspecting that police exaggerate or that things are different in the next village. What is irrational is not being influenced at all by the police warning; what is not irrational is being influenced more by goings-on closer at hand of which we have more intimate experience.

It follows from all this that we can only come to know that certain of our actions will have harmful consequences through prior experience (in some degree) of such harmful consequences. I come to know that drinking alcohol will give me a hangover most surely by having had it happen to me before, less surely by my having seen it happen to others before, less surely by others telling me that it has happened to them before, and least surely still by its being a remote prediction of some complex scientific theory. With the case of the worst evils it is not possible that my knowledge should be based on experience of what has happened to *me* before. I cannot know by experience that taking more and more heroin over a long period will cause death by having had it happen to me before. In such cases the most sure knowledge will be given by seeing it happen to many friends; less sure knowledge by seeing it happen on television (as in the British television documentary 'Gale is Dead'); still less sure knowledge by reading in a book that this happened before. Loss of limbs too is a consequence about which I can learn only by seeing or hearing of the experiences of others. But here too actually seeing a friend have to have his arm amputated as a result of standing too close to a dangerous machine in a factory and getting his arm trapped in it is rightly going to deter me from standing too close to the machine much better than is a notice which says 'Dangerous' (for the former gives me surer knowledge of the probable consequence of my action). It follows generally that my actions or negligence can only to my knowledge have really bad consequences if others have suffered such really bad consequences before. Among such really bad consequences are prolonged incurable suffering or death. These can only be among the evils which I can knowingly inflict on others, or through my negligence allow others to suffer, if others have suffered before.

Further, for any evil which men knowingly inflict on each other, there must have been a first time in human history at which this was done. There must have been a first murder, a first murder by cyanide poisoning, a first deliberate humiliation, and so on. The malevolent agent in each case knows the consequence of the result of his action (e.g. that imbibing cyanide will lead to death). *Ex hypothesi*, he cannot know this through having seen an agent give another cyanide for this purpose. His knowledge that cyanide poisoning caused death must come from his having seen or others' having told him that taking cyanide accidentally led to death. (If in my example, you think that knowledge of the effects of imbibing cyanide might be gained by seeing the effects of taking similar chemicals, the argument can be put more generally. Some man must have taken previously a similar poison by accident.) What applies to the malevolent agent also applies to the man who knowingly refrains from inflicting evil on another or stops evil occurring to another. There must be naturally occurring evils (i.e. evils not deliberately caused by men) if men are to know how to cause evils themselves or are to prevent evil occurring. And there have to be *many* such evils, if men are to have sure knowledge, for as we saw, sure knowledge of what will happen in future comes only by induction from many past instances. A solitary instance of a man dying after taking cyanide will not give to others very sure knowledge that in general cyanide causes death—may be the death on the occasion studied had a different cause, and the cyanide poisoning had nothing to do with it. And unless men have been bringing about evils of a certain kind deliberately recently, there have to be many recent naturally occurring evils if men are currently to have sure knowledge of how to bring about or prevent such evils.

Thus we know that rabies causes a terrible death. With this knowledge we have the possibility of preventing such death (e.g. by controlling the entry of pet animals into Britain), or of negligently allowing it to occur or even of deliberately causing it. Only with the knowledge of the effects of rabies are such possibilities ours. But for us to gain knowledge of the effect of rabies it is necessary that others die of rabies (when the rabies was not preventable by man), and be seen to have done so. Generally, we can only have the opportunity to prevent disease affecting ourselves or others or to neglect to do so, or the opportunity to spread disease deliberately (e.g. by indulging in biological warfare), if there are naturally occurring diseases. And men can only have the opportunity to prevent incurable diseases or to allow them to occur, if there are naturally occurring incurable diseases.

What applies to men applies also, *mutatis mutandis*, to animals. Higher animals too acquire knowledge by normal induction, knowledge of where to obtain food, drink, and fellowship; and also knowledge of the causes of pain, loss of health, and loss of life. Seeing the suffering, disease, and death of others in certain circumstances, they learn to avoid those circumstances. Animals, and especially the lower animals, do of course avoid many situations and do many actions instinctively; but in those cases they cannot be said to be doing the action or avoiding the situation through knowledge of its consequences. If it is good (as it might well appear) that they too should save their lives and those of their offspring through knowledge of consequences, this is only to be had by experience thereof. Other animals must suffer if some animals are to learn to avoid suffering for themselves and their offspring.

Reverting again to men, we may note that what applies to individuals in the short term, applies also in the longer term and to races. If men are to have the opportunity by their actions or negligence to bring about evil consequences in the distant future, or to avoid doing so, they must know the long-term consequences of their actions, and the most sure inductive knowledge of those consequences can only come from past human history. How are men to have the opportunity to stop future generations catching asbestosis, except through knowledge of what causes asbestosis, and how is that to be obtained except through records which show that persons in contact with blue asbestos many years ago have died from asbestosis thirty years later? Or suppose that men are to have the choice of building cities along earthquake belts, and so risking the destruction of whole cities and their populations hundreds of years later, or of avoiding doing so. How can such a choice be available to them unless they know where earthquakes are likely to occur and what their probable consequences are? And how are they to come to know this, unless earthquakes have happened due to natural and unpredicted causes, like the Lisbon Earthquake of 1755?

The scope for long-term choice available to future generations must not be underestimated. They may have the choice not merely of whether to build cities so as to avoid earthquakes, but of whether to drive the earth nearer to the sun or further from it, to take air and water to Mars and live there instead, to extend the life-span, to produce new man-like organisms in laboratories, and so on. But rational choices on these matters can only be made in the light of knowledge of the consequences of alternative actions. Sure knowledge can come only from our own experience or the records of the experiences of men who have experienced natural disasters or naturally caused changes of environment and constitution. If men are knowingly to determine the fate of future generations through making such choices they can do so most surely by having knowledge of the disasters and benefits which have befallen past generations.

I argued that what has happened to men very different from ourselves gives less sure knowledge of what will happen to us than does what has happened to ourselves. It does nevertheless give knowledge. And what has happened to sentient creatures other than men also gives knowledge of what will happen to us, though very much less sure knowledge. Indeed a great deal of our knowledge of the disasters for man which would follow some action come from study of the actual disasters which have befallen animals. For a long time it has been normal to discover the effects of drugs or surgery or unusual circumstances on man, by deliberately subjecting animals to those drugs or surgery or circumstances. Before putting men into space, men put animals into space and saw what happened to them. Such experiments do not give very sure knowledge of what would happen to men—because from the nature of the case there are very considerable differences between animals and men—but they do give considerable knowledge. The evils which have naturally befallen animals provide a huge reservoir of information for men to acquire knowledge of the choices open to them, a reservoir which men have often tapped—seeing the fate of sheep, men have learnt of the presence of dangerous tigers; seeing the cows sink into a bog, they have learnt not to cross that bog, and so on.

And as regards *very* long-term consequences of changes of circumstances, environment, or climate, the story of animal evolution provides our main information. Human history so far is too short to provide knowledge of the very long-term consequences of our actions (including the knowledge needed to make some of the choices to which I referred two paragraphs back). To take another example, future biologists will have the power to produce much good or ill by inducing various genetic mutations. Human history does not provide the data which will give them any knowledge of the consequences of their actions. Their surest knowledge of those consequences will come from a study of the evolutionary history of the consequences in animals of various naturally occurring mutations. It is not in the least far-fetched to suppose that evolutionary history could provide such detailed results. But in any case the story of pre-human nature 'red in tooth and claw' already provides some very general information crucially relevant to our possible choices. For suppose that animals had come into existence at the same time as man (e.g. 4004 BC) always in situations where men could save them from any suffering. Naturally it would then seem a well-confirmed theory that (either through act of God or nature) suffering never happens to animals except such as men can prevent. So men would seem not to have the opportunity to do actions which would cause suffering to later generations of animals of a subsequently unpreventable kind, or the opportunity to prevent such suffering. The story of evolution tells us that that is not so—the causation or prevention of long-term suffering is indeed within our power; such suffering can happen because it has happened. The story of pre-human evolution reveals to man just how much the subsequent fate of animals is in his hands—for it will depend on the environment which he causes for them and their genes which he may cause to mutate.

Like earlier examples, the above argument illustrates the more general point that if men are to have knowledge of the evil which will result from their actions or negligence, laws of nature must operate regularly; and that means that there will be what I may call 'victims of the system'. Thus I mentioned in the last chapter that among the advantages of the pain caused by fire is that it leads the sufferer to escape from the fire. But the pain still occurs when the sufferer is too weak or paralysed to escape from the fire. Would it not be better if only those able to escape suffered the pain? But if that were the case, then others would know that it mattered much less that they should help people to escape from fire and that they should prevent fire. And so the opportunities for men to choose whether to help others and guard against their future sufferings will correspondingly diminish. And in general if God normally helps those who cannot help themselves when others do not help, others will not take the trouble to help the helpless next time, and they will be rational not to take that trouble. For they will know that more powerful help is always available.

My main argument so far has been that *if* men are to have the opportunity to bring about serious evils for themselves or others by actions or negligence, or to prevent their occurrence, and if all knowledge of the future is obtained by normal induction, that is by induction from patterns of similar events in the past—then there must be serious natural evils occurring to man or animals. I have argued earlier that it is good that men should have the former opportunity. What of the possibility that God should give to man the necessary knowledge by a different route?

Normal inductive inference from the past is not our only route to knowledge of the future. In so far as what will happen lies within the power of an agent, we can learn what will happen, not merely by studying the regular patterns in the agent's past behaviour and so inferring by induction how he will behave in future, but by his telling us what he intends to do. I can learn that you will be in London tomorrow by your telling me so. I can learn that if I omit to pay your bills, you will prosecute me, by your telling me so. We can infer (inductively) from an agent's statement of his intentions to what he will do. Knowledge of the future obtained in this way I shall call verbal knowledge.[1] If there is a God, ought he not to convey to men knowledge of the consequences of their actions verbally, in order to avoid having to bring about natural evils? His giving us verbal knowledge of the consequences of our actions would involve his saying out loud such things as 'if you walk near the cliff, you will fall over', or 'if you want to kill your neighbour, cyanide is very effective'. Such a procedure would make men know for certain there was a God, with all that that involves. Then not merely would many men reasonably believe that there was a God; all men without exception would know for certain that all that happened (except for human actions) was due to the action of God. Whether morally good or bad, whether they would otherwise concern themselves with matters religious or not; the existence of God would be for them an

---

[1] There is no need to analyse here the inductive force of different statements of intention, i.e. which of an agent's statements are reliable indicators of what he intends to do. I am concerned only with statements which can reasonably be believed to come from God who presumably always tells the truth. If there are statements of doubtful origin or statements which come from a God of doubtful reliability, then they will have to be backed up by evidence of a normal inductive kind if they are to yield knowledge of the future, and the considerations of the last few pages all become relevant again.

item of evident common knowledge. Knowing that there was a God, men would know that their most secret thoughts and actions were known to God; and knowing that he was just, they would expect for their bad actions and thoughts whatever punishment was just. Even if a good God would not punish bad men further, still they would have the punishment of knowing that their bad actions were known to God. They could no longer pose as respectable citizens; God would be too evident a member of the community. Further, in seeing God, as it were, face to face, men would see him to be good and worshipful, and hence would have every reason for conforming to his will. In such a world men would have little temptation to do wrong—it would be the mark of both prudence and reason to do what was virtuous. Yet a man only has a genuine choice of destiny if he has reasons for pursuing either good or evil courses of action; for, as I argued in Chapter 5, a man can only perform an action which he has some reason to do. Further, in such a world, men could not choose whether to acquire knowledge for themselves or for future generations, or what kinds of knowledge to seek, but knowledge would surround them. In this way too men would have no choice of destiny.

I conclude that a world in which God gave to men verbal knowledge of the consequences of their actions would not be a world in which men had a significant choice of destiny, of what to make of themselves, and of the world. God would be too close for them to be able to work things out for themselves. If God is to give man knowledge while at the same time allowing him a genuine choice of destiny, it must be normal inductive knowledge. Proximity to God is no doubt a good thing; but a God has a reason to ensure that we only get to that state as a result of our own choice (e.g. in another world as a result of our conduct in this one). There is some reason for something of that importance not to happen to a man without his choosing that it should.

Clearly God could not give verbal knowledge to creatures without language. Only if animals had language could they acquire knowledge of the future consequences of their actions by a route other than the normal inductive one. It is difficult to see how animals could have language without being like men in all crucial respects including appearing to have free will. Hence if there are to be animals, beings of a simpler kind than men, their knowledge must be acquired by the normal inductive route.

Note that this general argument that God has reason to build natural evils into the world in order to give to man knowledge of how to cause or avoid them would only explain those evils which are physically necessitated or made physically probable by prior causes. Randomly occurring evil would not be explained. But in an orderly world there is no such evil. All natural evil occurs through physical processes which provide guidance as to how it can be attained in future.[1]

When men are contemplating any serious action, we feel that they should be *fully* alert to the consequences of that action. However well they think that they can imagine it, their imagination needs to be pulled into line by *seeing* how things really are. Reports given in language will necessarily fail to capture the detail and bring home the feel of those consequences, even if they were reports given by God, for necessarily language abstracts and renders impersonal. That full alertness to consequences can be gained only from the experience of similar consequences. We feel that those considering doing any action with serious consequences ought to have some experience of those consequences, in order to have full awareness of what they are doing. We feel that judges ought to spend a spell in prison before sending men to prison. Those contemplating dropping bombs ought to visit a few villages which have had bombs dropped on them. And so on. When a child is kidnapped, sometimes the distraught mother makes an appeal on television to the kidnappers. Why? Because some sort of contact with one of the sufferers might give to the kidnapper an awareness of what he is doing which mere words cannot give. Even if God could give verbal knowledge of the

---

[1] It may be objected to this argument for the need for actual evil, if men are to know how to cause or avoid evil, that men do not need knowledge in order to perform right actions, but that mere true belief is sufficient. Maybe my giving the kiss of life to a drowning man pulled out of the water would not count as doing an action in the *knowledge* that otherwise he would die, unless others who had not been given the kiss had been seen to die, but is not a mere true belief that the man would otherwise die enough to allow me to do the action in order to prevent his death? True beliefs need perhaps have no justification in experience. However, my conduct will only be rational and morally good, if it is conduct in the light of justified beliefs, and justified beliefs are beliefs backed up by the evidence of experience. (Knowledge is justified true belief, or a species thereof.) There is no merit in my acting on a belief for which I have not the slightest evidence; my conduct would rightly be held irresponsible. Men could perhaps be programmed to act on unjustified beliefs, but rational and morally good conduct needs justified beliefs. If God is not going to allow men to act in the light of justified beliefs, there would seem little point in having given to them free will; for they would have only beliefs as to how to achieve good ends, on which it would be irresponsible to act. Further it is of vast value in itself that agents should have and grow in knowledge; mere unjustified true belief is of far more dubious value.

consequences of our actions without impairing our choice of destiny, that knowledge would be less adequate than the knowledge obtained by induction from experience. It is a very deep philosophical truth that by and large all knowledge comes from experience, and that proximity to experience gives surer knowledge. Knowledge is awareness of how things are. The closer one is to something in one's consciousness of it, the more one knows about it.

The argument of this section fills gaps in the argument of the last chapter. In three places in the last chapter I made a claim about the most sure knowledge of the consequences of actions coming (of logical necessity) from experience of similar consequences. In this section I have provided the justification for that claim.

Two additional Arguments

A further argument why God might permit natural evils to be suffered by men is the argument from higher-order goods, the argument that various evils are logically necessary conditions for the occurrence of actions of certain especially good kinds. Thus for a man to bear his suffering cheerfully there has to be suffering for him to bear. Within limits a sufferer can choose whether to react to his suffering with cheerfulness or with self-pity. There have to be acts which irritate for another to show tolerance of them. Likewise it is often said, acts of forgiveness, courage, self-sacrifice, compassion, overcoming temptation, etc., can only be performed if there are evils of various kinds. Here, however, we must be careful. One might reasonably claim that all that is necessary for some of these good acts (or acts as good as these) to be performed is belief in the existence of certain evils, not their actual existence. You can show compassion towards someone who appears to be suffering, but is not really; you can forgive someone who only appeared to insult you, but did not really. But if the world is to be populated with imaginary evils of the kind needed to enable creatures to perform acts of the above specially good kinds, it would have to be a world in which creatures are generally and systematically deceived about the feelings of their fellows—in which the behaviour of creatures generally and unavoidably belies their feelings and intentions. But, it is plausible to suppose,[1] it would be a morally wrong act of a creator to create such a deceptive world. In that case, given a creator, then, without an immoral act on his part, for acts of

---

[1] In the tradition of Descartes. See his *Meditations* 4, 5, and 6.

courage, compassion, etc., to be acts open to men to perform, there have to be various evils. Evils give men the opportunity to perform those acts which show men at their best. A world without evils would be a world in which men could show no forgiveness, no compassion, no self-sacrifice. And men without that opportunity are deprived of the opportunity to show themselves at their noblest. For this reason God might well allow some of his creatures to suffer in various ways, since this suffering provides the opportunity for especially noble acts.

Objectors have rightly argued that the evincing of such virtues could not be the sole goods—there would be no point in my laying down my life for you unless you could enjoy your life subsequently by indulging the more primitive pleasures of eating, drinking, and doing philosophy. Nevertheless, in a world with much opportunity for enjoyment it is right that agents should have also the opportunity to show extreme nobility.

A related argument is that it is good that men should have experience of a full range of possible experiences. A world in which we did not know (except in the most formal way) of the logical possibilities of pain and disease, of rejection of lovers, of the desolation of orphans, etc., would be a world in which we would know little of the logical possibilities. 'It is good for me that I have been in trouble' sang the Psalmist, and he was right. A man looking back over his life may well be grateful for at any rate some of the pain which he has suffered and the emotional crises which have been his, not just because of the future benefits (e.g. in the way of coping with new troubles) which they bring in an imperfect world, but because of his exposure to and contact with the harsh possible realities. Why do we value watching a tragedy? Because we are glad of the small dose of emotional crisis, which second-hand participation gives us. If a parent had a drug which he could give to a child, which could ensure that the child would never feel pain, or desolation, or desertion, or maiming, in which he would never know the hard realities, he might for this reason alone well hesitate to give it. Of course once again such limited experience is to be valued, but there would be something wrong if most of most men's lives consisted in having such experiences. They do not, although most of some men's lives do; and this remains a difficulty for this defence, a reason why it needs to be backed up by other defences.

I have now outlined in this chapter a number of reasons why God might wish to bring about the more puzzling natural evils. I outlined in the last chapter reasons why God might wish to bring about moral evils and some of the less puzzling natural evils. The general defence has been in terms of the possible or actual greater good for which those evils provide the opportunity. If this general line of approach is accepted, there remain two crucial problems. First, in the scheme of things outlined necessarily some agents suffer harm for the benefit of other agents; they do not choose to suffer this harm, but it is imposed upon them. Does a God have the right to impose on one such harm for the benefit of another? Secondly, it may be felt that although these defences explain much of the evil in the world, there is more in kind and quantity than a God would have reason to bring about.

God's Right to Inflict Harm

I have been suggesting that it is good for God to allow men to have deep responsibility for other men, particularly their children; and for animals, who in turn have responsibility for their own offspring; and that it is good for God to allow men and animals to suffer for the sake of the knowledge provided to themselves and others, and for the sake of the opportunities provided for performing good actions and deepening knowledge. But even if this is correct, does God have the right to inflict harm on us for the sake of this greater good? Surely no one has this right to inflict harm on an agent for his greater good, let alone for the greater good of another, without the agent's consent. We judge that doctors who use people as involuntary guinea-pigs for medical experiments are doing something wrong.

However there are three crucial differences between the doctors and God, which have the consequence that God has the right to make choices for men which they do not have the right to make for each other. The first and most important difference is that the doctors *could* have asked the patients for permission; and the patients being free agents of some power and knowledge could have made an informed choice of whether or not to allow themselves to be used. God's choice is not about how to use already existing agents, but about the sort of agents to make and the sort of world into which to put them. In God's situation there are no agents to be asked. Thus in the last chapter I argued that it would be good that one agent *A* should have deep responsibility for another *B* who in turn would have deep responsibility for another *C*. Ought not God to have asked *B* if he wanted things thus? But this is not possible, for if *A* is to be responsible for *B*'s growth in freedom, knowledge, and power, there will not be a *B* with enough freedom and knowledge to make any choice before God has to choose whether or not to give *A* responsibility for him. The creator has to make the choice independently of his creatures, and he has a reason for choosing to make them deeply interdependent. Again, God has reason, we saw, to create a world in which some suffer, to give others knowledge. But men cannot choose in what sort of a world by what route they are to acquire knowledge, for until they have acquired knowledge they cannot choose anything. God has to make the choice for them.

Secondly, God as the author of our being would have rights over us which we do not have over our fellow men. To allow a man to suffer for the good of his or someone else's soul one has to stand in some kind of parental relationship towards him. I do not have the right to let some stranger, Joe Bloggs, suffer for the good of his soul or of the soul of Bill Snoggs, but I do have *some* right of this kind in respect of my own children. I may let the younger son suffer *somewhat* for the good of his and his brother's soul. I have this right because in small part I am responsible for the younger son's existence, its beginning, and continuance. If this is correct, then *a fortiori*, a God who is, *ex hypothesi*, so much more the author of our being than are our parents, has so many more rights in this respect. The third consideration is that a God knows exactly how much men will suffer and what the effects of their suffering will be. Part of the reason why we rightly hesitate sometimes to inflict suffering is that we do not know how much suffering we are inflicting and what its effects will be.

These latter two considerations also suggest that a God has a right to allow animals to suffer for the benefit of men under circumstances where men would not have that right. Clearly many men who have not created animals judge that nevertheless they have the right to cause animal suffering, in order to alleviate human suffering and to give men knowledge. Presumably they judge that animals have fewer rights than men in these respects, since they are not moral agents, having no free will and limited power and knowledge. In this connection it must be borne in mind that, as I claimed in Chapter 9, animal suffering is presumably far less intense than human suffering. For if man suffers and inanimate matter and plants do not, then suffering presumably increases with mental and nervous complexity. Animals in general are far less intelligent and have a far less developed nervous organization than men; one would expect their suffering to be correspondingly much less. Further there is the point that surely for many animals, as for many men, the good which they enjoy compensates for the harm which they suffer; a God in creating them compensates for that harm—which animal-experimenters who are not their creators do not.

So then God without asking men or animals has to choose for them between kinds of world in which they can live—basically either a world in which there is very little suffering, and correspondingly little creative opportunity; and a world in which there is suffering but there is also great benefit, and where the sufferers are not always those who benefit. How shall he choose? There are clearly reasons for both choices. But it does not seem to me that God would be immoral to presume that if (*per impossible*) the agents were able to choose, they would make the heroic choice. God's choice in that case is the choice which allows some to benefit others, although the latter can choose either to do so or not to do so. Of course in giving existence at all to an agent, God is in most cases giving him an immense benefit which is not outweighed even if harm comes with it. Although human parents are far less responsible for the existence of their children than is God, they sometimes find themselves in analogous situations. One which many parents of good education and comfortable background have recently faced is the choice of whether to send their children to the local comprehensive school or to send them to a paid private school. They may make that choice in the belief that their own children will be harmed by the local comprehensive (education will be bad and hostility shown towards middle-class children) but also in the belief that other children will benefit through the healing of divisions between communities. In such a case the parent will rightly be influenced by the relative amounts of harm and good which would be done, but where the amounts are not too slight, it would be hard to condemn either action as immoral. And God, as we have seen, has far more rights than parents in such a matter, just as his choice can sometimes be far more serious.

The Quantity of Evil

A man may accept the arguments of the previous two chapters in principle. He may agree that one does need a substantial amount of various kinds of evil in order to provide the opportunity for greater goods, and in particular a choice of destiny for men, to a significant degree. But he may feel that there is just too much evil in the world, and that less evil would produce adequate benefit. It might be said that a God could give to man choice enough by allowing him to inflict quite a bit of pain on his fellows, and could deter a man from harmful actions by some nasty headaches. In our world, the objection goes, things are too serious. There is too much evil which man can do to his fellow, and deterrents of too great seriousness, and so too unpleasant natural evils to give men knowledge thereof. The suffering of children and animals is something which rightly often appals us. The game, it may be said, is not worth the candle. This is, I believe, the crux of the problem of evil. It is not the fact of evil or the kinds of evil which are the real threat to theism; it is the quantity of evil—both the number of people (and animals) who suffer and the amount which they suffer. If there is a God, he has given man too much choice, the objection in effect says. He has inflicted too much suffering on too many people (and animals) to give knowledge to others for the sake of the freedom of the latter; he has given to man too much opportunity to do evil, and used too powerful deterrents to certain bad actions instead of just stopping men from doing them by force. With the objection that if there is a God, he has overdone it, I feel *considerable initial* sympathy. The objection seems to count against the claim that there is a God.

Clearly if there is a God, he must set a limit to the amount of suffering. Clearly too there is such a limit. There is a temporal limit constituted by death to the amount a given man can suffer. And there is also presumably a limit to the intensity of possible suffering, set by the constitution of the brain through which suffering comes to man. But the objection is that the limit is set too wide. It ought never to have allowed Hiroshima, Belsen, the Lisbon Earthquake, or the Black Death. But the trouble is that the fewer natural evils a God provides, the less opportunity he provides for man to exercise responsibility. For the less natural evil, the less knowledge he gives to man of how to produce or avoid suffering and disaster, the less opportunity for his exercise of the higher virtues, and the less experience of the harsh possibilities of existence; and the less he allows to men the opportunity to bring about large-scale horrors, the less the freedom and responsibility which he gives to them. What in effect the objection is asking is that a God should make a toy-world, a world where things matter, but not very much; where we can choose and our choices can make a small difference, but the real choices remain God's. For he simply would not allow us the choice of doing real harm, or through our negligence allowing real harm to occur. He would be like the over-protective parent who will not let his child out of sight for a moment.

Conscious of the *very* short temporal span of human and animal life (and to a lesser extent of the limits to the depths of pain and suffering within that life which can be experienced), my own final verdict is that God has good reason to bring about or allow to occur that amount of suffering which exists for the sake of the greater good which results. My conclusion is based on the grounds which I have given as to why a God might wish to produce such evils. But I have set them out only very briefly. Adequately to justify a moral viewpoint and to persuade others, not merely is a great deal of argument needed but also often a lot of personal experience of the kinds of goods and evils involved. For these reasons my arguments may not have been adequate to convince many a reasonable opponent. Also of course my own lack of experience of many of the harsher evils of the world may have led me to fail to appreciate their full horror. However the length of this book precludes further argument, and experience of worlds is no part of books; and so we must leave the argument here.

Clearly a God has *a* reason for making a world with the amount of natural evil and the possibilities for man-made evil which this world contains (a reason in the responsibility, etc. which are thereby given to man). Clearly too he has *a* reason for not making such a world (given by the evil involved in it). Fairly clearly too, I would judge, he does not have overriding reason for making such a world. There would be nothing wrong in his making a world without such evil. But, also, my own tentative conclusion, in the light of the considerations adduced, is that God does not have overriding reason for not making a world with this evil. For these reasons the existence of the evil which we find does not count against the existence of God. There is no good C-inductive argument from the existence of evil to the non-existence of God.

Everything turns on a quantitative moral judgement (i.e. a judgement about the *quantity* of evil which it is justifiable to bring about or to allow to occur, or the *quantity* of good which it is obligatory to create). Quantitative judgements are the hardest moral judgements on which to reach a sure conclusion. They are highly fallible, as can be seen by the fact that we frequently change our minds about them. Although we may hold throughout our lives certain general qualitative moral principles (e.g. that inflicting harm not for the sake of resultant good is always wrong), we normally through experience come to change our judgements on the detailed application of such principles; as we say after changing them, we grow in moral understanding. The two-year-old child who falls down and grazes himself, and bursts out crying would judge, if he could put his thoughts into words, that the evil of his suffering could never be justified by any higher good. When he grows up he is liable to think rather differently about the incident. We should bear in mind too that very great concern about non-extreme physical suffering is characteristic of contemporary Northern Europe and America. This is not to say that we are wrong to have such concern; it is only to draw attention to the fact that there are cultural differences, and that they should lead us to reflect on whether we are over-sensitive on this matter—and conversely not sensitive enough on other matters, about some of which other cultures have been very sensitive (e.g. the importance of responsibility, loyalty, freedom, knowledge, and right worship).

Saving Theism by Adding Hypotheses

However, clearly many persons of great moral sensitivity have reached a different conclusion from mine. Those who are inclined to follow them may well feel that although in itself the existence of evil does provide a good C-inductive argument against the existence of God, the argument will fail if we complicate somewhat the hypothesis of theism. We have already considered one way of doing this—adding to the hypothesis of theism the hypothesis of bad angels. Fairly clearly many, many years ago theism came to include this hypothesis for just this reason—to deal with the problem of evil. Another hypothesis added to theism partly also under the pressure of this problem is the hypothesis of life after death.[1] Men felt that God would only bring about or allow others to bring about great suffering if there was a life after death in which God could restore the victims to health of mind and soul. I have not myself argued along these lines, but I can see very strong reasons why a God would choose to bring about life after death, including the reason of the compensating for evils of life on earth. If any one wishes

---

[1] This hypothesis entered Judaism largely under the pressure of reflection on the suffering and untimely deaths of the Maccabean martyrs in the second century BC.

to add this hypothesis to theism to save it from the force of an argument from evil, he must however bear in mind that theism then becomes a more complicated hypothesis, and hence has less prior probability and so needs more in the way of confirming evidence to raise its over-all probability on evidence, to (e.g.) more than $\frac{1}{2}$.

A third extra hypothesis, which may be added to theism partly in order to deal with the problem of evil, is the hypothesis of redemptive incarnation. Men may feel that a God would only have the right to subject creatures to ills of the kind which they suffer if he were prepared to share with them the burden of the suffering and effort. The Christian religion has of course maintained that God knowing the worthwhileness of the conquest of evil and the perfecting of the universe by men, in fact shared with them this task by subjecting himself as man to the evil of the world, especially by accepting the Crucifixion. Similar considerations apply as apply to the additional hypothesis of life after death. I see abundant reason why a God should choose to bring about a redemptive incarnation. But to add this hypothesis to theism is to complicate theism so that it needs more in the way of confirming evidence, and I do not myself see the need to do this in order to save theism from a C-inductive counter-argument. However, I shall argue in the next chapter that there may be good grounds for believing in a redemptive incarnation which help to establish a theistic system rather than being dependent on one already established. I do not think that there are such grounds for believing in bad angels or in life after death. Arguments for the latter normally come through a belief in an independently established theistic system, e.g. through a belief about what a God would be expected to do, or through a belief that a particular person was a special messenger of God, may be God incarnate, and hence that the words which he uttered or that the teaching of the society which he founded is to be believed.[1]

Conclusion to Chapters 9, 10, and 11

We saw in Chapter 9 that the existence of conscious beings of the kind which exist in our world is something which would not have been expected to come about by normal physical processes, and

---

[1] There are arguments for life after death which do not come by these routes at all—e.g. arguments from the pronouncements of mediums at spiritualist seances—but considerations of space necessitate my ignoring these.

hence their existence counts in favour of the existence of God. Beginning in Chapter 9, and subsequently in Chapters 10 and 11, I considered the kinds of agents which a God would have reason to make, and the circumstances in which he would have reason to place them. He would have reason to create humanly free agents, that is, agents of limited free will, power, and knowledge, with the power to increase these, who are capable of marvelling at the order of nature and of worshipping God. The agents would have much pleasure, and enormous possibilities for creating more for themselves and for others. The agents would be subject to felt desires, including biologically useful ones; these desires would sometimes be for lesser goods which would mean that the agents were subject to temptation. They could therefore choose for themselves whether to do the morally right action and gradually become morally good beings. The agents would be greatly interdependent, capable of increasing each other's power, knowledge, and freedom, making each other happy or unhappy, and in this way, being subject to birth and death, capable of influencing distant generations. Such a world would be as it were a do-it-yourself world—a kit which a race over many generations could assemble for good or ill. It would also be a world in which suffering occurs in predictable ways in order that the increasing or the diminishing of suffering might be the alternatives before agents—which otherwise they could not be. It would contain much pleasure and enormous possibilities for more. It would contain too in the process enormous possibilities for generosity, courage, patience, self-sacrifice, resistance to temptation, sympathy, and persistence in love, giving and accepting forgiveness (as well as the possibilities of pursuing the converse vices). It would also contain simpler beings lacking free will but having some of the possibilities for good or evil which men have.

In all the respects which we can determine, our world is like this. Yet there might have been, instead of our world, a world with very different characteristics, which to all appearances God would have had overriding reason not to bring about. As I wrote at the end of Chapter 10, there might have been a world in which there were rational agents like men and animals lacking perfect freedom and knowledge but with the power to inflict endless suffering or suffering of infinite intensity. Reflection in this chapter on the reasons which God might have for bringing about or allowing the occurrence of evils suggests other such worlds which he might have overriding reason for not bringing about. One is a world in which rational agents suffered endlessly, not through the agency of other finite agents and not through any choice of their own. Another is a world in which there was a very large amount of randomly occurring suffering (see p. 213). For this would be evil which gives to agents no knowledge of how to avoid similar evil in future. Also among such worlds, I tentatively suggest, are a world of permanently isolated agents who could not co-operate with others, and a world in which agents had no natural or cultivable felt desires to help and co-operate with others. The fact that the world is our world and not one of the worlds described at the beginning of the paragraph (and perhaps that it is not one of the latter two worlds) confirms the claim that God made the world. For there exists a world which God has reason to bring about and not one of the worlds which he has overriding reason not to bring about, but which might if there were no God be equally likely to occur with our world.

The argument against this from the existence of such evil as we find in our world, I have claimed, stems from a failure to appreciate the deepest needs of men and other conscious beings, and a failure to appreciate the strength of the logical constraints on the kinds of world which God can make. The reader will sympathize with my verdict in so far as he believes that it is more important what an agent does (the choices he makes, the changes he produces in the world) than what happens to him (the sensations he experiences).

12

Arguments from History and Miracles

THE arguments for and against the existence of God which I have discussed so far have been arguments from very general and evident features of experience. The premiss of the cosmological argument, for example, that there is a universe, is both a very general feature of experience and one which is evidently true. The same applies to the argument against the existence of God from the existence of evil. The existence of evil in the world is evident to everyone, and it is a general feature of the world manifest at many places and many times. I am coming gradually to arguments for the existence of God from more particular goings-on. If there is a God, one might well expect him to make his presence known to men not merely through the over-all pattern of the universe in which he placed them, but by dealing more intimately and personally with them. In this chapter and the next chapter I shall consider claims that he has done so. In this chapter I consider the claim that God has made himself known in ancient and contemporary public events within history and the moulding of history thereby.

Many men have seen the hand of God in the sudden appearance of wise men, prophets, and great leaders on the historical scene, bringing great moral, political, or religious truths to their generation and inspiring them to act in accord with them. All theistic religions have in them central figures of this kind like Muhammad or Abraham, but they also have less central figures as well—men who have carried good news to new countries, reformed religious institutions, revived religious life, or applied religion to social and political affairs. From the work of such men of course whole traditions have flowed. Among the major theistic religions more has been claimed for one such phenomenon than for any others—and that phenomenon is of course the life, death, and Resurrection of Jesus of Nazareth. Here Christians have seen the hand of God not merely in what the individual taught and inspired, but in what he did and what was done to him. His life, according to Christian sources, was filled with miracles of healing the blind and dumb, the lame and mad, the socially inadequate and the psychologically maladjusted. His life had a generous and sacrificial character, and he gave bold and compelling moral and metaphysical teaching. His life was ended by his judicial murder, followed shortly, according to Christians, by his Resurrection from the dead. These Christian events gave rise to the Christian Church, a group of Galilean fishermen who suddenly announced the story of Jesus to the world. The Church grew rapidly, yet for proclaiming its news its members were persecuted violently by the civil authorities, and very many were executed. They never offered physical resistance to the authorities, and hundreds of thousands joined them—so many in fact that the persecutions had to cease and the illicit religion became the official religion of the Roman Empire. For many Christians these remarkable events have been evidence not merely that a God in whom they already believed was at work in a particular way, telling men a particular message, but evidence that there is a God.

Then we have particular events not central to a religious tradition, but ones which in some way occur within a religious tradition, and which have been seen by those who were close to them as especially compelling evidence of the hand of God in history and so of God's existence. I have in mind particularly striking miracles, generally believed to have occurred by the inhabitants of some small spatio-temporal region of the earth—sudden recoveries from cancer leaving no trace, a man growing a new limb from the stump of an amputated limb, or perhaps a striking and sudden recovery of sanity—these events occurring in the context of a religious tradition of prayer for them to happen. On some who have been close to such events, they have had a dramatic religious influence. Such events have in fact often formed an observer's religion for him. Then lastly there are the public events in a man's life which are of great importance to his own religion, but which have influenced no one else: the crisis when he suddenly discovered something worth doing or a point in his suffering; or the 'answering' of his prayers (sometimes by the literal fulfilment of those prayers, sometimes by an unexpected outcome which he feels to be equally satisfactory, in removing the concern which led him to prayer). Again, many men have come to believe that there is a God because they have attributed such events to his agency.

With regard to many of the events which I have mentioned there is little doubt that they have occurred and greatly influenced men's religious beliefs. But with regard to many others of them a crucial issue is whether they occurred at all, e.g. did the corpse of Jesus come to life? So we need, as well as arguments to show that if the events occurred God brought them about, arguments to show that they did indeed occur. It would not however be appropriate for one who is not professionally a detective or a historian or a New Testament scholar to discuss the historical evidence for and against certain detailed historical claims; nor is there space to do so in this book. All that I can do is to list the kind of evidence which is relevant to establishing disputed claims about whether certain historical events occurred; and to discuss generally what evidential force the occurrence of such disputed events would have (if they occurred), and the occurrence of other striking but non-disputed events does have, in pointing to the existence of God. It will be convenient to discuss the latter first.

Let us ask when e, the report of some historical going-on E, confirms h, the hypothesis that there is a God, given k—general background knowledge about how the world works of the kind which we have considered in earlier chapters in connection with other arguments (e.g. that there is a world governed by fairly deterministic natural laws, and that there are in it men who live and die, and have the capacity to grow in knowledge and power). What conditions have to be satisfied for $P(h/e.k) > P(h/k)$. By the relevance criterion, e has to be such that it is more to be expected, if there is a God, than it would be otherwise—$P(e/h.k) > P(e/k)$. As we saw earlier, this may occur for either of two reasons—either because it is very improbable that E would occur unless there is a God who brought it about (or allowed it to occur), that is, it is very improbable that E would occur through natural processes alone; *or* because although natural processes might well produce E, God has the character such that he would be more likely to produce E (or allow E to occur) than many other alternative phenomena which natural processes might equally well turn up if left to themselves—in symbols, either because $P(e/ \sim h.k)$ is low and so $P(e/k)$ is low; or because $P(e/h.k)$ is high.

Argument from the Power of God to bring about the Naturally Inexplicable

Let us concentrate, to begin with, on the first reason, and ask when is some particular historical event such that it is very improbable that it would occur through natural processes. It is not probable that natural processes will bring about *E* if our evidence makes it probable that physical objects do not have the power to bring about *E*. The powers of physical objects and their powers to exercise them are codified in natural laws (see pp. 41 f.). Hence it is not probable that natural processes will bring about an event *E* if the occurrence of *E* is incompatible with (or rendered highly improbable by) the universal operation of laws of nature, that is, if the only powers in the universe are those of physical objects codified in laws of nature. If the laws of nature in some field are universal laws, this will be because the odd event is contrary to the predictions of those laws and so what I shall call a 'violation' of them. If the laws of nature in some field are statistical, it will be because the odd event is very unlikely, given those laws and so is what I shall call a quasi-violation of them.[1]

Let me develop these points. As analysed so far in this book (see p. 25 as amended on p. 30) a universal law is a true generalization of the form 'all *A*'s are *B*' which is to be construed as making a claim about physical necessity—being *A* necessitating being *B*. As I argued in Chapter 3, the evidence that a purported law is a true law comes from its explanatory power and its prior probability. To take the example which I used there, suppose that you have observed many positions of planets, and propose a law that 'all planets move in ellipses with the Sun at one focus'. From the proposed law and some of the observed positions, you can predict all the other positions, positions which you would have no other reason for expecting—which gives the proposed law high explanatory power. The proposed law is a simple one, which (in the absence of relevant background knowledge of laws in analogous fields) suffices to give it high prior probability. All of this justifies the claim that the proposed law is a law of nature and hence justifies your expectation that it will hold in future without exception.

What, however, is to be said about an isolated exception to a purported law of nature? Suppose that one day Mars moves out of

---

[1] Here and for the next few pages my arguments are mainly condensed versions of those in my book *The Concept of Miracle* (London, 1971).

its elliptical path for a brief period and then returns to the path. There are two possibilities. This wandering of Mars may occur because of some current condition of the universe (e.g. the proximity of Jupiter drawing Mars out of its elliptical path), such that if that condition were to be repeated the event would happen again. In this case the phenomenon is an entirely regular phenomenon. The trouble is that what might have appeared originally to be a basic law of nature proves now not to be one. It proves to be a consequence of a more fundamental law that the original purported law normally holds, but that under circumstances describable in general terms (e.g. 'when other planets are close to Mars') there are exceptions to it. Such repeatable exceptions to purported laws merely show that the purported laws are not basic laws of nature. The other possibility is that the exception to the law was not caused by some current condition, in such a way that if the condition were to recur the event would happen again. In this case we have a non-repeatable exception to a law of nature. But how are we to describe this event further? There are two possible moves. One may say that if there occurs an exception to a purported law of nature, the purported law can be no law. If the purported law says 'all A's are B' and there is an A which is not B, then 'all A's are B' is no law. The trouble with saying that is that the purported law may be a very good device for giving accurate predictions in our field of study; it may be by far the best general formula for describing what happens in the field which there is. (I understand by a general formula a formula which describes what happens in all circumstances of a certain kind, but does not mention by name particular individuals, times or places.) To deny that the purported law is a law, when there is no more accurate general formula, just because there is an isolated exception to its operation, is to ignore its enormous ability to predict what happens in the field.

For this reason it seems not unnatural to say that the purported law is no less a law for there being a non-repeatable exception to it; and then to describe the exception as a 'violation' of the law. At any rate this is a coherent way of talking, and I think that it is what those who use such expressions as 'violation' of a law of nature are getting at. In this case we must amend our understanding of what is a law of nature beyond that attained in Chapter 2. To say that a generalization 'all A's are B' is a universal law of nature is to say that being A physically necessitates being B, and so that any A will be B—apart from violations.

But how do we know that some event such as the wandering of Mars from its elliptical path is a non-repeatable rather than a repeatable exception to a purported law of nature? We have grounds for believing that the exception is non-repeatable in so far as any attempt to amend the purported law of nature so that it predicted the wandering of Mars as well as all the other observed positions of Mars would make it so complicated and *ad hoc* that we would have no grounds for trusting its future predictions. It is no good, for example, amending the law so that it reads 'all planets move in ellipses with the sun at one focus, except in years when there is a competition for the World Chess Championship between two players both of whose surnames begin with K'. Why not? Because this proposed law mentions properties which have no other place in physics (no other physical law invokes this sort of property) and it mentions them in an *ad hoc* way (that is, the proposed new law has the form 'so-and-so holds except under such-and-such circum-stances', when the only reason for adding the exceptive clause is that otherwise the law would be incompatible with observations; the clause does not follow naturally from the theory). What we need if we are to have a more adequate law is a general formula, of which it is an entirely natural consequence that the exception to the original law occurs when it does.

In these ways we could have grounds for believing that an exception to a purported law was non-repeatable and so a violation of a natural law. Claims of this sort are of course corrigible—we could be wrong; what seemed inexplicable by natural causes might be explicable after all. But then we could be wrong about most things, including claims of the opposite kind. When I drop a piece of chalk and it falls to the ground, every one supposes that here is an event perfectly explicable by natural laws. But we could be wrong. Maybe the laws of nature are much more complicated than we suppose, and Newton's and Einstein's laws are mere approxima-tions to the true laws of mechanics. Maybe the true laws of mechanics predict that almost always when released from the hand, chalk will fall to the ground, but not today because of a slightly abnormal distribution of distant galaxies. However, although the true laws of nature predict that the chalk will rise, in fact it falls. Here is a stark violation of natural laws, but one which no one detects because of their ignorance of natural laws. 'You could be wrong' is a knife which cuts both ways. What seem to be perfectly explicable events might prove, when we come to know the laws of nature much better, to be violations. But of course this is not very likely. The reasonable man goes by the available evidence here, and also in the converse case. He supposes that what is, on all the evidence, a violation of natural laws really is one. There is good reason to suppose that events such as the following if they occurred would be violations of laws of nature: resurrection from the dead of a man whose heart has not been beating for twenty-four hours and who counts as dead by other currently used criteria; water turning into wine without the assistance of chemical apparatus or catalysts; a man growing a new arm from the stump of an old one.

So much for what is meant by saying that an event is, and how we can show that a certain event (e.g. a wandering of Mars) if it occurred would be, a violation of a law of nature.

Suppose now that the laws of nature in some field are statistical (see p. 26, as amended on p. 30). They will not then rule out any occurrence in the field and so the strict notion of a 'violation' of a law of nature will have no application. If a purported law says that '99.99% A's are B' (i.e. 'the physical probability of an A being B is 0.9999'), then however many A's which are not-B occur, their occurrence will not be ruled out by the law; because in the very, very long run 99.99% A's might still be B. However, there are clearly occurrences which are very, very improbable if a purported law is a true law, and which would be far more probable if some other law was the true law. For example if 1,000 out of 2,000 observed A's were found to be B, that would be very, very improbable if it were the law that '99.99% A's are B' and far, far more probable if the true law were '50% A's are B'. Among events compatible with some purported law L some are so improbable, given L, that their occurrence counts very strongly against its truth. Yet there may be no other general formula which predicts more accurately what happens. Under these circumstances it seems not unnatural to say that L is the true law of nature and that such an event E is a 'quasi-violation' of it. This involves amending our understanding of what is a statistical law of nature beyond that attained in Chapter 2, analogous to the amendment just made in respect of universal laws of nature. To say that 'n% A's are B' is a statistical law of nature is to say that being A makes being B physically probable to degree $n/100$, and so that n% A's will be B in the long run—apart from quasi-violations. Our grounds for supposing that some exception to a purported statistical law L is a quasi-violation of it will be that any attempt to replace L by another law L^1 would so add to the complexity of natural laws that there is every reason to suppose that its predictions would be false. Thus it is compatible with Quantum Theory (see p. 29 n. 1) that all the atoms in a block of C-14 should decay simultaneously in the next minute, but it is so vastly improbable that the occurrence of such an event would rightly be regarded as casting very grave doubt on that theory; because that event would be far, far more probable on another theory. Nevertheless there might be so much other evidence in favour of Quantum Theory that to amend it solely to deal with an apparent counter-instance would make it so complex as to make it unlikely that its other predictions will come off. In those circumstances we may reasonably conclude that a certain event is a quasi-violation of a statistical law.

Whether an event is a violation of a law of nature is a clear-cut matter; whether an event is a quasi-violation is not, since to be a quasi-violation the event has to be 'very, very improbable' on a law, and that is not a clear-cut notion. But to the extent to which some event is a quasi-violation, to that extent it is something which is too odd to be explained by science, and that is evidence that some other explanation is to be preferred. The explication of the last paragraph gives some idea what in practice would count as a quasi-violation. Even if the basic laws of nature are the statistical laws of Quantum Theory and all other laws are derivative from them and in consequence statistical in character, levitations, and spontaneous growths of new limbs from stumps would remain so very, very unlikely as to be beyond question quasi-violations of natural laws.

Now violations and quasi-violations are clearly events not explicable by natural processes. The structure of natural laws leads us to expect that they will not occur, and yet they do. (In so far as it is a matter of degree whether something is a quasi-violation of a natural law, the extent to which it is not explicable by natural laws is also a matter of degree.) Where k records that the world is governed by fairly deterministic natural laws and e records the occurrence of a violation or quasi-violation and h is the hypothesis of theism, $P(e/\sim h.k)$ will be low. For if there is no power beyond natural laws to determine what happens, one would expect what happens to accord with natural laws. Yet if natural laws operate because God makes them operate, then since God is equally able to make events occasionally occur not in occurrence with natural laws, the occurrence of the occasional violation or quasi-violation is much more to be expected. For then there is in being a power easily able to bring about such events; but otherwise all the powers in being are such as militate against the occurrence of such events. Hence $P(e/h.k) > P(e/\sim h.k)$ and so $P(e/h.k) > P(e/k)$. Hence the occurrence of violations and quasi-violations would confirm the existence of God. A violation or quasi-violation brought about by God may be called a miracle.

With respect to some of the kinds of event listed at the beginning of the chapter, as I wrote earlier, a crucial issue is whether they happened as reported. Normally those are the kinds of event about which there would be no doubt that if they did happen as reported, we would have a violation (or quasi-violation) of natural laws—and therefore by the argument just given, evidence for the existence of God. Among these events are the Resurrection of Christ, some of the Gospel miracles (such as the turning of water into wine),[1] and some miracles reported in Church history (e.g. levitations), or such Old Testament events as the sun staying still or moving backwards. The fact that such events if they occurred as reported, would have been violations (or quasi-violations) of natural laws, is in itself of course evidence against their occurrence, as Hume classically argued.[2] This is because if L is a law of nature, then it is vastly probable that what occurs will occur in accord with L; the past phenomena which make it (epistemically) probable that L is a law of nature make it probable that on the occasion in question, things conformed to L. But there may be much other evidence that an event E in fact occurred, which if it occurred would be a violation of a law of nature. There are four kinds of evidence about what happened on a particular past occasion. First each man has his own apparent memory of what happened—I seem to remember seeing John yesterday. Secondly, we have the testimony of others as to what they seem to remember—several people may claim to have seen John dead the day before yesterday. Thirdly, we have traces of the past, physical remains such as footprints, fingerprints, cigarette ash, Carbon-14, which allow us, given knowledge of laws of nature,

[1] There is of course some dispute as to exactly what the Gospel writers were claiming in some of these cases. In the case of the Resurrection there is, to my mind, little doubt that the Gospel writers are claiming a resurrection of Jesus in his old but transformed body, and so a violation of laws of nature—but some recent biblical commentators have their doubts about whether the Gospel writers were making this claim. In the case of other Gospel miracles, e.g. the turning of water into wine, there is much more serious doubt about how literally the Gospel writers intended their stories to be taken.

[2] See David Hume, *An Enquiry Concerning Human Understanding* (first published 1748), Sect. 10, 'Of Miracles'.

to retrodict what happened in the past. Knowing that cigarette ash is caused by smoking (or otherwise burning) cigarettes, and very rarely in any other way, we can retrodict from the presence of the ash that previously a cigarette was smoked (or otherwise burnt). Finally, we have our knowledge of the rest of the world (our background evidence about how things are), and in particular of how things behave on other occasions—and this acts as a corrective to discount some of the claims made on the basis of the first three kinds of evidence. If I report that I met a man ten feet tall, you will be suspicious of my report on the ground that men do not normally reach a height of ten feet. And crucially, if someone reports an event which, if it occurred, would be a violation (or quasi-violation) of a law of nature, this fact counts heavily against the report. However I see no adequate reason to suppose that it always counts decisively against the report.[1] Maybe so many careful witnesses report very clearly what happened that their evidence can outweigh the evidence of what normally happens; and so the weight of evidence shows that a violation of law of nature occurred. Certainly witness-reports can add to the probability that a violation occurred and so add to the probability that there is something not to be explained by natural processes. If e is merely witness-reports that a violation occurred, which are substantial evidence that a violation did occur (because the occurrence of the reports is not easily to be explained in some other way, e.g. in terms of the witnesses being misled by some non-miraculous phenomena), then e is more to be expected if a violation did occur than if it did not, and so marginally more to be expected if there is a God capable of bringing about violations than if there is not. The occurrence of much evidence of miracles is indirect evidence of the existence of God for it is evidence of the occurrence of events which natural processes do not have the power to produce. In so far as there is much such evidence, it would provide a good C-inductive argument to the existence of God.

The discussion in this chapter of violations of natural laws, has, in view of the programme of the book, concentrated on arguments from the occurrence of such violations, as witnessed by public historical evidence, to the existence of God. But note that the trail of evidence may go the other way as well. Other evidence (e.g. the existence and order of the universe) may confirm the hypothesis that God exists. This in turn will make it much more likely that

---

[1] I argue this point at some length against those who have held otherwise in *The Concept of Miracle*, Ch. 4.

occasionally there are violations of natural laws (because there exists a being with the power to intervene in the natural order), and so that a particular violation occurred, much more likely than the detailed historical evidence by itself would suggest. (Some violations which occur may of course be quite unnoticed by men.)

Argument about whether such particular events, as the Resurrection or levitations of saints occurred involves detailed historical argument, which I shall not pursue. All that I wish to point out is that in so far as there is evidence for the occurrence of such things, there is, by the argument given, evidence for the existence of God. There clearly is some slight evidence for the occurrence of such things—for there is serious historical argument about some of them (e.g. the Resurrection, or the miracles of Lourdes), but the issue which I cannot pursue is just how strong the evidence is.

However with regard to many of the events to which I referred at the beginning of the chapter, there is comparatively little doubt as to whether they occurred—no one will doubt that the history of the Church occurred roughly as I described it, or that people sometimes spontaneously recover from illness after prayers have been said for them. But a major issue is in which category the events lie. Are they violations of natural laws? To know this we would have to know what are the natural laws operative in this field, and what were the initial conditions prior to the occurrence of the event in question. Then we would see just what natural laws predict for the field, and whether the event in question is contrary to the predictions of those laws. We might find that the event was vastly improbable, given natural laws. Or that natural laws had nothing to say about whether it would occur. Or that it occurred entirely as predicted by natural laws. Our ignorance about what are the natural laws and initial conditions may not be total, and that may lead us to make reasonable estimates of the true situation; but in the case of the events which I have cited our ignorance is considerable. The way the early Christians behaved is contrary to the way most of us behave most of the time. But perhaps there are no laws in this field, and the unusual sometimes occurs. Or perhaps there are laws, and given the circumstances of Palestine in the first century AD, Christians behaved as the laws of sociology (as yet unknown by us) predict. Or again, a man prays for the recovery of his friend from depression and the friend spontaneously and permanently recovers. Do we have a violation here—who knows? Maybe human mental states are not subject to any more than the vaguest of statistical laws; or, if they are, we do not know. However, I repeat, although we are very unsure of the position, it may sometimes be more reasonable to suppose one thing than another; one supposition may be more probable than another. With regard to each of these events the arguments turn on points of medicine, psychiatry, or biblical criticism; and so it would be inappropriate to discuss them further in this book. All I have been concerned to do is to show the relevance of arguments in these fields. In so far as there is evidence for a violation (or quasi-violation), there is evidence for the existence of God.

Argument from the Character of God

Whichever way the argument goes as to whether such events are violations or quasi-violations, there is the further issue as to whether they are events such that God would have reason for bringing them about (or allowing them to occur). For, as we have seen, where e reports the occurrence of an event E, h is 'there is a God', and k is background knowledge of how the world works which we have considered in other chapters including the general operation of fairly deterministic natural laws, $P(e/h.k)$ may exceed $P(e/k)$ not because $P(e/\sim h.k)$ and so $P(e/k)$ are especially low (i.e. E is not to be expected given the operation of purely natural processes), but because $P(e/h.k)$ is quite high. E may be such that its occurrence is more to be expected if there is a God than if there is not. I argued earlier that God must do whatever there is overriding reason for him to do, and cannot do whatever there is overriding reason for him not to do or anything which he has no reason for doing. We may—though corrigibly—know what he has reason or overriding reason for doing or not doing. In so far as he has reason for bringing about some event, he may bring it about either by intervening in natural processes—in which case it will be a violation or quasi-violation; or by making the laws of nature such as to bring about the event in question at the appropriate time. If $P(e/h.k)$ exceeds $P(e/k)$ because God has reason, by either of these routes, to bring E about rather than some events which would otherwise be equally likely with E to occur, then the occurrence of E confirms the existence of God. (Qualifications must be added in the way set out in Chapter 6 to deal with cases where God has reason to allow others to bring about the occurrence or non-occurrence of E.) That the world is a world such as we might expect God to make is evidence that he did make it. So it remains to consider of the various particular events which I mentioned at the beginning of this chapter whether a God would have reason or overriding reason to bring them about, or not to bring them about (or allow others to do so).

I argued in earlier chapters that God has reason for giving men freedom and leaving them to work out their own destiny. But suppose they start to abuse that freedom; suppose they make wrong choices and fail to grow in moral and religious knowledge (in understanding the nature of God and their duties towards their fellows). What will God do? He has reason of concern and compassion to raise up prophets or leaders to announce moral and religious truths, and to encourage societies to pursue right paths. He has reason for not giving the leaders manifest 'supernatural' powers to overawe or dragoon societies into doing the right thing—for if he did, men would see as an evident truth (in the way I described towards the end of the last chapter) the coincidence of self-interest and moral rectitude in such a way as to bias them towards doing the good and take away their freedom of action (by taking away any genuine temptation to do the opposite). So the occasional appearance of wise men and great leaders is perhaps to be expected if there is a God—at any rate in so far as we can judge with our limited knowledge of what reasons God may have for acting. Parental analogy too suggests that God might act as I have described. When teenage children start going wrong, the good parent will not overrule their freedom (they have the right to make a mess of things); but he will not leave them without some instruction and encouragement. So the appearance of wise men and great leaders in times of crisis is not unreasonably seen as due to the hand of God. Things might so easily otherwise go from bad to worse—natural processes might so easily be such as not to throw up prophets to criticize bad systems.

Similarly God has reason for bringing about sudden recovery of the sick—for suffering is always something which God has reason to remove. And likewise God has reason for bringing about 'converting' events in a man's life.

But although God has reason for bringing these things about, he also has reason for not bringing them about or bringing them about too regularly. We have seen this at some length in the last three chapters in the case of suffering. But he also has reason for not bringing about guidance for communities who go astray or converting events in men's lives. The major such reason is that it is good that men should decide for themselves whether to warn or convert others, that men should have responsibility for the (immediate or long-term) spiritual destiny of their fellows. Hence God has reason for letting whether such events occur or not pass outside his control. But I cannot see that he has any reason for stopping such events ever occurring. And if that is right, their occurrence from time to time is somewhat more to be expected if there is a God than if there is not. (See the sixth possibility on p. 110.)

God does have reason for not violating the natural order too often in order to produce such events. For as we have seen in the last few chapters, only if there is a fairly deterministic order which produces in abundance consequences good and ill, will men have the ability or acquire the knowledge necessary for developing the world and for working out their own salvation. But it would not be unreasonable to expect God to do for men the sort of thing a good parent does when his children get into less serious[1] trouble that is, very occasionally bail them out, from a natural compassion, especially if requested; but otherwise leave them with the consequences of their actions, and leave them to cope themselves with natural disasters in order that they may learn by experience. So one would expect much healing of body and soul in accord with natural processes, and some contrary thereto—but one would not expect it to be too obvious that natural laws had been violated, at any rate very often. No parent advertises that he can be relied on to get his children out of difficulties—at least no parent who wants his children to grow up, advertises that.

An entirely regular world in which everything (apart from human choices) occurred in accordance with natural laws would not be a world in which God had any living interaction with men. It would be a world in which God had planned in advance what he wanted to happen if man did this or if man did that, and he would have so arranged natural laws that his responses to human actions and situations was built in to them. He would never respond to men's sins as they committed them, their requests and acts of worship as they made them. And that would give our dealings with him a very impersonal quality. He could of course still have made the world so

---

[1] When a good human parent's children get into more serious trouble, clearly he acts to save them from trouble immediately. But there are the disanalogies between God and the human parent of the kind to which in effect I drew attention on pp. 216-18 which suggest that God might allow men to suffer more serious evils, in the way in which a good human parent allows children to suffer less serious evils.

that different things happened to men according to the different free choices which they made. Thus he could have arranged it so that if a certain man started on a selfish path, he met a holy man who warned him of the consequences of his action. But it would have been built into the world in advance that this would happen; God would not have been responding to the man's choice of a selfish path as he made it. God has the reason of friendship to seek living interaction with the men which he has made, conscious beings and free agents like himself. Hence one would expect him to intervene in the natural order occasionally in response to the human situation, especially in answer to request (i.e. prayer) for good things. I cannot see that he has any reason never to intervene, although as we have seen, he has abundant reason not to intervene often. If that is right, in so far as there is evidence of occasional healings of body and soul, of individuals and nations, that too is evidence of his existence, not merely because of God's power, but also because of his character— there are the kinds of event which he would be expected to bring about occasionally.

Incarnation

It would be appropriate in conclusion to this chapter, to say something about one special event which God might be expected to bring about, a particular intervention of himself into the world which he made, an incarnation. Suppose that the human race gets into a really bad mess. Suppose that men so abuse their freedom that they teach others evil and not good. They do not altogether know which actions are right and which are wrong, and they conceal from themselves even what they do know. They show little interest in where they came from (e.g. whether they have a creator to whom thanks and service are appropriate), nor in whether their existence has any point and their race any destiny. They do not care for their fellows, but live for self. Now the Christian view is roughly that such was the human condition at the outset of civilization; and that but for various, especially Christian, influences from without, it still is. Now whether the Christian view is right here is of course a matter for argument which will turn both on issues of history and psychology and on moral issues; and once again there is no space to pursue these issues. However, few in the last quarter of the twentieth century would deny that this view has a certain plausibility. Suppose that this

Christian view of the human condition is correct. What does God have reason for doing about it?

There may be more than one thing which God has reason for doing about such a human condition; but one kind of response which God has reason to make is the following. He might conclude that things had gone so wrong that an atonement was needed; that the human race ought by sacrificial action to show to its creator and to itself its contrition. Yet he might also conclude that it was not within the capacity of a fallen race to make this kind of atonement; and that if atonement was to be made, it would have to be made on behalf of the race by a man preserved from the bad influences to which humanity was subject. Yet it would not be right of God to single out one man to make such a sacrifice. God could insist on the sacrifice of none other but himself. So God has a reason to bring about an incarnation of some kind of himself as man in order that atonement might be made. Once again, there are big Christian assumptions here which there is no space to discuss—e.g. whether atonement is morally good, or whether it is better for people just to forget wrongdoing; and there is also a big philosophical assumption—that it is coherent to suppose that a God can become incarnate (perhaps there is some self-contradiction in supposing a God to become man), and there is not space to discuss that issue either. But, in order to continue the argument further, let us suppose that the Christian moral view of the propriety of atonement is correct, and that the concept of an incarnation is coherent. As well as concluding that an incarnation to make atonement would be a good thing, God might also conclude that the human race needed a new start with a supreme leader and inspirer to found a society in which his work would be continued. The leader would need to teach the race new moral truths which it had only dimly perceived; perhaps, in virtue of his status, also to give it new moral laws, and to show it by example how to behave. Yet again, to preserve human freedom, the powers of the leader and of the society must not be too evident or too 'supernatural'. Thirdly, God might conclude that it would in any case be good that he should share the burden of evil, imposed for their ultimate good (in the way which I discussed in the last chapter) on the human race.

For these reasons, given the stated assumptions, if there is a God and if man's condition falls low, we may well expect there to appear among men a man who lived a humble and sacrificial life and suffered the evil that men do to men (e.g. by suffering an unjust death at their hands), who taught great moral and religious truths, who even suggested that he was God, and who founded a society to continue his work. He might manifest the divine compassion by healing, and the divine power by violating natural laws in order to do so. He might show to men that his atonement availed and that it was possible for them in his society to reform the world, by natural laws being violated in a supreme way by his resurrection from the dead. All of this however would be none too obvious in order that the option of rejecting it all might remain a genuine one for man. If we have evidence that things have happened like that, as in the Christian story of the life, death, and Resurrection of Jesus of Nazareth, and if we also have reason for believing the stated moral and other assumptions to be true, then that all confirms to some small degree the claim that there is a God, for God has reason for bringing about such a state of affairs—viz. the good of man. The analogy of the very good parent or very good spouse who makes a supreme sacrifice to save the lost child or spouse also suggests that some such thing is to be expected. Of course God may have reasons for not bringing about such a state; although I do not know them. There may be alternative states of affairs which he has good reason to bring about. But there are certainly alternative states of affairs which he would appear to have overriding reason not to bring about—e.g. the human race left eternally to make itself miserable through the original bad half-conscious choices of sinners in the centuries before Christ. Hence the occurrence of events of the type described is more probable if there is a God than if there is not, and so their occurrence would be evidence for his existence.

Whether there is evidence for a divine incarnation in the life, death, and alleged Resurrection of Jesus of Nazareth depends, we have seen, both on historical evidence and on moral and metaphysical assumptions, none of which there is space to discuss in this book. My concern here has been merely to point out what sort of evidence is relevant to this issue and to point out that such evidence would also be evidence for the existence of God, would provide a good C-inductive argument for his existence. It is of course very unlikely that I or the reader would think that God was very likely to do the sort of thing described unless we had had some contact with the Christian tradition or some religious tradition with similarities to the Christian one, and had thus come to believe that the condition of the human race was poor, and that there was a need for atonement and example. But that is no reason for supposing that what we think is not true. Unless I had been brought up in tradition of Western mathematics, I should be unlikely to believe that there is no greatest prime number, but what I believe is true—and the Western mathematical tradition has helped me to see it. Important moral and religious truths are learnt over a much longer time and in a much more complex way than mathematical truths—through experience and literature, through suffering, liturgy, and simple instruction; but they are truths none the less.

Conclusion

I argued in the previous section of this chapter that the character of God is such (he is omniscient and perfectly good, and therefore does what he has overriding reason to do, undeterred by temptation) that some of the events which I listed at the beginning of the chapter are ones (rather than others, equally likely to occur if there was no God) which he might be expected to bring about (or allow to occur) and hence that their occurrence very weakly confirms his existence. I argued earlier that some of those events, if they occurred, were ones which probably would not have occurred in the natural course of things, and hence their occurrence would confirm God's intervention and so his existence. I thus have argued that certain particular public events within history confirm theism (perhaps rather weakly), and many others would confirm theism if they occurred. So I defend the rationality of many who have been moved to religion by close acquaintance with such events. The argument of the chapter has, however, necessarily been incomplete in that I have not discussed whether many particular events, which if they occurred would clearly be violations (or quasi-violations) of natural laws, in fact occurred; nor have I discussed whether various events which clearly occurred and have influenced men's religious beliefs were in fact violations. And, in discussing one particular phenomenon—the life, death, and alleged Resurrection of Jesus of Nazareth—I have passed over crucial moral and philosophical questions, as well as questions of historicity. These issues are, alas, too big and controversial to be discussed within the covers of this book. There are inevitable crucial gaps in the argument of this chapter which there are not in earlier chapters.

However we need some result to carry forward to the next chapter. So I suggest that in view of the fact that some few occurrent events (which are not necessarily violations of natural laws) do confirm theism, and there is clearly some slight evidence of the occurrence of violations of natural laws (of a kind which God would have reason to bring about), that we say that there is a weak C-inductive argument from various particular events in history to the existence of God. If any reader after more detailed consideration of the historical evidence thinks that there is a stronger C-inductive argument or no good C-inductive argument to be had here, he will need to scale up (or down, as the case may be) my subsequent conclusions.

13

The Argument from Religious Experience

I F there is a God, one might well expect him not merely to concern himself with the progress of the human race by bringing about the occurrence of things prayed for, providing opportunity for men to do worthwhile things, or providing a revelation at a particular moment in history, or a society to continue that revelation; but also perhaps to show himself to and speak to at any rate some of the men whom he has made and who are capable of talking about God and worshipping him. Certainly one would not expect too evident and public a manifestation, for the reason which I gave in Chapter 11. If God's existence, justice, and intentions became items of evident common knowledge, then man's freedom would in effect be vastly curtailed. However, one might expect certain private and occasional manifestations by God to some men. The argument from religious experience claims that this has often occurred; many have experienced God (or some supernatural thing connected with God) and hence know and can tell us of his existence.

The Nature of Religious Experience

Let us begin by investigating the premiss. What are the 'religious experiences' whose occurrence is supposed to be evidence for the existence of God? An experience is a conscious mental going-on. It may be described in such a way as to entail the existence of some particular external thing apart from the subject, beyond the stream of his consciousness, normally the thing of which it is an experience; or it may be described in such a way as to carry no such entailment. Thus 'hearing the coach outside the window' is not unnaturally described as an experience; but if I have such an experience, if I really do hear the coach outside the window, then it follows that there is a coach outside the window. Yet if I describe my experience as 'having an auditory sensation which seemed to come from a coach outside the window', my description does not entail the existence of anything external of which the experience was purportedly an experience (or its non-existence). The former kind of description I will call an external description; the latter an internal description. Now when people talk about religious experiences, they often give external descriptions of them. Such external descriptions may be fairly precise—'I talked to God last night', or 'I saw Poseidon standing by the window', or, rather more vaguely, 'I became conscious of a timeless reality beyond myself'. The trouble with taking any external description as the premiss of an argument from religious experience is that there is going to be considerable doubt about the truth of the premiss; but once you accept the premiss, you are quite obviously most, if not all, of the way to your conclusion. If you accept that Joe talked to God last night, then of course there is a God—it hardly needs an argument to show it. If you accept that Joe became conscious of a timeless reality beyond himself, then, admittedly, that does not demonstrate the existence of God, but you are quite a lot of the way towards such a demonstration. So, it seems natural to say, all arguments from religious experience must be phrased as arguments from experiences given internal descriptions. There are various ways of giving internal descriptions of one's experiences, but in the case of most experiences, including those which the subject believes to be of something outside himself, a normal way is to describe how things appear or seem to the subject—one may say 'the room seemed to be going round and round', or 'the carpet appeared to be blue', or 'he appeared to be moving away from me'. One may use in giving such descriptions verbs which describe how things seem to the subject, the use of which is confined to connection with particular modalities of sense, verbs like 'looks' or 'feels' or 'tastes'—I may say 'It looked as if the coach was moving away from me' or 'it felt smooth' or 'it tasted of pineapple'.

There is a crucial distinction due to Chisholm between the epistemic and the comparative uses of such verbs as 'seems', 'appears', 'looks', etc.[1] To use such words in their epistemic use is to

[1] R. M. Chisholm, *Perception* (Ithaca, NY, 1957), Ch. 4. Chisholm attempted to distinguish a third ('non-comparative') use of such verbs, but there is some doubt

describe what the subject is inclined to believe on the basis of his present sensory experience. If I say 'the ship appears to be moving' I am saying that I am inclined to believe that the ship is moving, and that it is my present sensory experience which leads me to have this inclination to belief. If I am using 'looks' in this way when I say 'the figure looks elliptical', I am saying that I am inclined to believe that it is elliptical, and that my inclination to belief arises from my present visual experience. By contrast, to use 'looks', etc. in the comparative use is to compare the way an object looks with the way other objects normally look. In this use 'the penny looks elliptical' means 'the penny looks the way elliptical things normally look'. The speaker is not saying and does not imply that he is inclined to believe that the penny is elliptical; he may know very well that it is not. Again, in the comparative use 'from here it looks red' means 'from here, it looks the way red things normally look'. When I describe an experience in terms of the way things seem (epistemically) to the subject, I shall say that I describe it epistemically. A full internal description of a subject's experiences would seem to involve both kinds of internal description. When I look at a penny on the table from an angle, it looks (in the comparative sense) elliptical, and (in the epistemic sense) circular—and my experience is of it looking to me in both of these ways.

So much for what an 'experience' is and the ways in which we can describe it. But what constitutes a 'religious experience'? The concept of a 'religious experience' in ordinary use has as fuzzy a border as the concept of a religion, and in order to talk about arguments in this field, we need to make it moderately precise. For our present purposes it will be useful to define it as an experience which seems (epistemically) to the subject to be an experience of God (either of his just being there, or doing or bringing about something) or of some other supernatural thing.[1] The thing may be

about whether there is such a use, and I am concerned only with the epistemic and comparative uses.

[1] This definition rules out a lot of what has often been called 'religious experience'. For example, much 'religious experience' does not purport to be an experience of anything external. While many experiences in the religious traditions of Christianity, Judaism, and Islam are what Ninian Smart, following Otto, calls 'numinous', many deep experiences called 'religious' in the Buddhist tradition are not. (Smart defines a numinous experience as 'an experience of a dynamic external presence'. See his article on 'History of Mysticism' in P. Edwards (ed.), *Encyclopaedia of Philosophy* (New York, 1967). R. M. Gimello ('Mysticism and Meditation' in S. T. Katz (ed.), *Mysticism and Philosophical Analysis* (London, 1978)), claims (p. 193) that 'it is

a person, such as Mary or Poseidon; or Heaven, or a 'timeless reality beyond oneself', or something equally mysterious and difficult to describe. For the sake of simplicity of exposition, I shall for most of the discussion where no harm will be done, assume that religious experiences are ones which seem to be of God. At the end of the chapter however I shall also take other experiences into account.

The crucial feature of the definition to which I draw attention is that what makes an experience religious is the way it seems to the subject. This definition seems fair to the use of the expression 'religious experience' in our context—for the characteristics of such experiences have always been supposed to be that in some way they wore their religious origin on their face. What is it for the subject to be right, in fact to experience God, i.e. to be aware of God, and so in the very general sense to perceive God (believing that he is so doing)? (I talk of such awareness of God as a perception without implying that the awareness is necessarily mediated via the normal senses. 'Perceive' is the general verb for awareness of something apart from oneself, which may be mediated by any of the ordinary senses—e.g. it may be a matter of seeing or hearing or tasting—or by none of these.) It seems to me, for reasons which others have given at length, that the causal theory of perception is correct—that S perceives x (believing that he is so doing)[1] if and only if an experience of its seeming (epistemically) to S that x is present was caused by x's being present.[2] So S has an experience of God if and

certain that Buddhists do not ontologize the contents of their mystical experiences, nor people the cosmos with mystical entities, since their very purpose in having them is to "discern" their illusoriness'. Peter Moore ('Mystical Experience, Mystical Doctrine, Mystical Technique' in Katz (ed.)) also emphasizes the variety of 'mystical claims', that they involve both 'subjective' and 'existential' claims. Only religious experiences of the kind which my definition picks out have apparent evidential value in pointing towards the existence of God, and that is why I am concerned with them alone.

[1] There is a use of 'perceive' and other verbs of perception (e.g. 'see', 'hear') in which a subject may be said to perceive something which he does not believe that he is perceiving, e.g. I may be said to have perceived John without realizing that it was John whom I was perceiving. I am not concerned with perception of this kind, but only with perception of things which the subject believes that he is perceiving.

[2] The best presentation of the theory known to me is that by P. F. Strawson in his 'Causation in Perception' in his *Freedom and Resentment* (London, 1974). However, having given the conditions stated above, he argues that they are still insufficient, although necessary, for perception. He claims (pp. 79 f.) that there are further restrictions for different senses, e.g. that 'one can only see what is within one's arc of vision' or 'however loud the report of the cannon, if it is far enough away, it will be

only if its seeming to him that God is present is in fact caused by God being present.

Before going on to describe the different kinds of religious experiences, I need to make two further preliminary points. First, I need to distinguish between public and private perceptions. An object *x* may be such as to cause all persons rightly positioned with certain sense-organs and certain concepts who pay a certain degree of attention to have the experience of it seeming to them that *x* is present.[1] In that case we shall say that *x* is a public perception. Almost all our perceptions—e.g. my seeing a material object such as a desk—are in this sense public perceptions. For a desk is such as to cause all persons close to it (without any material objects between it and them) whose eyes are pointing at it, who are attentive, and have normal vision and the concept of a desk, to have the experience of its seeming to them that there is a desk there. But there may be objects *o* which cause certain persons to have the experience of its seeming to them that *o* is there without their having that effect on all other attentive persons who occupy similar positions and have similar sense-organs and concepts. This could be just because the causal chains which bring about perceptions of *o* are not at all deterministic—e.g. the laws of optics might be such that there was no guarantee that a suitably equipped observer would always see what was there. Or it could be because *o* is a person who can choose whom to cause to have the experience of its seeming to them that *o* is there. *o* may be a normally invisible man with the power of letting you but not me see him. If *S* has the experience of its seeming to him

out of earshot'. But such restrictions seem only to be correct if we suppose that the meaning of such expressions as 'within one's arc of vision' is defined by them. If there is an independent criterion of (e.g.) 'arc of vision'—say a geometrical one—then the stated restriction seems in no way obviously a necessary truth. There is nothing incoherent in supposing that some men can see round corners. I suggest therefore that my analysis gives sufficient, as well as necessary, conditions for perception. H. P. Grice in 'The Causal Theory of Perception', *Proceedings of the Aristotelian Society*, Suppl. Vol., 1961, republ. in G. J. Warnock (ed.), *The Philosophy of Perception* (London, 1967), pp. 85–112 (see pp. 102–6), argues in effect that if *S* is to perceive *x*, it is necessary that *x* cause *S*'s sense impression, but that this is not sufficient to guarantee perception. Grice's arguments against sufficiency however will not work if we understand by 'sense impression' its seeming to *S* that *x* is present, and if we take him as providing an analysis, not of '*S* perceives *x*', but of '*S* perceives *x* (believing that he is so doing)'.

[1] Of course what will constitute being 'rightly positioned' and what sense-organs and concepts are needed will vary with the sense and the kind of object, and are (as I urged on p. 247 n. 2) matters for empirical inquiry; and so too is the degree of attention which is needed.

that *o* is there, but either because of *o*'s choice or for some other reason, not every other attentive person rightly positioned and equipped would necessarily have the experience, then *S* has, I shall say, a private perception of *o*. If religious experiences are of anything, i.e. are perceptions, they are normally private perceptions. When one man has a religious experience, often his neighbour equally attentive and equally well equipped with sense-organs and concepts normally does not. The religious man's explanation of this is that God or gods give such experiences to those to whom they choose to give them, not to all and sundry.

Secondly, I call attention to a relation between experiences. One often perceives one thing in perceiving something else. In seeing a man dressed in such-and-such a way I may see John Smith. In seeing the print of such-and-such a shape in the sand I may see the footprint of a bear. In seeing an especially bright star in the sky I may see Venus near to the earth. In these cases my very same visual or other sensations (described comparatively) which bring about my perceiving the first thing also bring about my perceiving the second thing. In perceiving the second thing one does not see anything extra in the sense of a new item which had escaped one's notice before; rather one perceives the first thing as the second thing. In these cases one man may perceive both things, and another man perceive only the first thing and yet both have the same visual sensations. This relation which holds between perceptions may also hold between experiences described epistemically. In seeming (epistemically) to see the man dressed in such-and-such a way I may seem to see John Smith. In such cases the same sensations (described comparatively) which bring about the first experience also bring about the second. Two men may both have the same visual or other sensations (described comparatively) (e.g. a bright spot in the middle of their visual fields) and through having those sensations one may have a certain experience described epistemically (e.g. seeming to see a lighthouse in the distance) and the other may not. Or of course the same visual or other sensations may give rise to totally different experiences (described epistemically) in different men.

Five Kinds of Religious Experience

With these points in mind it will be useful to classify the different kinds of religious experience. In due course I shall make similar points about all of them, but it is worth while at this stage pointing out the diversity of experiences which fall under our definition. First, we have experiences which seem (epistemically) to the subject to be experiences of God or something else supernatural, but where he seems to perceive the supernatural object in perceiving a perfectly ordinary non-religious object. Thus a man may look at the night sky, and suddenly 'see it as' God's handiwork, something which God is bringing about (in the way in which a man may see a vapour trail in the sky as the trail of an aeroplane). He has, it may be said, an experience of contingency. Secondly, there are the experiences which men have in perceiving very unusual public objects. (The occurrence of the unusual object may or may not constitute a violation of a natural law.) The experiences had by those who witnessed 'the Resurrection appearances of Jesus' or the 'appearance of Mary' at Fatima, or (as far as the auditory phenomena are concerned) St. Paul's experience on the road to Damascus are in this category, if the accounts of these events are in any minimal way reliable. Take the appearance of the risen Jesus to the disciples as described in Luke 24: 36–49. A man looking and talking like Jesus who had been crucified three days earlier suddenly turned up among them and ate some fish (looking and talking like Jesus in the comparative sense, that is, looking and talking the way that Jesus used to look and talk). Yet in perceiving this public event, the disciples had the religious experience of taking the man to be the risen Jesus Christ. Their religious experience was that he looked like Jesus in the epistemic sense, and so they believed him to be. A sceptic might have had the same visual sensations (described comparatively) and yet not had the religious experience.

The other three classes of religious experiences are ones which do not involve taking public phenomena religiously. In them the divine is apprehended via something private to the subject. In the third place we have cases where the subject has a religious experience in having certain sensations private to himself, sensations of a kind describable by the normal vocabulary used for describing the sensations which result from the use of our five senses. In his dream described in Matthew 1: 20 f. Joseph dreamed that he saw an angel who said to him certain things. Here there were no public phenomena, but Joseph had certain private sensations which he might have been able to describe by means of normal sensory vocabulary —e.g. he had the visual sensation like the sensation which he would have had if he had been looking at a man dressed in white, and the auditory sensations which he would have had if someone had been saying such-and-such to him. (He might have been able to tell us the actual words which the angel seemed to be saying to him.) What made the dream a religious experience was that in having the sensations, *and* after he had woken up, it seemed to Joseph that an angel was talking to him, i.e. he took the man-in-the-dream to be a real angel and not a mere angel-in-a-dream, and the words-in-the-dream to be words uttered by the angel. (What the biblical author meant by saying that it was a dream is presumably that the experience was one had while the subject was by normal public criteria asleep, and that the experience was not of a public pheno-menon but that at the time, though not afterwards, it seemed to Joseph that it was of a public phenomenon.)

Fourthly, we have the case where the subject has a religious experience in having certain sensations private to himself, yet these are not of a kind describable by normal vocabulary. The subject has some sensation analogous to sensations of normal kinds, e.g. visual or auditory sensations, but only analogous—such that if his experience was of a public phenomenon we might say that it was the experience of a sixth sense. Presumably mystics and others who find it difficult if not impossible to describe their religious experiences, and yet feel that there is something to be described if only they had the words to do the describing, are having experiences of this kind. Fifthly and finally we have religious experiences which the subject does not have by having sensations. It seems to the subject, perhaps very strongly, that he is aware of God or of a timeless reality or some such thing, and yet not because he is having certain sensations; it just so seems to him, but not through his having sensations. Just as it may seem to me strongly that my hand behind my back is facing upward rather than downward, yet not because of any sensations. Many mystics who claim to experience God via 'nothingness' or 'darkness' may be making the point that their experience of God is not mediated via any sensations. More ordinary cases, however, also fall into this category. A man may be convinced that God is telling him to do so-and-so (e.g. follow such-and-such a vocation), and yet there are no auditory or other sensations occurring.

If the subject is asked 'What was it about your experience which made it seem to you that you were having an experience of God?'[1] in

---

[1] For ways of distinguishing between senses and so grounds for saying that we have a new sense, and for use of the 'what was it . . .' question, see H. P. Grice, 'Some Remarks about the Senses' in R. J. Butler (ed.), *Analytical Philosophy*, First Series (Oxford, 1962).

the case of experiences of the third and fourth kinds there is a partial answer, though in the case of experiences of the fourth kind we may lack the vocabulary to give it. In the case of experiences of the third kind, the partial answer will be 'because of such-and-such auditory or visual or other describable sensations which I had'. The answer will be partial because the mere fact that one was having such-and-such sensations does not make the experience seem to be of God; someone else could have those sensations without thereby having a religious experience. In the case of experiences of the fourth kind, the answer to the question will be 'because of the very unusual and virtually indescribable sensations which I had'. But in the case of experiences of the fifth kind, the answer to 'What was it about your experience which made it seem to you that you were having an experience of God?', will be 'It just did. There were no visual, auditory, or any other sensations which made it seem thus to me.'

So much for a classification of religious experiences. It is, I believe, both exclusive and exhaustive. For clearly an experience which seems to be of God, may or may not be mediated by something sensory (i.e. there may be an answer to the question 'What was it about your experience which made it seem to you that you were having an experience of God?'). If it is mediated by something, the something may be public or private. If it is private, it may or may not be describable by normal sensory vocabulary. If it is public, it may be a common, well-known phenomenon; or something very odd, the occurrence of which may be disputed. However, even though the classification is exclusive and exhaustive, it may sometimes be by no means obvious, even to the subject, into which class a given experience falls. For example, suppose I am alone and seem to see and talk to a figure dressed in white, which I take to be an angel. The correct classification of the experience depends on what others would have experienced if they had been there—this I may not know or have any means of finding out. If others also would have seen a figure dressed in white, then the experience is of the second kind; if not, it is of the third kind.

There is no doubt at all that very many men down the centuries have had religious experiences of one or more of the above kinds. Indeed that statement rather underplays the situation. For many people life is one vast religious experience. Many people view almost all the events of their life not merely under their ordinary description but as God's handiwork. For many people, that is, very many of the public phenomena of life are viewed religiously and so constitute religious experiences of the first type. What is seen by one man as simply a wet day is seen by another as God's reminding us of his bounty in constantly providing us with food by means of his watering plants. What is seen by one man as merely a severe illness is seen by another as God's punishing him for the sins of his youth. That God is at work is no inference for these men but what seems (epistemically) to be happening.

John Hick has called our attention to this phenomenon in various of his works but especially in *Faith and Knowledge*. He observes that:

The Old Testament prophets, for example, experienced their historical situation as one in which they were living under the sovereign claim of God, and in which the appropriate way for them to act was as God's agents; whereas to most of their contemporaries, who were 'experiencing as' in a different way, the situation did not have this religious significance. The prophets' interpretation of Hebrew history, as this is embodied in the Old Testament, shows that they were 'experiencing as' in a characteristic and consistent way. Where a secular historian would see at work various economic, social, and geographical factors bringing about the rise and fall of cities and empires, the prophets saw behind all this the hand of God raising up and casting down and gradually fulfilling a purpose. When, for example, the Chaldaeans were at the gates of Jerusalem, the prophet Jeremiah experienced this event, not simply as a foreign political threat but also as God's judgment upon Israel. . . . It is important to appreciate that this was not an interpretation in the sense of a theory imposed retrospectively upon remembered facts. It was the way in which the prophet actually experienced and participated in these events at the time.[1]

As well as such experiences of the first kind, very many men, both those who are much of the time religious believers and those who are not, have had many religious experiences of the other kinds.[2]

The question must now be faced as to the evidential value of all this. Is the fact that all these religious experiences have occurred evidence for the existence of God (or some other supernatural reality)?

---

[1] J. Hick, *Faith and Knowledge* (2nd edn., London, 1967), pp. 142f.

[2] For some modern 'religious experiences' (although ones of subjects almost entirely from an English Protestant background) see for example the recent volume summarizing a thousand reports of such experiences, provided in response to a public appeal—T. Beardsworth, *A Sense of Presence* (Oxford, 1977). Some are religious experiences on my criterion and some are not. The author is inclined to draw a conclusion from these experiences which is disputable in the light of some of the arguments put forward in this chapter.

The Principle of Credulity

In discussing religious experience philosophers have sometimes made the claim that an experience is evidence for nothing beyond itself, and that therefore religious experience has no evidential value. That remark reflects a philosophical attitude that those philosophers would not adopt when discussing experiences of any other kind. Quite obviously having the experience of it seeming (epistemically) to you that there is a table there (i.e. your seeming to see a table) is good evidence for supposing that there is a table there. Having the experience of its seeming (epistemically) to you that I am here giving a lecture (i.e. your seeming to hear me give a lecture) is good evidence for supposing that I am here lecturing. So generally, contrary to the original philosophical claim, I suggest that it is a principle of rationality that (in the absence of special considerations) if it seems (epistemically) to a subject that x is present, then probably x is present; what one seems to perceive is probably so. How things seem to be is good grounds for a belief about how things are. From this it would follow that, in the absence of special considerations, all religious experiences ought to be taken by their subjects as genuine, and hence as substantial grounds for belief in the existence of their apparent object—God, or Mary, or Ultimate Reality, or Poseidon. This principle, which I shall call the Principle of Credulity, and the conclusion drawn from it seem to me correct.[1] It seems to me, and I hope to my readers, intuitively right in most ordinary cases such as those to which I have just been referring, to take the way things seem to be as the way they are.

Note that the principle is so phrased that how things seem positively to be is evidence of how they are, but how things seem *not* to be is not such evidence. If it seems to me that there is present a

[1] C. D. Broad argues in this way for the prima facie justification of claims of religious experience in 'Arguments for the Existence of God' in his *Religion, Philosophy and Psychical Research* (London, 1953). Many philosophers have made the obvious point that no experience entails the existence of its purported object, but they seem to ignore the question whether it is prima facie evidence for it. Those who do discuss this question usually conclude that it is not prima facie evidence. For example, T. Penelhum in *Religion and Rationality* (New York, 1971), claims (p. 168) that 'an argument beginning with the occurrence, as psychological fact, of a given experience or set of experiences and ending with the ascription of them to a divine cause is either a poor explanatory hypothesis or a circular argument'. Such writers do not seem to me to be aware of the sceptical bog in which failure to accept the Principle of Credulity for other experiences will land them. And if it is all right to use it for other experiences, they need a good argument to show that it is not all right to use it for religious experiences.

table in the room, or statue in the garden, then probably there is. But if it seems to me that there is no table in the room, then that is only reason for supposing that there is not, if there are good grounds for supposing that I have looked everywhere in the room and (having eyes in working order, being able to recognize a table when I see one, etc.) would have seen one if there was one there. An atheist's claim to have had an experience of its seeming to him that there is no God could only be evidence that there was no God if similar restrictions were satisfied. They could not be—for there are no good grounds for supposing that if there is a God, the atheist would have experienced him.

I shall now argue that attempts to restrict the principle in ways designed to rule out its application to religious experience are either unjustified or unsuccessful. I shall consider two such attempts to argue that while its appearing to me that there are before me tables, chairs, houses, etc. is good grounds for supposing that there are (i.e. its seeming to me that I am seeing them is good grounds for supposing that I am), its appearing to me that the world before me is being sustained by God, or that there are present angels or Ultimate Reality is not good grounds for supposing that things are thus.

The first argument is that our supposing that the way things seem is the way they are is not an ultimate principle of rationality, but itself requires inductive justification, and that that inductive justification is available in the ordinary cases but not in the religious cases.[1] More particularly, a philosopher may claim that the fact that it appears that x is present is good grounds for supposing that x is present only if we have evidence that when in the past it appeared that x was present, it proved so to be; or at any rate the assumption that x is present has proved a successful assumption to work from. Hence, the philosopher might argue, it is all right to take what looks like a table as a table, because our past experience has shown that such appearances are not misleading; but he might go on to question whether we had the kind of inductive evidence which was necessary to justify taking religious experiences seriously.

One difficulty with this view is that it is ordinarily supposed that people are justified in taking what looks like a table to be one even if they do not at the same time recall their past experiences with tables,

---

[1] 'In order to infer the divine from an apparition we should have to have experience of a connection between them in the way in which we do have experience of the connection between smoke and fires.' A. MacIntyre, 'Visions', in A. Flew and A. MacIntyre (eds.), *New Essays in Philosophical Theology* (London, 1955), p. 257.

and even if they cannot immediately do so. So the principle would have to say that our justification for taking what looked like a table to be one was that we could remember such past experiences if we tried hard enough. It will not do to say that our merely having had the past experiences suffices to justify our present inference, whether or not we can remember those experiences. For if a claim is to be justified inductively, we must in some sense 'have' the evidence of past performance in order to be justified in making the inference. But then, an induction from past experiences to future experiences is only reliable if we correctly recall our past experiences. And what grounds have we got for supposing that we do? Clearly not inductive grounds—an inductive justification of the reliability of memory-claims would obviously be circular. Here clearly we must rely on the principle that things are the way they seem, as a basic principle not further justifiable; that we seem to have had such and such experiences is in itself good grounds for believing that we had. The principle that the rational man supposes that in the absence of special considerations in particular cases things are the way they seem to be, cannot always be given inductive justification. And if it is justifiable to use it when other justifications fail in memory cases, what good argument can be given against using it in other kinds of case when other justifications fail?

Another difficulty with the view of the first argument is that its suggested principle clearly needs modification to deal with cases where the subject has no past experience of x's but does have experience of properties in terms of which x is defined. Thus a centaur is defined as a being with the head, trunk, and arms of a man, and the body and legs of a horse. A subject has seen men and horses, but not centaurs before. It then appears to him that a centaur is present. Is that good reason to suppose that it is? Surely yes. So the principle behind the first argument had better be modified to read: the fact that it appears that x is present is good grounds for supposing that x is present only if we have evidence that when in the past it has appeared that x or any property by which x is defined is present they have proved so to be, or at any rate the assumptions that they were present proved successful assumptions to work from. But then the argument is quite inadequate to rule out taking religious experiences seriously. For 'God', like 'centaur', is defined in terms of properties of which most of us have had experience. He is defined as a 'person' without a 'body' who is unlimited in his 'power', 'knowledge', and 'freedom', and in terms of other similar properties, of all of which we have had mundane experience. A man might well, through visual, auditory, tactual, etc. experience of recognizing persons of various degrees of power, knowledge, and freedom be able to recognize when he was in the presence of a person of unlimited power, knowledge, and freedom. Indeed it is plausible to suppose that a man might be able to recognize extreme degrees of these qualities, even if he could not so easily recognize lesser degrees straight off without inductive justification. So once the inevitable modification is made to the first argument, whatever its merits, it has no force against the claims of religious experience.

The second attempt to restrict the application of the Principle of Credulity, allows that the principle holds in ordinary cases (without needing inductive justification) but denies that (in the absence of inductive justification) it holds in less usual cases. One writer who has thus restricted the principle is Chisholm. He claims that whenever we take something to have a certain sensible characteristic (or relation), we have adequate evidence for the claim that it does have this characteristic (or relation); but that whenever we take something to have some non-sensible characteristic (or relation), that is not in itself adequate evidence to suppose that it does. And what are these 'sensible' characteristics and relations? Chisholm writes:

The characteristics include being blue, red, green, or yellow; being hard, soft, rough, smooth, heavy, light, hot, or cold; and that of sounding, or making-a-noise. The relations include: being the same, or different with respect to any of the characteristics in question; being more like one object than another with respect to any of the characteristics, or with respect to hue, saturation, and brightness, or with respect to loudness, pitch, and timbre. The class of characteristics and relations also includes the 'common sensibles'—that is, 'movement, rest, number, figure, magnitude'—as well as what is intended by such terms as 'above', 'below', 'right', 'left', 'near', 'far', 'next', 'before', 'after', 'simultaneous', and 'to last', or 'to endure'. In short, the characteristics and relations in question are co-extensive with what Aristotelians have traditionally referred to as the 'proper objects of sense' and the 'common sensibles' and what Reid described as the objects of 'original' perception.[1]

So, according to Chisholm, if something seems (epistemically) to *S* to be brown or square or solid, that is good grounds for believing that it is. But if something seems to be a table, or a Victorian table, or a ship, or a Russian ship, that is in itself not good grounds for believing that it is. You can only have good grounds for believing

[1] Op. cit., p. 83.

that something is a table in terms of it looking brown, square, and solid and in terms of things which look like that having appeared (in the past) to be used for writing on (the notion of 'writing' perhaps being spelt out in terms of 'sensible' characteristics).

Let us say that if its seeming that an object x is present is grounds for supposing that is without need for further justification, then you have a *real experience* of x. But if this does not hold, then its seeming that an object x is present is an *interpretation* of your experience which stands in need of justification. If you have a real experience of x and if in fact x causes your experience, then you *really perceive* x; if you conclude that x is present without really experiencing x, then (even if your conclusion is correct and justifiable) you merely *infer* x. Attempts to draw such lines as Chisholm draws between real experience and interpretation, real perception and mere inference are of course as old as the empiricist tradition in philosophy. It is admitted by most of those who draw a line of this kind that even real experience may mislead. You may have a real experience of x, and therefore be justified in supposing that x is present, that x causes your experience, and so that you perceive x, when in fact x is not present at all. In that case you have a delusion, hallucination, or illusion of x, or are merely dreaming that x is present, or some such thing. However such cases are, on this view, to be distinguished from cases where although it seems that an object x is present, and you take it so to be when it is not, your mistake is one of misinterpretation of experience—a mistake which you would have been justified in making only if you had other grounds for believing the object x to be present.

That there is such a line to be drawn is a common and seldom argued assumption in many discussions of religious experience. Once the line is drawn, the consequences are evident. For the line always leaves the typical objects of religious experience as matters of interpretation rather than as true objects of real experience. It follows that even if it seems to you strongly that you are talking to God or gazing at Ultimate Reality, this fact is no reason in itself for supposing that you are. You are having an experience which is properly to be described in a much more mundane way—e.g. as the experience of hearing certain noises—which you *interpret* as the voice of God, but which you have no good reason for so doing unless further evidence is produced.

However, no such line as the one which Chisholm attempts to draw, can be drawn between real experience and interpretation. For clearly we are justified in holding many perceptual beliefs about objects having non-sensible characteristics which cannot be backed up in terms of beliefs about objects having 'sensible' characteristics. Few would doubt that I am justified in believing that a certain woman whom I see at the other side of a room is my wife. Yet if asked what it is about the woman I take to be my wife which makes me believe that she is my wife, I would be utterly unable to give a satisfactory answer. I could only give a very vague description of the Chisholmian 'sensible' characteristics by which I recognize her, a description which would fit tens of thousands of other women whom I would not for one moment mistake for my wife. That one can recognize does not entail that one can describe; nor does it even entail that (even if one cannot describe them) one knows what the features are by which one recognizes. I may be justified in claiming that you are tired or angry, just by looking at your face, and yet not know what it is about your face which makes you look tired or angry. Again, I can recognize my wife's voice over the telephone, although I certainly cannot say what it is about the noises which come through the telephone receiver which are especially characteristic of her voice. For senses such as smell and taste most of us have no vocabulary for describing sensible characteristics, other than in terms of the objects which cause them (e.g. as 'the taste of tea' or 'the smell of roses'). Asked about the liquid we are drinking 'What is it about it that makes it taste like tea?', we would be stuck for an answer. But that fact casts no doubt on our justification for believing that we are drinking a cup of tea. The fact that it tastes like tea is good reason in itself for supposing that it is—whether or not we can say in more primitive terms what it is about it which makes it taste like tea.

Men differ in the kinds of objects and properties which they learn to pick out. Sometimes they can pick out and even describe the 'sensible characteristics' of those objects and sometimes they cannot; and even if they can, the recognition of objects of some kind and their more sophisticated properties may be a more natural process than the description of their sensible characteristics. There is no reason of principle why we should not grow so adept at spotting Russian ships, or Victorian tables, or blue-dwarf stars, or elliptical galaxies that we can recognize them straight off, without being able to say what it is in the way of Chisholmian sensible characteristics about what we see which makes us identify them as we do.

So this second argument against the original Principle of Credulity fails, and the principle stands. If it seems (epistemically) to S that x is present, that is good reason for S to believe that it is so, in the absence of special considerations—whatever x may be. And it is good reason too for anything else to believe that x is present. For if e is evidence for h, this is a relation which holds quite independently of who knows about e. However, how things seem to S is clearly something of which S knows without inference, whereas others need S's testimony about how things seem to him in order to learn of his experiences. Our justification for relying on S's testimony about his experiences is an issue to which I shall come later in the chapter.

From all this it follows that if it seems to me that I have a glimpse of Heaven, or a vision of God, that is grounds for me and others to suppose that I do. And, more generally, the occurrence of religious experiences is prima facie reason for all to believe in that of which the reported experience was purportedly an experience.

Special Considerations which Limit the Principle of Credulity

It is time to list the special considerations which operate in particular cases and give to a man or to others grounds for holding that although his experience was that it seemed to him that x was present (and so he is inclined to believe that x was present), really x was not present. They are considerations which, when added to the report of the experience, prevent it from making it probable that x was present. Put symbolically, with e as 'it seems to S that x is present', h as 'x is present', and k as irrelevant background knowledge, they are considerations c such that although always $P(h/e.k) > \frac{1}{2}$, $P(h/e.k.c) \leqslant \frac{1}{2}$. If it seems to S that x is present, S is inclined to claim, at any rate to himself, that he perceives x. I shall describe what I am doing as listing the considerations which defeat the perceptual claim which S is inclined to make to himself. Having listed these considerations we can then see whether they will normally be able to show that religious experiences are not to be taken at their face value.

There are basically four kinds of special consideration which defeat perceptual claims. The first two show that the apparent perception was of a kind with others which proved in the past not to be genuine perceptions. First, one may show that the apparent perception was made under conditions or by a subject found in the past to be unreliable. Thus one may show that S's perceptual claims are generally false, or that perceptual claims are generally false when made under the influence of LSD, which is good inductive grounds for believing that a particular new perceptual claim made by S or made under the influence of LSD is false. Secondly, one may show that the perceptual claim was to have perceived an object of a certain kind in circumstances where similar perceptual claims have proved false. Thus if it seems to S that he has read ordinary-size print at a distance of a hundred yards, we can test him on a number of other occasions and see if he is able to read what is written at that distance; and if he is not we have good inductive evidence that the original claim was false.

One variant of the second kind of consideration is where one shows that S has not had the kind of experience which has been found empirically necessary to make a probably true perceptual claim of the kind in question. One might for example have evidence that only those who have actually tasted tea before and been told what it was that they were tasting, can (except by accident) make true perceptual claims to be tasting tea. It is not at all evident *a priori* what kinds of experience people need in order to make probably true perceptual claims; and clearly people vary enormously in this respect. Perhaps some of us who have only smelled tea but never tasted it before could in consequence recognize it by its taste at first tasting. Some of us can recognize people by descriptions. Some of us can only recognize people when we have seen them before.

The third and fourth considerations are ones concerned with the particular perceptual claim which do not involve inductive inference from the failure of similar claims. Since to perceive x is to have one's experience of its seeming that x is present caused by x's being present, one can challenge a perceptual claim to have perceived x either by showing that probably x was not present or by showing that even if x was present, it probably did not cause the experience of its seeming that x was present. The third consideration then which defeats a claim to have perceived x involves showing that on background evidence it is probable that x was not present. Now I suggest that in this case it is not enough that the background evidence makes it more probable than not that x was not present. It has to make it very improbable that x was present if it is to outweigh the force of S's experience sufficiently for it to remain more probable than not that S was not present. For, after all, most of the things which we think that we see are on background evidence less probable than not. It may seem to me, when I go to London, that I see Jones walking along the other side of Charing Cross Road. I may believe *a priori* that it is more probable than not that he is in

Dover where he lives; and that even if he is in London, the odds are against his being in Charing Cross Road at that particular moment. But my experience suffices to outweigh this background evidence. We would indeed be imprisoned within the circle of our existing beliefs, if experience did not normally have this force. However background evidence may make it very, very improbable that x is present—e.g. because it makes it very improbable that x exists at all, or very probable that he is somewhere else. If it is very probable on background evidence that John is dead, then it is very, very improbable that he is walking along the other side of Charing Cross Road at this moment; and my experience does not by itself suffice to push the latter into the category of the probable.

A similar point arises with respect to anyone who claims to have observed an entity of a kind rather different from those already known. If you claim to have seen a dodo on Mauritius, then if *a priori* it is probable, although not very very probable, that dodos become extinct in the seventeenth century, your perceptual claim remains over all probable. But if you claim to have seen a man twenty feet tall getting out of a space machine, then what you claim to have seen has such prior improbability that your claim needs backing up before it becomes probable.

There are various ways in which it can be shown that very, very probably x was not present. One may show that very probably x does not exist, or was in some other particular place at the time, or show that very, very probably x was not at the place in question more directly, in particular by showing that other observers who would very probably have had the experience of its seeming to them that x was there if x had been there, did not do so. If I claim to have seen John in the corridor, my claim may be defeated by showing that although there were many others in the corridor with eyes functioning correctly, who were looking out for John and knew what he looked like, they did not have the experience of its seeming that John was there. The application of this test requires us to know what sense-organs and training you need, and how attentive you need to be to perceive the object in question. We normally have or can get this evidence as a result of seeing what is needed for the detection of similar objects. Yet even when we know what kind of observers would very probably have had the requisite experience if x had been there, their not having the experience does not prove conclusively that he was not there. There will always be a doubt about whether the observers were sufficiently attentive, had their sense-organs working properly, etc. But clearly the more observers apparently rightly positioned with apparently the right sense-organs and concepts who fail to observe x, the less probable it is that x was there. But if some observers have the requisite experience, even if many others do not, that makes it probable that x was there. If x is an object very different in kind from others which have been investigated, we shall not have knowledge of which sense-organs, concepts, and degree of attentiveness are needed for perceiving x; and so we cannot have evidence against the claim, from those who would have had certain experiences if x had been present, but did not have such experiences. But clearly in so far as some do have the requisite experience, that makes it likely that x is there, even if some others do not have the experience, and we do not know why they do not have the experience (so long as we do not have positive reason for supposing that they would have had it if x had been there). The possibility always exists in such cases that the object is not a public object at all.

However, I am inclined to add that if we do not know what experience would count against some perceptual claim (because we do not know which observers could have been expected to have had an experience apparently of x if x had been there), that *somewhat* lessens the evidential force of an apparent perception—but only somewhat. This is because in that case we cannot have the confirming evidence of failure to find evidence which counts against the claim. There cannot stand in favour of the claim the fact that all witnesses who would have had the requisite experience, if the object was present, did so. If your claim could have been disconfirmed by certain phenomena, but the phenomena are shown not to occur, that very fact confirms the claim. If we do not know which observations count against a claim, there cannot be a failure to make such observations, which counts in favour of the claim. However, I stress the words 'only somewhat'; the diminishing force of the impossibility of being in a position to say that all witnesses who ought to have had the requisite experience did so, is not very great. For clearly if three witnesses saw the man in the distance, or the rainbow, or heard the high note, or felt the tremor, and three did not, that is substantial evidence in favour of the occurrence of the object reported, even if we do not know why others were unable to detect it.

Fourthly, the claim to have perceived x may be challenged on the grounds that whether or not x was there, x was probably not a cause of the experience of its seeming to me that *x* was there. One obvious way in which this can be done (without casting any doubt on other of my perceptual claims) is by showing that (probably) something else caused my experience. We challenge the claim by producing a causal explanation of why it seemed to me that *x* was there, which does not involve *x* at any stage. If you show me the actor who was dressed up to look like John and who walked down the corridor, I realize that the experience of its seeming to me that I had seen John was probably caused by the actor, and so that I have no grounds for believing that John was in the corridor.

These four ways which I have listed are all ways in which we or others challenge ordinary perceptual claims. Let us take another example of how they work. Suppose that I wake up startled and, because it so looked to me, I claim to have seen a man dressed in a toga looking up the chimney, who disappeared straight away when I looked at him. You may deny my claim by pointing out (1) that I have become addicted to LSD which has led me to claim to see things which are not there quite a bit recently; or (2) that tests on other occasions show that I cannot recognize a toga when I see one; or (3) that my wife was awake, but did not see the man, and so probably he was not there; or that I have good inductive reason from long experience to believe that men cannot just vanish, and so that it is unlikely that things happened as I claimed; or (4) that there was on the walls a pattern of shadows which could naturally have been interpreted as a man in a toga, and so there was a cause of my experience of 'its looking to me as if there was a man in a toga' other than a man in a toga. Yet if none of these challenges can be made, my claim ought to be accepted. Any claim such as a claim to have seen a man in a top hat walking down the street, which cannot be defeated by any of these challenges, ought to be accepted.

If one of these challenges works, the onus of proof shifts. The subject now needs to prove his experience to be genuine (i.e. that he perceives what he thinks he does). He can do this by producing positive evidence in support of his perceptual claims which can come from consideration of any of the other possible challenges. Thus, to revert to the toga example, I have good evidence from long experience to show that men in togas do not just vanish up chimneys. So a challenge of type (3) counts substantially against my perceptual claims. But I may be able to show (1) that I am in general a very reliable witness, (2) that I know what togas look like, and that I am reliable in reporting things immediately on waking up, (3) that my wife also saw the man, and (4) that there was nothing else which might plausibly have been mistaken for a man in a toga. In such cases we must weigh the conflicting evidence. Our criteria for doing so (e.g. for how much weight we should give to considerations of type (4) against considerations of type 3)) are by no means clear. There is a large border region of possible cases in which it is unclear which way the balance of probability tilts, but clearly if there is enough positive evidence of the kind described, it suffices to outweigh an initially successful challenge to a perceptual claim.

Note that some experiences are very much more forceful than others—some experiences are very clear and unavoidable and leave a very strong impression; it may have seemed that an object was very close and that I could not be mistaken about it. In so far as an experience has such a character, clearly it needs more in the way of challenge to defeat it. If I am really convinced that I saw John in the corridor, it needs to be *very* probable that it was the actor who caused my experience before my perceptual claim becomes improbable.

How far are the above challenges available to defeat the claims of those who claim to have experienced God, or Poseidon, or Ultimate Reality? The first challenge may defeat a few such claims, but it is hardly generally available. Most religious experiences are had by men who normally make reliable perceptual claims, and have not recently taken drugs. The second challenge would consist in showing that normally religious perceptual claims were unreliable. If there was a good proof of the non-existence of God or anything similar, then of course that could be done. But the point here is that the onus of proof is on the atheist; if he cannot make his case the claim of religious experience stands.

It might be thought that there was a general proof of the unreliability of the claims of religious experience in the fact that so many of them conflict with each other. Thus, Flew:

Religious experiences are enormously varied, ostensibly authenticating innumerable beliefs many of which are in contradiction with one another . . . The varieties of religious experience include not only those which their subjects are inclined to interpret as visions of the Blessed Virgin or senses of the guiding presence of Jesus Christ, but also others more outlandish presenting themselves as manifestations of Quetzalcoatl or Osiris, or Dionysus or Shiva.[1]

Now of course devotees of different religions describe their religious

---

[1] A. Flew, *God and Philosophy* (London, 1966), pp. 126f.

experiences in the religious vocabulary with which they are familiar. But in itself this does not mean that their different descriptions are in conflict—God may be known under different names to different cultures (as both Old and New Testaments acknowledge—see Exodus 6: 2 f. and Acts 17: 23). Likewise a Greek's claim to have talked to Poseidon is not necessarily in conflict with a Jew's claim to have talked to the angel who watches over the sea; it is so only if to admit the existence of Poseidon is to commit one to a whole polytheistic theology, and there is no need to suppose that generally it is.

Admittedly, sometimes the giving of one description to the object of religious experience does carry commitment to a doctrine regarded as false by devotees of another religion. Claiming to have experienced the heavenly Christ commits one to a belief in an Incarnation which an orthodox Jew would not admit. But in these cases if the opponent of the doctrine can produce good grounds for regarding it as false, that is reason for the subject of the experience withdrawing his original claim. Among those grounds may be that others have had conflicting experiences and that their experiences are more numerous and better authenticated; but there may be many grounds of other kinds as well. The subject of the religious experience need not in such a case withdraw his original claim totally; he need only describe it in a less committed way—e.g. claim to have been aware of some supernatural being, not necessarily Dionysus (as originally claimed). The fact that sometimes (and by no means as frequently as Flew suggests) descriptions of the object of a religious experience are in conflict with descriptions of the object of another religious experience, only means that we have a source of challenge to a particular detailed claim, not a source of scepticism about all the claims of religious experience. Babylonian astronomers reported the movements of holes in the firmament; Greek astronomers reported the movements of physical bodies in the heavens. The conflict between them did not mean that there were no specks in the sky of which both groups were giving further descriptions. But it did mean that the perceptual claims of each group constituted arguments against the perceptual claims of the other group; and, given that the perceptual claims of both groups were equally weighty in number and conviction, that further arguments were needed to adjudicate between them. Eventually the Babylonian astronomers had to admit that they had somewhat misdescribed what they saw. But this process need hardly lead to general scepticism about astronomical observation; nor need the similar process in religion.[1]

However, it does follow that if there were a substantial number of religious experiences which entailed the non-existence of a particular supernatural being, that would cast significant doubt on the credibility of claims to have perceived that being. There certainly does not exist evidence of this kind sufficient to cast significant doubt on the credibility of claims to have perceived God. Religious experiences in non-Christian traditions are experiences apparently of beings who are supposed to have similar properties to those of God, or experiences apparently of lesser beings, or experiences apparently of states of affairs, but hardly experiences apparently of any person or state whose existence is incompatible with that of God. If there were vastly many experiences apparently of an omnipotent Devil, then that sort of evidence would exist; but there are not such experiences.

Another general objection under the heading of this second challenge might be that those who make claims of religious experience have not had the kind of experience which is needed to make claims of this kind which are probably true. The argument might be that your claim to have recognized a person is only likely

[1] There was a tradition in the description of mystical experience, typified by W. T. Stace (see his *Mysticism and Philosophy*, London, 1961), which claimed that all mystical experiences are in essence the same. It was simply that Christians, Muslims, Buddhists, etc. read into them their own different interpretations, or no interpretations. We have seen (p. 258 f.) that any distinction between the real experience and the interpretation superimposed upon it is going to be hard to justify, if the experience is supposed to be of some external object. However the natural way to interpret Stace's claim is as a claim that all subjects have in essence the same kinds of sensory experiences, i.e. the same kinds of experience described comparatively (see pp. 245 f.) which give rise to different kinds of experience described epistemically, i.e. lead the subjects to hold different beliefs. Stace distinguished mystical experiences from other religious experiences, such as voices and visions, but even so his claim is disputable. (See the discussion by S. T. Katz, 'Language, Epistemology, and Mysticism', in his collection *Mysticism and Philosophical Analysis*, London, 1978). Yet even if it were correct, there would only be a situation of conflicting experiences, giving rise to the situation described in the text, if the subjects were to describe their experiences as experiences apparently of objects which could not both exist together (e.g. an omnipotent God and an omnipotent Devil). The fact that one subject describes his experience solely in comparative terms ('I had the sort of experience which you have if you look at a very bright light'), and another describes his experience in a more committed way ('I had an experience apparently of a very Pure Being') does not give rise to this situation. We can accept the claims of the subjects of both experiences. The Principle of Credulity suggests that we should draw an ontological conclusion from the second, but not from the first, i.e. it suggests that there is some object which the first subject fails to recognize, but which the second subject does recognize.

to be correct if you have previously perceived that person (and been told who he is) or if you are previously given a detailed description of his appearance (appropriate to the modality of sense by which you claim to recognize him—e.g. you would need previously to have been given a description of his visual appearance, before your claim to have seen him is likely to be correct).[1] But this argument seems clearly mistaken. I can come to recognize people whom I have never perceived before after being given descriptions of them which can hardly be regarded as descriptions of their appearance appropriate to the modality of sense involved. Thus I may be told that Smelinowski is the only Ruritanian with a really English sense of humour, or that General Walters is the most commanding personality whom I am ever likely to meet in a lifetime; and these descriptions may be perfectly adequate for me to be able to recognize Smelinowski or General Walters. The description of God as the one and only omnipotent, omniscient, and perfectly free person may indeed suffice for a man to recognize him—by hearing his voice, or feeling his presence, or seeing his handiwork, or by some sixth sense. Even if some of us are not very good at recognizing power, or knowledge, or freedom in the human persons whom we meet, we might well be able to recognize extreme degrees of these qualities when we cannot recognize lesser degrees. Nor of course if a man has the ability to recognize something, does it follow that he can imagine in advance what the experience of recognition would be like. What you tell me about an entirely new colour may enable me to recognize that colour when I see it, even if I cannot visualize the experience in advance. This objection certainly has no compelling force, but it does seem to me to have some small force. Great power, knowledge, or freedom are not characteristics

---

[1] In the case of visions of persons now dead who formerly lived on earth, such as the saints, one must be careful not always to suppose that the person will continue to look and otherwise appear as he did on earth, in his more superficial aspects. No doubt character and some memory may be expected to continue, as more intimately connected with personal identity; but one would not expect dress necessarily to be the same and linguistic competence to be confined to the tongue which the person spoke on earth. Thus sceptics are apt to deny the claim of some Portuguese peasant to have seen Mary, on the grounds that the description which the peasant gives of the way Mary was dressed does not fit the way Mary used to dress in Palestine, but corresponds closely to the way she is pictured on the walls of Portuguese churches. That seems to me to count not at all against the peasant's claim. For if Mary has survived death, what reason is there to suppose that she has now to dress the way she did in Palestine? If she is to manifest herself in bodily form the obvious way for her to dress is the way in which she would be recognized by those to whom she appears.

which we easily learn to recognize by hearing a voice, or by seeing some object which might be an agent's handiwork, or by feeling. And *some* mild suspicion is cast on a subject's claim to have recognized an agent with these qualities by the qualitative remoteness of his previous experiences from what he claims to have detected—but for the reasons which I have given, only *some* mild suspicion.

The third challenge to a claim of religious experience would consist, in the case of a purported experience of God, in a demonstration that very, very probably God was not present to be perceived, and so the subject could not have perceived him. But if there is a God, he is everywhere. He is only not present if he does not exist. So to use this challenge, you have to prove that very, very probably there is no God, and, as stated above, the onus is on the atheist to do so.[1] As we have seen, it will not do to show that some people with similar equipment and concepts to those who do have experiences of God, do not have such experiences. For we do not know that all persons with certain equipment and concepts could be expected to have experiences of God, if he was there. Clearly, if he so chose, an omnipotent God could cause a private experience, in the way that a table could not. Clearly too some people with similar equipment and concepts do have experiences apparently of God. But, as we have also seen, the fact that there are no obvious disconfirming observations (no observations of the absence of God) which could be made, has the consequence that the original perceptual claim is, on its own, somewhat less evidence of the existence of God.

The fourth challenge would consist in showing that the religious experience had a cause other than its purported object, e.g. God. But this is a particularly awkward challenge to apply when we are dealing with a purported experience of God—as opposed to, say, Mary or Poseidon. My religious experience will no doubt be caused by goings-on in my brain. It is an experience of Mary if Mary belongs to the causal chain which brings about those goings-on, by her presence where she appears to be. Since Mary is not omnipresent, she will appear to be here rather than there; and since she is not the sustainer of the world, she can only be responsible for some causal processes in it. It is possible to show that the causal chain

---

[1] For religious experiences of other persons or things, e.g. of Mary or Poseidon, you need to show either that the person does not now exist, or that he is not where the subject said that he was.

which produced my experience involved events only at places other than where she appeared to be or involved causal processes which would have operated whether or not she had been there. It is possible to show that she was not involved in the process, without in any way tending to disprove her existence. But if there is a God, he is omnipresent and all causal processes only operate because he sustains them. Hence any causal processes at all which bring about my experience will have God among their causes; and any experience of him will be of him as present at a place where he is. And so if there is a God, any experience which seems to be of God, will be genuine—will be of God. He may bring about that experience either by intervening in the operation of natural laws (producing an event other than natural laws would ordinarily produce) or by sustaining their normal operation. (The scientifically inexplicable phenomena for which by the Principle of Credulity God is invoked as cause, are either the occurrence of religious experiences in violation of natural laws, or the fact that natural laws are such as to bring about religious experiences.) But a demonstration that God was not responsible for the processes which caused me to have the religious experience can only be attained by demonstrating that there is no God—for if he exists as defined, clearly he is responsible both for the normal operation of natural laws and for any occasional violation.[1]

The upshot of all this is that there are two qualifications which somewhat diminish the evidential force of religious experience apparently of God. One is the qualitative remoteness of subjects' past experiences from what they claim to have recognized, viz. God. The other is the fact that there cannot be perceptions of the absence of God. But for these qualifications, I would have concluded that a religious experience apparently of God ought to be taken at its face value unless it can be shown on other grounds that very, very probably God does not exist. The qualifications lead me to modify the 'very, very probably', and to suggest that a religious experience apparently of God ought to be taken as veridical unless it can be shown on other grounds significantly more probable than not that God does not exist.

Religious experience purportedly of other supernatural persons or things may have more difficulty in getting taken at its face value—it is open to the fourth challenge (and it may be more open

---

[1] This simple point is well made in W. J. Wainwright, 'Natural Explanations and Religious Experience', *Ratio*, 1973, **15**, 98-101.

to the objection that there are religious experiences of persons whose existence is incompatible with that of the purported objects of the original experiences).

To return to the main thread—the issue with regard to the evidential force of experiences apparently of God is just how improbable is the existence of God, on background evidence, that is, that general knowledge of the world and its operations, together with reports of miracles and revelation, considered in Chapters 7 to 12. Is the existence of God significantly more probable than not, so that an experience apparently of God should not be taken at its face value?

We saw that any apparent perception of what is on background evidence too improbable to be believed (i.e. for what is apparently perceived to be improbable over all on all the evidence) may become credible if backed up by positive evidence that the experience is genuine. This positive evidence can take the form of others' having corroborating experiences. It is a further important principle of rationality that, in the absence of reason for challenge, we believe what people tell us about their experiences.

The Principle of Testimony

The Principle of Credulity is concerned with a subject's grounds for believing that things are as they seem to him. Clearly in ordinary life we use a wider principle, for we usually believe to have occurred what other people tell us that they perceived occurring. Other things being equal, we think that what others tell us that they perceived, probably happened.

By 'other things being equal' I mean the absence of positive grounds for supposing that the others have misreported or mis-remembered their experiences, or that things were not in fact as they seemed to those others to be. Clearly most of our beliefs about the world are based on what others claim to have perceived—beliefs about geography and history and science and everything else beyond immediate experience are thus based. We do not normally check that an informant is a reliable witness before accepting his reports. And we *could* not do so because we form our beliefs about what they are saying, the meaning of the claims which they are making, on the assumption that other people normally tell the truth.

We can see this by considering how an anthropologist comes to learn the language of a native tribe. He listens to what the natives say, and observes correlations between what they say and how things are—e.g. he finds that on the day before a festival natives often say 'p' but they do not say 'p' at any other time. If he takes this as evidence that 'p' means 'there will be a festival tomorrow', he must already assume that normally natives tell the truth. What applies to the anthropologist applies to a child learning his first language or additions to it. When people point to a colour and say 'this is green', the child believes that 'green' is the name of that colour—because he has already made (implicitly) the assumption that people normally tell the truth. The assumption itself cannot be tested—because if it is up for test whether people normally tell the truth, then we would have to see whether there are correlations between the propositions people utter and how things are—yet we should not know what propositions they were uttering (i.e. what they meant by their sentences), unless we had already made the assumption up for test.

The assumption that things are (probably) as others claim to have perceived them has two components. One is the Principle of Credulity—that (in the absence of special considerations) things are (probably) as others are inclined to believe that they have perceived them. The other component is the principle that (in the absence of special considerations) the experiences of others are (probably) as they report them. This latter principle I will call the Principle of Testimony. I used this principle in claiming (on the basis of what they tell us) that very many people have religious experiences. The special considerations which lead us to doubt a subject's reports of his experiences are evidence that generally or in matters of a particular kind he misremembers or exaggerates or lies. But in the absence of such positive evidence we have good grounds to believe what others tell us about their experiences.

In general there are no special considerations for doubting what subjects report about their religious experiences, although sometimes there are such considerations. There may be evidence from what he says about other matters on other occasions that a subject is a habitual liar, or tells a lie whenever he can gain attention by so doing, or exaggerates, or misremembers. In these cases his reports on his religious experiences are to be viewed with scepticism. But this is not the normal situation.

One ancient test which may be used where there is doubt about the veracity of a subject's report of some religious experience is to see whether the subject's life-style has undergone a change. Suppose that Jones claims to have had an overwhelming experience which strongly seemed to him to be of God. If he really did have that experience, one would expect his faith in God to be much deeper and this to make a great difference to his way of living. Our grounds for this expectation are that if it really seems to you that you have seen x, then you will believe that x exists. If you believe that x exists, that will make a difference to your behaviour in appropriate circumstances. (This may or may not be an analytic truth as some philosophers have claimed, but it is certainly a generalization which normally holds.) If it really seems to you that you have talked with God, then it will be much more natural for you to act as if there is a God (unless you are set to spite God); prayer, worship, and self-sacrifice will be more natural occupations.[1]

Since (probably) others have the experiences which they report, and since (probably) things are as a subject's experience suggests that they are, then (with some degree of probability) things are as others report. However the degree of probability is less in the conclusion than it is in either of the premisses. If p is evidence for q, and q is evidence for r; then p is normally less evidence for r than it

---

[1] One kind of case where more than normal scepticism about a subject's reports of his experience is perhaps called for is where the subject claims that God has told him to do something. More than normal scepticism is called for because there is a natural tendency of many men to believe that others, and so *a fortiori* God, wish them to do what they want to do anyway. Men tend to read approval into the attitudes of others towards their actions. The more a subject is seen to be liable to this tendency, the more his reports of this kind of religious experience ought to be treated with caution. Independent evidence (e.g. from considerations of morality) about what God (if there is a God) would wish the subject to do can to some extent be used to check both that the subject is not deceiving himself and others about how things seem to him to be, and that things are as they seem to him to be. In this connection note that the mere fact that a subject A has an experience apparently of God telling him to do X, and subject B has an experience apparently of God telling him to stop A doing X does not automatically entail that one or other experience is not veridical. Thus a Muslim may have an experience of being told by God to defend Jerusalem against the infidel, while a Christian has the experience of being told by God to attack it. This might be explained by the fact that in the course of human history as a result of factors for which men are much to blame, Muslim and Christians have come to have different and very limited understandings of God. God is very anxious that human understanding of God should develop through human experience, effort, and co-operation, and should not always be revealed by divine intervention; yet he is also very anxious that at any time in history men should live and die by the ideals which they then have. He therefore tells Muslim and Christian each to live by their current ideals; knowing that the experience of so doing may lead them to a deeper understanding. On a human level, a sage might well sometimes give to each of two persons who sought his advice the advice to oppose the other, thinking it for the good of both that they should seek to develop their independence and authority.

is for *q*. If the fingerprint is evidence of Jones's presence at the scene of the crime, and Jones's presence at the scene is evidence that he did the crime; the fingerprint is less evidence for Jones's having done the crime than it is for his presence at the scene of the crime. Hence if *S* reports that it seems (epistemically) to *S* that *x* is present, then that is reason for others also to believe that *x* is present, although not as good reason as it is for *S* if in fact he is having the experience which he reports. However, clearly it is quite good reason. As we have seen, our whole system of beliefs about the world beyond our immediate experience is based on trusting the reports of others. And of course in so far as a number of others give similar reports that greatly increases their credibility.

Conclusion

One who has had a religious experience apparently of God has, by the Principle of Credulity, good reason for believing that there is a God—other things being equal—especially if it is a forceful experience. We have seen that the only way to defeat such a move is to show that it is significantly more probable than not that there is no God. If the prior probability of the existence of God on the evidence discussed in Chapters 7 to 12 is significantly less than half, then an individual's religious experience needs backing up by the testimony of others to having had similar experiences. That testimony is evidently available. Only if the prior probability of the existence of God is very low indeed will this combined weight of testimony be insufficient to overcome it. Everything turns on just how improbable on background evidence is the existence of God. To that issue I will come in the final chapter.

One who has not himself had an experience apparently of God is not in as strong a position as those who have. He will have less evidence for the existence of God; but not very much less, for he will have testimony of many who have had such experiences.

Not all religious experiences are apparently of God. Within the Christian tradition men have claimed to have perceived angels and saints, Heaven and Hell. Within other traditions men have claimed to have perceived various beings and things, largely, I have urged, ones compatible with the claims of theism. Many of these experiences are experiences of persons or things which are more likely to exist if there is a God than if there is not. Thus an experience of The Blessed Virgin Mary is an experience of a person as present, who is much more likely to be present if there is a God who has preserved her in existence after death than if there is no God. In so far as an experience is of this kind, its occurrence is evidence for the existence of something which is in its turn evidence of the existence of God—but clearly much less evidence than is an experience apparently of God.

My conclusion about the considerable evidential force of religious experience depends on my Principle of Credulity that apparent perceptions ought to be taken at their face value in the absence of positive reason for challenge. This principle is a very fundamental and very simple principle for the interpretation of experience. It is because of its fundamental and simple character, that I did not need to interpret the issues of this chapter via the apparatus of Bayes's theorem. However, since by the argument of this chapter, with h as 'there is a God', e as the evidence of very many religious experiences, and k the phenomena considered in previous chapters, $P(h/e.k) > P(h/k)$, we can use the relevance criterion in reverse to infer that $P(e/h.k) > P(e/k)$, and so $> P(e/\sim h.k)$. It may indeed be to some extent probable that men will have experiences apparently of God, even if there is no God. There is a certain probability that (in an orderly world containing men and animals, etc.) the laws of nature might be such as to lead to men having such experiences anyway. But if there is a God, there is a greater probability that they will have such experiences—because if men have a basic ability to detect how things are, it is more likely that they will have an experience apparently of x (i.e. an experience inclining them to believe that x is present), if x is present than if x is not. And that they do have this basic ability is what in effect the Principle of Credulity is claiming.

I stress that the Principle of Credulity is a very fundamental principle for the interpretation of experience. There is no primitive description of what is perceived in terms of which all other claims to have perceived things need justification. When we learn our first language, we acquire a conceptual scheme, no one part of which is more basic or more central than any other one. In terms of this we must operate and describe what we perceive. The language game is played. If someone denies one of our claims on good grounds (formulated within the terms of our conceptual scheme), then we can withdraw it and redescribe the experience. And by this process whole conceptual schemes may be radically transformed—but, as in Neurath's famous analogy, like a ship at sea, only one plank at a time. Initial scepticism about perceptual claims—regarding them as guilty until proved innocent—will give you no knowledge at all. Initial credulity is the only attitude a rational man can take—there is no half-way house. However, claims which can subsequently be shown unreasonable can be weeded out. But the onus remains on the challenger. Unless we take perceptual claims seriously, whatever they are about, we shall find ourselves in an epistemological Queer Street. Religious perceptual claims deserve to be taken as seriously as perceptual claims of any other kind.

14

The Balance of Probability

In previous chapters I have urged that various occurrent phenomena are such that they are more to be expected, more probable if
there is a God than if there is not. The existence of the universe, its
conformity to order, the existence of animals and men, men having
great opportunities for co-operation in acquiring knowledge and
moulding the universe, the pattern of history and the existence of
some evidence of miracles, and finally the occurrence of religious
experiences, are all such as we have reason to expect if there is a
God, and less reason to expect otherwise. For each of these
phenomena e $P(e/h.k) > P(e/k)$, where h is the hypothesis of theism,
k are the phenomena previously taken into account (i.e. tautological
evidence where e is the existence of the universe; the existence of the
universe where e is its conformity to order, and so on). Hence, by
principles of probability which I discussed in Chapter 6 for each e
$P(h/e.k) > P(h/k)$ and so each argument from e to h was a good C-
inductive argument for the existence of God. I also argued that one
or two phenomena which have been considered to be confirming
evidence of the existence of God are not such evidence—e.g. the
existence of morality. I also discussed, mainly in Chapter 11, the
main argument against the existence of God from the existence of
evil; and I argued that the existence of evil did not count against the
existence of God. With e as the amount and kind of evil which there
is in the world, $P(h/e.k) = P(h/k)$.

I believe that I have stated in outline what is the main evidence for
and against the existence of God. However, only for the evident
general public evidence have I been able to analyse the evidence in
detail and assess its force. With respect to the important evidence
from some of the detailed historical phenomena considered in
Chapter 12, I was able only to consider what would be the evidential

force of various phenomena if they occurred, not whether in fact the direct evidence (of witnesses, traces, etc.) shows that they did occur. So I could not reach a final conclusion on just how strong a C-inductive argument was to be had here. (We also saw in Chapter 13 that within limits the exact force of an argument from religious experience would depend on whether the subject had himself had religious experiences, on their strength, and on the extent of his knowledge of the religious experiences of others.) In Chapters 9, 10, and 11 I had to omit discussion of a crucial issue—whether men have free will. I assumed that it was not demonstrable that they do not. My argument of those chapters would fail if men do not have free will. But there was no space to discuss an issue which demands (and often gets) a book to itself. If any reader believes that it is probable that men do not have free will, he will judge the arguments of those chapters to have correspondingly less force; and if any reader believes that it is probable that men do have free will, those arguments will have correspondingly more force. My failure to discuss these two issues is my most glaring omission. But of course there is a lot more to be said, indeed infinitely more to be said, on every issue discussed in this book. Nevertheless, I believe that I have explored with some rigour the evidential force of the most evident relevant phenomena on the question of the existence of God, and it is now time to draw my threads together to reach a conclusion. The crucial question remaining for discussion is just how probable all of the evidence which I have considered makes the hypothesis of theism. Where all the relevant factual evidence is included in e, and k is mere tautological evidence, what is the value of $P(h/e.k)$? We may not be able to give it an exact numerical value, but the important issue is whether $P(h/e.k) > P(\sim h/e.k)$ and so $> \frac{1}{2}$. Do we have a good P-inductive argument to the existence of God?

It seems fairly evident to me that an argument from the occurrence of all the phenomena which I have described to the existence of God is not a good deductive argument, for the same reason as the reasons which I gave for a cosmological argument not being a good deductive argument (pp. 119 f.) and for a teleological argument not being a good deductive argument (pp. 143 f.). The reason is simply that the description of a world in which all the phenomena described occur, but there is no God seems, with apparent obviousness, to be a coherent description, to contain no buried self-contradiction. And in that case there is no valid argument from the occurrence of those phenomena to the existence of God. Now certainly what seems to be coherent may in fact not be. But the world described seems to be a coherent world. Attempts to discover self-contraditions within it notoriously fail, and it seems easy enough to spell out one or more ways in which our world could be such a world. For example, our universe of material objects could behave in a law-like way, some of them being conscious agents of limited knowledge and power. Reports of miracles would occur because of men's excessive credulity; and men's claims to have perceived God would be the result of some delusion. No one would have limitless power or know everything, and the world would depend on no agent for its existence. Its existence might be an ultimate brute fact.

This picture of how things might be could be spelt out at great length and does not appear to contain any self-contradition (although of course what is described may be improbable). Hence in the absence of positive arguments to the contrary it seems fairly evident to me that there is no good deductive argument from the occurrence of all the phenomena described to the existence of God (and hence of course no good deductive argument from any of the phenomena separately to the existence of God—as I urged in connection with the cosmological and teleological arguments, but did not bother to urge in connection with other arguments). So I return to the question of just how probable all the evidence taken together makes the hypothesis of theism.

I have taken for granted our ordinary criteria for what confirms what, and for what makes what probable, criteria which seem to us to be intuitively right; and I have been concerned to apply these criteria to investigate the probability of theism. I have derived our ordinary criteria by meditating upon what we say about cases in science, history, or other ordinary areas of discourse. For example, I urged that a theory is more likely to be true in so far as it is simple. I reached this conclusion by pointing out from scientific and other examples that we regard a theory h_1 as more probable than another theory of equal scope (i.e. telling us about things of similar kinds) h_2 where both are equally successful in leading us to expect the phenomena which we observe ($P(e/h_1 . k) = P(e/h_2 . k)$) but where h_1 is simpler than h_2 (e.g. in the number of entities or the mathematical relations between them which it postulates). A study of what seems intuitively the right thing to say in many cases in science, history, or other areas (e.g. detective work) about when evidence confirms this theory, or confirms this theory more than that one, enables us to extrapolate criteria which we can apply to the issue of theism. It was that which enabled us to say that this and that confirmed theism. However, when we come to judgements about whether a hypothesis is more probable than not, there is a shortage of suitable examples from science, history, and other areas, from which to extrapolate criteria for evidence making a theory more probable than not.

There are certainly cases where it is intuitively obvious (and almost all would agree) that evidence makes a theory over-whelmingly probable or overwhelmingly improbable, at any rate where that theory is a theory about a particular past or future occurrence. On the evidence available to us it is overwhelmingly probable that the sun will rise again within the next twenty-four hours, that my study will not suddenly disintegrate, that there really was a Roman Empire, and so on. Juries find prisoners guilty, when the evidence points to their guilt 'beyond reasonable doubt'. Similarly there are cases where theories are wildly improbable. But when we get anywhere near the border between the probable and the improbable, there is a shortage of examples; examples of theories which, it is intuitively obvious, are more probable than not, without being overwhelmingly probable; or less probable than not without being overwhelmingly improbable. Once there is genuine doubt about, say, some historical theory, historians will seldom agree about whether the theory is more probable than not. And when there is genuine doubt about the predictions of a scientific theory scientists will seldom agree about whether those predictions are more probable than not. The same applies in other areas. The situation is even worse when we are dealing, not with hypotheses about particular past or future events, but with universal scientific theories, that is, theories making claims about infinitely distant regions of space and time. Is Quantum Theory more probable than not? Or is the General Theory of Relativity? The answer is in no way clear.[1] So any difficulty in reaching a conclusion about whether

---

[1] Some philosophers have claimed that all universal scientific theories have zero probability on any evidence. There is however no compelling argument for this claim and it seems to run counter to what scientists and others naturally wish to say about scientific theories. Most scientists of the eighteenth century would have said that on the evidence then available Newton's theory of gravitation was overwhelmingly probable. Today perhaps the majority of scientists would say that they think that on present evidence Quantum Theory is probable. Further, almost all scientists are prepared to say that among theories compatible with the evidence, some are more probable than others; and often that one such is more probable than any other. Yet clearly one theory can only be more probable than a second if the first does not have zero probability. Also scientists often affirm that they believe that Quantum Theory is true, that the evidence points to its truth rather than its falsity. Yet you can only

theism is more probable than not is not in any way to the special discredit of theism.

However, the situation is by no means hopeless; and so let us proceed, conscious, however, of the considerable difficulty of making judgements of this kind. The reader will recall that by Bayes's Theorem, the probability of a hypothesis *h* on empirical evidence *e* and background knowledge *k* is a function of its explanatory power and its prior probability.

$$P(h/e \cdot k) = \frac{P(e/h \cdot k)}{P(e/k)} \times P(h/k).$$

believe something if you also believe that that thing is not totally improbable (i.e. if you believe that its probability is not zero); and you can only hold that the evidence points to the truth rather than to the falsity of a theory, if you hold that on the evidence the theory is more probable than not. Talk of scientific theories being probable or improbable does seem to be embedded in or implied by the way in which we naturally talk about these matters. The claim that all universal scientific theories have zero probability on any evidence is in no way forced upon us if we suppose as I suppose (see my *An Introduction to Confirmation Theory*) that the axioms of the probability calculus have application to talk about the probability of scientific theories. True, if one assumed that each of an infinite number of universal scientific theories had equal prior probability, one would have to conclude that the prior probability of each was zero; and from that it would follow, given the calculus, that the posterior probability of each on any evidence would also be zero. But there is no need to make that implausible assumption. If simplicity is evidence of truth, as I have claimed in this book, the simpler a theory the greater its prior probability; and hence prior probabilities differ as simplicity differs. Mary Hesse has argued recently that although scientists do talk about scientific theories being probable, such talk ought not to be taken literally. (See her *The Structure of Scientific Inference*, London, 1974.) Talk about a scientific theory being probable ought rather to be construed as talk about the theory probably operating in our spatio-temporal region. However Professor Hesse's discussion of positive arguments for her thesis is very brief and seems mainly to rely on an appeal to the claim (p. 182) that 'it is not reasonable to suppose that any lawlike generalization . . . in current or any future science will remain forever unqualifiedly true in every instance.' But why is it not reasonable? No adequate answer is given. Science has only been a serious pursuit for a few hundred years, and we may not yet have found the true laws of nature which hold over endless space and time. But why is it unreasonable to suppose that in a few million years we may find them? I do not know of good positive arguments why we should understand our talk about theories being probable in the way which Hesse suggests. Even if a reader does accept Mary Hesse's view, that provides no ground for taking a similar view about the probability of theism. For if one scientific theory *T* only holds within a limited spatio-temporal region *S*, this will be a consequence (in view of the special conditions within *S*) of the fact that a more general theory *T* holds in a wider region (or universally). But if theism explains phenomena in some region, it must hold universally. It follows from the nature of theism that if it holds for one place and time, it is true universally (if there is an eternal, omnipotent being at one place and time, there will be one at all places and times) and if it is true, nothing further explains why it is true (see p. 105).

The explanatory power of a hypothesis is a function of $P(e/h.k)$ which I term its predictive power, and $P(e/k)$ the prior probability of the evidence. $P(e/h.k)$ is a matter of how likely it is if h is true (and k holds) that e will occur. $P(e/k)$ is a matter of how likely e is to occur at all, whether or not h is true. $P(h/k)$ is the prior probability of h, how likely h is to be true *a priori*—that is whether or not e holds.

We now take h as the hypothesis of theism, 'God exists'. Let k be mere tautological knowledge, and so $P(h/k)$ be the intrinsic probability of theism. We saw in Chapter 3 that prior probability depends on simplicity, fit with empirical background knowledge, and scope. Where the prior probability is intrinsic probability, the second factor does not play any role—for k does not include any empirical background knowledge. There are not any accepted theories for neighbouring fields with which h ought to fit. We saw also, by the example of Newton's theory that where we are dealing with a theory of large scope, scope is of far less importance than simplicity in determining prior probability. The intrinsic probability of theism seems to depend mainly on just how simple a theory theism is.

I argued in Chapter 5 that theism is an extremely simple theory. It postulates that all explanation is reducible to personal explanation. Personal explanation explains a phenomenon in terms of it having been brought about by an agent for a purpose. According to theism, explanations of the other kind, i.e. scientific explanations, are reducible to personal explanation in the sense that the operation of the factors cited in the scientific explanations is to be explained in personal terms. Newton's laws work because God keeps them in operation. There are planets because God is responsible for the operation of the law which brought about their evolution from pre-existing matter, and so on. Theism is simple in postulating that in this way explanation is all of one kind.

Further, as the cause of the existence and powers of all other things, theism postulates the existence of the simplest kind of person which there could be. A person is a being with capacities, beliefs, and intentions. The theist postulates that God has capacities as great as they logically can be. He is infinitely powerful, that is omnipotent. That there is an omnipotent God is a simpler hypothesis than the hypothesis that there is a God who has such-and-such limited power (e.g. the power to rearrange matter, but not the power to create it). It is simpler in just the same way that the hypothesis that some particle has zero mass or infinite velocity is simpler than the hypothesis that it has a mass of 0.34127 of some unit, or a velocity of 301,000 km/sec. A finite limitation cries out for an explanation of why there is just that particular limit, in a way that limitlessness does not. There is a neatness about zero and infinity which particular finite numbers lack.

According to the theist, God's beliefs have a similar infinite quality. Human persons have some few finite beliefs, some true, some false, some justified, some not. In so far as they are true and justified (or at any rate justified in a certain way), beliefs amount to knowledge. It would seem most consonant with his omnipotence that an omnipotent being have beliefs which amount to knowledge (for without knowledge of what you are doing you can hardly have the power to do any action). The simplest such supposition is to postulate that the omnipotent being is limited in his knowledge, as in his power, only by logic. In that case he would have all the knowledge that it is coherent to suppose that a person could have, i.e. he would be omniscient.

For a person to act he has to have intentions. His intentions might be determined by factors outside his control, or at any rate, as are those of humans, greatly influenced by them. It would however seem more consonant with his omnipotence for an omnipotent being to be entirely uninfluenced in his choice of intentions on which to act by factors outside his control, i.e. to be perfectly free. (For an omnipotence which you cannot but use in predetermined ways would hardly be worth having.) The theist postulates that God is perfectly free. It is clearly simpler to suppose that the ultimate principle of explanation, the final source of things, has always been the same—rather than to suppose that only for example in 4004 BC did God come to be and reign—and so to suppose that God has existed eternally. Theism thus postulates a person of an incredibly simple kind—one with such capacities, beliefs, and intentions, that there are no limits (apart from those of logic) to his capacities, to the extent of his justified true belief, and to his choice of intention; and no limits of time to his existence. I argued in Chapter 5 that the other defining properties of God are possessed necessarily by a being who possesses the ones which I have just considered. I conclude that the hypothesis of theism is a very simple hypothesis.

It remains to me, as to so many who have thought about the matter, a source of extreme puzzlement that there should exist anything at all. And maybe for that reason $P(h/k)$ is low. But there does exist something. And if there is to exist something, it seems impossible to conceive of anything simpler (and therefore *a priori* more probable) than the existence of God. The intrinsic probability of theism may be low; but it is, I suggest, relative to other hypotheses about what exists, very high. The crucial factor with which we shall need to compare $P(h/k)$ will be $P(e/k)$, and to that I shall come shortly.

Our evidence e are the phenomena which I have described in Chapters 7 to 13; but I shall find it convenient to exclude for the moment the evidence of religious experience which I described in Chapter 13, and confine myself to the evidence of the existence and general character of the world described in Chapters 7 to 11 together with the evidence of the occurrence of certain undoubted historical events, together with some evidence confirming the occurrence of violations of natural laws described in Chapter 12. Let us summarize that evidence. There is a universe, in which throughout the vast spatio-temporal region of which we have knowledge, material bodies have identical powers. They attract or repel each other in identical ways on earth and on Mars, and, as far as we can tell, on the most distant galaxy, this year and last year and millions of years ago. The powers of things are identical. The universe is a beautiful universe. In it there are many conscious beings, and among them men, agents of limited power and knowledge and, quite possibly limited free will in the sense in which I have defined this. They have the power to grow in these or to abandon them. They are capable of marvelling at the order of nature and of worshipping God. Men are subject to felt desires, including biologically useful ones; these desires are sometimes for lesser goods, which means that men are subject to temptation. They are therefore able to choose for themselves whether to do the morally right action, and may in the course of time develop a morally good character. Men are greatly interdependent, capable of increasing each other's power, knowledge, and freedom, making each other happy and unhappy, and in this way, being subject to birth and death, capable of influencing distant generations. The world is thus a providential world both in the respect that man is often able to satisfy his bodily needs, and more importantly in the respect that provision is made for his deeper needs. The world contains much evil, but the evil is not endless and it is either evil brought about by men, or evil of a kind which is necessary if men are to have knowledge of the evil consequences of possible actions (without that knowledge being given in ways which will curtail their freedom), and which provides the other benefits described in Chapter 11. All of this forms the general character of the world in which we live—the human condition. The world is a do-it-yourself world, one which men can make and in which they can make themselves, and make themselves fit for a different kind of world if such there be. Within this world there are further relevant particular phenomena—there is the work of prophets and wise men encouraging men to the worship of God, and knowledge of God and the universe and the service of their fellows, encouraging them towards an 'upwards march' especially when selfishness dominates. And there is too some slight evidence of violations of natural laws from time to time in religious contexts for good and religious ends.

With this e, what is the predictive power of theism? How likely is it if theism is true that things will be thus?

Now the existence of God does not entail that there will be a universe of the kind described. The traditional view, for example, is that it was up to God whether or not he should make a universe; God's goodness did not require him to make a universe. We have however seen in the preceding chapters that God has reason for bringing about (or allowing to occur) the universe with all the various characteristics described above. Further, it seems sometimes to be the case that if he brings about certain of these things, he has overriding reason for bringing about others, e.g. I argued (p. 147) that if he brings about a universe, he has overriding reason for making it an orderly universe. Some other worlds are such that God has overriding reason for not bringing them about. One such world, I claimed, was any world in which some human beings suffer *for ever*, without their having in some way chosen so to do. This would be an evil too great to justify any resultant good. I claimed also that theism rules out a world in which there is an *enormous* amount of *uncaused* suffering—for the occurrence of such suffering would not provide any knowledge for man. (For its occurrence would not reveal any natural processes by which future suffering could be increased or diminished. There might, however, be some good served by *some* such suffering.) Other worlds are such that we cannot see reason why God should bring them about, but there may of course be such reason. All of these considerations make $P(e/h.k)$, although low, not too low. The world is such that, given God's character, he might well bring it about.

What, finally, of the prior probability of e? I shall argue that this is a very low value indeed, much lower than $P(h/k)$.

It follows from the axioms of the probability calculus that the probability of any proposition on any other proposition is the sum of the probabilities of each of the different ways in which the first proposition could be true on the evidence of the second proposition —e.g. $P(p/r) = P(p.q/r) + P(p. \sim q/r)$. Examples make this intuitively obvious. The probability on some evidence that Jones did the crime is the sum of the probability that Jones did the crime together with Smith, and the probability that Jones did the crime, but not together with Smith. So, for our stated, h, e, and k, $P(e/k)$ is the sum of the intrinsic probability that e holds and there is a God, and the intrinsic probability that e holds and there is no God. $P(e/k) = P(e.h/k) + P(e. \sim h/k)$. Now $P(e.h/k)$ is the product of the two factors whose value we have so far been considering, $P(h/k)$ and $P(e/h.k)$.[1] $P(e.h/k) = P(h/k) \times P(e/h.k)$. So everything turns on $P(e. \sim h/k)$. This is the probability *a priori* that there be a universe with all the listed characteristics, but no God who sustains it in being. There would be such a universe without a God if either there was some alternative explanation of its existence, or there was no explanation at all.[2]

Clearly, as I argued in Chapter 7, there can be no scientific explanation of the existence of a universe; for all that science can do is to explain how a present state of the universe was brought about by a past state. It cannot explain why there is a universe at all. For a similar reason, as I argued in Chapter 8, science cannot explain why there are the most basic laws of nature that there are—e.g. why, if Newton's laws are the basic laws, they, rather than some other laws, are the basic laws. I argued in Chapter 9 that it was rather unlikely that science would be able to explain the existence of conscious agents. The regular correlations between brain-events and mental events which belong to a conscious agent are not explicable within the terms of anything like our current science (how can its chemical constitution explain why salt tastes salty rather than sweet, or its

---

[1] For argument in support of this axiom of the probability calculus see my *An Introduction to Confirmation Theory*, Ch. 5.

[2] $P(e. \sim h/k) = P(e/\sim h.k) \times P(\sim h/k)$. $P(h/k) + P(\sim h/k) = 1$. Given that, as I suggested earlier (pp. 283 f.), $P(h/k)$ is fairly low, although very high relative to that of other hypotheses about what exists; $P(\sim h/k)$ will be fairly high, not too far below 1. In that case the value of $P(e. \sim h/k)$ will be close to and largely determined by the value of $P(e/\sim h.k)$, the probability that there will be a universe with the various listed characteristics if there is no God. We have discussed in previous chapters the value of $P(e/\sim h.k)$ for various e and the considerations adduced there are consequently relevant for determining the value of $P(e. \sim h/k)$ and will be repeated here.

electrical properties explain why a brain-event is correlated with something looking blue rather than red?). Nor is it readily conceivable how *any* science could explain such correlations—for it would have to find something in common between this brain-event and something looking blue, and that brain-event and something looking red, such that these correlations are to be expected in a way that the opposite correlations (e.g. the former brain-event being correlated with something looking red) would not be expected. It is very hard indeed to see how that could be done.

The general pattern of the nature and circumstances of men and animals which I discussed in Chapters 9, 10, and 11, together with some of the historical phenomena which I discussed in Chapter 12, was no doubt a consequence of the operation of natural laws on primeval matter. But the laws of nature might so easily have been such as not to produce such a pattern—the behaviour of agents might be so instinctive that they would not be influenced by rational considerations, and so by the good or bad behaviour of previous generations. And so on. What science cannot explain is why the laws of nature are of the character they are. Finally, we saw in Chapter 12 there was some evidence that there occur particular scientifically inexplicable events. So science cannot explain our data. If there is an explanation of these things, it must be a personal explanation, because that is the only other kind of explanation which we have.

I suggest that theism is very, very much more probable than any rival personal explanation of the existence, orderliness, and other characteristics of the universe. A personal creator of the universe must be a person of immense power and to suppose that he has very great but finite power would be, as we saw earlier, to propose a much less simple hypothesis than the hypothesis that he has infinite power. It would raise the enormous problem of why he had just the amount of power which he had and what, if anything, limited his power in this way. Some other force would, as it were, stand against God limiting him. Similar points apply to hypotheses that the personal creator of the world has limited knowledge or freedom. The other alternative hypotheses postulating a limited creator of the universe are very, very much less probable than the hypothesis that God made it. The only plausible alternative to theism is the supposition that the world with all the characteristics which I have described just is, has no explanation. That however is not a very probable alternative. We expect all things to have explanations.

Above all, as I argued in Chapter 4, it is probable that things which are inert, diverse, complex, and yet show manifold correlations, have explanations.

I argued in Chapters 7 and 8 that the universe existing and conforming to natural laws has just this character of complex and diverse regularity. The world is a complicated thing. There are lots and lots of different bits of matter, existing over endless time (or possibly beginning to exist at some finite time). The bits of it have finite and not particularly natural sizes, shapes, masses, etc.; and they come together in finite, diverse, and very far from natural conglomerations (viz. lumps of matter on planets and stars, and distributed throughout interstellar space). There is just a certain finite amount of matter, or at any rate finite density of it, manifested in the particular conglomerations; and a certain finite amount, or at any rate finite density of energy, momentum, spin, etc. Matter is inert and has no powers which it can choose to exercise; it does what it has to do. Yet each bit of matter behaves in exactly the same way as similar bits of matter throughout time and space, the way codified in natural laws. Each electron attracts each positron, and repels each other electron in accord with the same natural laws throughout endless space and time. Yet natural laws are not entities; talk of natural laws is just talk of the powers and properties of bodies. So, we may say, all electrons throughout endless space and time have exactly the same powers and properties as all other electrons (properties of attracting, repelling, interacting, emitting radiation, etc.); all photons have the same powers and properties as all other photons, etc., etc. Matter is complex, diverse, but regular in its behaviour. Its existence and behaviour need explaining in just the kind of way that regular chemical combinations needed explaining; or it needs explaining when we find all the cards of a pack arranged in order. Further, as I argued in Chapter 9, the regular correlations between brain-events and mental events have just this characteristic of complexity (many, many, different correlations) and yet regularity (allowing predictions of mental events from brain-events, and vice versa) which needs explaining.

For all of these reasons I conclude that $P(e. \sim h/k)$, the intrinsic probability of there being a universe such as ours and no God is very much lower that $P(h/k)$, the intrinsic probability of there being a God. It remains perhaps passing strange that there exists anything at all. But if there is to exist anything, it is far more likely to be something with the simplicity of God than something like the universe with all its characteristics crying out for explanation without there being God to explain it.

By Bayes's Theorem

$$P(h/e.k) = \frac{P(e/h.k) \times P(h/k)}{P(e/k)}$$

We saw that $P(e/k) = P(e.h/k) + P(e.\sim h/k)$ and so $=$

$\{P(e/h.k) \times P(h/k)\} + P(e.\sim h/k)$. Hence

$$P(h/e.k) = \frac{P(e/h.k) \times P(h/k)}{\{P(e/h.k) \times P(h/k)\} + P(e.\sim h/k)}$$

We have concluded that $P(h/k)$ may be low, but $P(e.\sim h/k)$ is very, very much lower, and that $P(e/h.k)$ is low, but not too low. If $P(e/h.k)$ is not too low, $P(e/h.k) \times P(h/k)$ will equal $P(e.\sim h/k)$ and the probability of theism on the evidence so far considered ($P(h/e.k)$) will be $\frac{1}{2}$. If it is lower, then $P(h/e.k)$ will be less than $\frac{1}{2}$.

All this so far is very imprecise, but, as we have seen we just do not have the criteria for very precise estimation of probabilities in science or history or most other fields. However I now suggest that it is reasonable to come to the following qualitative judgement about the force of the evidence *so far* considered (i.e. all the evidence apart from the evidence of religious experience). Theism does not have a probability close either to 1 or to 0, that is, on the evidence considered so far, theism is neither very probable nor very improbable. It does not have a probability close to 1 because it does not have high predictive power $P(e/h.k)$. It is compatible with too much. There are too many different possible worlds which a God might bring about. Hence $P(e/h.k) \times P(h/k)$ will be very low, and this will tend to make $P(h/e.k)$ none too high. On the other hand, theism is a very simple hypothesis with a remarkable ability to make sense of what otherwise is extremely puzzling. $P(e.\sim h/k)$ is very low and $P(h/k)$ is much higher. For this reason $P(h/e.k)$ is not too close to 0.

My claim then is that although the predictive power ($P(e/h.k)$) of theism is quite low, and so too is its prior probability $P(h/k)$, nevertheless, its over-all probability $P(h/e.k)$ is well away from 1 or 0, because the prior probability of the evidence $P(e/k)$ is very low indeed (due to $P(e.\sim h/k)$ being very low).

A theory may not make the occurrence of its data e very probable, and the theory may not have very high prior probability; but if it provides the only possible explanation of e, or the only remotely plausible explanation of *e*, and if the occurrence of *e* uncaused would be a great puzzle, then *e* is very strong evidence for the theory. We can see this by taking a fairly mundane example, where *k* includes general empirical background knowledge. A man Jones is found killed by shooting in a room locked on the inside, all the windows being locked on the inside and there being no other means of access. No gun is to be found near, which rules out a hypothesis of suicide. Jones has only one known enemy—Smith, who was seen near the scene of the crime at the time when it was committed and whose fingerprints are found on certain items in the room, and who is found to possess money proved to have been stolen from Jones. Let us represent by *e* all the evidence about the locked room, the sightings of Smith, and the money—i.e. what the detectives subsequently discovered; and by *k* general background evidence including Smith's known hostility to Jones. We represent by *h* the hypothesis that Smith murdered Jones. $P(h/k)$ is not too low, but it is not very high, because the mere general background evidence does not by itself give a very high degree of probability to Smith's murdering Jones. The trouble is however that *h* does not make *e* too probable—if Smith indeed murdered Jones, the defence counsel may well object, we would expect to find some way by which he got out of the room. So $P(e/h.k)$ is none too high. What, however, will incline a jury to accept the hypothesis *h* is that any other explanation of what happened is far more puzzling than *h* (if it is supposed that someone else did the murder, the same problems arise about the locked door; and yet there is not the slightest bit of evidence against anyone else), and it would be incredibly puzzling to say that there was no explanation of Jones's being shot. $P(e/k)$ is very low because of the lack of possible explanations of *e* other than one which leaves crucial unanswered questions. And that is why $P(h/e.k)$ is none too low. *h* leaves unanswered questions, but a rational detective will accept it because it is the only remotely plausible hypothesis.

Things are like this, I am suggesting, with theism. The phenomena which we have been considering are puzzling and strange. Theism does not make their occurrence very probable; but nothing else makes their occurrence in the least probable, and they cry out for explanation. *A priori*, theism is perhaps very unlikely, but it is far more likely than any rival supposition. Hence our phenomena are substantial evidence for the truth of theism.

My conclusion so far then has been that the probability of theism is none too close to 1 or 0 on the evidence so far considered. However, so far in this chapter I have ignored one crucial piece of evidence, the evidence from religious experience. (I have ignored this evidence so far, because I had a somewhat different approach to it from the approach to all other evidence, which involved the use of Bayes's theorem.) I concluded the last chapter (p. 274) with the claim that unless the probability of theism on other evidence is very low indeed, the testimony of many witnesses to experience apparently of God suffices to make many of those experiences probably veridical. That is, the evidence of religious experience is in that case sufficient to make theism over all probable. The argument of Chapter 13 was that the testimony of many witnesses to experiences apparently of God makes the existence of God probable if it is not already on other evidence very improbable. I believe that I have shown in this chapter that that condition is well satisfied and hence the conclusion of Chapter 13 applies. On our total evidence theism is more probable than not. An argument from all the evidence considered in this book to the existence of God is a good P-inductive argument. The experience of so many men in their moments of religious vision corroborates what nature and history shows to be quite likely—that there is a God who made and sustains man and the universe.

APPENDIX A

Reply to Mackie[1]

MACKIE'S posthumous book on the philosophy of religion, *The Miracle of Theism*, contains a number of detailed criticisms of versions of inductive arguments for the existence of God offered in my own book, *The Existence of God*. In this paper I argue that what I take to be the three main criticisms have no force.

Mackie discusses in detail my treatment of the cosmological argument, the argument from design, and the argument from consciousness. One general counter-argument which occurs in a number of places in his book (especially pp. 100, 129 f., 149) is that my theistic hypothesis is not nearly as simple as I suppose.

My category of 'personal explanation' (explaining a state of affairs as brought about intentionally by an agent) is not a simple one. For, he writes (p. 100):

The key power, involved in Swinburne's use of 'personal explanation', is that of fulfilling intentions *directly*, without any physical or causal mediation, without materials or instruments. There is nothing in our background knowledge that makes it comprehensible, let alone likely, that anything should have such a power. All our knowledge of intention-fulfilment is of *embodied* intentions being fulfilled *indirectly* by way of bodily changes and movements which are *causally* related to the intended result, and where the ability thus to fulfil intentions itself has a *causal*

[1] This is a shortened version of a paper originally published under the title 'Mackie, Induction, and God' in *Religious Studies*, 1983, **19**, 385–91. Page references to Mackie's book are to *The Miracle of Theism* (Oxford, 1982). I wrote this paper with some reluctance. John Mackie was a good friend of mine. We argued about these matters over many years: we first debated in public about the existence of God in 1965. It would in a way have been courteous to have left the last word with him, who is no longer in a position to continue the debate. However, the issues are of such importance that I felt that I must reply. I am sure that John, with his great charity and love of truth, will understand.

history, either of evolutionary development or of learning or of both. Only by ignoring such key features do we get an analogue of the supposed divine action.

Mackie has not taken seriously my intention expressed in many places in the book (see especially p. 63 n.), in judging the worth of such general arguments, to start without any factual background knowledge (and to feed all factual knowledge gradually into the evidence of observation), and so to judge the prior probability of theism solely by *a priori* considerations, namely, in effect, simplicity. The simplicity of a hypothesis is not a matter of its familiarity, whether or not it is exemplified in the world of experience. We could understand and judge to be highly simple the notion of two (logically) distinct variables being linearly related to each other (i.e. x and y having the relation $x = ky$, where k is a constant), even if all actual observable variables measured by us were related in more complicated ways. And the model of billiard balls interacting by collision remains a simple model even if it is proved that actual billiard balls never really touch but exert on each other some force at a distance. The simplicity of the relation between intention and its realization has nothing to do with whether this very simple relation is instantiated. It is a very simple relation—the occurrence of an event E being brought about by a person intending to bring about E under a description thereof built into the intention. And we have experience of such a relation being instantiated (and hence derive our understanding of it) before we come to realize that in practice, often, there are intermediate unintended links in the causal chain. I experience my efficacy in getting my hand to move through having the intention so to do, before I learn of the intermediate unintended links. The need in many normal cases for physical links between an intention and the intended effect must not obscure from us the simplicity of the relation.

Suppose that we now take account of Mackie's point that intentions are normally fulfilled in humans via a complex chain. Does the hypothesis of theism, that God acts directly on the universe, make it improbable that there be agents whose intentions are fulfilled indirectly? Why should it? Let us define an agent's range of direct control as those states of affairs which he can bring about without doing so via a causal chain whose efficacy does not depend on him. The region of direct control for humans is their brain-states. For given that our intentions do cause our bodily movements via a chain of neural states, clearly they cause directly various brain-states. Let us define an agent's range of easy control as those states of affairs which he can bring about simply by having the intention so to do without having the intention to bring about some cause or effect of those states. The range of easy control for humans includes initially many bodily movements, and also certain internal bodily states and states caused by bodily movements, such as the utterances of words, in a way unknown to the agent. But humans have the power to extend or diminish their range of easy control. They can spread the range of easy control of states far beyond the body—learning perhaps to control a rocket at a distance and forgetting which bodily movements they need to make in order so to do. Or they can narrow the range of easy control until it coincides with the region of direct control. They can come to learn to bring about directly (without any intermediate causal chains) some brain-state under its neurological description (e.g. 'C-fibres firing'), not simply under the description of 'whatever brain-state is necessary to produce such-and-such a bodily movement'. For given that now my intention causes the movement of my arm indirectly by causing my C-fibres to fire directly, when I learn the details of this process, I shall be in a position to bring about the firing of my C-fibres directly under that description. It is good that agents have the power to extend or diminish their range of easy control; for that is just one more power which those agents can choose whether or not to exercise, and so help to control their own future life and the lives of their descendants. One very obvious way in which agents can have this power is by having initially a range of easy control and then coming to be able to extend or contract it through acquiring beliefs about the causes or effects of their actions, then bringing about those causes or effects via the original actions, and then losing the need to think consciously of those original actions. First I learn to tie my shoelace by moving my fingers in certain ways; then the process becomes so natural that I forget which finger-motions are needed.

God, being omnipotent, cannot rely on causal processes outside his control to bring about effects, so his range of easy control must coincide with his range of direct control and include all states of affairs which it is logically possible for him to bring about. There is no need for these ranges initially or ever to coincide in the case of humans, and God may have some good reason for giving us a start in expanding our range of easy control by making it lie beyond the range of direct control. The complexity of our bodies, which are the vehicle of our easy control, makes it possible for medical science to improve or neglect them. That our range of easy control should arise through a process of learning is good, since parents' having responsibility to encourage or neglect it is good. And the fact that it evolves through a process of evolution is also good— evolution is a very beautiful process and one which is now available to men to influence for good or ill, giving them yet further responsibility—which is good (despite all its deficiencies— see my pp. 154 f ., 196 f. and Chapter 11).

The point remains, however, that although certain physical conditions of the brain need to occur if human agents are to have intentions which are efficacious, the human model suggests a simpler model in which such limitations are removed. While our experience of collisions may be limited to medium-size composite objects, such as billiard balls, made of all sorts of molecules, it clearly suggests the possibility of collisions between non-composite fundamental particles. The compositeness of participating objects is not of the essence of a collision; no more is the existence of necessary conditions for operation and intermediate causal links of the essence of personal explanation. It is simpler without these limitations. He who seeks simpler explanations will not postulate such limitations unless it is necessary to do so.

The naturalness of the connection between the intention to bring about E and E allows us to explain Es which are puzzling because they are diverse and complex, e.g. the many diverse correlations between brain-states and mental states which they cause, such as sensations; and so the answers to Mackie's questions:

Has God somehow brought it about that material structures do now generate consciousness? But then is this not almost as hard to understand as that material structures should do this *of themselves*? (p. 131)

are 'yes' and 'no' respectively.

A different objection to the simplicity of personal explanation is that the 'particularity', the detailed features of the phenomena to be explained, has not been removed by postulating an intention to bring about those phenomena:

The particularity has not been removed, but only shelved; we should have to postulate particularities in God, to explain his choice of the particular universe he decided to create. (Mackie, p. 100; see also his p. 149, ll. 15 ff.)

The structure of my counter-argument to that is already there in *The Existence of God*. First, as I wrote earlier, a perfectly free, omnipotent, and omniscient person can only bring about states of affairs which he has reason to bring about and no overriding reason not to bring about (see my p. 111). Clearly not all states which some agent might bring about are like this, and I gave arguments for supposing with respect to each of the states discussed that they were like this. I described the reasons a good God would have for bringing about a universe, an orderly universe, the existence of conscious agents, etc. And I also gave grounds for supposing that some other existing states of affairs which might seem to be states which God would have overriding reason not to bring about (e.g. pain suffered by children) were really not so, because they were necessary conditions of a greater good. But I pointed out that there were some states of affairs which could not be justified along the lines along which I justified existing evils, and which were therefore to all appearances ones which God would have overriding reason not to bring about, e.g. undeserved suffering of infinite intensity or duration, and hence we had an explanation of why such suffering did not occur (viz. what happens must be permitted by God; God would not have permitted such suffering—see my pp. 223 ff.).

Further, the occurrence of some one rather than any other of a number of equally good states of affairs is made more comprehensible if it is seen as resulting from a personal choice rather than from some random mechanism—for personal choice among equally good alternatives is a mechanism which we see intuitively to be a simple and natural mechanism for selecting alternatives; it is a mechanism, indeed the only mechanism, of which we have inside experience and whose operation is thus comprehensible (see my p. 103).

As well as criticizing my claim about the simplicity and so prior probability of the theistic hypothesis, Mackie claims in various ways that the evidence of observation is not nearly as improbable *a priori*, as I allege—not nearly as unlikely to occur, if the theistic hypothesis is false, as I allege. In particular I alleged that the totally regular and simple ways of behaviour of physical objects— or, as we should say in order to avoid hypostatizing laws of nature, the vast coincidence that there are objects of a very few kinds (electrons, photons, etc.) all of each kind having identical powers and liabilities—is a very striking coincidence which is *a priori* very unlikely. The hypothesis of a common creator explains the coincidence, since he has the power to bring it about and reason to do so. (The regularities of behaviour are beautiful and give creatures a tool for making a difference to the world.) Such is my version of the argument for design.

Mackie objects:

> Inductive extrapolation would not be reasonable if there were a strong presumption that the universe is really completely random, that such order as we seem to find in it is just the sort of local apparent regularity that we should expect to occur occasionally by pure chance, as in a series of random tosses of a coin we will sometimes get a long run of heads, or a simple alternation of heads and tails over a considerable number of throws. Swinburne holds, and his argument requires, that inductive extrapolation is reasonable, prior to and independently of any belief in a god. But, I would argue, this would not be reasonable if there were a strong presumption that the universe is completely random. So he cannot consistently say that, without the theistic hypothesis, it is highly improbable *a priori* that there are any regularities; for the latter assertion of improbability is equivalent to saying that there is a strong presumption of randomness. (p. 148)

Mackie's argument seems to be that in holding that regularities which we observe are typical of wider regularities in regions of space and time outside the region immediately observed (as I do in rebutting the suggestion that we are observing an untypical segment of space and time), I am already committed to denying the strong presumption of randomness.

Before showing what is wrong with Mackie's argument, it is worth while to show it in action in another case. Suppose that there are before us, ready for use, many packs of cards. On examining some of them at random we find that they are all arranged in order of suits and seniority. That allows us to infer that the other packs which we have not examined will also be so arranged. Any normal observer would then immediately suspect that these coincidences are to be explained in terms of something beyond themselves, e.g. an agent or a machine constructed by an agent which arranged the packs in order. There is, after all, a modest prior probability that there is such an agent who has the power to arrange the cards and a motive for doing so. Mackie, however, if we are to take his argument seriously, would not so react. The mere fact that we can reasonably predict that the unobserved packs will be arranged in order shows that order in packs of cards is a normal thing to be expected, not in need of further explanation.

What has gone wrong? Mackie has misconstrued the argument for design. There is indeed a strong presumption of randomness. But then we observe the regular and simple behaviour of all of the many objects which we observe. We argue that if all objects behave in regular and simple ways (h_1), our observation will be made; but if only a few objects behave in regular and simple ways (h_2), our observation is very unlikely to be made. Although *a priori* h_1 has a much smaller probability than h_2, the observations are so much more likely to be observed if h_1 than if h_2 that the posterior probability of h_1 significantly exceeds that of h_2. (It is because there are so few ways in which objects can behave regularly and so many ways in which they can behave irregularly that, while each hypothesis of the former kind has greater prior probability than each hypothesis of the latter kind, overall h_2 has greater prior probability than h_1.) We then inquire how such an unlikely hypothesis as h_1 comes to be true; we seek a higher hypothesis which explains it. Faced with the choice between saying that there are simply brute coincidences in the behaviour of objects and saying that their behaviour is brought about by a common cause, a person, we choose the latter on the grounds that its simplicity is high and it gives some probability to what we observe. That, after all, is how we argue with regard to the packs of cards. Analogy demands that we argue in the same way with respect to the regularities in nature.

It is very unlikely indeed *a priori* that there should be a universe made of matter behaving in totally regular ways, giving rise to conscious beings capable of changing themselves and others, making themselves fit for the heaven of which they have a glimpse in religious experience. Hence the reason which we use about science and history demands that we postulate a simple explanation of these phenomena in terms of a creator and sustainer God. Mackie's reasons for rejecting that view are not adequate.

APPENDIX B

The Argument from the Fine-Tuning of the Universe[1]

I

IN this appendix I seek to examine the force of an argument to the existence of God from the widely discussed fact that the boundary conditions of our universe and the laws of its evolution are of a very special kind which alone could lead to the evolution of intelligent life and in fact make it probable.

In considering the force of this evidence, I shall assume that there is a universe and that there are laws of nature, and shall consider whether the fact that those laws have a particular form, and the boundary conditions of the universe have a particular form which alone permit the evolution of intelligent life and in fact make it probable, provides a good C-inductive argument for the existence of God. In the pattern of argument of the book this appendix thus provides an argument lying between the arguments from the existence of the universe and from its conformity to laws of nature (discussed in Chapters 7 and 8) and the argument from consciousness (discussed in Chapter 9). It is a form of argument from design or teleological argument which appeals both to spatial order and to a certain aspect of temporal order. A full-length account of the recent scientific work relevant to such an argument has been given by J. D. Barrow and F. J. Tipler in their book *The Anthropic Cosmological Principle*,[2] and I shall assume that the detailed scientific facts are as they state them. My concern is to

---

[1] This is a shortened version of a paper first published in J. Leslie (ed.), *Physical Cosmology and Philosophy* (New York, 1989). I am most grateful to Dr. W. E. Parry for advice on points of physics discussed herein.

[2] Oxford, 1986.

assess the evidential force of the work which they describe. In doing so I take further the argument of some recent philosophical work of John Leslie.[3]

I argued in this book that the existence of intentional agents of limited power and knowledge is a good which God has reason for bringing about. I also argued briefly (p. 160) that God has reason for bringing about embodied agents of this kind, such as humans. Humans are embodied in the sense that it is through stimuli landing on their bodies that they are caused to have sensations and acquire beliefs, and it is through their bodies that they execute their purposes. Through my eyes and ears I learn about the world, and through my legs and arms I make a difference to it. What reason has a God to make creatures with a mental life who are embodied? Why not creatures who know about the world without needing eyes to see with, or ones who can move the furniture without needing to do so by means of arms and legs?

The answer is that embodiment allows us to learn (or to choose not to learn) to control our mental life and to grow in power over and knowledge of the world. The natural world is a world governed by simple natural laws. If our sensations are caused by events in that world we can observe which events cause which sensations, and then put ourselves into positions where (because of the predictable conformity of events to scientific laws) causes will bring about those events which are the immediate cause of those sensations we want to occur and not those we do not. If I find that fire causes my hand to burn and the burning causes acute pain, then, knowing the predictable behaviour of fire, I can avoid this source of pain in the future by not allowing my hand to go near the fire. We can learn also to improve the quality and quantity of our justified beliefs. If our beliefs are caused by stimuli impinging on bodies, we can find out (by cross-checking with other beliefs) when these stimuli are misleading and then discount beliefs

---

[3] He has argued from the fine-tuning of the universe in a series of articles beginning with 'Anthropic Principle, World Ensemble, Design', *American Philosophical Quarterly*, 1982, **19**, 141–51, culminating in a full-length discussion in his book *Universes* (London, 1989). He regards the explanation by the action of God to which the argument from fine-tuning leads us not, as I have claimed, as explanation by the intentional action of an omnipotent agent, but rather as explanation by 'ethical requiredness'. For this latter see his *Value and Existence* (Oxford, 1979). I shall not discuss here this aspect of his views, but rely instead on the positive reasons which I shall articulate to see the fine-tuning of the universe as providing evidence for a God of the traditional kind.

acquired in a certain kind of way. And we can find out which stimuli are reliable indicators of things new or small or distant, and thus extend the range of our justified beliefs. We can learn the principles of optics and apply them to constructing telescopes, looking through which will allow us to have perceptions and so beliefs about remote events. And, finally, learning what causes what, we can extend the range of our control. Learning the laws of mechanics, we can apply them to send space-rockets to the moon. One of the ways in which we can grow in knowledge and control is by acquiring knowledge of how to communicate with others (learning to use foreign languages, the telephone, and radio) and thereby learning how to exercise control which results from co-operative effort. Embodiment in a world of simple natural laws puts us in a framework where causes and effects operate independently of us, and thus allows us to grow in knowledge by seeing how effects are signs of causes, and in control by using causes to bring about effects. But we cannot choose to grow unless there are procedures of knowledge-acquisition and control which we can acquire; and there cannot be procedures unless there is an independent realm of simple (and so understandable and reliable) scientific laws. Enmeshed in such a world, we have the power to choose what sort of beings to be: to grow or to neglect to grow. And among the knowledge we will acquire is knowledge of the beauty of a marvellous world. A God has good reason for making not merely conscious agents, but embodied conscious agents, agents with bodies through which they acquire sensations and beliefs and through which they make a difference to things, bodies which are constituents of a world conforming to simple scientific laws.

Now I argued in Chapter 9 that there cannot be a scientific explanation of consciousness; science cannot explain why the organisms which evolution produced were conscious beings rather than unconscious robots; and I argued there that that fact provides a further argument for the existence of God. My concern here is not, however, with the evolution of consciousness, but with the fact that there are human and animal bodies suited for the embodiment of conscious beings. For the rest of this paper, I shall understand my datum that there exist intelligent organisms, more precisely than I have understood it hitherto, as the datum that there exist bodies which are suitable vehicles for the embodiment of conscious beings. For the reasons which I have given, a God would both be able and have reason to produce intelligent organisms.

If this production of intelligent organisms is to have value, the world has to be governed, as we have seen, by simple scientific laws (which the conscious beings could come to understand and manipulate). God has another and quite different reason for making an orderly universe: order is beautiful, total chaos is ugly. Even if God alone perceives the universe, he has reason for making it beautiful. But he has the power and abundant reason for putting in such a universe intelligent organisms. He could do so either directly (as most, but not all, thinkers before Darwin supposed that he had done) or indirectly, making the world with boundary conditions and scientific laws such as to give rise to intelligent organisms. All the evidence accumulated by scientists over the past 200 years shows overwhelmingly that present-day intelligent organisms (i.e. human and animal bodies) evolved gradually from inanimate matter in accord with scientific laws over thousands of millions of years. So God did not produce intelligent organisms directly. But if all the evidence is that the occurrence of boundary conditions and laws such as to permit and make probable the evolution of intelligent organisms are *a priori* (that is, unless there is a God) very unlikely, then (by the pattern of argument used extensively in this book) that is evidence that God brought them about, and thereby indirectly brought about the existence of intelligent organisms. He made an intelligent-organism-producing universe. With e as laws and boundary conditions such as to make likely the evolution of intelligent organisms, h as the hypothesis of theism, k as the existence of a universe governed by some laws of nature or other, $P(h/e.k) > P(h/k)$, indeed $P(h/e.k.) \gg P(h.k.)$[4]. In the main body of the book I commented (p. 136) that the occurrence of life was a rare event in the vast spaces and many millennia of world history, and so supposed that its occasional occurrence would not be unexpected given the operation of some laws of nature or other, and so not very strong evidence of a Creator. I did not take seriously the fact that laws and boundary conditions had to lie within a certain range if there was to be life at all; and for that reason I underestimated the strength of an argument of this kind.

---

[4] '$\gg$' means 'is very much greater than', '$\ll$' means 'is very much less than'.

II

Now what features does a body have to have to be a vehicle of the kind described for the expression of consciousness? It needs to turn the incoming stimuli (light, sound, touch, etc.) into sensations and into true-belief-correlates, that is, brain-states which are correlates of true beliefs about features of the stimulus source; and to turn purpose-correlates, that is, brain-states which vary with the purposes which agents seek to execute, into limb-movements which will effect those purposes. The kind of complexity needed depends on the kind of belief and purpose which the agent has. For complex beliefs and purposes of the kind described in the previous section, a complex brain is needed. To acquire quickly many true beliefs of varying kinds useful for the execution of their purposes, organisms need limbs to give them mobility. For learning and ratiocination to be possible, memory is crucial; and substantial, embodied memory involves brain-states stable over long periods as the correlates of memory beliefs. To be effective over a continuing period and changing environment, the organism needs to have a mechanism of self-repair. And, unless inorganic material had the power spontaneously to give rise to more life, organisms need—in order to have responsibility for children—to have the power of self-reproduction.

So intelligent organisms need a large, stable body, with sense-organs (sensitive to a diversity of stimuli), an information processor, a memory bank, an energy processor, and limbs giving mobility. A life based on carbon, in combination with certain other elements, expecially hydrogen, oxygen, and nitrogen, has just these features. With a valence of 4, carbon can enter into many different chemical combinations. Carbon compounds are stable over long periods of time; but are also metastable in that they can easily be induced to interact further. Hence, 'more information can be stored in carbon compounds than in those of any other elements'.[5] Together with hydrogen, nitrogen, and oxygen, carbon can form long, complex chain molecules; and, together with calcium giving skeletal rigidity, such an information-processing system can be made a continuing independent component of the universe. For reproduction we need self-replicating molecules transmitting organism-forming instructions by a genetic

[5] Barrow and Tipler, *Anthropic Cosmological Principle*, p. 547.

code; the nucleic acids formed of the crucial molecules of carbon, hydrogen, nitrogen, and oxygen have these properties.[6] Carbon-based life requires for its stability a moderate range of temperature and pressure—and, for its purposes to have much effect, a solid planet on which to live.

Given the present constituents of the universe (energy and fundamental particles) and the laws of their behaviour, it is highly doubtful whether there could be any other kind of intelligent life. It has sometimes been suggested that silicon could replace carbon in its central role, but this seems doubtful in that silicon compounds do not have the stability of carbon compounds.[7] Another recent suggestion has been that intelligent systems of particles relying on the 'strong' interaction for their organization might exist inside neutron stars; but it seems doubtful whether they could have nearly as much information-processing capacity as does carbon-based life on Earth.[8] So let us suppose, plausibly enough, that carbon-based life is the only possible kind of life (given the present constituents of the universe and the laws of their behaviour). If silicon-based life is possible, the argument below would not need much alteration (for the conditions necessary for its evolution are very similar to those necessary for the evolution of carbon-based life), and neutron-star life is too speculative a suggestion to be taken into account at this stage.

III

Laws of nature determine which states of the universe give rise to which succeeding states. The present consensus of evidence is that certain *a priori* very unlikely features of laws are necessary for the occurrence of carbon-based life.

This section may not be fully comprehensible to those without adequate scientific background. I suggest, nevertheless, that such readers read through these pages; they will get the main message, that laws of nature need to have very special features indeed if carbon-based life is to occur.

Given the four fundamental forces and the basic array of fundamental particles (photons; leptons, including electrons; mesons; and baryons, including protons and neutrons), the strengths of forces and masses of particles have to have to each

---

[6] On self-reproduction and self-repair, see ibid., pp. 510–23.
[7] Ibid., pp. 545 ff.   [8] Ibid., pp. 343–6.

other ratios within certain narrow bands if the larger chemical elements, including carbon, are to occur at all, and the Pauli exclusion principle has to hold. This principle (applying to all fermions, e.g. electrons and protons) says that in one system (e.g. one atom) only one particle of the same kind can be in a given quantum state. In consequence there are only a small number of possible energy states for the electrons of an atom, and only a small number of electrons can be in each state. While the basic laws of quantum theory ensure the stability of the atom—electrons do not collapse onto the nucleus—the Pauli principle leads to the electrons being arranged in 'shells'. Hence atoms of a finite number of different kinds can be formed by different numbers of electrons surrounding the nucleus, and molecules can be formed by bonds between the electrons of different atoms. No exclusion principle, no chemistry. But not much chemistry unless there is plenty of possibility for different structures to be built up, to be relatively stable, to interact, and to form new structures. For that we need atoms to be large structures with plenty of empty space between well defined central nuclei and electrons. For that we need both of two crucial dimensionless numbers to be small: α the fine structure constant, $e/hc \sim (137)^{-1}$, and β, the electron-to-proton mass ratio, $m_e/m_n \sim (1836)^{-1}$. Their small value makes possible the long chains of molecules, such as DNA, which make life possible.[9] But α and β too small would not give stable enough atoms. Another dimensionless number is crucial for the existence of the right kind of nuclei to form atoms of many different elements—α_s ($\equiv g_s^2/4\pi \sim 0.2$), a crucial constant in the nuclear force. There are three possible systems (nuclei or components of nuclei) with two nucleons—the deuteron (proton + neutron), the diproton (proton + proton), and the dineutron (neutron + neutron). But with the present value of α_s neither the dineutron nor the diproton is in a stable state. An increase in α_s of 0.3% would bind the dineutron (i.e. allow the formation of a stable dineutron) and one of 3.4% would bind the diproton. If the diproton were bound, all the hydrogen would have been burned to helium in the early stages of the big bang, and so no hydrogen compounds or long-lived stable stars could be formed. A decrease in α_s of 9% would unbind the deuteron, and this would prevent the formation of elements heavier than hydrogen.[10] Either

[9] Ibid., pp. 295–305.   [10] Ibid., pp. 321 ff.

variation would have the consequence that the larger elements, including carbon, could not exist. A slight increase in electro-magnetic force (and so in α) would have the same effect.[11] Other constants are possibly also crucial, such as the value of Δm, the neutron–proton mass difference which approximately equals m_e, the mass of the electron; if this value were much different, protons would decay before they could form stable nuclei.[12] And so on.

Further, given the actual laws of nature or laws at all similar thereto, boundary conditions will have to lie within a narrow range of the present conditions if intelligent life is to evolve (or else they will have to lie well outside that range; this point will be discussed later). If the universe had a beginning, the boundary conditions are the arrangements and properties of the stuff of the universe at the time—the way the universe started off. Present evidence suggests (much more strongly than the evidence available when I first wrote *The Existence of God*) an initial singularity, the formation of the universe by explosion from a 'big bang' some 15,000,000,000 years ago. For the formation of intelligent life in a universe expanding from an initial singularity, conditions at the time of the big bang have to be (within narrow ranges) just right (or, more precisely, as going backward we approach the time of the big bang asymptotically, conditions must asymptotically approach values within certain narrow ranges). The initial rate of expansion is critical. If (for the actual value of the gravitational and other constants) the initial velocity of expansion were slightly greater than the actual initial velocity, stars and so the heavier elements would not form; if it were slightly less, the universe would collapse before it was cool enough for the elements to form.[13] It has been calculated that (barring a possible qualification from 'inflation theory' to which we shall come shortly) a reduction in the rate of expansion of one part in a million million would lead to premature collapse, and an increase by one part in a million would have prevented the evolution of stars and heavier elements.[14] Some initial inhomogeneity in the distribution of radiation is needed if galaxies, and so stars, are to be produced. Too much would lead to black holes being formed before stars could form.[15] In the beginning there was a very slight excess of baryons over anti-baryons; all but the excess baryons became

---

[11] Ibid., p. 326.   [12] Ibid., p. 400.   [13] Ibid., pp. 410 ff.
[14] Papers by S. W. Hawking and by R. H. Dicke and P. J. E. Peebles cited in Leslie, *Universes*, p. 29.   [15] Barrow and Tipler, pp. 414–19.

radiation. If the excess number were even slighter, there would not be enough matter for galaxies or stars to form. If it were greater, there would be too much radiation for planets to form.[16] And so on. The universe has to start with the right density and amount of inhomogeneity of radiation and velocity of expansion, and that means (within a very narrow range) the actual amount.

IV

So, for both laws and boundary conditions, crucial variables must lie within a narrow range. Such is what the current physics seems to show. But this branch of physics is highly unstable; new theories are produced each year. Changes are possible which would have the consequence that variables can vary within a much wider range and yet life still evolve. One possible change, though in my amateur judgement an unlikely one, is that it be discovered that the boundary conditions are significantly different from what has been supposed, e.g. that the universe did not evolve from an initial singularity, but from a very dense state resulting, perhaps, from a prior collapse, or perhaps from a quantum mechanical fluctuation of the 'vacuum'.[17] Such a change, probably going with the adoption of the view that the universe was infinitely old, would have the consequence that a far wider range of boundary conditions would give rise to life.

The role of 'boundary conditions' in a backwardly eternal (i.e. infinitely old) universe may need clarification. Imagine a billiard table sealed under a glass cover in which the balls move in a vacuum (and that any energy transfer to or from the outside can be discounted). The laws of collision govern the interaction of the balls which bounce off each other and off the walls for the indefinite future. It could have been that this process was started off by someone arranging the balls and giving them an initial push before the table was sealed. In that case the boundary conditions would be the initial conditions (arrangement and velocity of balls), and they together with the laws of collision would determine all the subsequent behaviour of the balls. The positions of the balls would be determined by the initial conditions. Some initial conditions would allow the balls to arrange themselves in all the (logically) possible arrangements during the course of a subsequent infinite

---

[16] Ibid., pp. 401–8.
[17] Ibid., pp. 440 ff.

time. Yet some initial conditions (e.g. the balls moving initially with velocities parallel to each other and to the walls) will ensure that the balls occupy only a few of the possible arrangments even in the course of infinite time. Suppose, on the other hand, that the process has been going on for ever (i.e. is not merely forwardly but backwardly eternal). Then the set-up may still have certain features at a given time which ensure that only a narrow set of possible arrangements either ever have been or ever will be occupied (e.g., again, if at one time the balls are moving parallel to each other and to the walls), or, much more likely, features which ensure that in the course of infinite time backward and forward all possible arrangements of those balls occur. However, the sealing of the table still ensures that the only possible arrangements are arrangements of those balls—there cannot be more or fewer balls in the past or future. The 'boundary conditions' of an infinite universe are those features of its conditions at any one time (e.g. in a Newtonian universe, the quantity of energy) which determine the possible future and past states.

Now, if the universe is backwardly eternal, its present state may be such that we can infer that it must pass through such and such a range of states in the course of infinite time. These might include all the logically possible states of matter-energy; but that is not very likely, for some kind of principle of conservation of energy (within quantum limits) will ensure that past (and future) states are limited to rearrangements of the existing amount of energy. However, although all of this would have to be worked out, it is highly plausible to suppose that (for given scientific laws) life is much more likely to evolve at some time in the course of the history of our universe if it has an infinite past than if it has a finite past. There is more time for more possible arrangements of the constituents of the universe. Nevertheless, the present evidence suggests a finite age of some 15,000,000,000 years.

The alternative change in physics might be discovery that the laws are other than previously supposed, in particular that the laws are such as to bring forth intelligent life out of a much wider range of boundary conditions than had hitherto been supposed. 'Inflation theory' suggests just that. Inflation theory tells us that regions of the universe with certain features may be subject, soon after the big bang, to a random, vast faster-than-light expansion leading to a cooler homogeneous and isotropic region.[18] So features such as

[18] Ibid., pp. 430–40.

310 *Appendix B*

homogeneity and isotropy for which a narrow range of initial conditions were thought vital are now said to be expected, given certain laws, to arise from a wider range of initial conditions. However, it seems difficult to get a satisfactory version of inflation theory which is not highly complex, and so ill-justified by data; and it is doubtful whether the range of critical conditions necessary for intelligent life would be significantly widened by such a theory.[19] What is most unlikely is that physicists will change their views about the values of the constants of those laws which have to operate for the very existence of life (as opposed to those which have to operate if it is to evolve from certain boundary conditions), e.g. the values of α and β.

Our judgements as to just how narrow are the ranges within which crucial variables of boundary conditions and some of the constants of scientific laws have to lie in order to permit the evolution of intelligent life must be very tentative. However, the significant balance of evidence, as, following Barrow and Tipler, I have assessed it, is that, given boundary conditions and physical laws of the kind which in fact operate in our universe, these variables have to lie within very narrow ranges—for instance, given the four forces and the kind of formula which governs their operation (e.g. approximately an inverse square law of gravitational attraction), the constants which appear in those laws have to lie within very narrow ranges; and given an initial singularity, the initial velocity of recession has to lie within a very narrow range.

Now certainly if we vary a number of different constants of laws, or even change the laws entirely, and alter the boundary conditions in a large way (e.g. suppose no initial singularity), then no doubt intelligent life could evolve as a result of a quite different mechanism. There is no logical necessity tying its evolution to the particular laws and boundary conditions which we have. But the crucial point is that any slight variation in these would make life impossible. John Leslie compares the situation to a dart transfixing a cherry hanging on a wall, surrounded by a cherryless region, which would be no less impressive even if there were plenty of cherries in distant regions.[20]

One must go on to add that even if the necessary conditions for intelligent life are satisfied, it is still, in Barrow and Tipler's estimate, only likely to occur very rarely. In their estimate,

[19] Ibid., pp. 438 ff. and p. 502.
[20] 'Anthropic Principle, World Ensemble, Design', p. 143.

hominoid life (i.e. life with the kind of intelligence arising from a genome of the human type) is likely to occur on planets immensely many light-years apart, and so on at most three or four planets within the visible universe. Intelligent life of the kind which I have analysed will occur somewhat, though not very much, more frequently. They reach their estimate by pointing out that, given the occurrence of heavy elements on a planet at the right temperature, ten crucial steps were needed for the evolution of man:[21] the origin of the genetic code, of aerobic respiration, of glucose fermentation, of photosynthesis, of mitochondria, of the precursors of neurons, of an eye precursor, of the endoskeleton, of the chordates, and finally of the intelligence characteristic of *Homo sapiens*. They suggest that each of these steps is crucial and that the probabilities of their occurrence during the length of time a biosphere can continue (i.e. the length of time that the stars continue on main sequence) are each so low as to yield the above estimate of the probability of the occurrence of hominoid life. If the universe is spatially infinite, there will no doubt (given the crucial range of laws and initial conditions) be an infinite number of occurrences of hominoid life. Dependent on the exact form of laws and boundary conditions, the same may hold if the universe is an oscillating universe—in the course of infinite time, hominoid life may evolve an infinite number of times. The infrequency of hominoid life or of intelligent life generally is, however, irrelevant to the argument. The argument appeals only to the fact that certain conditions are necessary for intelligent life at all.

Any moderately precise estimate of what proportion of logically possible laws and boundary conditions would allow life seems impossible. There is no obvious way of setting about counting here. All that is clear is that, within the kind of region of laws and boundary conditions for which we can get some feeling of proportions, the range allowing life is probably very small indeed. In these circumstances, the best policy for assessing the worth of the argument from fine-tuning would seem to be initially to add to our background knowledge (k), that the universe began from an initial singularity and that laws have the form of our four-force laws, and then consider the force of the further evidence (e) that the initial conditions and constants of laws had just those values which allowed life to evolve. *A priori* this is very unlikely, but, for the reasons given earlier, much to be expected if there is a

---

[21] Barrow and Tipler, pp. 556–70.

God (h). Hence, since $P(e/h.k) \gg P(e/k)$; $P(h/e.k) \gg P(h.k)$. That evidence has significant confirming value for the hypothesis that there is a God. If we suppose that we can have some idea of the relative proportion of set-ups among all logically possible laws and boundary conditions which would yield life, then we can transfer the information treated above as background knowledge into e and simply take as the background knowledge the conformity of nature to scientific laws. My guess is that the proportion might be somewhat higher without the restriction to an initial singularity (for the reason that any arrangement of matter is more likely to occur given an infinite time than given only a finite time), but somewhat lower among laws of quite different forms. (For example, it is well known that orbits of bodies travelling around a centre of force are not stable if the attractive force varies with an inverse power of 3 or greater.) But in the absence of more definite theory, while allowing for some overestimate (arising from the restriction to an initial singularity), we must go on the evidence and theory we have available, and what that shows is that (with background knowledge simply the conformity of nature to scientific laws) to the extent to which we can have some reasonable assessment of the force of the evidence, the peculiar values of the constants of laws and variables of initial conditions are substantial evidence for the existence of God, which alone can give a plausible explanation of why they are as they are.

v

How can the conclusion that such life provides substantial evidence for the existence of God be avoided? There seem to be two 'ways out' considered in the current literature.

The first is by a certain kind of interpretation of the 'anthropic principle'. An anthropic principle says, roughly, that laws and boundary conditions must be such that life evolves, for otherwise no one would be observing it. Precise statements of the 'weak anthropic principle' and 'strong anthropic principle' vary some-what, and the variation often turns a trivial truth into an obvious falsity or vice versa. As interpreted by Barrow and Tipler,[22] the weak anthropic principle says simply that the obvious datum that there are observers now at the present region of space and time (distinguished by the general character of Earth and solar system,

[22] Ibid., p. 16.

present distribution and density and evolved state of galaxies, etc.) tells us that all theories with laws and boundary conditions such that they have the consequence that there will not be observers in such a region of space and time are false. So interpreted, the principle is a trivial truth; to be true, a theory must be compatible with evidently true data of observation. However, Barrow and Tipler easily slide into careless expositions of the principle, carrying interpretations which would render it obviously false— e.g. 'Many observations of the natural world, although remarkable *a priori*, can be seen in this light as inevitable consequences of our own existence.'[23] The suggestion might seem to be that our existence is in some sense the *cause* of the laws of nature and boundary conditions being the way they are (because if they were not that way we would not be able to observe them). That suggestion is nonsense. The laws of nature and boundary conditions cause our existence; we do not cause theirs.

A fuller answer to objections of the above kind is to be found on pp. 137 f., but I emphasize the main point by telling another parable which brings it out. On a certain occasion the firing squad aim their rifles at the prisoner to be executed. There are twelve expert marksmen in the firing squad, and they fire twelve rounds each. However, on this occasion all 144 shots miss. The prisoner laughs and comments that the event is not something requiring any explanation because if the marksmen had not missed, he would not be here to observe them having done so. But of course the prisoner's comment is absurd; the marksmen all having missed is indeed something requiring explanation, and so too is what goes with it—the prisoner being alive to observe it. And the explanation will be either that it was an accident (a most unusual chance event) or that it was planned (e.g. all the marksmen had been bribed to miss). Any interpretation of an anthropic principle which suggests that the evolution of observers is something which requires no explanation in terms of boundary conditions and laws being a certain way (either inexplicably or through choice) is false.

Other interpretations of anthropic principles turn them into interesting and probably false contingent scientific claims. Thus, for Barrow and Tipler, the 'strong anthropic principle' originally expressed, ambiguously, as: 'The Universe must have those properties which allow life to develop within it at some stage in its

---

[23] Ibid., p. 219.

history' is then supposed to have the implication that 'The constants and laws of Nature must be such that life can exist.'[24] This I understand as claiming that the laws are such that, whatever the boundary conditions, life will evolve at some time. That seems very dubious. As I claimed earlier, science suggests that the laws are such that if the universe had begun with an even bigger 'big bang', life would never have evolved.

Anthropic principles serve only to obfuscate.

VI

A marginally more plausible way to avoid the theistic conclusion is by postulating many worlds or universes. Suppose that our universe is one of many, some of which have different laws and some of which have different boundary conditions from ours. Many of these are such that intelligent life will not evolve in them, but ours of course is such that it will. Ours is a universe within a super-universe of universes of different kinds. If there are millions of executions, it is to be expected, given that even good marksmen sometimes miss, that just occasionally all the marksmen will miss with all their shots. A hundred tosses of heads in a row is by itself an event which leads to suspicion of cheating; but if it is but one series of tosses among at least 2^{100}, such series generated by the same process, the suspicion is perhaps unwarranted—the unusual sometimes happens in a large enough collection of events.

Now if we have reason to believe that there are such other universes, it will form part of our background knowledge by which to assess the worth of the argument that our universe is life-evolving. Let k_2 be the background knowledge that there are a trillion orderly universes with different laws and boundary conditions from each other, and k be the background knowledge that there is at least one orderly universe; let e be the evidence that there is a universe which is life-evolving, and h the hypothesis that there is a God. Then $P(e/k_2)$ will be quite high, not significantly different from $P(e/k_2 \cdot h)$, and so e will certainly be no significant evidence for h, whereas $P(e/k)$ looks very low and so much lower than $P(e/k \cdot h)$, and so e is evidence for h. If we have the background knowledge incorporated in k_2, the argument to h will not work. But do we?

[24] Ibid., p. 21.

What is meant by a 'universe'? Sometimes cosmologists under-stand by 'our universe' the physical objects (galaxies, dust, energy, etc.) currently observable by us, or (which on some physical theories is wider) those which are or will be at some future time observable from Earth, or which were at some time observable from Earth, and there are variants of these kinds, distinguishing universes by the physical objects which lie within some 'horizon'[25] of the Earth. Then other 'universes' are other regions of space (of similar size) lying spatially beyond our universe in one of these ways. Reasonable inductive principles certainly suggest that there are such universes. If we cut up our universe into many regions, varying in their distance and direction from Earth, evidence of observation shows that at the same instant of cosmic time equally dense matter is to be found in each, and so that beyond each equally dense region lies another one.[26] That is good reason for supposing that the same holds when we pass beyond the horizon. But the same evidence which shows that there are in this sense other universes shows also that they have the same general character as our own—both in respect of boundary conditions and in respect of laws.

That the laws of nature are the same in distant regions as in our own is indeed an assumption which could not in general be shown false. For to learn the character of those regions we suppose that laws of nature which hold in our region hold in the intervening space, and that enables us to interpret certain data in our region (e.g. marks on our telescopes' photographic plates) as caused by certain events in those regions. Supposing that light travels in straight lines with the same velocity as in our region, we infer from the marks on our telescopes' photographs the density of galaxies in those regions. Without the assumption that in general the same laws held, we could have no knowledge of how matter-energy did behave in distant regions. True, the assumption that most of the laws were the same in the distant region might allow us to make inferences about the behaviour of matter in that region which showed that one or two laws were different. But I know of no such evidence. And we could have no evidence for a general difference

[25] See (e.g.) my *Space and Time* (2nd edn., New York 1981), Ch. 12.

[26] The approximate homogeneity and isotropy of the universe within the region observable by telescope, after making allowance for the fact that we observe more distant regions as they were at periods of time longer ago, is well evidenced by observation. See Barrow and Tipler, pp. 414–30.

of laws. By 'laws' I mean 'fundamental laws', that is, highest-level laws not derivable from laws of even higher level. We could have evidence that in our region matter behaved in certain ways because of some peculiar feature of this region (e.g. the density of matter here). And that evidence would show us that matter would behave in different ways in a region which had a different character. But we could only reach that conclusion because we had the evidence of how the behaviour of matter varied with that feature of the region, that is, because we had evidence of a place-independent law showing how the behaviour of matter varied with variation in that feature.

We could, however, in principle obtain evidence that the current arrangement of matter-energy (e.g. the number and kind of galaxies, their density and velocity) was very different in some distant region. But the evidence is abundant that that is not so; the universe in different regions is everywhere approximately the same in the arrangement of its matter-energy at the same cosmic instant. The most striking evidence of this comes from the observable isotropy of the universe: distant regions seen from telescopes in the southern sky look just the same as distant regions seen from telescopes in the northern sky.

So, even if we treat spatially distant regions as different universes, we have good reason to suppose that they are like our own in boundary conditions and laws, and, like our own, life-evolving. The same applies, and for similar reasons, if we treat temporally distant parts of our spatial region as different 'universes'. If we have reason to believe that there was such a universe (viz. that there was matter-energy here) billions of years ago, that can only be because it is the simplest explanation of many present data that they were caused by states of that universe billions of years ago. Since that 'universe' belongs to and is causally continuous with our universe, it has by definition the same boundary conditions. The ultimate constituents of our 'universe' are the same. We extrapolate backward by assuming certain laws to hold then and during the intervening period. But the only laws we are justified in supposing to hold are those which form part of a set giving the simplest explanation of present data. True, the extrapolation backward of most such laws might allow us to infer with justification a state of affairs in which some one or two laws which now hold did not hold. But there could be no evidence that in general the laws of nature were different, and again I know of no evidence for supposing that even one law differed in its operation in the past. Again, in talking about laws, I am talking about fundamental laws. We could have evidence for supposing that there are certain regularities of behaviour characteristic of our temporal era, deriving from some general feature thereof, such as the density of matter, which would not hold in the past 'universe', but that evidence would be evidence that there is time-invariant law showing how these regularities depend on that general feature; we would have evidence of the latter fundamental law because it provided the simplest explanation of a vast range of present data, including those irregularities. But we could not have any evidence of any general, random, non-law-dependent change in the patterns of the behaviour of matter as we go backward in time. We could not, for example, have any evidence that certain 'constants' of nature change over time in a non-law-dependent way.[27] The only past 'universes' of which we have evidence are those with the same boundary conditions and laws as our own; and so they will be, eventually (either during their existence or during that of their successor 'universe'), life-evolving. What goes for past universes goes for future 'universes' too, by a similar pattern of argument; so they too, or their predecessor universe, must be life-evolving. That any past and future 'universes' for the existence of which we have evidence, have in general the same laws and boundary conditions as our own, is, I have been arguing, a necessary truth (the necessity of which follows from the very criteria we use of what is evidence for what). That the same is so of spatially distant 'universes' is a contingent truth, but one very well evidenced by data (including above all, the observable isotropy of the universe). The difference between the two cases arises from the fact that the boundary conditions of past and future universes in our spatial region are (by definition) the same as our own. The similarity of the boundary conditions of spatially distant universes to those of our own is a contingent truth. Similar conclusions with respect to the similarity of laws and boundary conditions follow by extrapolation to 'universes' distant in both space and time from our own; we extrapolate to a spatially distant universe and thence to an earlier or later universe in that spatial region and reach the conclusion that there too boundary conditions and laws are

---

[27] P. A M. Dirac postulated that the gravitational 'constant' varied with time in a law-dependent way. See Barrow and Tipler, pp. 20 ff. Even this hypothesis did not prove well justified.

quantitatively the same. Also we may extrapolate backwards to an earlier state of our spatial region of the universe (e.g. as it was immediately after the 'big bang') and then forward again to other regions now spatially distant from us but having the same earlier state (i.e. their present state was caused by the same earlier part of the universe as ours), and thus gain information about those regions, other than by direct observation of them. In this case we might conclude (because the processes which separated the regions were such as to produce later regions of different kinds from each other) that there could not exist intelligent life now or later in those regions. It would still remain the case that those regions have laws and boundary conditions which (unlike the vast majority of logically possible laws and boundary conditions) are life-evolving even if not productive of life in those regions at this time. (The boundary conditions would be such because they would be those of our region, where they have produced life). So the evidence is that in all regions of space and time spatially related to (i.e. at some distance in some direction from) and temporally related to (i.e. earlier than or later than) our own, laws and boundary conditions are quantitatively the same, and thus, at some time and place, life-evolving. If we insist on calling these regions different 'universes', in the crucial respects they are the same as our own. It is, I think less misleading to talk of them as regions of one universe (the whole physical universe consisting of all the physical objects spatio-temporally related to ourselves, as I defined it on p. 116).

What of the possibility of other 'universes' not spatially related to ourselves? We can only have knowledge of them if at some time they have interacted with our own (either causing effects in our world or as effects of a common cause which had effects in our world). The only such universes seriously discussed in the scientific literature are the many worlds of Everett's 'Many Worlds Interpretation' (MWI) of quantum theory.[28] The ψ-function of quantum theory describes the deterministic evolution of a system; however, when a measurement is made on the system, there is a 'collapse of the wave packet'—the ψ-function yields for observation only one of a number of possible values; which one is not entailed by a description of the function. The quantum cosmologist seeks a ψ-function for the evolution of the whole universe and

---

[28] Barrow and Tipler, pp. 472–96.

interprets the notion of the 'measurement' of this function as the occurrence of any processes external to the development of the function, such as the occurrence of a non-gravitational field which would define a scale-length,[29] which give values to variables of the system. MWI then seeks to save the determinism of quantum theory by saying that every measurement splits the universe into a number of different universes, each realizing one of the possible values of the ψ-function. We are only in one of those universes and so only observe the value realized in our universe. Measurement, MWI holds, does not indeterministically select only one of the possible evolutions of the function. (Barrow and Tipler claim that often only the measuring instrument is split, not the whole universe; the only difference between the two universes after a measurement with two possible outcomes is that one contains an instrument having one record, and the other contains an instrument having a different record. But although this may be the only qualitative difference, it remains the case that, on MWI, there exist two numerically different universes, although the qualitative differences between them concern only a small part of the two universes. For the other parts of one universe are such that observers there can be affected only by one value of the measurement, and the other parts of the other universe are such that observers there can be affected only by the other value. Everything has been split).

Now this understanding of quantum theory does indeed involve postulating many worlds, infinitely many worlds. Barrow and Tipler claim[30] that MWI suggests a preference for certain forms of quantum theory over others (e.g. certain constraints on cosmological boundary conditions), and those forms have observable consequences, and that is one of its advantages. The other suggested advantage is an advantage common to all 'many worlds' theories, that we do not need to postulate that its boundary conditions lie within a very narrow range in order to explain why our universe has various features rather than others. We avoid that need if we say that all possible universes exist (each starting from a different development in early stages); ours is just one of infinitely many.

I cannot, however, see that MWI could ever be a justified interpretation of any form of quantum theory, whatever form is

---

[29] Ibid., pp. 499 ff.   [30] Ibid., pp. 493–6.

best supported by observation. For its basic idea is to postulate an infinity of worlds, the states of which will never produce *any* observable effects in our world. And the reason for doing this is to save the determinism of the ψ-function and to avoid the need for very detailed boundary conditions. But MWI would have to postulate so many worlds! To start with, it has to say that 'measurements', and so world-splitting, are very frequent. Further, since some outcomes of measurements are more probable than others, this can only be interpreted by MWI by saying that for each outcome there are more possible worlds in which there is that outcome than worlds in which there is the other outcome. So, although there may be only a finite number of possible outcomes of each measurement, for each outcome (varying with the outcome) there are a considerable number of possible worlds. And among the things which the measurement duplicates are the observers; every time a measurement is made by a human observer, he is split into two.[31]

It should now be apparent that if postulating infinitely many worlds were necessary to save the determinism of quantum theory and to avoid having to postulate that the boundary conditions lie within a very narrow range, it would be best instead to interpret the ψ-function indeterministically, as a probability-wave describing the physical probabilities of the behaviour of the real constitutents of the universe, and to postulate that the boundary conditions do lie within the narrow range. It is a crucial tenet of the scientific method that entities are not to be postulated beyond necessity. We are right to postulate unobservable entities of a few kinds and simple patterns of behaviour, if their behaviour would explain many complex or coincidental observations. And if a logical consequence of postulating, for these reasons, some entities is that there are other entities which will not causally affect our observations, that is acceptable, so long as our theory does not get too top-heavy. But to postulate infinitely many worlds in order to save a preferred interpretation of a formula, which is in no way obviously simpler than the alternative explanation, and to avoid having to postulate a very narrow range of boundary conditions (which have to lie within a certain range anyway) seems crazy.

---

[31] I have noted elsewhere that there are considerable philosophical difficulties in supposing that persons can be split. See (e.g.) *The Evolution of the Soul* (Oxford, 1986), pp. 149 ff.

MWI is like an enormous inverted pyramid of theory resting on a vertex of observation.

We can only have knowledge of worlds not spatially related to our own if our own is different from what it would be if there were no such worlds. MWI does not provide that evidence. It is the main scientific contender to do so on grounds other than the fact that our universe is life-evolving. That is, we do not have independent background knowledge of the type k_2. As far as our background knowledge is concerned, we have no reason for supposing that there are worlds other than our own with significantly different laws and boundary conditions.

What, finally, of the suggestion that, although we do not have any other reason (background knowledge) for supposing the existence of 'many worlds', the fact that our world is productive of intelligent life is reason for supposing that there are, more or as much reason for supposing that there is a God? The supposition (h_2) would be that an infinity of worlds with varying laws and boundary conditions exists, not caused by anything else, our intelligent-life-producing world (e) being but one of them. With h as the existence of God, the suggestion is that (with k as the existence of—at least—one orderly universe) $P(h_2/e \cdot k) \geq P(h/e.k)$.

This suggestion does not deny that e confirms (that is, raises the probability of) h. It suggests only that e confirms h_2 equally well. Given that, roughly speaking, both h and h_2 lead us to expect e equally well $[P(e/h \cdot k) = P(e/h_2 \cdot k)]$, whether e makes h or h_2 more probable depends on whether, apart from e, h or h_2 is more probable anyway. That depends on whether h or h_2 is the simpler theory—the one postulating fewer entities, mathematically simpler modes of behaviour, less arbitrary coincidences, etc. Such factors determine the theory's prior probability on the background knowledge k. In symbols, the prior probability of h is represented by $P(h/k)$, of h_2 by $P(h_2/k)$. By Bayes's theorem, if $P(e/h \cdot k) = P(e/h_2 \cdot k)$, $P(h/e \cdot k) > P(h_2/e \cdot k)$ if only if $P(h/k) > P(h_2/k)$. Scientists can always construct an infinite number of theories (some of them highly complex) able to predict any finite set of data. If they are ever to be justified in saying that one of these theories is more probably true than any other (or that its predictions are more probably true than those of any other such theory), it can only be on the basis of factors such as those I stated, determining simplicity. On any reasonable understanding of simplicity, I suggest, $P(h_2/k)$ will be absurdly low compared to $P(h/k)$. The postulation of God, as I argued in Chapter 5, is the postulation of *one* entity of a simple kind (the simplest kind of person there could be, having no limits to his knowledge, power, and freedom). To postulate the actual existence of an infinite number of worlds, between them exhausting all the logical possibilities, many of them consisting of an infinite quantity of matter-energy behaving in accord with simple laws over infinite time which are not caused by anything else, which do not causally affect each other, but which between them exhaust the logical space without any one being qualitatively identical to any other, is to postulate complexity and non-prearranged coincidence of infinite dimensions beyond rational belief. Hence, $P(h_2/e \cdot k) \ll P(h/e \cdot k)$. The existence of God is much more likely on the evidence of our life-producing world than the existence of 'many worlds'.

There are no good grounds for adopting any form of 'many worlds' hypothesis, except ones which postulate 'universes' belonging to the same spatio-temporal realm as our own, which have the same intelligent-life-producing properties. The existence of our world, with its power to produce intelligent life (and of the other such worlds if they exist), is therefore strong confirming evidence of the existence of God.

Index